CASES AND SOLUTIONS IN INTERNATIONAL FINANCIAL REPORTING STANDARDS

4th Edition

Derry Cotter, FCA

Chartered Accountants Ireland

Published by
Chartered Accountants Ireland
Chartered Accountants House
47–49 Pearse Street
Dublin 2
www.charteredaccountants.ie

The opinions expressed in this publication are those of the author and do not necessarily represent the views of Chartered Accountants Ireland. The text is designed to provide accurate and authoritative information in regard to the subject matter covered. It is sold on the understanding that Chartered Accountants Ireland is not engaged in rendering professional services. If professional advice or other expert assistance is required, the services of a competent professional should be sought.

ISBN: 978-1-910374-30-6

First published 2008
Second edition 2009
Third edition 2012 (reprinted as a single volume 2014)
Fourth edition 2015

Typeset by Deanta Global Publishing Services
Printed and bound by Grafo, S.A.

To the students of Chartered Accountants Ireland and UCC, whose courtesy and kindness has made teaching such a great pleasure

Acknowledgements

I wish to thank Michael Diviney for commissioning the 4th edition of this book. I also want to acknowledge the invaluable administrative support provided by Liam Boyle and Becky McIndoe.

I am especially indebted to David Ahern and Brendan Doyle, for their insightful comments and suggestions. Any errors or omissions, however, are entirely the responsibility of the author.

TABLE OF CONTENTS
(with Case Study Topics)

Page

INTRODUCTION

The Case Study Approach

It is generally perceived that the use of case study material significantly enhances student learning. Case studies are seen as an invaluable educational resource, one that is entirely complementary to other methods of teaching. Where conventional textbooks typically provide a discipline's core knowledge material, case studies can assist in developing the students' critical and analytical skills, and enhance their capacity for problem-solving. This is often achieved by presenting challenging scenarios, which require the students to integrate and apply the material contained in conventional texts.

The Aim of this Book

Cases and Solutions in International Financial Reporting Standards offers a broad range of case study material in the area of international financial reporting standards. Each case provides many examples of how International Accounting Standards (IAS) and International Financial Reporting Standards (IFRS) are applied in practice. The book is targeted both at accounting practitioners and at undergraduate students who have completed an introductory course in Financial Reporting, as well as those preparing for examinations set by the professional accountancy bodies. From a lecturer's perspective, it is envisaged that this case study book would provide an ideal tutorial pack.

Cases and Solutions in International Financial Reporting Standards also offers a range of case study material in the core area of financial reporting. Several case examples focus on *Reporting Financial Performance*, with coverage of key issues such as the presentation of financial statements, earnings per share, interim financial reporting, share-based payment, non-current assets held for sale and discontinued operations, accounting policies, events after the reporting period, leases, revenue from contracts with customers, employee benefits, the effects of changes in foreign exchange rates, related party disclosures, operating segments and financial instruments. There is extensive coverage of *Accounting for Assets*, which includes inventories, property, plant and equipment, asset impairment and intangible assets. There is also a focus on *Accounting for Liabilities* such as income taxes, and provisions and contingent liabilities. Finally, many aspects of *Group Accounts* are addressed, including business combinations and investments in associates and joint ventures.

Tips and guidance for using this book

Two indices are provided to facilitate quick and easy access to material:

- The first, at the front of the book, identifies the case study questions in which *specific IASs or IFRSs* are addressed.

- The second index, which is at the back of the book, provides an alphabetical listing, *by subject topic,* referenced to the case study questions.

- The cases are set at a level that assumes that student users will have completed an introductory course in financial reporting.

- The cases are written so that they can be used in an open-book environment, whereby students can refer to their own notes and other sources of information when preparing their answer.

- Past FAE Financial Reporting papers, included in the 4th edition, have been updated to fully reflect all subsequent changes in IFRS.

- These solutions have been prepared as a resource to lecturers when using this book in a lecture or tutorial format. The solutions are numbered as per the case book and presented in the same order. The solutions in this text have been drafted in accordance with standards issued on or before 30 June 2015.

- The following acronyms are used in journal entries throughout the book:
  - ° *SOCI* for the statement of comprehensive income
  - ° *P/L* for profit or loss
  - ° *OCI* for other comprehensive income
  - ° *SOFP* for the statement of financial position.

Index to Case Studies

Reference is to Case Study *Question*

Topic	Versatile	Vorster	Webster	Hayward	Black Bay	Target	Magna	Harrington	O'Neill	Fitzwilliam	Harding
Conceptual framework				(b)				(a)			
IFRS 1											
IFRS 2										(d)	
IFRS 3	(a)	(1)			(a)		(b) (i)	(e)			(c) (i)
IFRS 5	(a)	(3)	(b)	(a)					(2)		(a) (ii)
IFRS 8											
IFRS 9			(e)		(b)						
IFRS 10	(a)	(3)			(a)						a (ii)
IFRS 11		(2)					(a)				
IFRS 15	(c)		(d)	(c)						(a)	
IAS 1	(a)										
IAS 2	(c)										
IAS 8			(c)	(c)							(b)
IAS 10											
IAS 12			(a)								
IAS 16	(b)				(c)	(1)		(b) & (c)		(b)	(d)
IAS 17						(2)		(d)		(c)	(b)
IAS 20											
IAS 21					(b)						
IAS 23					(b)	(1)					
IAS 24	(a)		(c)	(b)		(1)				(b)	
IAS 27											
IAS 28				(d)				(e)			
IAS 36	(b)					(4)	(b) (ii) & (c)	(b)			
IAS 37				(a) & (c)		(3) & (4)			(1)	(a)	(a) (i)
IAS 38	(d)						(d)				(c) (ii)
IAS 39			(e)		(b)					(b)	
IAS 40											

PART 1

CASES

PART 1

CASES

BELLMOTH GROUP

You are the audit senior in a firm of Chartered Accountants and Registered Auditors, Goodman Hart and Co. You are currently reviewing the draft consolidated financial statements of Bellmoth Holdings Limited and its subsidiary companies, Caterpillar Limited and Butterfly Limited.

Your firm's audit partner, Yvonne Russell, has sent you a memo containing the following information:

- Background to the group companies: Appendix I below

- Matters arising from the 2x05
  audit of the group: Appendix II below
- Draft consolidated statement of
  financial position and statement
  of comprehensive income for the group: Appendix III below

Requirement:

On the basis of the information provided by Yvonne Russell, draft a memorandum to her outlining:

- Recommendations as to how the accounting issues arising should be dealt with. You should include an explanation of your reasons for the proposed accounting treatment.
- The journal entries necessary to adjust the draft financial statements.
- Disclosure requirements (outline *not* detailed notes) relating *only* to Caterpillar's investment in Bumble Bee (see matters arising, Appendix II).

Note: you are *not* required to redraft the financial statements.

50 marks

FRS 102

Outline the key differences in accounting treatment if the financial statements were prepared in accordance with the requirements of FRS 102 *The Financial Reporting Standard applicable in the UK and Republic of Ireland.*

Appendix I

Background to the Group Companies

The Bellmoth Group comprises the following companies:

Bellmoth Holdings Limited (Bellmoth) – A holding company employing 16 people and providing services to the other group trading companies.

Caterpillar Limited – A 100% subsidiary of Bellmoth, acquired several years ago. Caterpillar is a major supplier of food products, employing 220 staff located throughout the major cities in Ireland.

Butterfly Limited – Butterfly was established in the United States on 1 January 2x05 by Bellmoth. Butterfly manufactures high quality carpets to customers' specifications. The company, which employs 100 staff, is an 80% subsidiary of Bellmoth. It operates on an autonomous basis, only referring to Bellmoth in relation to matters of strategic importance.

Appendix II

Matters Arising from the 2x05 Audit of the Bellmoth Group

(1) Caterpillar

    (i)   *Restructuring*

In October 2x05 Caterpillar announced that it was investigating the possibility of rationalising its provision of foodstuffs with a short shelf life. Following a feasibility study, a detailed plan was drawn up in December for the sale of surplus non-current assets, and for the redeployment of staff. The plan has been approved in principle by members of staff who will be affected.

It has been estimated that the downsizing of short-life foodstuff sales would necessitate a provision of €2 million at 31 December 2x05. This provision is analysed as follows;

	€000
Loss on disposal of non-current assets	650
Redundancy settlements	350
Warehouse re-design costs	220
Marketing costs to refocus company's sales promotion on continuing lines	380
Future operating losses of short-life foodstuffs sales	400
	2,000

No provision has been made in the financial statements at 31 December 2x05.

(ii) *Warranty provisions and refunds*

- It is estimated that the discounted value of future warranty claims against goods supplied by the company during 2x05 amounts to €1.5 million at 31 December 2x05.

- Additionally, Caterpillar has a policy of making cash refunds or exchanging goods at their customers' request. Although there is no legal obligation to do so, it is believed that the policy has promoted a greater than average level of customer loyalty to the company.

  From past experience it is estimated that cash refunds relating to 2x05 sales will amount to €800,000 in 2x06. Additionally, it is estimated that €200,000 of goods sold in 2x05 will be exchanged in 2x06. Caterpillar earns an average gross margin of 50% on sales.

  No provisions have been made in the draft 2x05 accounts, either in respect of warranty provisions or refunds, and the full amount of sales consideration has been recorded in trade receivables and revenue.

(iii)   *Staff retraining costs*

Legislative changes at European level during 2x05 have resulted in more stringent requirements relating to product design. Consequently, staff retraining costs over the next three years are estimated as follows:

	€000
2x06	300
2x07	400
2x08	500

(iv)   *Joint venture*

On 1 January 2x05, Caterpillar set up Bumble Bee as a joint venture initiative with Thompson Products Limited. Caterpillar obtained a 50% stake in Bumble Bee and, along with Thompson Products Ltd, participated actively in the company's financial strategy and day-to-day running.

Caterpillar's investment in Bumble Bee cost €1 million, which was financed by a term loan. Caterpillar paid €20,000 to an advisor, who negotiated the finance on the company's behalf, and administrative fees of €25,000 were charged by the bank and retained out of the loan proceeds.

Caterpillar made sales amounting to €1 million to Bumble Bee during 2x05, on which the profit margin was 30%. Of these sales, half were still held in inventory by Bumble Bee at 31 December 2x05.

Bumble Bee had sales of €5 million, and cost of sales of €2 million for the year ended 31 December 2x05. The company's profit for the year was €1.4 million, all of which was retained.

With the exception of the sales by Caterpillar to Bumble Bee, no entries have been made by Caterpillar (or in the draft consolidated financial statements) in respect of its investment in the joint venture.

(v)   *Tangible non-current assets*

- On 1 January 2x04 Caterpillar purchased a plot of land for €600,000. The land was revalued at €800,000 at 31 December 2x04, and was sold during 2x05 for €1.3 million. The disposal has not been reflected in the draft 2x05 financial statements, and the land continues to be included in tangible non-current assets at a valuation of €800,000.

- On 1 January 2x03 Caterpillar purchased a commercial property for investment purposes. The property, which cost €500,000, was included in the Statement of Financial Position at its fair value of €700,000 at 31 December 2x04. During 2x05 a rezoning decision had reduced the value of the property to €300,000. No account of the rezoning decision has been taken in preparing the 2x05 draft financial statements.

(2) Butterfly

Inventory
Butterfly purchased inventories of wool over the last quarter of 2x05 as follows:

Month	Tons purchased	Cost per ton	Tons in inventory at end of month
Oct	10	$50,000	8
Nov	11	$60,000	15
Dec	9	$70,000	17

In accordance with normal accounting practice in the United States, the closing inventory of wool has been valued on a LIFO basis, and this basis has been applied in the draft consolidated financial statements.

The normal valuation basis in the Bellmoth Group is FIFO. The net realisable value of the wool at 31 December 2x05 was $30,000 per ton.

The rate of exchange at 31 December 2x05 was €1 = $1.50, and this was also the rate throughout the last quarter of the year.

It can be assumed that the carpets, which will use the above inventories of wool, will be sold at a profit.

Appendix III

Draft Consolidated Financial Statements

Draft Statement of Comprehensive Income
for the Year Ended 31 December 2x05

	€000
Revenue	36,800
Cost of sales	(18,600)
Gross profit	18,200
Distribution costs	(4,800)
Administrative expenses	(3,900)
Other expenses	(1,500)
Finance costs	(300)
Profit before tax	7,700
Income tax expense	(700)
Profit for the year from continuing operations	7,000
Other comprehensive income:	
Items that will not be reclassified to profit or loss:	
Gains on property revaluation	450
Total comprehensive income for the year	7,450
Profit attributable to:	
Owners of the parent	6,200
Non-controlling interests	800
	7,000
Total comprehensive income attributable to:	
Owners of the parent	6,650
Non-controlling interests	800
	7,450

Draft Statement of Financial Position as at 31 December 2x05

	Notes	2x05 €000	2x04 €000
Assets			
Non-current assets			
Property, plant and equipment		18,000	
Goodwill		14,000	
		32,000	
Current assets			
Inventories		9,000	
Trade and other receivables		5,000	
Cash and cash equivalents		3,000	
		17,000	
Total assets		49,000	
Liabilities			
Current liabilities			
Trade and other payables		9,500	
Current tax payable		1,000	
		10,500	
		10,500	
Non-current liabilities			
Convertible debentures		2,000	
10% Preference shares		300	
Provisions		5,500	
Other payables		6,000	
		13,800	
Total liabilities		24,300	
Net assets		24,700	
Equity			
Capital and reserves attributable to equity holders of the parent			
Share capital		600	
Share premium account		4,800	
Revaluation reserve		1,200	
Retained earnings		14,800	
		21,400	
Non-controlling interests		3,300	
Total equity		24,700	

CROMPTON PLANT AND FERTILISER GROUP

The Crompton Plant and Fertiliser Group comprises Crompton Holdings Limited and its subsidiary companies which it has held for several years. Only one subsidiary, Ingston Limited, in which Crompton Holdings Limited holds 90% of the equity shares, is not wholly owned. In your capacity as Group Financial Accountant you are currently reviewing the draft consolidated accounts of the group. The Finance Director has requested that you prepare a memorandum outlining any issues which may require amendment. The financial statements are being authorised by the Board of Directors on 20 July 2x06.

In its separate financial statements, Crompton Holdings accounts at cost for investments in subsidiaries.

(1) Acquisition of Plant Life Limited

On 31 May 2x06 the parent company, Crompton Holdings Limited, acquired 100% of Plant Life Limited. The Group has regularly purchased goods from Plant Life Limited in each of the last five years (purchases amounted to €2.5 million in the year ended 31 May 2x06), and the acquisition was seen as being strategic in copper-fastening the Group's presence in the residential market for house plants.

Consideration for the acquisition comprised the following:

- 1 million €1 equity shares of Crompton Holdings Limited. The market value of these shares on 31 May 2x06 was €6 each.

- 100,000 shares in Grafton Bank Plc which had been purchased as an investment by Crompton Holdings on 1 October 2x05 for €1 million. The market value of these shares at 31 May 2x06 was €1.35

million, though the increase in value has not been reflected in the financial statements.

- Cash consideration of €400,000, payable on 1 June 2x08, which is contingent on certain profitability parameters being achieved by Plant Life Limited over the next two years. At 31 May 2x06 the directors of Crompton Limited were confident that this consideration would not become payable, but a new contract awarded to the company on the 1 July 2x06 means that the required profitability targets are likely to be achieved. Borrowed funds are normally available to Crompton Holdings Limited at 10% per annum.

No entries have been made in the consolidated accounts, or the accounts of Crompton Holdings Limited, relating to this consideration.

Having requested additional details relating to the new subsidiary, the following information is brought to your attention:

(i)   The draft financial statements of Plant Life Limited for the year ended 31 May 2x06 are included in Appendix I.

(ii)   At 31 May 2x06 the finished goods inventory of Plant Life Limited was valued on a first in first out (FIFO) basis. The goods were subsequently sold for €200,000 less than their value in the statement of financial position at 31 May 2x06.

(iii)   At a Board meeting in November 2x05, the Directors of Plant Life Limited had committed the Company to a reorganisation programme costing €250,000, which commenced in June 2x06. No provision has been made for these costs in the financial statements at 31 May 2x06. This will also result in the immediate disposal of machinery for €300,000, net of selling costs. These machines had a net book value of €400,000 at 31 May 2x06. Negotiations with the Board of Crompton Holdings Limited commenced in January 2x06.

(iv)   Crompton Holdings Limited has incurred professional fees of €100,000 relating to the acquisition of Plant Life Limited. No provision has been made for these expenses, which are payable in August 2x06. Additionally, general management expenses amounting to €85,000 have been included in other receivables in the consolidated financial statements of the Crompton Group at 31 May 2x06. It is intended to treat these expenses as part of the cost of acquiring Plant Life Limited.

(v)   In February 2x06 Plant Life Limited took a legal action against one of its suppliers on the basis that goods supplied were faulty. An amount of €100,000 was included under trade and other receivables at 31 May 2x06, as the minimum amount of the gain expected from this action. On 28 June 2x06, Plant Life received a settlement of €320,000 from the supplier in respect of its claim. The financial statements of the group are due to be authorised for issue on 20 July 2x06.

(vi)   The fair value of the land and buildings of Plant Life Limited at 31 May 2x06 was €2.5 million. Buildings have not been depreciated as their residual value is expected to exceed their cost price.

(vii)   A dividend of €600,000 was paid by Plant Life Limited in July 2x06 out of profits of the year ended 31 May 2x06. This was **not** provided for in the financial statements at 31 May 2x06.

(2) Group Accounts

The Group Accounts have also been prepared in draft form (see Appendix II below). These accounts do *not* include the new subsidiary Plant Life Limited. The following accounting issue relating to the group accounts has not been fully resolved:

On 1 June 2x05 Ingston Limited commenced the construction of a leisure centre for the company's employees. The premises were completed in May 2x06 at a total cost of €3 million. It has been agreed by the trustees of the employees' pension scheme that the cost of the building will be offset against a deficit on the fund, which has been accrued as a provision in the Group financial statements at 31 May 2x06.

Ingston Limited has the full use of the property for the next five years, at which point ownership will transfer to the pension fund. A five-year contract has been signed with a leisure company for the rental of the centre at a net annual rent of €120,000, the first instalment being payable on 31 May 2x07.

The property has been included as an investment property in Ingston Limited's financial statements at 31 May 2x06 at its fair value of €4 million.

Appendix I

Draft Financial Statements of Plant Life Limited

Draft Statement of Comprehensive Income for the year ended 31 May 2x06

	2x06 €000	2x05 €000
Revenue	11,800	
Cost of sales	(7,950)	
Gross profit	3,850	
Distribution costs	(300)	
Administrative expenses	(500)	
Other expenses	(400)	
Finance costs	(400)	
Profit before tax	2,550	
Income tax expense	(1370)	
Profit for the year from continuing operations	1,180	
Other comprehensive income:		
Items that will not be reclassified to profit or loss:		
Gains on property revaluation	250	
Total comprehensive income for the year	1,430	

Draft Statement of Financial Position of Plant Life Limited
at 31 May 2x06

	Notes	2x06 €000	2x05 €000
Assets			
Non-current assets			
Land and buildings		2,298	
Plant and equipment		4,645	
		6,943	
Current assets			
Inventories of finished goods		1,469	
Trade and other receivables		1,395	
Cash and cash equivalent		1,155	
		4,019	
Total assets		10,962	
Liabilities			
Current liabilities			
Trade and other payables		2,215	
Income tax payable		1,350	
		3,565	
Non-current liabilities			
Term loan		820	
Provisions		300	
		1,120	
Total liabilities		4,685	
Net assets		6,277	
Equity			
Share capital		100	
Share premium account		250	
Revaluation surplus		1,000	
Retained earnings		4,927	
Total equity		6,277	

Appendix II

Draft Consolidated Financial Statements of the Crompton Group

Draft Consolidated Statement of Comprehensive Income
for the year ended 31 May 2x06

	2x06	2x05
	€000	€000
Revenue	52,000	
Cost of sales	(27,950)	
Gross profit	24,050	
Distribution costs	(4,800)	
Administrative expenses	(9,500)	
Finance costs	(1,240)	
Gain on revaluation of investment property	1,000	
Profit before tax	8,130	
Income tax expense	(2,150)	
Profit for the year from continuing operations	5,980	
Other comprehensive income:		
Items that will not be reclassified to profit or loss:		
Gains on property revaluation	720	
Total comprehensive income for the year	6,700	
Profit attributable to:		
Owners of the parent	5,480	
Non-controlling interests	500	
	5,980	
Total comprehensive income attributable to:		
Owners of the parent	6,200	
Non-controlling interests	500	
	6,700	

Draft Statement of Financial Position of the Crompton Group at 31 May 2x06

	Notes	2x06 €000	2x05 €000
Assets			
Non-current assets			
Property, plant and equipment		31,550	
Investment property		4,000	
		35,550	
Current assets			
Inventories		3,444	
Investments		1,000	
Trade and other receivables		3,395	
Cash and cash equivalents		2,155	
		9,994	
Total assets		45,544	
Liabilities			
Current liabilities			
Trade and other payables		6,965	
Income tax payable		4,150	
		11,115	
Non-current liabilities			
Convertible debentures		1,600	
Term loan		2,120	
Provisions		3,400	
		7,120	
Total liabilities		18,235	
Net assets		27,309	
Equity			
Equity attributable to owners of the parent holders of the parent			
Share capital		1,000	
Share premium account		1,700	
Revaluation surplus		3,904	
Other reserves		900	
Retained earnings		19,205	
		26,709	
Non-controlling interests		600	
Total equity		27,309	

Appendix III

Crompton Holdings: Group Structure

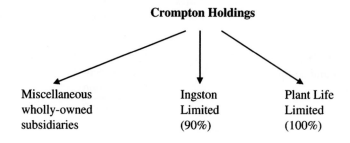

Crompton Holdings

| Miscellaneous wholly-owned subsidiaries | Ingston Limited (90%) | Plant Life Limited (100%) |

Requirement:

You are required to draft a memorandum to the Finance Director of the Crompton Group, outlining your recommendations in respect of the accounting issues relating to:

(a)   Plant Life Limited
(b)   The Group

You are also required to show the calculation of goodwill relating to the acquisition of Plant Life Limited.

Your recommendations should be in accordance with generally accepted accounting practice.

The capital gains tax rate for all companies in the Group is 20%.

No temporary differences exist at 31 May 2X06, except in relation to the land and buildings of Plant Life Limited.

FRS 102

Outline the key differences in accounting treatment if the financial statements were prepared in accordance with the requirements of FRS 102 *The Financial Reporting Standard applicable in the UK and Republic of Ireland.*

CURRENT ISSUES GROUP

The Current Issues Group has a major presence in the newspaper industry. You have recently been appointed as Group Financial Accountant, having worked with a competitor company for a number of years. Your appointment has come at a busy time as the Group is currently reviewing its accounts for the year ended 31 December 2x05.

In their separate/individual financial statements, all companies within the Group account at cost for investments in subsidiaries, joint ventures and associates.

The following investments have been made in recent years;

(1) On 1 January 2x02, Current Issues Limited acquired 80% of Big Times Limited at a cost of €800,000. The fair value of the net identifiable assets of Big Times at the date of acquisition was €500,000. The fair value of non-controlling interests was €120,000, and this was the basis on which non-controlling interests were measured at the acquisition date.

(2) During 2x05 Current Issues Limited acquired 25% of the equity share capital of Sometimes Limited. Current Issues has representation on the Board of Directors of Sometimes Limited, and exercises significant influence over its financial policy decisions.

(3) On 31 March 2x05 Current Issues Limited acquired 75% of the equity share capital of Blow the Whistle Limited, the consideration being equal to the fair value of the identifiable net assets acquired by Current Issues. Non-controlling interests at the acquisition date were measured at their proportionate share of the identifiable net assets of Blow the Whistle Limited.

Inter-company sales from Current Issues to Blow the Whistle during 2x05 amounted to €600,000, 30% of these arising during the first three months of the year.

(4) On 1 January 2x05 Current Issues purchased 80% of the equity share capital of Worthit Limited for €450,000. The fair value of the net identifiable assets of Worthit Limited at that time was €700,000, analysed as follows:

	€000
Machinery	600
Inventory	350
Creditors	(250)
	700

Non-controlling interests at acquisition date were measured at the proportionate share of the fair value of the net assets acquired.

Accounting Transactions

The following transactions occurred during the year ended 31 December 2x05:

(a) *Related party issues*

(i) On 31 March 2x05, Current Issues gave a loan of €1 million to one of its executive directors, Mr Smith. The purpose of the loan was to assist Mr Smith in repairing subsidence damage to his house.

(ii) On 8 May 2x05, Current Issues sold a printing press to Big Times at less than half its market value of €2.5million. On the same date, Sometimes Limited made a gift of an old printing press, which had a market value of €1 million, to Big Times.

(iii) During 2x05 Sometimes Limited bought a large quantity of dye from Fine Tune Limited, which is owned by Tom Osborne, whose wife Margaret is the controlling shareholder of Sometimes Limited.

(b) *Sale of assets*

(i) On 1 January 2x05 Current Issues sold freehold land to Money Limited, a wholly-owned subsidiary of an investment bank. The land, which had cost €600,000 in 2x01, was sold for €700,000. Money Limited had an option to resell the land to Current Issues for €931,700 on 31 December 2x06. Current Issues had a call option to repurchase the land on the same basis.

(ii) On 1 January 2x02 Current Issues purchased freehold buildings for €300,000. The buildings were revalued to €500,000 in the financial statements at 31 December 2x03, and sold for €600,000 in

March 2x05. It is group policy to depreciate buildings over 50 years on a straight-line basis from the date of purchase. The useful economic life did not change as a result of the revaluation. A full year's depreciation is charged in the year of purchase, and no depreciation is charged in the year of disposal.

(c) *Financing*

    (i)   On 1 January 2x05 Current Issues entered into a joint venture with Money Limited. A new company was set up, Fudgeit Limited, in which both Current Issues and Money held 50% of the shares. Under the terms of the joint venture agreement, Money advanced a loan of €500,000 to Fudgeit which was used to buy new equipment currently being used by Current Issues until Fudgeit begins trading. Current Issues has a majority of the Board members in Fudgeit, and has the power over decision making in that company.

        Fudgeit Limited is included in the financial statements of the Group, using the equity method.

    (ii)   On 30 September 2x05, Current Issues signed an agreement with Advance Factors. The following details are available:

- Advance Factors would give Current Issues an advance equal to 75% of its gross trade receivables. These funds were advanced primarily on a non-recourse basis, although Current Issues would be liable for the first €10,000 of bad debts. The normal level of bad debts incurred by Current Issues amounts to 3% of gross debtors.
- The remaining (25%) of trade receivables will continue to accrue to Current Issues.
- A facility fee of 1% of funds advanced would be charged.
- A fee equal to 1.5% of sales invoiced would be charged by Advance Factors in connection with the operation of the sales ledger of Current Issues.
- Interest at 12% per annum would be charged on funds advanced.
- At 31 December 2x05, Current Issues had received advances of €750,000 from Advance Factors, gross debtors standing at €1 million on that date. The following expenses were correctly accrued: interest €12,000, facility fee €7,500 and sales ledger fees of €30,000.

(d) *Titles*

Over the years Current Issues has expended large sums in promoting the group's titles. At 31 December 2x04 Current Issues had included €450,000 in the statement of financial position as an intangible asset in respect of these titles. An additional amount of €100,000 was also capitalised, this being the cost of titles procured from No Time Limited which had gone into liquidation during 2x04.

(e) *Impairment of assets*

In January 2x01 Current Issues had set up a division within the company to investigate the direction of the group's strategy in dealing with the rapid technological advances in the industry. Significant investment was made in developing an e-learning division. By 2x05 it had become clear that the e-learning division would be an insignificant market player. In accordance with IAS 36 *Impairment of Assets*, an impairment review of the e-learning division was carried out at 31 December 2x05.

(i)

	€000
Book value of net assets of division in statement of financial position	1,200*
Fair value less costs to sell of net assets of division	500

	€000
Goodwill	300
Generic software development	400
Tangible non-current assets carried at cost less accumulated depreciation	500
	1,200*

(ii) Value in use

Efforts are currently in progress to convert the e-learning division to a commercially viable database. This work is at an advanced stage, and the results are extremely promising. The following information is available in respect of the value in use of the net assets of the division:

The cumulative values of future cash flows of the division at 31 December 2x10 are estimated as follows. These figures are based on the company's approved budgets for the next five years.

	€000
Total cash flows from operations before taxation	2,830*
Software development costs	(2,000)
Finance costs	(1,000)

*This figure includes inflows of €1,400,000 which will result from planned development expenditure.

The company's pre-tax weighted average cost of capital (WACC) is 12%, but it is considered that an additional risk premium of 4% should be added to reflect the risk profile of this project.

(f) *Miscellaneous impairment issues*

An impairment review of the local newspaper division of Current Issues Limited took place in 2x03 with the result that the following write-downs were made in that year:

(i) Printing presses which had originally cost €400,000 were five years old on 31 December 2x03 when they were written down on 31 December 2x03 to their recoverable amount of €60,000.

Up to 2x04 the printing presses had been depreciated at 10% per annum on a straight-line basis. Depreciation in 2x04 was charged on a straight-line basis over the assets' remaining life of 5 years.

A positive change in consumer preferences during 2x05 has meant that the reasons which led to the original impairment have now been reversed.

(ii) Land which had been purchased in 2x00 for €300,000 was revalued to €500,000 in 2x02. As part of the impairment review it was written down on 31 December 2x03 to its recoverable amount of €200,000.

The write-down was recorded as follows:

	DR €	CR €
Revaluation surplus – OCI	200,000	
Impairment write-down – P/L	100,000	
Land – SOFP		300,000

Due to a revision of consumer preferences in 2x05, it is believed that there are grounds for reversing the original impairment.

(iii) Titles

As part of the 2x03 impairment review, the book value of purchased local newspaper titles had been written down by €250,000. In retrospect this appears to have been unnecessary following improvements in content which have resulted in more positive findings on consumer preferences in 2x05.

(g) *Miscellaneous provisions and contingency issues*

(i) Legal action

On 30 November 2x05 a well-known celebrity took a libel action against Current Issues Limited. The case is due to come before the courts in June 2x06 and the plaintiff has refused to accept an unconditional apology together with a cash settlement of €80,000.

On 31 March 2x06 (the date on which the directors of Current Issues authorised the accounts for issue), the company's legal advisors were of the opinion that there was a 75% probability that the plaintiff would be awarded damages of €100,000. Additionally, they estimated that there was a 25% probability that damages as high as €200,000 could be awarded.

Current Issues have sought to recover part of the award from a publicity group which allegedly leaked false information about the celebrity. On 31 March 2x06 it seemed probable that a cash settlement of €20,000 might be agreed.

(ii) Review of provisions

In finalising the 2x05 accounts, the Board of Directors of Current Issues Limited is carrying out a review of provisions:

- A decision to restructure a division within Current Issues Limited was taken at a Board meeting in December 2x04, and a provision of €250,000 was made at that time. An outline plan for the restructuring was finalised in December 2x05.

- A provision for the ongoing repair of printing presses was increased by 20% to €300,000 during 2x05. It is expected that a significant proportion of this provision will be required during 2x06.

- At 31 December 2x05, the present value of future un-provided decommissioning expenses of printing presses purchased during the year ended 31 December 2x05 was estimated at €300,000.

(iii) Payments to retired employees

Due to legislative changes in 2x05, Current Issues Limited has been forced to agree to make additional pension payments to retired employees as part of the company's defined benefit scheme. The additional amounts which will be payable are as follows:

	€
2x06	150,000
2x07	200,000
2x08	250,000
2x09	280,000
2x10	320,000
2x11	350,000

(h) *Tangible non-current assets*

(i) Capitalisation of costs

During 2x05 Current Issues decided to construct a specialised mini-printing press for the production of advertising leaflets which were to be circulated as newspaper inserts. The following costs were incurred during 2x05:

	€
Purchase of machine part components (before deducting trade discount of 5%)	20,000
Option premium to guarantee availability of external labour personnel paid in January 2x05*	3,000
External labour costs	10,000
Labour costs of own employees	13,000
Safety and clearance check procedures	2,000
Correction of design errors	3,000

Marketing costs associated with advertising leaflets	
- incurred during construction	1,000
- incurred after completion of construction	1,000
Trial print runs	2,000
Interest costs**	3,000
Estimated present value cost @ 31/12/2x05 of dismantling mini-printing press	1,500
	59,500

*Option premium was paid when it was probable that construction of the mini-printing press would proceed.
**Interest costs were incurred during the construction of the mini printing press.

At 31 December 2x05 it was apparent that the proposal to produce the advertising inserts was not going to be as profitable as first thought. At this point it was estimated that the printing press had the following values:

- Net selling price €40,000.
- Value in use €42,000.

Printing presses are depreciated at 10% on a straight-line basis. A full year's depreciation is provided in the year of purchase/production. The residual value of the mini-printing press is estimated at €5,000 (€7,000 based on future prices).

(ii) Subsequent expenditure
The following items have been capitalised by Current Issues Limited in the year ended 31 December 2x05:

- Costs of the annual overhaul of the company's printing presses, amounting to €200,000.
- Removal of partitioning in factory to increase worker productivity costing €100,000.
- Replacement of lifts in the company headquarters, costing €200,000. The original lifts were depreciated at 10% per annum on a reducing-balance basis. The office headquarters building is depreciated at 2% per annum on a straight-line basis.

- Relocation costs of printing presses amounting to €30,000.
- Extension of warehouse, costing €120,000.

(iii) Revaluation gains

    (a) Current Issues Limited purchased an office building in 2x02 for €1 million. The building has been used by company staff and has been depreciated at 2% per annum on a straight-line basis. On 31 December 2x05 an external valuer has estimated the fair value of the property to be €1.5 million.

    (b) Current Issues purchased a factory building in 2x03 for €500,000. The building was being depreciated on a straight-line basis over a useful life of 50 years with zero residual value. On 31 December 2x04 the building was revalued to €300,000, and was further revalued to €490,000 on 31 December 2x05.

(iv) Revaluation losses

    (I) Current Issues Limited purchased a site in 2x02 for €400,000, which was intended to be used for the construction of a paper storage warehouse. In 2x05 it was decided not to proceed with the construction of the warehouse. The market value of the site at 31 December 2x05 is estimated at €300,000.

    (II) At 31 December 2x04 a property which had been purchased by Current Issues Limited in 2x03 for €750,000 was revalued to €1 million. Due to a general fall in property values, the fair value of the property at 31 December 2x05 was estimated at €600,000. The property was depreciated on a straight-line basis over 50 years with zero residual value.

(v) Disposals

During 2x05, Current Issues Limited disposed of land which had cost €200,000 in 2x02 and had subsequently been revalued to €310,000 during 2x04. The net proceeds of disposal amounted to €370,000.

(i) *Accounting policy issues*

    (i) Research and development

At 31 December 2x04, Current Issues had €2 million of development costs included under intangible assets in the Statement of Financial Position. Previously, development costs had been written off in accordance with the expected sales revenue of future periods. The directors have decided however that, commencing in 2x05, development costs should be written off by reference to the expected time horizon of future sales as new information indicates that this would better reflect the consumption of the future economic benefits of the development expenditure.

(ii)   Investment property

Current Issues Limited purchased a freehold premises in 2x03 for €3 million. The premises, which was used by company personnel, was included in the financial statements at cost and was not depreciated.

In December 2x05, the premises was no longer used by company personnel, and it was let to an unrelated party at a market rental. The premises is included in the financial statements at 31 December 2x05 at its fair value of €5 million.

(j)   *Profit before taxation*

The profit before taxation of the Current Issues Group for the year ended 31 December 2x05 amounted to €850,000.

Requirement:

You are required to write a report to the Finance Director of the Current Issues Group, outlining how the above transactions should be accounted for in the consolidated financial statements and, where appropriate, in the financial statements of the individual companies in the group. *(Ignore tax)*

The Current Issues Group has a weighted average cost of capital of 8%. This equates to 12% on a pre-tax basis.

The structure of the Current Issues Group is outlined in Appendix I.

FRS 102

Outline the key differences in accounting treatment if the financial statements were prepared in accordance with the requirements of FRS 102 *The Financial Reporting Standard applicable in the UK and Republic of Ireland.*

Appendix I – Group Structure

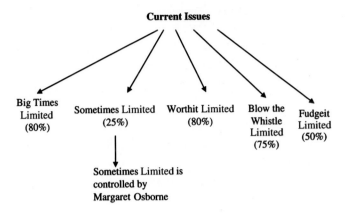

Other Companies:

(1) **Fine Tune** – owned by Margaret Osborne's husband

(2) **Money Limited** – A wholly-owned subsidiary of a merchant bank, Money Limited owns the other 50% of Fudgeit

(3) **No Time Limited** – No relationship with Current Issues Group

FRONTPAGE GROUP

Introduction

You are an audit senior in a firm of Chartered Accountants, Rockwell, Spate & Co. It is February 2x06 and you are currently reviewing the draft financial statements of the Frontpage Group which has recently become a client of your firm.

Frontpage Limited is a publishing company which was set up by John Walker. In 2x00 Frontpage Limited acquired 100% of the equity share capital of Backpage Limited.

In 2x02 Frontpage Limited purchased 30% of Sideissue Limited for €5 million. John Walker had been a director of Sideissue Limited since 2x02, but resigned from the Board on the disposal of Frontpage Limited's interest in Sideissue for €9 million on the 30 September 2x05. Sideissue had been included in the Group accounts using the equity method of accounting.

A number of accounting issues have arisen in respect of the audit of the Frontpage Group for the year ended 31 December 2x05. The audit manager, Patrick Queally, has requested that you review these issues and send him a memorandum. Your report should set out the appropriate accounting treatment and disclosure in respect of each accounting issue, together with any necessary associated journal adjustments.

The accounting issues and the draft financial statements are set out in Appendix I and Appendix II respectively.

Requirement

Based on the accounting issues given in Appendix I and the draft financial statements in Appendix II, prepare a memorandum to the audit manager of Rockwell Spate & Co. setting out your advice in relation to the accounting treatment, together with any journal adjustments and disclosures required in respect of each of the following accounting issues that arose during the 2x05 audit:

(1)	Inventory	**11 marks**
(2)	Financing arrangement	**4 marks**
(3)	Disposal of shares in Sideissue Limited, and related issues	**10 marks**
(4)	Construction of office building	**9 marks**
(5)	Legal and miscellaneous issues	**8 marks**
(6)	Deferred tax	**8 marks**

Total 50 marks

For each issue include the impact, if any, on:

(i)   the separate/individual financial statements of the respective companies;

(ii) the consolidated financial statements of the Frontpage Group.

Notes:

- **Re-drafted financial statements are NOT required. However, your report should include the journal entries in respect of any accounting adjustments required in respect of each accounting issue.**

- **The Frontpage Group currently pays corporation tax at 25%, but it is possible that this rate will increase to 40% in 2x06. Capital gains tax is levied on chargeable gains at 20%.**

- **In its separate financial statements, Frontpage Limited accounts at cost for investments in subsidiaries, joint ventures and associates.**

FRS 102

Outline the key differences in accounting treatment if the financial statements were prepared in accordance with the requirements of FRS 102 *The Financial Reporting Standard applicable in the UK and Republic of Ireland.*

Appendix I

Accounting Issues Arising in Respect of the 2x05 Financial Statements

(1) Inventory in Frontpage Limited

(i) *Publishing delay*

Work on a history book had been scheduled for completion in December 2x05. It has been discovered, however, that a series of illustrations which had been photographed on location have been misplaced. These were re-taken in January 2x06, and the book will now be published in April 2x06. It had been hoped to publish before a rival publication from Associated History Books Ltd, but it is unlikely that this will now be achieved. Consequently, sales are expected to be only 60% of the budgeted sales level of €750,000.

Costs incurred at 31 December 2x05, which have been included in inventory, are as follows:

	€000
Materials	100
Production salaries*	150
Depreciation of equipment	20
General administration	40
Selling and distribution costs	80
	390

*Includes €30,000 in respect of misplaced book illustrations.

Further costs are estimated as follows, of which 50% have already been incurred in January/February 2x06:

	€000
Production salaries**	90
Selling and distribution costs	220
	310

**Includes €40,000 in respect of book illustrations

(ii) *Printing stationery*

In previous years Frontpage had outsourced its printing needs, but printing has been performed in-house since 1 January 2x05.

15,000 reams of printing stationery are included in inventory at 31 December 2x05. This inventory is held in a sealed warehouse and additional reams of paper are stored on top of existing reams. During 2x05 five consignments of printing stationery were received, each containing 10,000 reams. The cost per ream of the first consignment was €11.40 (net of a trade discount of 5%) and increased by 5% for each of the other four consignment lots received. Stationery inventory has been included in the financial statements on a last in first out (LIFO) basis at 31 December 2x05.

During 2x05, the inventory of stationery did not fall below 10,000 reams at any time. After the second consignment was received, the level of stationery inventory did not fall below 15,000 reams. Inventories of stationery have been included in the financial statements at 31 December 2x05 on a LIFO basis.

(iii) *Excess dye*

Frontpage Limited's production process gives rise to a dye residue, which is sold to a nearby furniture manufacturer. Frontpage had inventories of dye with a net realisable value of €50,000 on hand at the 31 December 2x05. This has resulted from two months of printing production.

No record of the inventories of dye has been made in the financial statements at 31 December 2x05.

(2) Financing Arrangement

The trade receivables of €10.3 million were factored by Frontpage Limited in December 2x05. The factor provided an immediate advance of €8 million. The balance of €2.3 million will continue to accrue to Frontpage Limited.

The funds were advanced by the factor on the following basis:

In respect of the trade receivables of €10.3 million, Frontpage Limited is liable for the first €3.3 million of bad debts.

All of the funds advanced by the factor were included as a current liability in the financial statements of Frontpage Limited at 31 December 2x05.

A bad debts provision of 5% of gross debtors should be provided for at 31 December 2x05. A provision of €250,000 was included in the Statement of Financial Position at 31 December 2x04.

In January 2x06 one of the company's best customers unexpectedly went into liquidation. The balance on that debtor's account at 31 December 2x05 amounted to €500,000. No adjustment has been made to the financial statements in respect of the customer's liquidation.

(3) Disposal of Shares in Sideissue Limited, and Related Issues

(i) Sideissue had retained earnings of €4 million when Frontpage acquired its interest in 2x02. On 31 December 2x04, the retained earnings of Sideissue had increased to €7 million.

Sideissue earned profit before taxation of €2 million in the nine months ending 30 September 2x05, and incurred taxation of €600,000 on these profits.

(ii) In the nine months ending 30 September 2x05, Backpage Limited recorded sales of €900,000 to Sideissue at cost plus 10%. Backpage normally earns a mark-up of 50% on sales. None of these goods are included in the inventory of Sideissue at 30 September 2x05.

(iii) Sideissue was included in the Group Financial Statements using the equity method of accounting.

(4) Construction of Office Building

On 1 January 2x03 Backpage Limited commenced the construction of a new office building, which was completed on 30 November 2x03. It was discovered, however, that planning laws had been contravened and it was not possible to occupy the offices due to a restraining order imposed by the Council. Costs of €1 million had been incurred and these were written off in full in Backpage Limited's 2x03 financial statements.

On 1 March 2x05 planning permission was granted retrospectively and the costs previously written off were reinstated and credited to profit or loss by Backpage Limited.

Backpage depreciates buildings at 2% per annum on a straight-line basis. A full year's depreciation is charged in the year of purchase or construction; no depreciation is charged in the year of disposal. Depreciation of €20 million has been charged on the office building for the year ended 31 December 2x05.

In December 2x05 the Board capitalised €300,000 of interest costs as part of buildings. These costs were incurred in respect of the financing of the new office building for the following periods:

	€000
1 January 2x03 – 30 November 2x03	100
1 December 2x03 – 1 March 2x05	200
	300

(5) Legal and Miscellaneous Issues

(i)   In November 2x05 another publishing group threatened to take legal action against Frontpage, claiming breach of copyright. In a phone call to John Walker, the company's marketing director accused Frontpage of infringing their exclusive rights to publish a Brazilian musician's collected works and threatened to sue for sales rights amounting to €0.5 million. In mid-February 2x06 no further action had been taken and John Walker has dismissed the claim as ludicrous, maintaining that Frontpage would be able to lodge a counter-claim for copyright infringement against the same company for a similar amount.

(ii) In December 2x05 a local art expert maintained that a painting in Frontpage Limited's headquarters was worth in the region of €700,000. On 10 January 2x06, while still awaiting confirmation of its value, the painting was sold for €350,000 to Margin Limited, a company in which John Walker's son, Thomas, had a controlling interest.

On 21 January 2x06 the value of the painting was confirmed at €700,000. The painting had been purchased for €10,000 several years ago and, at 31 December 2x05, it is included in property, plant and equipment at its net book value of €8,000.

(6) Deferred Tax

General issues

At 31 December 2x05, the following issues arose in respect of Frontpage Limited:

(i)   The net book value of plant and machinery at 31 December 2x05 was €1.4 million. The tax written down value of this plant and machinery amounted to €900,000 at the same date.

(ii) Pension costs of €300,000 were accrued at 31 December 2x05, and deposit interest, included as a receivable in the financial statements, amounted to €80,000. It should be assumed that pension costs are allowed for tax purposes when paid, and that deposit interest is taxed on a cash receipts basis.

(iii) There was a revaluation surplus of €500,000 in respect of land at 31 December 2x05. It is intended to retain the land within the group for the foreseeable future.

(iv) Development costs capitalised at 31 December 2x05 amount to €250,000, all of which has been paid and fully claimed for tax purposes. Frontpage Limited writes off development costs at 20% per annum, on a straight-line basis.

(v)   Frontpage Limited had recognised a liability for deferred taxation of €100,000 at 31 December 2x04, and this liability was unchanged at 31 December 2x05. None of the liability at 31 December 2x04 related to the revaluation of land referred to in (iii) above.

Appendix II

Draft Statement of Comprehensive Income of the Frontpage Group for the year ended 31 December 2x05

	€000
Revenue	14,500
Cost of sales	(6,900)
Gross profit	7,600
Distribution costs	(400)
Administrative expenses	(700)
Other expenses	(3,500)
Share of profit of associate	600
Profit on disposal of Sideissue Ltd	4,000
Finance costs	(600)
Profit before tax	7,000
Income tax expense	(750)
Profit for the year from continuing operations	6,250

Other comprehensive income:
Items that may subsequently be reclassified to profit or loss:

Share of other comprehensive income of associate	250
Cash flow hedges	750
Total comprehensive income for the year	7,250

Profit attributable to:

Owners of the parent	6,250
Non-controlling interests	–
	6,250

Total comprehensive income attributable to:

Owners of the parent	7,250
Non-controlling interests	–
	7,250

Draft Statement of Financial Position of the Frontpage Group at 31 December 2x05

	Notes	€000
Assets		
Non-current assets		
Property, plant and equipment		15,500
Current assets		
Inventories		1,500
Trade and other receivables		10,900*
Cash and cash equivalents		700
		13,100
Total assets		28,600
Liabilities		
Current liabilities		
Trade and other payables		14,200
Income tax payable		1,600
		15,800
Non-current liabilities		
Term loan		1,200
Deferred income taxes		100
		1,300
Total liabilities		17,100
Net assets		11,500
Equity		
Equity attributable to owners of the parent		
Share capital		1,000
Share premium account		3,000
Revaluation surplus		1,500
Retained earnings		6,000
Total equity		11,500

*Includes trade receivables of €10.3 million

HARDCOURT GROUP

Introduction

You are an audit senior in a firm of Chartered Accountants, Comerford Lane & Co. It is February 2x06 and you are currently reviewing the draft financial statements of the Hardcourt Group which has recently become a client of your firm.

The Hardcourt Group consists of Hardcourt Limited and its subsidiary company, Claycourt Limited, which was acquired during 2x05. The Group's principal area of business is focused on the sale of timber products and ancillary activities. A number of accounting issues have arisen in respect of the audit of the Hardcourt Group for the year ended 31 December 2x05. The audit manager, Beatrice Lambe, has requested that you review these issues and send her a memorandum. Your report should set out the appropriate accounting treatment and disclosure in respect of each accounting issue, together with any necessary associated journal adjustments.

The accounting issues and the draft financial statements are set out in Appendix I and Appendix II respectively.

Requirement:

Based on the accounting issues outlined in Appendix I, and the draft financial statements in Appendix II, prepare a memorandum to the audit manager of Comerford Lane & Co. setting out your advice in relation to the accounting treatment, together with any journal adjustments and disclosures required in respect of each of the following accounting issues that arose during the 2x05 audit:

(1)	Acquisition of Claycourt Limited	**20 marks**
(2)	Revaluation of land	**4 marks**
(3)	Restructuring	**10 marks**
(4)	Land	**4 marks**
(5)	Capital grants	**7 marks**
(6)	Financing arrangement	**5 marks**
		Total 50 marks

For each issue include the impact, if any, on:

(i)   the separate/individual financial statements of the respective companies;

(ii)   the consolidated financial statements of the Hardcourt Group.

Notes:

- **Re-drafted financial statements are NOT required. However, your report should include the journal entries in respect of any accounting adjustments required in respect of each accounting issue.**

- **The Hardcourt Group pays capital gains tax @ 20%. The corporation tax rate is 30%.**

- **It is group policy to measure non-controlling interests at acquisition date at their proportionate share of the identifiable net assets of a subsidiary.**

FRS 102

Outline the key differences in accounting treatment if the financial statements were prepared in accordance with the requirements of FRS 102 *The Financial Reporting Standard applicable in the UK and Republic of Ireland.*

Appendix I

Accounting Issues Arising in Respect of the 2x05 Financial Statements of the Hardcourt Group

(1) Acquisition of Claycourt Limited

On 1 July 2x05, Hardcourt Limited acquired 85% of the ordinary share capital of Claycourt Limited for €8.5 million in cash. The book value of the identifiable net assets of Claycourt Limited at that time was €7 million. The following details are relevant to the acquisition:

- It has since transpired that work in progress inventory of Claycourt, which had a book value of €500,000 on 1 July 2x05, was subsequently sold for €400,000. Completion costs relating to this inventory amounted to €70,000.
- The costs of a due diligence investigation of Claycourt Limited amounted to €400,000. This was written off to the Statement of Comprehensive Income of Hardcourt Limited.
- Quoted investments with a book value of €300,000, held as current assets by Claycourt Limited, had a market value of €800,000.
- Sales of timber products by Claycourt Limited to Hardcourt Limited amounted to €200,000 per calendar month during 2x05. Hardcourt Limited had one month's inventory on hand at 31 December 2x05, which had been acquired from Claycourt Limited at a mark-up of 25% on cost.

No entries, other than the write-off of due diligence costs, have been made in respect of the acquisition of Claycourt Limited.

(2) Revaluation of Land

Land purchased by Hardcourt Limited in 2x03 for €1 million had been revalued to €1.5 million in 2x04. A rezoning decision in 2x05 has reduced the value of the land to €700,000 at 31 December 2x05.

(3) Restructuring

During 2x05 a detailed restructuring plan for Hardcourt Limited was drawn up, involving the closure of the timberland division, details of which were announced to the staff in October. However, operating activities cannot cease until 31 May 2x06 due to contractual commitments with customers. It is estimated that operating losses during the first five months of 2x06 will amount to €600,000. It is intended to dispose of all of the saleable assets of the division as part of a single transaction.

It is expected that the following additional costs will be incurred:

Redundancy costs
Redundancy costs are expected to amount in total to €1 million. It is believed, however, that there is a 60% probability of re-deploying some staff, which would result in €200,000 of the redundancy costs being avoided.

(4) Land

A land site owned by Hardcourt Limited is surplus to requirements and, in December 2x05, the site was put on sale at an amount which is €300,000 more than its value in the statement of financial position at 31 December 2x05. It is expected that the site will be sold for this amount during 2x06.

The land had been purchased several years ago for €800,000, and is valued in the financial statements at 31 December 2x05 at €1.7 million. Selling costs are estimated at €30,000.

(5) Capital grants

Hardcourt Limited has always recorded amounts of grants received on a cash receipts basis. The Board of Directors has now decided that grants should be recorded in the financial statements when Government commitments are in place. This decision has been taken on the grounds that an accruals basis will provide information that is reliable and more relevant.

At 31 December 2x05 Hardcourt Limited had received commitments for grants of 25% in respect of machinery costing €800,000 purchased during November and December.

One of the machines was transferred to Claycourt Limited at its cost price of €200,000 soon after the date of purchase.

Appendix II

Draft Statement of Comprehensive Income of the Hardcourt Group for the year ended 31 December 2x05

	2x05 €000
Revenue	17,900
Cost of sales	(5,850)
Gross profit	12,050
Distribution costs	(700)
Administrative expenses	(600)
Other expenses	(2,100)
Finance costs	(620)
Profit before tax	8,030
Income tax expense	(750)
Profit for the year from continuing operations	7,280
Other comprehensive income:	
Items that will not be reclassified to profit or loss:	
Gains on property revaluation	1,230
Items that may be subsequently reclassified to profit or loss:	
Cash flow hedges	750
Total comprehensive income for the year	9,260
Profit attributable to:	
Owners of the parent	6,450
Non-controlling interests	830
	7,280
Total comprehensive income attributable to:	
Owners of the parent	8,430
Non-controlling interests	830
	9,260

Draft Statement of Financial Position of the Hardcourt Group at 31 December 2x05

	Notes	2x05 €000	2x04 €000
Assets			
Non-current assets			
Property, plant and equipment		20,943	
Current assets			
Inventories		4,469	
Trade and other receivables		5,395	
Cash and cash equivalents		1,155	
		11,01	
Total assets		31,962	
Liabilities			
Current liabilities			
Trade and other payables		3,565	
Non-current liabilities			
Term loan		1,120	
Total liabilities		4,685	
Net assets		27,277	
Equity			
Equity attributable to owners of the parent			
Share capital		100	
Share premium account		5,250	
Revaluation surplus		7,500	
Retained earnings		12,927	
		25,777	
Non-controlling interests		1,500	
Total equity		27,277	

HEALTHFIRST GROUP

Introduction

You are an audit senior in a firm of Chartered Accountants, Lantry Mansfield & Co. It is February 2x06 and you are currently reviewing the draft financial statements of the Healthfirst Group which has recently become a client of your firm.

Healthfirst Limited is a medical goods company set up by Edward Smithson some years ago. Healthfirst Limited has a number of subsidiaries, including an 85% shareholding in Scanright Limited, acquired on 1 April 2x05, with a view to diversifying into a growth area in the diagnostic goods sector. All other subsidiaries are 100% owned by Healthfirst Limited.

A number of accounting issues have arisen in respect of the audit of the Healthfirst Group for the year ended 31 December 2x05. The audit manager, Susan Gilmartin, has requested that you review these issues and send her a memorandum. Your memorandum should set out the appropriate accounting treatment and disclosure in respect of each accounting issue, together with any necessary associated journal adjustments.

The accounting issues and the draft financial statements are set out in Appendix I and Appendix II respectively.

Requirement:

Based on the accounting issues outlined in Appendix I, and the draft financial statements in Appendix II, prepare a memorandum to the audit manager of Lantry Mansfield & Co. setting out your advice in relation to the accounting treatment, together with any journal adjustments and disclosures required in respect of each of the following accounting issues that arose during the 2x05 audit:

(1)	Goodwill on the acquisition of Scanright Limited, and relevant disclosures	**10 marks**
(2)	Inter-company sales	**9 marks**
(3)	Deferred tax	**13 marks**
(4)	Investment property	**8 marks**
(5)	Sale of franchise	**10 marks**
		Total 50 marks

For each issue include the impact, if any, on:

(i)   the separate and individual financial statements of the respective companies;

(ii) the consolidated financial statements of the Healthfirst Group.

Notes:

- **Re-drafted financial statements are NOT required. However, your report should include the journal entries in respect of any accounting adjustments required in respect of each accounting issue.**

- **The Healthfirst Group currently pays corporation tax at 25%, but it is possible that this rate will increase to 40% in 2x05. Capital gains tax is levied on chargeable gains at 20%.**

- **In its separate financial statements, Healthfirst Limited accounts at cost for investments in subsidiaries, joint ventures and associates.**

- **It is group policy to measure any non-controlling interest in subsidiaries at acquisition date at fair value.**

FRS 102

Outline the key differences in accounting treatment if the financial statements were prepared in accordance with the requirements of FRS 102 *The Financial Reporting Standard applicable in the UK and Republic of Ireland.*

Appendix I

Accounting Issues Arising in Respect of the 2x05 Financial Statements

(1) Goodwill Arising on Acquisition of Scanright Limited

On 1 April 2x05 Healthfirst paid €6.5 million for an 85% interest in Scanright. Scanright had the following shareholders' funds at this date:

	€000
Equity share capital	1,000
Reserves	3,800

The fair value of non-controlling interests in Scanright at 1 April 2x05 was €1.147 million. The Healthfirst Group values NCI at its fair value on the date that a subsidiary is acquired.

It was estimated that the market value of Scanright's land holdings was €800,000 greater than their net book value at that time.

Finished goods included in Scanright's inventory at 1 April 2x05 have been in the company's warehouse since 31 December 2x04. They were included in the statement of financial position of Scanright at their production cost of €395,000.

These goods were sold in June 2x05 for €300,000.

(2) Intragroup Sales

During 2x05 Scanright sold goods evenly throughout the year to Healthfirst Limited for €960,000. Scanright charged a mark up of 25% on cost, and 20% of the goods remained in the inventory of Healthfirst at 31 December 2x05. The latter goods had been purchased from Scanright after 1 April 2x05.

(3) Deferred Tax

At 31 December 2x05, the following information is available in respect of the Healthfirst Group (excluding Scanright Limited):

(a) Land purchased in 2x00 for €1 million was revalued at €1.4 million at 31 December 2x05.

(b) Deposit interest of €50,000 was recorded in the financial statements of the Group at 31 December 2x05, but was not received until February of 2x06.

(c)   The tax written down value of plant and machinery at 31 December 2x05 was €1.4 million. The net book value at that date was €2 million.

(d)   Development costs are allowed for taxation purposes when paid, and are expensed to the statement of comprehensive income of the Health-first Group over five years, commencing at the point of commercial production. All expenditure incurred was capitalised and has been paid for in full at 31 December 2x05.

(e)   During 2x05 the Healthfirst Group incurred fines amounting to €100,000 for a breach of planning guidelines.

(f)   A liability of €100,000 had been recognised at 31 December 2x04 for deferred taxation.

(4) Investment Property

An office building, purchased in 2x01 for €700,000, was let to a third party at a market rental. This building was included in the financial statements of the Healthfirst Group as an investment property at its fair value – €1.3 million at 31 December 2x04.

On 1 January 2x05 the lease agreement terminated and the building was used by the Healthfirst Group as a staff office. The Healthfirst Group depreciates buildings at 2% per annum on a straight-line basis.

(5) Sale of Franchise

In 2x01, Suretime Limited, a 100% subsidiary of Healthfirst Limited, purchased a franchise for a lifestyle drug for €1 million. This amount was capitalised and was not amortised. On 1 November 2x05 the franchise was sold by Suretime Limited to a US pharmaceutical firm for $2.5 million, the sales proceeds being included in turnover at the spot rate on that date.

On 20 December 2x05 Suretime Limited received full payment from the US purchaser of the franchise. In the expectation of a rise in the value of the dollar, the $2.5 million sales proceeds were held in a $ bank account. Following a strength-ening of the dollar, the funds were converted into euro on 15 February 2x06.

Exchange rates were as follows:

1 November 2x05:   €1 = $1.1
20 December 2x05:   €1 = $1.05

31 December 2x05:   €1 = $1
15 February 2x06:   €1 = $.95

Appendix II

**Extract from Draft Statement of Comprehensive Income of the
Healthfirst Group for the year ended 31 December 2x05**

	2x05 €000
Revenue	15,500
Cost of sales	(5,400)
Gross profit	10,100
Distribution costs	(400)
Administrative expenses	(700)
Other expenses	(1,500)
Finance costs	(600)
Share of profit of associate	600
Profit before tax	7,500
Income tax expense	(750)
Profit for the year from continuing operations	6,750
Other comprehensive income:	
Items that will not be reclassified to profit or loss:	
Gains on property revaluation	750
Items that may be subsequently reclassified to profit or loss:	
Cash flow hedges	200
Total comprehensive income for the year	7,700
Profit attributable to:	
Owners of the parent	6,450
Non-controlling interests	300
	6,750
Total comprehensive income attributable to:	
Owners of the parent	7,350
Non-controlling interests	350
	7,700

Draft Statement of Financial Position of the Healthfirst Group
at 31 December 2x05

	Notes	€000
Assets		
Non-current assets		
Property, plant and equipment		6,000
Development costs		800
		6,800
Current assets		
Inventories		1,500
Trade and other receivables		14,000
Cash and cash equivalents		1,300
		16,800
Total assets		23,600
Liabilities		
Current liabilities		
Trade and other payables		5,800
Non-current liabilities		
Term loan		1,200
Deferred income taxes		100
		1,300
Total liabilities		7,100
Net assets		16,500
Equity		
Equity attributable to owners of the parent		
Share capital		1,000
Share premium account		3,000
Revaluation reserve		2,100
Retained earnings		9,300
		15,400
Non-controlling Interest		1,100
Total equity		16,500

MAINPART GROUP

Introduction

You are an audit senior in a firm of Chartered Accountants, Witherspoon Holt & Co. It is February 2x06 and you are currently reviewing the draft financial statements of the Mainpart Group, which has recently become a client of your firm.

The Mainpart Group consists of Mainpart Holdings Limited and two wholly-owned subsidiary undertakings, Mainpart Limited and Rent Part Limited. The group's principal area of business is the sale of cement products and ancillary activities. A number of accounting issues have arisen in respect of the audit of the Mainpart Group for the year ended 31 December 2x05. The Senior Partner of Witherspoon Holt & Co., Judith Holt, has requested that you review these issues and prepare a report for the Board of Directors of Mainpart Holdings Limited. Your report should set out the appropriate accounting treatment and disclosure in respect of each accounting issue, together with any necessary associated journal adjustments.

The accounting issues and the draft financial statements are set out in Appendix I and Appendix II respectively. The Group structure is outlined in Appendix III.

Requirement:

Based on the accounting issues outlined in Appendix I, and the draft financial statements in Appendix II, prepare a report to the Board of Directors of Mainpart Holdings Limited setting out your advice in relation to the appropriate accounting treatment, together with any journal adjustments and disclosures required in respect of each of the following accounting issues that arose during the 2x05 audit:

(1)	Construction of building	**20 marks**
(2)	Disposal of subsidiary	**13 marks**
(3)	Restructuring	**12 marks**
(4)	Disposal of land	**5 marks**
		Total 50 marks

For each issue include the impact, if any, on:

    (i)   the separate/individual financial statements of the respective companies; and

    (ii) the consolidated financial statements of the Mainpart Group.

Notes:

- **Redrafted or consolidated financial statements are not required. The Group's weighted average cost of capital (WACC) is 12%.**

- **In their separate financial statements, Mainpart Holdings Limited accounts at cost for investments in subsidiaries, joint ventures and associates.**

FRS 102

Outline the key differences in accounting treatment if the financial statements were prepared in accordance with the requirements of FRS 102 *The Financial Reporting Standard applicable in the UK and Republic of Ireland.*

Appendix I

Accounting Issues Arising in Respect of the 2x05 Financial Statements of the Mainpart Group Companies

(1) Construction of Building

Mainpart Limited commenced the construction of a new factory premises on 1 January 2x05. The building was completed on 31 October 2x05, and the following costs were incurred and capitalised as part of the land and buildings of Mainpart Limited:

	€000
Site preparation costs	100
External labour costs (Note 1)	700
Materials (Note 2)	1,500
Overheads:	
- production (Note 3)	400
- general management	100
Re-design cost due to planning restrictions	170
Location map and brochure sent to customers	10
Recruitment costs of security personnel who commenced work in December 2x05	20
Interest costs (from 1 January to 31 October 2x05)	300
Official opening luncheon	30
	3,330

Note 1: External labour costs
This work was carried out by Small Part Limited, a company in which Mainpart Limited has a 22% shareholding.

A two-months' delay was caused by a work stoppage in July 2x05, which increased the total labour costs by €100,000. Funds borrowed were put on temporary deposit for the stoppage period, earning interest of €12,000.

Note 2: Materials
Materials are inclusive of VAT at 10% and before deducting a trade discount of 5%.

Note 3: Production overheads

Staff recruited for project	100
Administrative staff redeployed from other Mainpart locations	80
Salary of safety officers	140
Other variable overheads	80
	400

Note 4: Depreciation

Buildings are depreciated at 2% per annum on a straight-line basis. A full year's depreciation is charged in the year of purchase or construction. No depreciation is charged in the year of disposal.

(2) Disposal of Subsidiary

On 1 July 2x05 Mainpart Limited sold 90% of its shares in Subpart Limited, which supplies ancillary cement products. Disposal proceeds were €32 million in cash. One hundred per cent of Subpart Limited had been acquired on 1 January 2x03 at a cost of €22 million. The assets less liabilities of Subpart Limited were included in the Group's statement of financial position at €26 million on the 1 July 2x05. Goodwill of €2 million relating to the acquisition of Subpart Limited was also included in the Group's statement of financial position at 1 July 2x05. The fair value of the 10% stake retained was €3.5 million at 1 July 2x05.

Mainpart Limited agreed to buy directly from Subpart Limited after the disposal date so as to continue to service the needs of a select number of its customers. Purchases from Subpart Limited for the six months ended 31 December 2x05 amounted to €1.5 million.

(3) Restructuring

During 2x05 a re-structuring plan for Mainpart Limited's gardening division was drawn up and implemented. The following costs were incurred.

	€000
Redundancy settlements (Note 1)	800
Enhanced pensions for staff laid off (Note 2)	2,640
Provision for continuing losses expected in 2x06 and 2007	1,000
	4,440

Note 1: Redundancy settlements

These amounts were paid early in 2x06. It is likely that further redundancy costs of €300,000 will be incurred. It is believed, however, that these costs can be avoided, and that the staff can be redeployed elsewhere within the company. This would necessitate a retraining programme, which would cost in the region of €100,000.

Note 2: Enhanced pensions

It has been agreed to pay an enhanced pension to staff who have been laid off. This will cost €220,000 per annum for the next 12 years. The first annual instalment was paid by the company on 1 January 2x06.

Note 3: Other costs

A five-year lease agreement was signed on 1 January 2x05 in respect of a building which is now being vacated. The terms of the lease require the payment of annual lease instalments of €90,000, payable in advance. Mainpart Limited is confident that half of this amount can be recouped by subletting the premises to another tenant.

(4) Disposal of Land

On 28 December 2x05, land in a newly-acquired subsidiary, Rent Part Limited, was sold for €2 million to Robert Thompson, the Managing Director of that company. Settlement was deferred until February 2x06. The land had cost €800,000 in 2x02, and the disposal has been accounted for in accordance with IAS 16 *Property, Plant and Equipment*. On 12 January 2x06, the land was re-purchased by Rent Part Limited for €2 million.

Appendix II

Draft Financial Statements for the year ended 31 December 2x05

Statement of Financial Position as at 31 December 2x05

	Mainpart Holdings Limited	Mainpart Limited	Rent Part Limited
	€000	€000	€000
Non-current assets			
Property, plant & equipment	300	21,000	9,200
Financial assets:			
Mainpart Limited	5,700	–	
Small Part Limited	10,000	–	–
Rent Part Limited	15,000		
	31,000	21,000	9,200
Current assets			
Inventories	–	4,400	4,500
Trade and other receivables	–	3,600	2,700
Cash and cash equivalents	–	1,900	1,100
	–	9,900	8,300
Total assets	31,000	30,900	17,500
Liabilities			
Current liabilities			
Trade and other payables	250	4,000	2,900
Non-current liabilities			
Convertible debentures	10,000	–	–
Total liabilities	10,250	4,000	2,900
Net assets	20,750	26,900	14,600
Equity			
Share capital	17,000	1,000	1,000
Revaluation surplus	–	1,460	–
Retained earnings	3,750	24,440	13,600
Total equity	20,750	26,900	14,600

Statements of Comprehensive Income for the year ended
31 December 2x05

	Mainpart Holdings Limited	Mainpart Limited	Rent Part Limited
	€000	€000	€000
Revenue	–	28,000	22,000
Cost of sales	–	(16,000)	(12,000)
Gross profit	–	12,000	10,000
Other income	3000	–	–
Distribution costs	–	(1,500)	
Administrative expenses	(800)	(2,000)	(3500)
Other expenses	–	(500)	
Finance costs	(1500)	(1,000)	(700)
Profit on disposal of land	–	–	1,200
Profit on sale of Subpart Ltd	–	10,000	–
Profit before tax	700	17,000	7,000
Income tax expense	(350)	(4,500)	(2,600)
Profit for the year from continuing operations	350	12,500	4,400
Other comprehensive income: Items that will not be reclassified to profit or loss:			
Gains on property revaluation	–	340	–
Total comprehensive income for the year	350	12,840	4,400

Appendix III

Group Structure

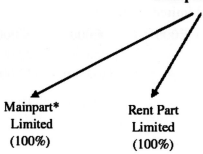

Mainpart Holdings Limited

Mainpart*
Limited
(100%)

Rent Part
Limited
(100%)

*Mainpart Limited held a 100% interest in Subpart Limited until 1 July 2x05.
On that date it disposed of 90% of its shareholding in Subpart Limited.

MILLENNIUM GROUP

The Millennium Group has a substantial presence in the technology field. The Group comprises Millennium Plc and a number of wholly-owned subsidiary companies which have been acquired over a number of years. The draft consolidated financial statements of the Group for the year ended 31 December 2x05 are set out in Appendix I. As the newly-appointed Financial Accountant of the Group you are reviewing the draft financial statements and the following matters have come to your attention:

(1) Sale of Land

On 1 December 2x05, Millennium Plc has agreed to sell a block of land for €1,500,000 which had cost €1,000,000 in 2x01. Consideration for the purchase is being deferred until 1 July 2x06 to allow time for the purchaser, a newly-established building firm, to apply for planning permission for the construction of a housing development.

The land had been revalued to €1,200,000 at 31 December 2x04 in the consolidated financial statements of the Millennium Group. The sale has been recorded by Millennium Plc and the deferred consideration has been included in trade receivables.

(2) Depreciation of Building

On 1 January 2x05, a subsidiary of Millennium Plc, Century Limited, purchased a building for €1,600,000. The building has an estimated useful life of 50 years, but it is expected that it will be sold by the Group in 10 years' time.

The estimated residual value in 10 years' time, based on 2x05 prices, is €1,500,000 (€2 million including expected inflation). On the basis that the expected residual value exceeds the cost of the building, Century Limited has not charged depreciation on the asset for the year ended 31 December 2x05.

(3) Sale of Subsidiary

On 1 July 2x05 Millennium Plc sold a wholly-owned subsidiary, Leading Edge Limited. Up to the time of its disposal Leading Edge Limited had contributed 50% of the Group's data backup sales. The remaining customers in this sector will continue to be fully serviced by the other companies in the Group.

Leading Edge Limited had turnover of €3 million and operating profit of €1 million for the six months ended 30 June 2x05, and its results have been included in the draft consolidated financial statements in accordance with IFRS 3 *Business Combinations.*

(4) Software Costs

During 2x05 a number of issues have arisen in respect of software costs. All of the costs incurred have been included under intangible assets in the consolidated statement of financial position of the Group; no amounts have been amortised to date.

(a)   Externally purchased software

During the year, Millennium Plc purchased a variety of software to assist the operation of the Group's inventory control packages for internal purposes. The total cost amounted to €800,000, and the software, on average, is expected to have a useful life of five years.

However, one package included in the above total cost €100,000 and was acquired specifically to run the Group's mainframe computer, which is due to be replaced in January 2x08. It is expected that the existing software will not be compatible with the new mainframe.

The Group depreciates non-current assets on a straight-line basis over their expected useful lives, charging a full year's depreciation in the year of purchase, and charging no depreciation in the year of disposal.

(b) Software development

A number of additional programmers were employed during 2x05 to develop software for the Group's own use. Costs incurred up to 31 December 2x05 amounted to €500,000 and the new software is due to become operational in the second half of 2x06. The costs incurred were included as an intangible asset in the financial statements.

(c) Software acquired for development work

Software costs of €400,000 were incurred in 2x05 to assist in the development of a new product-costing system that the Group intends to market in 2x06. Initial market research had proved very promising, and the product is on course to deliver fully on its potential. Other costs associated with this project have been capitalised as development costs. The software costs of €400,000 have been expensed to the statement of comprehensive income.

(5) Investment in Future Developments Limited

- On 1 April 2x05, Millennium Plc purchased Future Developments Limited in partnership with Twentieth Century Limited, which is not related in any way to the Millennium Group. Both companies have agreed to manage the entity jointly, and the contract of agreement stipulates that the new entity is intended for long-term development. Both Millennium Plc and Twentieth Century Limited own 50% of the equity share capital of Future Developments Limited.

- The fair value of the identifiable net assets of Future Developments Limited at 1 April 2x05 was €500,000 in excess of their book value (this excess fair value has *not* subsequently been reflected in the financial statements). The book value of net assets at 1 April 2x05 was €4,883,000, and retained earnings at the same date were €3,533,000.

- On 1 July 2x05, Future Developments Limited sold a plot of land (which had cost €300,000) to Millennium Plc for €600,000. It should be assumed that this gain will not incur a tax charge.

- On 1 October 2x05, Century Limited (a wholly-owned subsidiary of Millennium Plc) sold a large quantity of inventory to Future Developments Limited for €1 million. The cost of the goods to Century

Limited had been €750,000. The inventory is still held by Future Developments at 31 December 2x05.

- The draft financial statements of Future Developments for the year ended 31 December 2x05 are included in Appendix I.

Requirement:

(a) Explain what adjustments should be made to the draft financial statements of the Group in respect of the above transactions to comply with recommended accounting practice.

(35 marks)

(b) Document the journal entries which will be necessary to effect the changes outlined in (a) above.

(15 marks)

Notes:

- **It should be assumed that any adjustments to the draft financial statements will have no tax implications.**

- **The Group Structure is outlined in Appendix II.**

FRS 102

Outline the key differences in accounting treatment if the financial statements were prepared in accordance with the requirements of FRS 102 *The Financial Reporting Standard applicable in the UK and Republic of Ireland.*

Appendix I

Draft Statement of Comprehensive Income for the year ended
31 December 2x05

	Millennium Group €000	Future Developments Limited €000
Revenue	16,800	4,300
Cost of sales	(7,950)	(2,780)
Gross profit	8,850	1,520
Distribution costs	(600)	(100)
Administrative expenses	(420)	(80)
Other expenses	(280)	(30)
Finance costs	(620)	(418)
Profit on disposal of subsidiary	800	–
Profit on disposal of land	300	300
Profit before tax	8,030	1,192
Income tax expense	(750)	(206)
Profit for the year from continuing operations	7,280	986
Profit attributable to:		
Owners of the parent	7,280	
Non-controlling interests	–	
	7,280	

Draft Statement of Financial Position as at 31 December 2x05

	Millennium Group €000	Future Developments Limited €000
Assets		
Non-current assets		
Property, plant and equipment	12,943	6,105
Intangible assets	4,000	–
Investment in joint venture at cost	4,000	–
	20,943	6,105
Current assets		
Inventories	4,469	1,240
Trade and other receivables	5,395	972
Cash and cash equivalents	1,155	1,130
	11,019	3,342
Total assets	31,962	9,447
Liabilities		
Current liabilities		
Trade and other payables	3,565	2,715
Non-current liabilities		
Term loan	1,120	1,035
Convertible debentures	2,000	–
	3,120	1,035
Total liabilities	6,685	3,750
Net assets	25,277	5,697
Equity		
Share capital	100	100
Share premium	3,250	250
Revaluation surplus	9,000	1,000
Retained earnings	12,927	4,347
Total equity	25,277	5,697

Appendix II

Group Structure

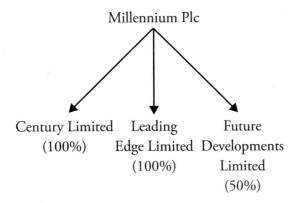

Millennium Plc

Century Limited
(100%)

Leading
Edge Limited
(100%)

Future
Developments
Limited
(50%)

Other companies:
Twentieth Century Limited – Millennium Plc's joint venture partner in Future Developments Limited.

NORMAN EPSTOW LIMITED

Introduction

Several years ago, Norman Epstow realised a childhood ambition when he founded a toy soldier factory in Galway. As a child he had been fascinated by these miniature men of war, and much of his youth was spent supervising enormous battles full of surprise attacks and tactical manoeuvres. At the age of eighteen Norman registered as a Commerce student in University College Galway. He graduated with an honours degree and found employment as a trainee Chartered Accountant. Although quite adept at all aspects of his work, Norman did not find a sense of fulfilment, and he left his firm before sitting his final examination. Having worked in a variety of jobs Norman had accumulated a modest amount of savings, and it was a chance meeting with an old friend, Stewart Dunston, that gave him the idea for his new venture. As Norman and Stewart discussed childhood memories attention inevitably focused on Norman's fascination with toy soldiers. Stewart recalled a trip to a toy soldier factory in Birmingham the previous year and, as he described the visit, Norman had already begun to consider the potential for a business idea.

After several months spent assessing the viability of a toy soldier enterprise Norman set up in business, operating at first from his family home. Initially it seemed that he would be unable to survive, but his dogged commitment to the business bought him some time, and the liquidation of a rival firm was to provide a lifeline. Eventually Norman Epstow Limited acquired a new premises, and a skilled and dedicated workforce provided the inspiration for continued growth.

The most significant change in the company's business since incorporation had been the necessity to expand the product range. The toy soldier market had been on a declining trend for some time, and the company had diversified into the manufacture and distribution of giftware and 'classic miniatures'. This latter product was a miniature reproduction of characters from the classics of authors such as Charles Dickens. The manufacturing process required the development of master moulds into which liquid lead is poured, which then hardens to produce the desired miniature. The miniatures can then be painted to make the figures appear more attractive. The development of 'master moulds' was an expensive investment, but the focus on classics provided a long shelf life for the company's products.

Over the years Norman Epstow Limited had developed a large mail-order business, with orders being received from up to 20 countries. There have been two main categories of sales:

- *Kit sales*
  This comprises the sale of miniature moulds, together with a solid block of the lead-based compound. Customers would use the kits to make their own figures which they could then paint if desired.

- *Item sales*
  This involves the in-house manufacture of completed products, encompassing the giftware and miniature range. Customers would be presented with a finished product, which had been moulded and painted by the company's employees.

Children comprise 80% of the kit sales market, the remaining 20% being sold to adults with a particular interest in hobby casting. Item sales are primarily an adult market.

Norman Epstow Limited has never employed a qualified accountant to operate its accounting systems or to prepare its annual financial statements. Norman himself has always kept an eye on this side of the business and has been involved in preparing the draft accounts for the year ended 31 December 2x05 (attached in Appendix I).

As audit manager for Compston & Co. Chartered Accountants you are reviewing the draft accounts and your attention has been drawn to the following matters by I. Ambright who has worked as a senior on the job.

(i) *Termination of toy soldier item sales*
  In April 2x05, Norman Epstow decided to terminate the production of toy soldier item sales and to sell off assets being used for this purpose. This decision was based on declining sales, plus the fact that the

product was labour intensive and earning a lower margin than other products in the item sales range. This decision was put into effect by 30 June 2x05, when all uncompleted mail-order sales had been filled. However, for public relations and company image purposes, the toy soldier range would remain in the company's catalogue, and occasionally an individual piece would be supplied to one of the company's most important customers. For this reason, Norman Epstow regarded toy soldier item sales as an ongoing activity.

Toy soldier item sales comprised 40% of the value of total item sales in 2x01, but declined at the rate of 25% per annum in each subsequent year. Toy soldier item sales have had a gross margin of 15% for several years and have accounted for 10% of net operating expenses.

Item sales comprised 20% of the company's total sales value for the last three years.

(ii) Research and development

The growth in kit sales has been restricted in recent years by health concerns related to their high lead content. For several years Norman Epstow has been researching the possibility of developing an alternative substance, which would continue to have the essential hardening characteristics. A major breakthrough was achieved early in 2x05, and it is now probable that the lead content can be reduced to insignificant levels. This is likely to materially increase the level of kit sales.

The company has incurred the following expenditure in the last two years relating to this project:

- €50,000 in 2x04 – written off to the statement of comprehensive income when incurred, but credited to the same statement in 2x05 and included under trade and other receivables at 31 December 2x05.
- €70,000 in 2x05 – included as a prepayment under trade and other receivables at 31 December 2x05.

In addition, a machine was purchased in February 2x05 for €30,000 to assist in the research project. The company normally depreciates machinery over five years on a straight-line basis, a full year's depreciation being charged in the year of purchase. In view of the successful research developments however, no depreciation has been charged in respect of this machine.

(iii) Sale of production rights

In 2x04 Norman Epstow Limited spent €250,000 on the limited rights to produce miniature figures of characters in the film *When We Were Kings,* based on the life of boxer, Muhammad Ali. The production rights were included in the Statement of Financial Position as an intangible asset at 31 December 2x04.

In 2x05 these rights were unexpectedly sold for €550,000, 'a nice killing' according to Norman Epstow. The sales proceeds were included as revenue in the Statement of Comprehensive Income in 2x05, and the intangible asset was retained in Norman Epstow's financial statements.

(iv) Sale of premises

On 30 November 2x05 Norman Epstow Limited sold a premises for €300,000. This asset had been purchased in 2x02 for €120,000, and was now regarded as surplus to requirements due to the termination of toy soldier item sales. The premises had been revalued to €200,000 in the financial statements at 31 December 2x03. Depreciation had been provided over a 50-year useful economic life on a straight-line basis with zero residual value. It is the company's policy to charge a full year's depreciation in the year of purchase and to not depreciate an asset in the year of disposal.

The premises has been sold subject to an agreement by Norman Epstow Limited that the purchaser would be compensated for the costs of eliminating dry rot, a problem which was identified in an engineer's report commissioned by the purchaser. At 31 December 2x05, the purchaser maintained that the repair costs would amount to €30,000, but on 2 February 2x06 a settlement of €20,000 was agreed.

Norman Epstow Limited has made no provision for repair costs, and has made no record of the disposal of the premises in the 2x05 financial statements.

(v) Joint venture with Checkmate Limited

On the 1 January 2x05, Norman Epstow Limited entered into a joint venture arrangement with Checkmate Limited. This initiative involved the manufacture of themed chess pieces to supply the increasing demand for this specialist market. Under the terms of the joint venture agreement, Checkmate Limited will design a range of chess sets and bear all of the associated design costs. The sets will be manufactured by Norman Epstow, who will take responsibility for all manufacturing and selling costs. It was agreed that sales revenue would be split between Norman Epstow and Checkmate on a 60:40 basis respectively.

During 2x05, Norman Epstow purchased new machinery costing €200,000 for use in connection with the manufacture of chess pieces. Machinery is depreciated over five years on a straight-line basis, with a full year's depreciation being charged in the year of purchase.

Manufacturing costs during 2x05 amounted to €250,000 (including depreciation of machinery), and cash sales of €600,000 were realised during the period. Inventories of chess sets on hand at 31 December 2x05 had been produced at a cost of €100,000 (included in the costs of €250,000 above). These chess sets are 50% complete, and it is estimated that selling costs will amount to €3,000.

(vi)   *Jointly-controlled property*

On 1 July 2x05, Norman Epstow jointly purchased an investment property with Telstar Limited. The property, which cost €700,000, is owned equally by both companies. Net rental income for the six months ended 31 December 2x05 amounted to €20,000, all of which was received. The fair value of the property at 31 December 2x05 was €900,000.

Norman Epstow Limited recorded its share of the cost of €350,000 under property, plant and equipment. No further entries have been made.

Requirements:

(a)   Explain what adjustments are required to the draft financial statements in respect of the issues outlined in (i)–(vi) above.

(35 marks)

(b)   Summarise the journal entries that are necessary in order to implement the adjustments in (a).

(15 marks)

Ignore taxation

Total   **50 marks**

FRS 102

Outline the key differences in accounting treatment if the financial statements were prepared in accordance with the requirements of FRS 102 *The Financial Reporting Standard applicable in the UK and Republic of Ireland.*

Appendix I

Draft Statement of Comprehensive Income of Norman Epstow Ltd for the year ended 31 December 2x05

	2x05 €000	2x04 €000
Revenue	1,800	1,300
Cost of sales	(950)	(780)
Gross profit	850	520
Distribution costs	(120)	(90)
Administrative expenses	(80)	(85)
Other expenses	(100)	(35)
Finance costs	(20)	(18)
Profit before tax	530	292
Income tax expense	(148)	(106)
Profit for the year from continuing operations	382	186

Draft Statement of Financial Position of Norman Epstow Ltd as at 31 December 2x05

	2x05 €000	2x04 €000
Assets		
Non-current assets		
Property, plant and equipment	1,693	555
Intangible assets	250	250
	1,943	805
Current assets		
Inventories	269	240
Trade and other receivables	395	322
Cash and cash equivalents	155	130
	819	692
Liabilities		
Current liabilities		
Trade and other payables	365	315
Non-current liabilities		
Term loan	120	135
Net assets	2,277	1,047
Equity		
Share capital	200	100
Share premium	1,150	402
Revaluation surplus	85	85
Retained earnings	842	460
Total equity	2,277	1,047

Norman Epstow owns 60% of the called-up equity share capital, the remaining shares being held by family members and close friends.

RIGHT TYPE GROUP

Introduction

You are an audit senior in a firm of Chartered Accountants, Dartry Maunsell & Co. It is February 2x06 and you are currently reviewing the draft financial statements of the Right Type Group which has recently become a client of your firm.

Right Type Limited is the parent company of a group which operates in the construction industry. The Group has a presence across both the residential and commercial sectors and, based on its progress to date, it is regarded as a serious player in the industry. Right Type Limited was founded by Michael Simpson, who focused initially on the residential market. A number of small acquisitions were made subsequently, resulting in the Group diversifying into the commercial sector.

A number of accounting issues have arisen in respect of the audit of the Right Type Group for the year ended 31 December 2x05. The audit manager, Martina O'Sullivan, has requested that you review these issues and send her a memorandum. Your memorandum should set out the appropriate accounting treatment and disclosure in respect of each accounting issue, together with any necessary journal adjustments.

The accounting issues and the draft financial statements are set out in Appendix I and Appendix II respectively.

Requirement:

Based on the accounting issues outlined in Appendix I, and the draft financial statements in Appendix II, prepare a memorandum to the audit manager of Dartry Maunsell & Co. setting out your advice in relation to the accounting treatment, together with any journal adjustments and disclosures required in respect of each of the following accounting issues that arose during the 2x05 audit:

(1)	Establishment of Side Type Limited	**11 marks**
(2)	Intangible assets	**16 marks**
(3)	Commercial contract	**9 marks**
(4)	Expenditure on assets	**14 marks**
		Total 50 marks

In your memorandum include the impact, if any, on:

(i) the separate/individual financial statements of the respective companies;

(ii) the consolidated financial statements of the Right Type Group.

Note:

- **Re-drafted financial statements are NOT required. However, your report should include the journal entries for any accounting adjustments required in respect of each accounting issue.**

- **In their separate financial statements, all companies within the Group account at cost for investments in subsidiaries, joint ventures and associates.**

FRS 102

Outline the key differences in accounting treatment if the financial statements were prepared in accordance with the requirements of FRS 102 *The Financial Reporting Standard applicable in the UK and Republic of Ireland.*

Appendix I

Accounting Issues Arising in Respect of the 2x05 Financial Statements

(1) Establishment of Side Type Limited

On 1 April 2x05 Right Type Limited, in conjunction with Bellair Construction, set up Side Type Limited. The rationale for the establishment of Side Type Limited was the belief that both groups could benefit by joint ownership of a parts warehouse complex located five miles outside Belfast. Right Type Limited and Bellair each own 50% of the ordinary shares of Side Type Limited.

The cost of establishing Side Type Limited amounted to €3 million, related to the acquisition of a premises. The Managing Director of Bellair is a personal friend of Michael Simpson but, apart from their joint ownership of Side Type Limited, there is no other relationship between Bellair and the Right Type Group.

From the outset the management of Side Type Limited was outsourced to Milton Property Care, which manages the operation of the warehouse and provides the total staffing requirement. An annual fee of €1 million each is paid by both Right Type and Bellair to Milton. Surplus warehouse space is rented to third parties. Total rental income from third parties amounted to €300,000 during the nine months ended 31 December 2x05, shared equally between Right Type Limited and Bellair Construction.

(2) Intangible Assets

(a) The Right Type Group has invested heavily in promoting the quality of their brand name over the last three years. €1.2 million was invested in promotion and marketing of the Group brand during 2x03, and the cumulative investment in the Right Type brand has increased annually by 20% since then. On the basis that the brand value significantly enhances that of the Group, it is carried as an asset in the Group Statement of Financial Position. Bellair Construction operates a similar policy in respect of expenditure incurred on brand promotion.

(b) On 1 July 2x05 the Right Type Group paid €3 million for the Well Build brand name, which was previously held by a competitor company. At that time Michael Simpson believed that it had been acquired at a discount of 25% of its market value, and it was included in the statement of financial position of the Right Type Group at its fair value. Consequently, a gain on a bargain purchase was recorded, and this has been maintained in the statement of financial position of the Group. On the basis that the Well Build brand name will increase in value, it is not being amortised in the Group financial statements.

(3) Expenditure on Assets

(i) Replacement of lift

On 1 January 2x05 Right Type Limited replaced the lift in the company's head office building. The replacement lift cost €300,000, not including future decommissioning costs which were estimated at a present value of €30,000 based on a discount rate of 10%. It was estimated that the lift will have a useful life of 10 years, and a residual value of €20,000 (this is estimated to increase to €35,000, based on prices that are expected to apply in 2x16).

The only entry made by Right Type Limited in respect of the new lift is to record it as an addition to land and buildings at its cost of €300,000. Right Type Limited depreciates land and buildings at 2% per annum on a straight-line basis.

(ii) Compliance with fire regulations

In July 2x05 the Right Type Group invested a total of €400,000 in meeting the requirements of new government fire regulations. This cost has been included in fixtures and fittings, and has been depreciated at 10% on a reducing-balance basis. The Right Type Group depreciates land and buildings at 2% per annum on a straight line basis. Fixtures and fittings are depreciated by 10% per annum on a reducing-balance basis. A full year's depreciation is charged in the year of acquisition in all cases.

The total cost incurred relates to the following items:

	€000
Repair of fire doors	50
Installation of fire escapes	250
Additional fire extinguishers and miscellaneous safety equipment	100
	400

(4) Revenue Issues

(i) Sale of residential homes

During 2x05 the Right Type Group completed the construction of a residential estate of 24 houses. Sales were significantly down on previous developments, primarily as the result of planning permission being granted for a waste management plant adjacent to the estate.

At 31 December 2x05 sales of 12 houses had been completed at a selling price of €300,000 per house.

Deposits of €20,000 per house had been taken on another four, the sales being dependent on an engineer's report and on the purchaser being able to raise finance. Deposits are refundable if the sale does not proceed.

For the remaining eight, Michael Simpson decided to allow potential purchasers to occupy them on a three-month lease, each lessee paying €1,000 per month in advance. The eight lease agreements were signed on 1 October 2x05, and all lease payments were received at the due date.

On 2 December 2x05, two of the lessees signed unconditional contracts to purchase a house for €300,000, and it was agreed that the December lease instalment would be set-off against the purchase price.

Each house had a completed construction cost of €170,000. No accounting entries have been made in respect of the above.

(ii) *Provision of security service*

While employing security personnel to safeguard the housing estate prior to handover, Right Type Limited decided to provide a security service to other developers. On 1 October 2x05 a two-year contract was signed with Property Sites Limited whereby the latter agreed to pay €1,200 monthly in advance, with immediate effect. Should any damage or break-ins occur, Property Sites would be entitled to a full refund of that month's service charge. In addition, they would receive a 50% reduction on the following month's charge.

A break-in occurred on one of Property Sites' properties during November 2x05.

(5) Land

Right Type Limited acquired an area of land several years ago at a cost of €1 million with a view to using it for house building. The land was revalued to €1.5 million during 2x05. It now appears possible that the planning permission will be rescinded and, in that event, the land would be used for agricultural purposes, at a value of €400,000.

(6) Village Living Concept

During 2x05 Right Type Limited was engaged in finalising plans for the development of a new concept known as 'Village Living'. This would involve future housing estates being built on a much larger scale and equipped with services, such as a mini-shopping complex. It is expected that the 'Village Living' concept will be finalised in the first quarter of 2x06 and that construction will commence later in 2x06.

During 2x05 Right Type Limited incurred the following costs in connection with the 'Village Living' concept, both of which were charged as expenses:

	€000
Labour	300
Lease payments on equipment	100

The lease payments relate to the acquisition of a mobile information office. The terms of the lease were as follows:

- Eight half-yearly payments of €100,000 in the primary lease period, commencing in advance on 1 July 2x05. Right Type Limited can retain the information office during the subsequent secondary lease period for an annual payment of €1.

At the date of the inception of the lease, the mobile office had a useful life of five years and its cash price was €600,000. The present value of the minimum lease payments was also €600,000.

In January 2x06 Right Type Limited announced a 1 for 3 rights issue to finance the further development of the 'Village Living' concept. The rights issue was fully subscribed before the end of February.

Right Type Limited uses the sum of digits method to allocate interest on finance leases.

Appendix II

Draft Statement of Comprehensive Income of the Right Type Group (excluding Side Type Limited) for the year ended 31 December 2x05

	€000
Revenue	19,100
Cost of sales	(6,900)
Gross profit	12,200
Distribution costs	(700)
Administrative expenses	(250)
Other expenses	(150)
Finance costs	(600)
Profit before tax	10,500
Income tax expense	(750)
Profit for the year from continuing operations	9,750
Other comprehensive income	
Items that will not be reclassified to profit or loss:	
Remeasurements of defined benefit pension plans	(750)
Items that may be reclassified subsequently to profit or loss:	
Cash flow hedges	(250)
Other comprehensive income for the year, net of tax	8,750
TOTAL COMPREHENSIVE INCOME FOR THE YEAR	18,500

All profit and total comprehensive income is attributable to the owners of the parent.

Draft Statement of Financial Position of the Right Type Group (excluding Side Type Limited) at 31 December 2x05

	€000
Assets:	
Non-current assets	
Property, plant and equipment	6,460
Goodwill	500
Right Type brand	1,728
Well Build brand	4,000
	12,688
Current assets	
Inventories	1,500
Trade and other receivables	5,000
Amounts recoverable on contracts	6,200
Cash and cash equivalents	1,300
	14,000
Total assets	26,688
Liabilities	
Current liabilities	
Trade and other payables	5,300
Income tax payable	500
	5,800
Non-current liabilities	
Term loan	200
Deferred income taxes	100
Negative goodwill	1,000
	1,300
Total liabilities	7,100
Net assets	19,588
Equity	
Capital and reserves attributable to holders of the parent	
Share capital	1,000
Share premium	6,000
Revaluation surplus	1,500
Retained earnings	11,088
Total equity	19,588

TRACER GROUP

Introduction

You are an audit senior in a firm of Chartered Accountants, Clarke, Scriven & Co. It is March 2x06 and you are currently reviewing the draft financial statements of the Tracer Group which has recently become a client of your firm.

Tracer Plc is a conglomerate group, comprising a number of subsidiary companies in which dominant influence is exercised by the group parent company, Tracer Limited. The shares of Tracer Plc are listed on the Dublin and London stock exchanges.

A number of accounting issues have arisen in respect of the audit of the Tracer Group for the year ended 31 December 2x05. The audit manager, Julie Crimson, has requested that you review these issues and send her a memorandum with your observations and recommendations.

It should be noted that in their separate/individual financial statements all companies within the Group account at cost for investments in subsidiaries, joint ventures and associates.

It is Group policy to measure any non-controlling interest in subsidiaries at the non-controlling interest's proportionate share of the acquired company's identifiable net assets.

The accounting issues are set out below and relevant financial information is set out in Appendix I. It should be assumed that the financial statements are authorised for issue on 28 February 2x06.

Accounting Issues Arising in Respect of the 2x05 Financial Statements

Issue (a) – Construction of Head Office Building

On 1 January 2x05 Tracer Limited commenced the construction of a new head office. The new building was scheduled for completion on 30 June 2x05 but, due to a work stoppage from 1 April–30 June, the building was eventually completed on 30 September 2x05.

The various costs associated with the construction, paid by Tracer Limited, are summarised as follows:

Item	1 Jan 2x05 €000	1 Apr 2x05 €000	30 Sep 2x05 €000	Total €000
Site clearance	200			200
Legal fees	70			70
Construction and fitting out		1,600	1,900	3,500
General administration overhead allocation		200	200	400
Total	270	1,800	2,100	4,170

From 1 January 2x05 Tracer Limited paid the amounts outlined, based on architects' certificates obtained at each due date. To finance the construction, Tracer Limited used bank funds obtained for general company use. The interest rate charged on these funds was bank base rate plus 3%. On 1 January 2x05, the bank base rate was 5%, and this increased to 6% on 1 July 2x05.

The total costs of €4.17 million were capitalised as buildings by Tracer Limited at 30 September 2x05. The asset was valued on 31 December 2x05 at €6 million, and was included in the financial statements at that valuation.

Tracer Limited depreciates buildings at 2% per annum on a straight-line basis.

Issue (b) – Government Grant

Comps Limited, a 100% subsidiary of Tracer Limited, purchased a machine on 1 January 2x04 at a cost of €500,000. A government grant of €100,000 was received, which was netted off against the machine in the Group financial statements at 31 December 2x04. In July 2x05, a Government Inspector found that Comps Limited had failed to meet the conditions of the grant agreement, relating to employee numbers, and a demand was issued for the repayment of the grant.

Comps Limited has appealed the Inspector's decision and, on 28 February 2x06, it was estimated there was a 40% probability that Comps would meet the employment targets, albeit behind schedule, and be able to retain the grant.

It is the policy of the Tracer Group to depreciate plant and machinery at 10% per annum on a reducing-balance basis, and depreciation has been charged for 2x05 and 2x04.

Comps Limited has made no entries relating to the repayment of the grant in its financial statements for the year ended 31 December 2x05. Nor has any record been made in respect of the decommissioning costs of the machine, which were estimated on 1 January 2x04 to amount to €10,000 at the end of the asset's life.

Issue (c) – Share Options

On 31 December 2x03, Tracer Limited issued share options to 10 of its key executives, giving each executive the option to purchase 100,000 shares at €1 per share. The fair value of each option at that date was €0.80.

The exercise of the share options was conditional on the completion of two-years' service from 31 December 2x03. The nominal value of the shares of Tracer Limited was 50 cent.

The company's share price on subsequent dates was as follows:

31 December 2x04 €2.70
31 December 2x05 €3.50

In March 2x05, after the 2x04 financial statements were authorised for issue, one of the executives unexpectedly resigned her position in the company. In

April 2x05 a second executive, Patrick Cudmore, was dismissed. Mr Cudmore immediately instigated legal proceedings against Tracer Limited, and it was probable, on the 28 February 2x06, that he would be deemed to have completed the two-year qualifying period of his share option agreement. Legal advice at that time was that he was also likely to be awarded €500,000 in compensation, and that it was possible that this could rise to €900,000.

The eight remaining executives exercised their options on 31 December 2x05.

Issue (d) – Disposal of Shares

On 30 September 2x05 Tracer Limited disposed of 60% of the share capital of Airlight Limited, a subsidiary undertaking in which it had held a 90% stake. The proceeds of disposal amounted to €12 million. Tracer Limited's residual interest of 30% in Airlight Limited allowed it to exercise significant influence over that company.

The 90% stake in Airlight Limited had cost Tracer Limited €9 million on 1 January 2x02 when the identifiable net assets in the statement of financial position of Airlight Limited amounted to €5 million. Goodwill had suffered no impairment loss since acquisition.

Airlight Limited had retained earnings of €3 million on 1 January 2x02; this figure had increased to €7 million at 31 December 2x04. Airlight Limited had profit after tax of €2 million for the year ended 31 December 2x05.

The fair value of the identifiable net assets of Airlight Limited has always been identical to the carrying value of the identifiable net assets in Airlight Limited's statement of financial position. The fair value of the holding retained was therefore judged to be equivalent to its net asset value.

The Tracer Group measures its non-controlling interests at the acquisition date at its proportionate share of the subsidiary's identifiable net assets.

Requirement:

Issue (a) – Construction of Head Office Building

Review all of the costs involved in the construction of the head office building, and:
- outline your recommended accounting treatment;
- provide relevant journal entries;
- draft Tracer Limited's accounting policy note relating to its treatment of borrowing costs.

17 marks

Issue (b) – Government Grant

Explain how the government grant should be treated in the financial statements of Comps Limited for the year ended 31 December 2x05. Provide relevant journal entries.

8 marks

Issue (c) – Share Options

Explain how the share options should be treated in the financial statements of Tracer Limited in 2x04 and 2x05. Provide relevant journal entries.

9 marks

Issue (d) – Disposal of Shares

(i) Compute the profit or loss on the disposal of Airlight Limited shares in the *separate financial statements* of Tracer Limited, and provide the relevant journal entry.

4 marks

(ii) Compute the profit or loss on the disposal of Airlight Limited shares in the Group financial statements. Provide the relevant journal entry to record this profit and to reclassify Airlight Limited in the Group financial statements.

9 marks

(iii) Outline the disclosure requirements relating to the disposal of Airlight Limited shares in the financial statements of the Group.

3 marks

Total 50 marks

Notes:
- Re-drafted financial statements and consolidated financial statements are **not** required.
- The Tracer Group pays capital gains tax at 20% on chargeable gains.

FRS 102

Outline the key differences in accounting treatment if the financial statements were prepared in accordance with the requirements of FRS 102 *The Financial Reporting Standard applicable in the UK and Republic of Ireland.*

Appendix I

Consolidated Statement of Comprehensive Income of the Tracer Group for the year ended 31 December 2x05

	€ million
Revenue	29,000
Cost of sales	(13,800)
Gross profit	15,200
Distribution costs	(3,000)
Administrative expenses	(4,000)
Other expenses	(2,000)
Finance costs	(2,600)
Profit before tax	3,600
Income tax expense	(1,500)
Profit for the year from continuing operations	2,100
Other comprehensive income:	
Items that will not be reclassified to profit or loss:	
Gains on property revaluation	1,000
Items that may subsequently be reclassified to profit or loss:	
Cash flow hedges	450
Other comprehensive income for the year, net of tax	1,450
TOTAL COMPREHENSIVE INCOME FOR THE YEAR	3,550
Profit attributable to:	
Owners of the parent	1,800
Non-controlling interests	300
	2,100
Total comprehensive income attributable to:	
Owners of the parent	3,100
Non-controlling interests	450
	3,550

Consolidated Statement of Financial Position of the Tracer Group as at 31 December 2x05

	€ million	€ million
Assets		
Non-current assets		
Land and buildings	9,600	
Plant and machinery	4,000	
Fixtures and fittings	800	
Investment property	2,600	
Development costs	1,600	
		18,600
Current assets		
Inventory	3,000	
Trade and other receivables	18,000	
Bank	2,600	
		23,600
Total assets		42,200
Liabilities		
Current liabilities		
Trade and other payables	8,400	
Current tax payable	3,200	
		(11,600)
Non-current liabilities		
Term loan		(7,400)
Deferred income taxes		(200)
		(7,600)
Net assets		23,000
Equity		
Capital attributable to owners of the parent		
Called up share capital		2,000
Share premium		6,000
Revaluation surplus		3,000
Retained earnings		10,800
		21,800
Non-controlling interests		1,200
Total equity		23,000

Consolidated Statement of Financial Position of the Tracer Group as at
31 December 20X5

	£ million	£ million
Assets		
Non-current assets		
Land and buildings	2,000	
Plant and machinery	4,000	
Fixture and fittings	800	
Investment property	2,600	
Development costs	2,600	
		15,000
Current assets		
Inventories	4,500	
Trade and other receivables	18,000	
Bank	2,500	
		25,000
Total assets		42,200
Liabilities		
Current liabilities		
Trade and other payables	8,000	
Current tax payable	3,500	
		(11,000)
Non-current liabilities		
Term loan	(7,200)	
Deferred income tax	(800)	
		(9,000)
Net assets		23,000
Equity		
Capital attributable to owners of the parent		
Called up share capital	5,000	
Share premium	6,000	
Revaluation surplus	3,000	
Retained earnings	10,500	
		21,600
Non-controlling interests		1,200
Total equity		23,000

VERSATILE GROUP

Introduction

You are an audit senior in a firm of Chartered Accountants, Turnbull Bramston & Co. It is February 2x06 and you are currently reviewing the draft financial statements of the Versatile Group which has recently become a client of your firm.

Versatile Plc is a conglomerate group, comprising a number of subsidiary companies in which dominant influence is exercised by the group parent company, Versatile Limited. The shares of Versatile Plc are listed on the Dublin and London Stock Exchanges.

A number of accounting issues have arisen in respect of the audit of the Versatile Group for the year ended 31 December 2x05. The audit manager, Frank DeCourcey, has requested that you review these issues and send him a memorandum with your observations and recommendations.

It should be noted that in their separate/individual financial statements all companies within the Group account at cost for investments in subsidiaries, joint ventures and associates.

It is Group policy to measure any non-controlling interest in subsidiaries at the non-controlling interest's proportionate share of the acquired company's identifiable net assets.

The accounting issues are set out below and relevant financial information is set out in Appendix I.

Accounting Issues Arising in Respect of the 2x05
Financial Statements

Issue (a) – Sale of Subsidiary

On 30 September 2x05 Versatile Limited sold a subsidiary undertaking, Excess Limited, which although previously a separate major line of business, was no longer considered to be part of the Group's core operations.

Eighty per cent of the shares of Excess Limited had been purchased in 2x00 for €62 million in cash, when Excess Limited had retained earnings of €25 million. The fair value of Excess Limited's identifiable net assets at that time was €40 million, and these values were fully reflected in the statement of financial position of Excess Limited. To date there has been no evidence that goodwill relating to the acquisition of Excess Limited has become impaired in value.

Excess Limited had retained earnings of €100 million on 30 September 2x05, and the disposal proceeds amounted to €250 million.

Versatile Limited has provided an indemnity to the purchaser against unrecorded taxation or other liabilities. It was estimated at 31 December 2x05 that unrecorded liabilities of approximately €5 million were likely. On 23 February 2x06 (the date on which the financial statements of the Versatile Group were authorised for issue) it was probable that unrecorded liabilities would amount to €10 million.

Goods costing €200 million were sold by Mercer Limited (a wholly-owned subsidiary undertaking of Versatile Limited) to Excess Limited, at a mark-up of 25%, evenly during the year ended 31 December 2x05. Half of the goods purchased by Excess Limited were in that company's inventory at 31 December 2x05.

Issue (b) – Revaluation of Land

Mercer Limited purchased a plot of land for €15 million in 2x03 for storage of the Group's building supplies. In 2x04 the area adjacent to the land was identified as the development site for a new shopping centre; Mercer Limited revalued the land to €80 million at 31 December 2x04 due to its newly acquired development potential. No deferred tax has been provided in respect of the revaluation surplus.

During 2x05 a protest campaign by local residents resulted in the local council withdrawing permission for the commercial development, and at 31 December 2x05 the land was revalued to €30 million. At that time, most of the area was being utilised for storage, with a small section being fenced off for parking by Group personnel.

Issue (c) – Contract Work in Progress/Development Site

Minstrel Limited, a wholly-owned subsidiary undertaking of Versatile Limited, has been engaged in the construction sector for several years. On 1 January 2x05 a large site was acquired for the production of retail units on which construction was scheduled to commence in 2x07. The cost of this site was €20 million and, following an escalation in property values, it was revalued to €35 million at 31 December 2x05.

At 31 December 2x05 a contract involving the construction of an office block for a client company was in progress. Work on this contract had begun on 1 April 2x05 and was scheduled to be completed on 31 May 2x06. The following information is available in respect of this contract at 31 December 2x05:

Contract 6211Y

	€ million
Costs to date	15.5
Cost of work certified	12.2
Costs to complete	7.7
Value of work certified	15.0
Progress billings	8.8
Amounts received from client	6.3
Contract price	28.5

In accordance with the contract agreement, the client obtains control of the work in progress asset when work done is certified by the architect.

Issue (d) – Research & Development

During 2x05 Mercer Limited incurred costs of €6.5 million in connection with the development of a new product, the 'wizmo', which will be launched in the marketplace in late 2x06. The results of all tests to date have been positive and market research suggests that the 'wizmo' will be exceptionally well received by consumers.

On 1 January 2x05 a machine was purchased, at a cost of €2.5 million, to carry out final tests on the new product. The Versatile Group depreciates machinery at 20% per annum on a straight-line basis; depreciation on this machine is *not* included in the €6.5 million costs incurred in respect of the 'wizmo'.

Requirements:

Issue (a)

(i) Explain the correct accounting treatment of the acquisition and disposal of Excess Limited in the group financial statements **and** in the separate financial statements of Versatile Limited.

(ii) Set out the journal entries required to reflect your recommended accounting treatment together with the relevant disclosures.

The journal entries should cover the period from the date of acquisition to the date of sale and should include:

– journal entries relating to the group; *and*

– journal entries relating to the separate financial statements of Versatile Limited.

20 marks

Issue (b)

(i) Explain the correct accounting treatment of the land since its purchase in 2x03.

(ii) Set out the journal entries required to reflect your recommended accounting treatment.

9 marks

Issue (c)

(i) Explain the correct accounting treatment of the site acquired by Minstrel Limited and set out relevant journal entries.

(ii) Explain the correct accounting treatment of Contract 6211Y, and set out the journal entries required.

(iii) Provide Statement of comprehensive income and statement of financial position extracts in respect of Contract 6211Y.

15 marks

Issue (d)

(i) Explain the correct accounting treatment in respect of the research and development expenditure incurred by Minstrel Limited.

(ii) Set out the journal entries required to reflect your recommended accounting treatment.

6 marks

Total 50 marks

Note:

- **Re-drafted financial statements and consolidated financial statements are NOT required. The capital gains tax rate should be assumed at 20%.**

FRS 102

Outline the key differences in accounting treatment if the financial statements were prepared in accordance with the requirements of FRS 102 *The Financial Reporting Standard applicable in the UK and Republic of Ireland.*

Appendix I

Statement of Comprehensive Income of the Versatile Group for the year ended 31 December 2x05

	€ million
Revenue	14,500
Cost of sales	(6,900)
Gross profit	7,600
Distribution costs	(1,600)
Administrative expenses	(2,000)
Other expenses	(900)
Finance costs	(1,300)
Profit before tax	1,800
Taxation	(750)
Profit for the year from continuing operations	1,050
Other comprehensive income for the year, net of tax	
Items that will not be reclassified in profit or loss:	
Gains on property revaluation	205
TOTAL COMPREHENSIVE INCOME FOR THE YEAR	1,255

Statement of Financial Position of the Versatile Group as at 31 December 2x05

	€ million	€ million
Assets		
Non-current assets		
Land and buildings	2,300	
Plant and machinery	2,000	
Fixtures and fittings	400	
Investment property	1,300	
Development costs	800	
		6,800
Current assets		
Inventory	1,500	
Trade and other receivables	9,000	
Bank	1,300	
		11,800
Total assets		18,600
Liabilities		
Current liabilities		
Trade and other payables	4,200	
Current tax payable	1,600	
		(5,800)
Non-current liabilities		
Term loan		(1,200)
Deferred income taxes		(100)
		(1,300)
Net assets		11,500
Equity		
Equity attributable to owners of the parent		
Called up share capital		1,000
Share premium		3,600
Revaluation surplus		1,500
Retained earnings		5,400
Total equity		11,500

VORSTER GROUP

Vorster Ltd produces a range of equipment for the automobile industry. In recent years the Managing Director, Michael Hayes, has led a policy of corporate acquisition and investment in an effort to increase market share. The following are details of acquisitions and disposals.

(1) Acquisition of Motor Factors Limited

On 31 October 2x05, Vorster Ltd acquired 80% of the ordinary share capital of Motor Factors Limited for €1,475,000 which was paid in cash. The following information relates to the acquisition:

- Motor Factors Limited had 200,000 issued ordinary shares of €1 nominal value at 31 October 2x05, along with retained earnings of €850,000.
- Vorster Limited paid professional fees of €25,000 in evaluating whether it should invest in Motor Factors Limited. In the financial statements of Vorster Limited this amount was included in the cost of investment.
- Land and buildings of Motor Factors Limited were worth €100,000 in excess of their book value at 31 October 2x05.
- There was a disputed tax liability of €180,000 at 31 October 2x05 which was not recorded by Motor Factors Limited. This amount was subsequently confirmed as being due at that date.
- Vorster Limited intends to carry out a significant reorganisation of Motor Factors Limited. The total cost of this programme is estimated at €90,000; this has been provided for in Motor Factor Limited's statement of financial position at 31 October 2x05 and

charged in its statement of comprehensive income for the year ended 31 October 2x05.

- It is group policy to value the non-controlling interest at its proportionate share of the subsidiary's identifiable net assets.

(2) Investment in Auto Parts Limited

On 1 January 2x04, Vorster Limited signed a joint venture agreement with Magnus Limited to set up a new company, Auto Parts Limited, which would specialise in buying scrapped cars and storing the parts for sale. Under the terms of the joint venture agreement each company received 50% of the ordinary shares in Auto Parts Limited. Vorster Limited and Magnus Limited each have three directors on the Board of Auto Parts Ltd, and each of the investing companies participates equally in its management.

At 31 December 2x05 Auto Parts Limited has €300,000 of goods that were purchased from Vorster Limited. These goods were supplied at a mark-up of 25% on cost.

(3) Disposal of Cycle Accessories Ltd

As part of its long-term strategy to concentrate on the motorised industry sector, Vorster Limited disposed of a subsidiary company, Cycle Accessories Ltd, on 30 September 2x05. This company had been acquired on 1 January 2x03 at a cost of €200,000 for 100% of its equity shares. At that time Cycle Accessories Ltd had 100,000 issued ordinary shares of €1 each nominal value and retained earnings amounted to €100,000. No goodwill arose on the acquisition of Cycle Accessories in 2x03.

The proceeds on disposal of Cycle Accessories amounted to €900,000, all of which was received in cash.

(4) Financial Statements

The financial statements of Auto Parts Limited and of companies in the Group at 31 December 2x05 are set out below.

Statement of Financial Position

	Vorster Ltd at 31/12/05 €000	Vorster Ltd at 31/12/04 €000	Motor Factors Ltd at 31/10/05 €000	Auto Parts Ltd at 31/12/05 €000
Assets				
Non-current assets				
Land and buildings	800	500	300	200
Plant and machinery	800	650	400	180
Investments at cost:				
Shares in Motor Factors	1,500	–	–	–
Shares in Auto Parts	5	5	–	–
Shares in Cycle Accessories	–	200	–	–
	3,105	1,355	700	380
Current assets				
Inventory	1,200	900	350	300
Receivables	1,100	950	400	450
Bank	700	350	250	200
	3,000	2,200	1,000	950
Total assets	6,105	3,555	1,700	1,330
Equity and liabilities				
Ordinary share capital	450	250	200	10
Capital reserves	200	200	–	–
Retained earnings	2,885	1,755	850	770
Total equity	3,535	2,205	1,050	780
Non-current liabilities				
Long-term loan	970	–	–	–
Current liabilities				
Trade and other payables	1,200	1,050	450	400
Current tax payable	400	300	200	150
Total liabilities	2,570	1,350	650	550
Total equity and liabilities	6,105	3,555	1,700	1,330

Draft Statement of Comprehensive Income

	Vorster Ltd y/e 31/12/05 €000	Motor Factors Ltd y/e 31/10/05 €000	Autoparts Ltd y/e 31/12/05 €000
Revenue	4,000	2,100	1,900
Cost of sales	(2,500)	(900)	(800)
Gross profit	1,500	1,200	1,100
Other income	330		
Distribution costs	(350)	(320)	(275)
Administrative expenses	(450)	(280)	(225)
Finance costs	(200)	(20)	(30)
Profit on disposal of Cycle Accessories	700		
Profit before tax	1,530	580	570
Income tax expense	(400)*	(200)	(150)
Profit for the year	1,130	380	420

* Includes €175,000 capital gains tax on the disposal of shares in Cycle Accessories Limited.

(5) Financial Statements of Cycle Accessories Limited

The financial statements of Cycle Accessories, which was sold by Vorster Limited on 30 September 2x05, are set out below.

Statement of Financial Position of Cycle Accessories Limited

	31 December 2x04 €000	31 December 2x05 €000
Non-current assets		
Land and buildings	200	250
Plant and machinery	150	200
	350	450
Current assets		
Inventory	480	580
Trade and other receivables	300	400
Bank	100	200
	800	1,100
Total assets	1,230	1,630

Equity and liabilities

Ordinary share capital	100	100
Retained earnings	530	780
Total equity	630	880

Current liabilities

Trade and other payables	450	600
Current tax payable	150	150
Total liabilities	600	750
Total equity and liabilities	1,230	1,630

Statement of Comprehensive Income of Cycle Accessories Ltd for year ended 31 December 2x05

	€000
Revenue	1,000
Cost of sales	(300)
Gross profit	700
Distribution costs	(120)
Administrative costs	(80)
Interest	(100)
Profit before tax	400
Income tax expense	(150)
Profit for the year	250

It should be assumed that the profit of Cycle Accessories Limited accrued evenly over the year.

Requirements:

You are required to prepare the following statements in respect of the **Vorster Group**:

- Statement of Comprehensive Income for the year ended 31 December 2x05.
- Statement of Financial Position as at 31 December 2x05.

Notes:

- **It should be noted that, in their separate/individual financial statements, all companies within the Group account at cost for investments in subsidiaries, joint ventures and associates.**

- **It is Group policy to measure any non-controlling interest in subsidiaries at the non-controlling interest's proportionate share of the acquired company's identifiable net assets.**

- **All companies in the Vorster Group pay capital gains tax at a rate of 25%.**

FRS 102

Outline the key differences in accounting treatment if the financial statements were prepared in accordance with the requirements of FRS 102 *The Financial Reporting Standard applicable in the UK and Republic of Ireland.*

WEBSTER GROUP

Introduction

You are an audit senior in a firm of Chartered Accountants, Craughwell James & Co. It is February 2x07 and you are currently reviewing the draft financial statements of the Webster Group which is a client of your firm.

Webster Plc is a conglomerate group, comprising a number of subsidiary companies in which control is exercised by the Group parent company, Webster Holdings Limited. The shares of Webster Plc are listed on the Dublin and London stock exchanges.

A number of accounting issues have arisen in respect of the audit of the Webster Group for the year ended 31 December 2x06. The audit manager, Pamela Deane, has requested that you review these issues and send her a memorandum with your observations and recommendations.

The accounting issues are set out below and the Group's financial information is set out in Appendix I.

Accounting Issues Arising in Respect of the 2x06 Financial Statements

Issue (a) – Deferred Tax

The following details relate to the Group's taxation affairs for the year ended 31 December 2x06:

   (i)   During 2x06 the Webster Group generated a large surplus cash balance, which was put on deposit pending a decision on a capital project which was under consideration. Deposit interest accrued in the consolidated statement of financial position at 31 December 2x06 amounted to €2.4 million. The Webster Group will incur a tax charge when the deposit interest is received.

(ii) A land site which the group had purchased in 2x02 for €220 million was revalued to €370 million at 31 December 2x06. This site is the proposed location for the Group's new head office building. This was the first revaluation of this site.

(iii) A building acquired in 2x05 for €25 million was subsequently let to Mercer Limited, a company in which Webster Holdings owns 25% of the equity share capital. At 31 December 2x06 the building was included in the consolidated statement of financial position as an investment property at a valuation of €40 million.

(iv) During 2x06 First Limited sold goods for €36 million to Second Limited. First Limited charged a mark-up of 33% on these sales. Half of the goods are included in the inventory of Second Limited at 31 December 2x06. Both First Limited and Second Limited are 100% subsidiaries of Webster Holdings.

(v) Plant and machinery and fixtures and fittings held by the Group had a total net book value of €4,820 million at 31 December 2x06. These assets had a total tax written down value of €4,420 million at the same date.

(vi) There were no other temporary differences at 31 December 2x06.

(vii) All companies in the Webster Group pay corporation tax at 12.5%, six months after their accounting year end. The capital gains tax rate is 20%. The balance on deferred tax in the consolidated statement of financial position at 31 December 2x05 amounted to €20 million and this balance has been retained at 31 December 2x06. The entire €20 million existing balance was originally charged through profit or loss.

Issue (b) – Closure of Division

On the 30 November 2x06 the activities of the export division of First Limited, a 100% subsidiary undertaking of Webster Holdings, were terminated. The division had been loss-making for some time, therefore the decision did not come as a surprise. Fortunately it was possible to relocate the entire workforce, thus eliminating the necessity for redundancies.

The assets of the division were available for immediate sale and it was considered to be highly probable that their sale would be completed early in 2x07.

At 30 November 2x06, the book value of the net assets of the export division (which included buildings carried under the cost model) was €72.6 million. This included inventory of €30 million, which was estimated to have a net realisable value of €26 million at 30 November 2x06.

At the 30 November 2x06, the net assets of the export division had a fair value less costs to sell of €63.9 million.

The export division made a loss before taxation of €96 million for the 11 months ended 30 November 2x06. The loss will be available against other profits of the Webster Group, and will reduce the Group taxation charge for 2x06 by €12 million.

Issue (c) – Interest Incurred on Construction of Factory Buildings

On 1 January 2x05, Second Limited, a 100% subsidiary undertaking of Webster Holdings, commenced the construction of a new factory building for its own use. Building work was projected to be completed on 30 June 2x06, but continued until the 30 September 2x06 as work was suspended for three months on 1 April 2x06 due to the discovery of a design error.

Construction costs have been incurred as follows, with payment being made by Second Limited following the submission of an architect's certificate by the contractor.

	Year ended 31 December 2x05	Year ended 31 December 2x06
Site clearance: 1 January certificate	€46 million	–
Purchase of building materials: 1 April certificate	€120 million	€140 million
Direct labour and production overheads: 1 June certificate	€60 million	€100 million
General overheads: 1 June certificate	€100 million	€80 million

Second Limited paid for the construction costs from its general borrowing facilities. The bank base rate was 5% on 1 January 2x05; this rate increased to 6% on 1 January 2x06. Second Limited can borrow funds at 2% above the bank base rate.

Second Limited wrote off the interest as an expense in its 2x05 financial statements, but decided to capitalise the interest as part of the cost of the building in 2x06. However, the consolidated financial statements have not been amended for either 2x05 or 2x06 to reflect the new treatment.

Issue (d) – Revenue

First Limited commenced a special promotion during 2x06 whereby customers whose monthly purchases exceed €100,000 could defer making payment for the goods for one year.

The promotion proved more successful than expected, and total sales for 2x06 on a deferred payment basis amounted to €340 million. First Limited earns a profit margin of 25% on deferred payment sales and gives a discount of 10% to cash customers.

It is predicted that 4% of deferred payment customers outstanding at 31 December 2x06 will return their goods to First Limited; 90% of goods returned can be resold, with the other 10% considered to have a zero resale value.

Issue (e) – Financial Instruments

(i) *Loan stock*

Second Limited purchased loan stock in B Limited for €10 million on 1 January 2x06. The loan stock carries no coupon and will be redeemed on 31 December 2x08 for €13,310,000.

The loan stock was purchased with the intention of being held to maturity by Second Limited. The effective interest rate is 10% per annum. No other factor affects the contractual cash flows.

(ii) *Purchase and disposal of shares*

Second Limited purchased shares in Smile plc for €85 million on 1 January 2x06. The shares are held for trading.

At 31 December 2x06, Second Limited has an entitlement to €3 million in respect of dividends declared by Smile plc in November 2x06. The shares held by Second Limited had a fair value of €97 million at 31 December 2x06; they were sold for €103 million in February 2x07.

Requirements:

Issue (a)

(i) Compute the correct balance for deferred tax in the consolidated financial statements of the Webster Group at 31 December 2x06.

(ii) Set out the journal entry required to reflect your adjustment to the deferred tax balance of the Group.

12 marks

Issue (b)

(i) Explain the correct accounting treatment of the closure of the export division of First Limited.

(ii) Set out the journal entries required to reflect your recommended accounting treatment together with the relevant disclosures.

10 marks

Issue (c)

(i) Explain the correct accounting treatment for the interest incurred in respect of the construction of the building by Second Limited. It should be assumed that all interest expenditure relating to the construction is incurred **after the 1 January 2009**.

(ii) Draft the accounting policy note which will appear in the 2x06 financial statements of Second Limited.

12 marks

Issue (d)

(i) Explain the correct accounting treatment in respect of the deferred payment sales by First Limited.

(ii) Set out the journal entries required in the 2x06 financial statements to reflect your recommended accounting treatment.

8 marks

Issue (e)

(i) Outline the correct accounting treatment in respect of the loan stock purchased by Second Limited, and provide journal entries covering all years from issue to maturity.

4 marks

(ii)   Explain the correct accounting treatment in respect of the shares purchased by Second Limited in Smile Limited. You should also provide journal entries for all transactions between the purchase and disposal dates.

4 marks

Total 50 marks

Note:

- **Re-drafted financial statements and consolidated financial statements are *not* required.**

FRS 102

Outline the key differences in accounting treatment if the financial statements were prepared in accordance with the requirements of *FRS 102 The Financial Reporting Standard applicable in the UK and Republic of Ireland.*

Appendix I

Statement of Comprehensive Income of the Webster Group for the Year Ended 31 December 2x06

	€ million
Revenue	3,625
Cost of sales	(1,725)
Gross profit	1,900
Distribution costs	(625)
Administrative expenses	(500)
Finance costs	(325)
Profit before tax	450
Income tax expense	(187)
Profit for the year	263
Other comprehensive income:	
Items that will not be reclassified to profit or loss:	
Gains on property revaluation	400
TOTAL COMPREHENSIVE INCOME FOR THE YEAR	663

Profit attributable to:

Owners of the parent   263

Total comprehensive income attributable to:

Owners of the parent   663

Statement of Financial Position of the Webster Group as at 31 December 2x06

	€ million	€ million
Assets		
Non-current assets		
Land and buildings	2,300	
Plant and machinery	4,015	
Fixtures and fittings	410	
Investment property	335	
Development costs	800	
Financial assets	395	
		8,255
Current assets		
Inventory	3,550	
Trade and other receivables	3,350	
Bank	700	
		7,600
Total assets		15,855
Liabilities		
Current liabilities		
Trade and other payables	4,150	
Current tax payable	1,550	
		(5,700)
Non-current liabilities		
Term loan		(1,330)
Deferred tax		(20)
		(1,350)
Net assets		8,805

Equity
Equity attributable to owners
  of the parent

Called-up share capital	600
Share premium	4,230
Revaluation surplus	750
Retained earnings	3,225
Total equity	**8,805**

THE HAYWARD GROUP*

Introduction

You are an audit senior in a firm of Chartered Accountants, Parker Russell & Co.

It is March 2x10 and you are currently undertaking the audit in respect of the 2x09 financial statements of one of your firm's largest clients, the Hayward group. The Hayward group comprises:

(1) Hayward Holdings Ltd ('Hayward Holdings'), a holding company employing 25 staff;

(2) Hayward Forms Ltd ('Hayward Forms'), a manufacturer of business forms and stationery employing 110 staff; and

(3) Hayward Flexo Ltd ('Hayward Flexo'), a manufacturer of packaging for the food industry, employing 375 staff.

The Hayward group is a fourth-generation family business. The current Chairman, Jim Hayward, and the Managing Director, Robert Hayward, are father and son. The Board of Directors also includes two other members of the Hayward family who are no longer directly involved with the day-to-day operation of the business, and one other non-executive director.

The ordinary share capital of Hayward Holdings is owned 80% by Jim Hayward, with Robert Hayward owning the balance. Hayward Holdings holds 100% of the share capital of Hayward Forms and Hayward Flexo.

A number of accounting issues have arisen in respect of the audit of the Hayward Group for the year ended 31 December 2x09. The senior partner of Parker Russell & Co., David Parker, has requested that you review the various issues and prepare a report for Jim and Robert Hayward which sets out the appropriate

*Based on 2000 Paper 2(i) in the Final Admitting Examination of the Institute of Chartered Accountants in Ireland.

accounting treatment and disclosure in respect of each accounting issue together with any necessary associated journal adjustments. The report is to be issued to Jim and Robert Hayward and discussed at a meeting to take place next week.

The accounting issues and the draft financial statements are set out in Appendix I and Appendix II respectively.

Requirement:

Based on the accounting issues outlined in Appendix I and the draft financial statements in Appendix II, prepare a report to Jim and Robert Hayward setting out your advice in relation to the appropriate accounting treatment together with any journal adjustments and disclosures required in respect of each of the following accounting issues that arose in respect of the 2x09 audit:

(a)	Business rationalisation	12 marks
(b)	Head office building	12 marks
(c)	Flexible packaging	12 marks
(d)	New opportunity	14 marks

Include in the report the impact, if any, on:

(i)   the separate/individual financial statements of the respective companies; and

(ii)   the consolidated financial statements of the HAYWARD group.

Total 50 marks

Notes:

- **Re-drafted and consolidated financial statements are not required. However, your report should include journal entries in respect of any accounting adjustments required in respect of each accounting issue.**

- **It should be noted that, in their separate/individual financial statements, all companies within the Group account at cost for investments in subsidiaries, joint ventures and associates.**

FRS 102

Outline the key differences in accounting treatment if the financial statements were prepared in accordance with the requirements of FRS 102 *The Financial Reporting Standard applicable in the UK and Republic of Ireland.*

Appendix I

Accounting Issues Arising in Respect of the 2x09 Financial Statements of the Hayward Group Companies

(a) Business Rationalisation

In early 2x09 Hayward Holdings prepared a development strategy for the Hayward Group which identified the options for the future of the various businesses within the group. The strategy recognised that, as a result of advances in office technology, the business forms and stationery market would rapidly become increasingly competitive and ultimately unprofitable. This had already become apparent in the decreasing profitability of Hayward Adhesives, a division within Hayward Forms Ltd.

Robert Hayward was tasked with identifying new development opportunities for the group and for preparing an exit plan under which the group would withdraw from the adhesives market. The exit plan was presented at a meeting of the Board of Directors in October 2x09 and agreed unanimously in principle. Robert Hayward wants the costs of implementing the exit plan to be provided for in full in the 2x09 accounts of Hayward Forms, although no provision has yet been made. The exit plan, which would take approximately six months to implement, involves the following:

- **Disposal of continuous printing equipment currently used by Hayward Adhesives.** The equipment would have a limited second-hand market locally but is readily saleable, by an agent, to buyers in the Far East. The agent has already identified an interested buyer. The equipment, which has not been revalued, has a net book value at 31 December 2x09 of €2,000,000 and, on sale, is estimated to realise €1,000,000 before deduction of the agent's fee of 10% of the sale price. The equipment, which has not been used for six months due to a lack of orders, is likely to have a limited ongoing value in use to Hayward Adhesives whether or not the exit plan is implemented. All other equipment in Hayward Adhesives can be usefully re-deployed to Hayward Forms.

- **Staff redundancies**. A total of 110 staff are currently employed in Hayward Adhesives. If the exit plan is implemented, 10 staff are likely to be re-deployed elsewhere within the group but the remainder will face compulsory redundancy. The cost of implementing the redundancy programme will be in the region of €1 million. As the exit plan remains confidential, the redundancy terms have not yet been discussed with staff or their Union representatives. However, given that the terms are well in excess of statutory entitlements, the Board believes that they are likely to be accepted.

- **Other costs to implement the plan.** In addition to the items noted above, other costs associated with the implementation of the plan, such as legal and professional fees, are estimated at €100,000.

- **Operating losses.** Hayward Adhesives is forecast to make a trading loss of approximately €200,000 in the period up to the full implementation of the exit plan.

(b) Head Office Building

In order to raise finance for new ventures, Hayward Holdings entered into a binding agreement on 31 December 2x09 to sell its head office building to Alpha Investments Ltd for €2 million. This is €500,000 below the estimated open market value of the property, but €500,000 in excess of the net book value at 31 December 2x09.

The terms of the agreement are as follows:

- Hayward Holdings will continue to occupy the building for a period of five years.

- At any time during the five-year period Hayward Holdings has an option to re-purchase the building, while Alpha Investments Ltd has an option to sell the property back to Hayward Holdings. Under either option, the price will be calculated on the basis of €2 million plus indexation at the bank base lending rate for the period between 1 January 2x10 and the date of re-purchase or re-sale. This option will activate automatically at the end of the five-year period.

- Each quarter in advance, for a period of five years, Hayward Holdings will pay rent to Alpha Investments Ltd. The rent will be calculated on the basis of the average daily bank base rate plus 5% charged on €2 million. Hayward Holdings will settle directly all other outgoings in respect of the property.

This agreement has not yet been reflected in the draft 2x09 financial statements of Hayward Holdings.

Alpha Investments Ltd is a company jointly owned and controlled by Jim Hayward and his wife, Iris.

(c) Flexible Packaging

Hayward Flexo has been manufacturing packaging for the food industry for a number of years using a range of printing equipment and materials. Hayward Flexo has a number of large contracts with supermarket multiples and their suppliers both in the United Kingdom and in mainland Europe.

1. *Danish Customer*

    During December 2x09 Hayward Flexo manufactured a significant order in respect of Danobuy, a major customer based in Denmark. The order, which had a sales value of €400,000, was invoiced to Danobuy on 20 December 2x09 and the sale is reflected in the draft financial statements of Hayward Flexo.

    As part of the year-end inventory count procedures on 31 December 2x09, the company's premises and vehicles were inspected by the auditors. During this inspection, a 40-foot container parked at the rear of the company's premises was found to contain the entire Danobuy order. Although it had been included in pre-year-end despatches on the company's management information system, it was not due for shipment until late January as Danobuy did not want to accept delivery until after its year end on 31 January 2x10.

    The materials cost on the Danobuy order is estimated to be 30% of the sales value. In addition, relevant production overhead is estimated to average in the region of 15% of material cost.

    No adjustments have been made to the draft financial statements in respect of this matter since the inventory count.

2. *French Customer*

    As part of its recent expansion, Hayward Flexo launched a new packaging range that was guaranteed as safe and suitable for direct food contact. The first order for product of €500,000 was invoiced and shipped to a major French customer, 'Supermarche', in November 2x09.

However, in early December 2x09, it became apparent that the product was defective and was failing food hygiene tests in France as the ink was leaving traces on food stored within the packaging.

On further investigation by independent experts during December, it was confirmed that the problem had arisen as a result of a combination of defective ink and the manufacturing process, which was at temperatures which were insufficient to dry the ink properly. Hayward Flexo has been fully involved in the investigation into the causes of the problem, which was instigated by its French customer, and it is clear that the problem had arisen because of the defective product supplied by Hayward Flexo.

Although no subsequent batches produced by Hayward Flexo of this food packaging product type have been affected, the initial problem has caused such embarrassment and disruption to Supermarche that it has not paid the initial invoice, has cancelled all further orders with Hayward Flexo and refused to accept any more Hayward Flexo product.

To settle the matter in full, Hayward Flexo will have to issue a credit note for the full value of the goods invoiced, and pay €100,000 in costs incurred by Supermarche. The ink supplier has committed in writing to Hayward Flexo that it will meet 50% of the total cost of the settlement.

The initial sale of the product to Supermarche has been reflected in the draft financial statements of Hayward Flexo but no further entries have been made.

(d) New Opportunity

The Group development strategy noted above also recognised the opportunities presented to organisations such as the Hayward Group by the Internet and e-commerce. As a result, on 1 October 2x09, Hayward Holdings purchased a 25% equity stake in Virtual Inc. ('Virtual'), a local company engaged in website design and the re-sale of computer hardware. Robert Hayward believes the fit with Virtual to be particularly appropriate because of Hayward Group's customer base and in-house design skills, allied to Virtual's website expertise. Both Robert and Jim Hayward have been appointed to the eight-member Board of Virtual and are actively involved in identifying new products and markets for Virtual and in its strategic development.

The purchase of 1 million €1 ordinary shares in Virtual on 1 October 2x09 cost €7.3 million cash. The shares were purchased from Dave Foster, founder and Chief Executive of Virtual, who previously held 100% of the share capital. For Dave Foster the deal provided an opportunity to raise personal funds without losing overall control of the company. Copies of the draft financial statements of Virtual for the year ended 31 December 2x09, which are stated at fair value, are set out in Appendix III.

To date, the only entry which has been made in the accounts of Hayward Holdings in respect of this transaction is to debit investments €7.3 million and credit bank €7.3 million.

In its separate financial statements, Hayward Holdings accounts at cost for investments in subsidiaries, joint ventures and associates.

Appendix II

Draft Financial Statements for the year ended 31 December 2x09

Statement of Financial Position as at 31 December 2x09

	Hayward Holdings Ltd	Hayward Forms Ltd	Hayward Flexo Ltd
	€000	€000	€000
ASSETS			
Non-current assets			
Property, plant and equipment	2,700	2,500	10,000
Investments			
HAYWARD Forms	100		
HAYWARD Flexo	4,000		
VIRTUAL Inc	7,300		
	14,100		
Current assets			
Inventory		200	2,000
Trade Receivables	500	500	3,000
	500	700	5,000
Total assets	14,600	3,200	15,000
EQUITY AND LIABILITIES			
Share capital	500	100	4,000
Retained earnings	900	1,500	6,000
Total equity	1,400	1,600	10,000
Non-current liabilities			
Long-term loans	10,000		
Current liabilities			
Trade creditors	200	800	2,000
Accruals		200	1,000
Bank overdraft	3,000	600	2,000
Total current liabilities	3,200	1,600	5,000
Total equity and liabilities	14,600	3,200	15,000

Statement of Comprehensive Income for the year ended 31 December 2x09

	Hayward Holdings Ltd	Hayward Forms Ltd	Hayward Flexo Ltd
	€000	€000	€000
Revenue	1,000	3,500	13,000
Cost of sales		800	6,000
Gross profit	1,000	2,700	7,000
Administration costs	750	1,500	2,000
Distribution costs	–	1,000	2,500
Finance costs	750	50	500
Profit/loss before tax	(500)	150	2,000
Income tax expense	–	100	500
Profit/loss for the period	(500)	50	1,500

Appendix III

Draft Financial Statements

Virtual Inc.

Statement of Financial Position at
31 December 2x09

	€000
Non-current assets	
Property, plant and equipment	7,000
Current assets	
Inventory	–
Trade receivables	2,000
Cash	4,000
Total assets	13,000
Equity and liabilities	
Share capital	4,000
Retained earnings	6,150
Total equity	10,150
Non-current liabilities	
Long-term loans	2,000
Current liabilities	
Trade creditors	150
Bank overdraft	700
Total liabilities	2,850
Total equity and liabilities	13,000

Statement of Comprehensive Income for the year ended
31 December 2x09

	€000
Revenue	80,000
Cost of sales	61,500
Gross profit	18,500
Administration costs	17,000
Distribution costs	–
Interest	900
Profit before tax	600
Income tax expense	
Profit for year	600

BLACK BAY BOATS*

Introduction

It is March 2x13 and you are an audit senior in a firm of Chartered Accountants and Registered Auditors. You are currently undertaking a range of accounting and auditing assignments on behalf of the firm. Each member of staff in the firm is allocated to a practice team for work scheduling and management purposes. One of the audit managers on your practice team is attending a residential training course for a week but has asked you, during his absence, to review some accounting issues which have arisen in respect of the 2x12 audit of one of the firm's clients, Black Bay Boats Ltd ('Black Bay Boats'). In order to provide the background information you need to undertake this work he has sent you an e-mail which contains three attachments:

Appendix I: Background briefing note to Black Bay Boats Ltd

Appendix II: Draft financial statements for the year ended 31 December 2x12

Appendix III: Foreign currency rates for the year ended 31 December 2x12

*Based on 2001 Paper 2(i) in the Final Admitting Examination of the Institute of Chartered Accountants in Ireland.

Requirement

Based on the accounting issues outlined in Appendix I and the draft financial statements in Appendix II, prepare a memorandum to the audit manager setting out your advice in relation to the appropriate accounting treatment together with any journal adjustments and disclosures required in respect of each of the following accounting issues that arose in respect of the 2x12 audit of Black Bay Boats:

(a) Investment in Pleasure Craft Inc.
   ('Pleasure Craft')   **26 marks**

(b) Foreign currency loan   **10 marks**

(c) Revaluation of showroom   **10 marks**

(d) Black Bay Boats: motor craft   **4 marks**

                                                   Total 50 marks

Include in the memorandum the impact, if any, on:

- the separate financial statements of Black Bay Boats; and

- the consolidated financial statements of the Black Bay Boats group.

Notes:

- **Re-drafted or translated financial statements are NOT required. However, your report should include the journal entries in respect of any accounting adjustments required in respect of each accounting issue.**

- **Ignore taxation implications of recommended accounting adjustments.**

- **It should be noted that, in their separate/individual financial statements, all companies within the group account at cost for investments in subsidiaries, joint ventures and associates.**

- **It is group policy to measure any non-controlling interest in subsidiaries at the non-controlling interest's proportionate share of the acquired company's identifiable net assets.**

FRS 102

Outline the key differences in accounting treatment if the financial statements were prepared in accordance with the requirements of FRS 102 *The Financial Reporting Standard applicable in the UK and Republic of Ireland.*

Appendix I

Background Briefing Note to Black Bay Boats Ltd

Black Bay Boats is a privately-owned company which has been trading for a number of years and is owned and controlled by Mr Jim Kennedy and his wife, Doris, who between them own 100% of the share capital of Black Bay Boats.

Black Bay Boats sells and services luxury motor cruisers from its coastal show-room and stocks a range of craft supplied by some of the world's leading boat manufacturers. The market for luxury motor cruisers, which generally sell for between €100,000 and €1 million each, is closely linked to general economic conditions. As the economy has been growing successfully in recent years Black Bay Boats has expanded and become highly profitable.

Investment in Pleasure Craft Inc.

The financial success of Black Bay Boats has encouraged Jim Kennedy to look abroad for opportunities to expand the business and, in particular, to seek to break into the lucrative US market. During 2x11 Jim commenced negotiations with a pleasure cruiser distributor based in Miami, Florida, Pleasure Craft. This company is owned and managed by Bill and Ted Powers, twins in their early 60s, and who have been attempting to realise some cash from Pleasure Craft to fund their impending retirement.

The negotiations continued into 2x12 and on 31 March 2x12 Black Bay Boats acquired 10% of the ordinary share capital of Pleasure Craft for 1 million US dollars ($). The initial investment did not give Jim Kennedy any strategic or management input to the company as Bill and Ted Powers were reluctant to dispose of a larger share of the equity until they knew that they could "get on", both professionally and personally, with their new fellow-shareholder. After six months Bill and Ted Powers agreed to sell a further 40% of the share capital to Black Bay Boats on 30 September 2x12 for $5 million. At the same time Jim Kennedy was appointed Managing Director of Pleasure Craft, assuming day-to-day control over company policy and decision making; Bill and Ted Powers effectively withdrew from the management of the business. As a result, Black Bay Boats has taken financial and operational control of Pleasure Craft. Therefore, at 30 September 2x12, the shareholders of Pleasure Craft were as follows:

Bill Powers	25%
Ted Powers	25%
Black Bay Boats	50%

The net assets of Pleasure Craft in US dollars during 2x12 are as follows:

1 January 2x12	31 March 2x12	30 September 2x12	31 December 2x12
$000	$000	$000	$000
9,000	9,280	9,840	10,120

(For foreign currency rates refer to Appendix III.)

As part of the review exercise undertaken by Black Bay Boats in respect of the second stage investment in September 2x12, the following items were noted:

- A property valuation report dated 1 January 2x12. This had been undertaken by professional valuers acting on behalf of Pleasure Craft which indicated that the company's primary property had increased by $1 million in value compared to its carrying amount in the accounts of Pleasure Craft. The previous valuation was carried out in 2x07.

- A major customer of Pleasure Craft filed for bankruptcy on 1 September 2x12. At that time the customer owed Pleasure Craft $200,000. It is believed that nothing will be recovered from the bad debt.

Notes:

- **Neither of these items have been adjusted in the net assets or draft financial statements of Pleasure Craft.**

- **It should be assumed that the fair value of the net assets of Pleasure Craft at 30 September 2x12 is equal to the fair value of the company at that date.**

Foreign Currency Loan

The purchase of the investment in Pleasure Craft was funded in part by a 10-year loan taken out by Black Bay Boats, denominated in US dollars and drawn on the First American Bank. The rationale for using a US dollar loan was to try and offset, in part, any adverse movements on the €:$ rate. The loan was drawn down in two parts: $500,000 on 31 March 2x12 and a further $2.5 million on 30 September 2x12. (For foreign currency rates refer to Appendix III.)

To date the investment in Pleasure Craft has been accounted for in the books of Black Bay Boats as follows:

Account	DR €000	CR €000
Investment in Pleasure Craft	625	
Bank		312.5
Bank loan		312.5
Investment in Pleasure Craft	3,125	
Bank		1,562.5
Bank loan		1,562.5
Being entries in respect of two investments in Pleasure Craft.		

Black Bay Boats: Showroom Revaluation

Black Bay Boats has been trading from a coastal showroom for the last 13 years. The showroom had been acquired at a cost of €6.25 million. Approximately three years ago there were major concerns over the future suitability of the showroom as the area where it is located was suffering from significant coastal erosion and prone to potential flooding. However, a major development programme in the area, including the strengthening of coastal defences and the development of a 300-berth marina, has addressed the issues and provided a significant boost to local property values.

Details of recent revaluations of the showroom property undertaken by the same firm of professional valuers in 2x10 and 2x12 are noted below:

- 1 January 2x10 valuation €3 million. This compared to the then carrying value of €5 million. As a result, a €2 million revaluation loss was taken to the statement of comprehensive income of Black Bay Boats.

- 31 December 2x12 valuation €6 million.

The depreciation policy of Black Bay Boats for land and buildings is to write them off straight-line over 50 years. A full year's depreciation is charged in the year of purchase. Although the results of the 2x12 revaluation have not yet been reflected in the draft financial statements, the directors have indicated that this valuation should be incorporated in the financial statements.

Black Bay Boats: Motor Craft

Black Bay Boats is a distributor for a number of manufacturers of luxury motor craft. In early 2x12 it obtained distribution rights for an Italian manufacturer, Baggio Boats ('Baggio'). The distribution rights are subject to an agreement. At 31 December 2x12 Black Bay Boats had three craft supplied by Baggio. The craft were delivered in May 2x12. These craft are all variants of the same basic model with a list price cost at 31 December 2x12 ex Baggio of €150,000 each. Under the terms of the agreement, this cost, if not previously settled in full, can vary from time to time as Baggio reviews prices on a quarterly basis.

At 1 December 2x12 Black Bay Boats had another Baggio craft but this was transferred at the direction of Baggio to another dealer in mainland Europe who had a customer awaiting delivery. The remaining three craft were to be paid for on 1 December 2x12, but Baggio has agreed a further six-month payment extension in respect of these craft.

In early 2x12, as part of the agreement, Black Bay Boats paid a refundable inventory deposit to Baggio of €100,000. The inventory deposit is the only aspect of this trading relationship which has been reflected in the books of Black Bay Boats. It was accounted for as follows: CR Bank and DR Trade Payables.

Appendix II

Black Bay Boats Ltd

Draft Financial Statements for the year ended
31 December 2x12

Statement of Financial Position as at
31 December 2x12

Assets	€000
Non-current assets	
Property, plant and equipment	6,500
Investments:	
Pleasure Craft Inc.	3,750
Total non-current assets	10,250
Current assets	
Inventory	15,000
Trade receivables	1,000
Cash	5,000
Total current assets	21,000
Total assets	31,250
Equity and Liabilities	
Share capital	1,500
Retained earnings	19,575
Total equity	21,075
Non-current liabilities	
Long-term loans:	
Bank loans	2,500
US Dollar loan	1,875
Total non-current liabilities	4,375
Current liabilities	
Trade and other payables	5,000
Current tax payable	500
Overdraft	300
Total current liabilities	5,800
Total liabilities	10,175
Total equity and liabilities	31,250

Statement of Comprehensive Income for year ended 31 December 2x12

	€000
Revenue	23,000
Cost of sales	10,000
Gross profit	13,000
Administration costs	2,500
Distribution costs	3,500
Interest	500
Profit before tax	6,500
Income tax expense	1,500
Profit for the year	5,000

Appendix II

Pleasure Craft Inc.

Draft Financial Statements – Stated in US Dollars

Statement of Financial Position as at
31 December 2x12

		US $000
Assets		
Non-current assets	5,000	
Current assets		
Inventory	8,000	
Trade receivables	1,200	
Cash	500	
Total assets		14,700
Equity and liabilities		
Share capital		2,000
Retained earnings		8,120
Total equity		10,120
Current liabilities		
Trade creditors		4,000
Accruals		280
Overdraft		300
Total liabilities		4,580
Total equity and liabilities		14,700

Statement of Comprehensive Income for year ended 31 December 2x12

	US $000
Revenue	16,000
Cost of sales	8,000
Gross profit	8,000
Administration costs	4,000
Distribution costs	1,000
Interest	500
Profit before tax	2,500
Income tax expense	1,380
Profit for the year	1,120

Appendix III

Foreign Currency Rates for the year ended 31 December 2x12

Currency rates over the year were as follows:

Date	$ to €
1 January 2x12	1.50
31 March 2x12	1.60
30 September 2x12	1.60
31 December 2x12	2.00
Average for year 2x12	1.75

TARGET GROUP*

Introduction

It is April 2x02 and you are an audit senior in a firm of Chartered Accountants and Registered Auditors, Brown, Black & Co.

You are undertaking the audit of a major client of the firm, the Target group of companies, which comprises:

- Target Holdings Ltd ('Target Holdings'); and
- Target Engineering Ltd ('Target Engineering').

Target Holdings owns 100% of the share capital of Target Engineering. The share capital of Target Holdings is owned equally by Derek and Steve Rogers, two brothers who formed the company 10 years ago following successful careers in the engineering sector. The Target Group designs, manufactures and installs production facilities for pharmaceutical and food processing companies. The group has benefited significantly from the increasing number of such companies developing manufacturing facilities in Ireland.

Target Holdings provides administrative and management support to the other Group company. Target Engineering undertakes the construction and installation of production facilities.

The audit of the Target Group is 80% complete and a number of accounting issues now require resolution. Your audit manager is due to undertake an assignment review with you in the near future and he has requested that you consider

---

*Based on 2002 Paper 2(i) in the Final Admitting Examination of the Institute of Chartered Accountants in Ireland.

the accounting issues which have been identified and make recommendations as to the options for their accounting treatment. The outcome of the assignment review can then form the basis for a future meeting with the client at which these matters can be resolved.

The accounting issues requiring resolution are noted below. Draft statements of comprehensive income and financial position for the two group companies are set out in Appendix I.

Accounting Issues

Issue 1: Head Office Building

Until this year the Target group had no permanent head office building to accommodate the design and administrative functions of the Group companies. Instead, connecting temporary buildings had been used to provide office space. This had been economically prudent as the companies grew and investment was focused on specialised plant and equipment to generate revenues and improve productivity. However, the temporary buildings had become increasingly impractical from an operational perspective and did not create the appropriate impression for existing and potential customers.

On 1 January 2x01 Target Holdings acquired a site adjacent to its main production facility for the development of a Head Office building. On 1 January 2x01 final plans were agreed and clearance of the site commenced. Construction continued for approximately a further nine months until the building was available for occupation and came into use on 1 October 2x01.

The various costs incurred by Target Holdings associated with the construction during 2x01 are summarised in the table below:

Element	1 Jan 2x01 €000	31 Jan 2x01 €000	31 Mar 2x01 €000	30 Sep 2x01 €000	Total €000
Acquisition of site	2,700				2,700
Legal fees	90				90
Architect's fees	100	60		60	220
Site clearance and preparation		240			240
Construction and fitting out			480	1,200	1,680
General administration overhead allocation			100	100	200
Total	**2,890**	**300**	**580**	**1,360**	**5,130**

From 31 January 2x01 onwards the costs, as indicated in the above table (excluding the general administration overhead allocation), were certified by architect's certificates issued on each date. These were paid by Target Holdings on the date of issue using funds drawn down from the company's overdraft facility.

In order to fund the purchase of the site and development of the Head Office building, Target Holdings arranged an extension to its bank overdraft facility from €4 million to €8 million for a period up to 31 December 2x01. An arrangement fee in respect of this extension of €28,700 was charged by the company's bankers and debited from the account on 1 January 2x01. The interest rate charged on the facility throughout the year was bank lending base rate plus 4%. On 1 January 2x01 base rates were 5% increasing to 5.75% on 31 March 2x01, at which level they remained until December 2x01. The use of the extended bank overdraft was intended as a temporary funding mechanism to cover the period of construction only.

In the non-current assets of Target Holdings at 31 December 2x01 the building has been capitalised at a total cost of €4,820,000, comprised as follows:

- Acquisition of site €2,700,000
- Site clearance and preparation €240,000
- Construction and fitting out €1,680,000
- General administration overhead allocation capitalised €200,000.

All the other costs noted in the table on the previous page have been expensed to the statement of comprehensive income. No depreciation has been charged to date on the head office building in this financial year (2x01) although the depreciation policy of the company in respect of land and buildings is to write them off, straight-line, over 50 years from the date of coming into use.

Interest capitalisation

Derek Rogers is an engineer but throughout the trading history of the Group he has taken Board level responsibility for company accounts and financial issues, in conjunction with the in-house bookkeeper/accountant. During the course of the audit Derek has indicated to you that he is aware of other companies which have capitalised interest charges on construction projects and he would like the advice of the company auditors in this respect with regard to the head office building.

Construction & fitting out

The construction and fitting out of the Head Office building was undertaken by Acorn Developments Ltd ('Acorn'). Acorn is a company which is 40%-owned by Steve Rogers and it undertakes general construction assignments for a number of clients. As a result of the commitment required by his involvement in the Target Group, Steve Rogers has no executive role within Acorn nor is he a director of the company.

Tenders for the construction and fitting out work were sought from four potential contractors. Three contractors, including Acorn, submitted tenders. All of the submitted tenders met the required technical and build quality criteria. The Acorn tender, which was ultimately successful at €1.680 million, was the highest priced received and was €400,000 higher than the lowest tender submitted.

Issue 2: Head Office Building Disposal

On 31 December 2x01 the recently completed head office building was disposed of to Fitzpatrick Properties Ltd ('Fitzpatrick') for €6.5 million. The terms of the disposal were as follows:

- Fitzpatrick pays €6.5 million to Target Holdings on 31 December 2x01;
- Target Holdings enters into a five-year agreement with Fitzpatrick to occupy the property at an annual rent payable quarterly in advance. The rent is €575,000 per annum;
- Target Holdings has no option to repurchase the property; and
- Target Holdings is responsible for all repairs and upkeep during the lease period.

In December 2x01 Target Holdings commissioned a valuation of the property by its property advisers. The property advisers estimated the open market value (fair value) of the property to be €5.5 million.

Notes:

- **The only entry to have been made in the draft accounts of Target Holdings in respect of this transaction is to DR Bank Overdraft €6.5 million; CR Other Payables €6.5 million.**

Issue 3: Third-party Claim

Target Engineering has two trading divisions, the Pharmaceutical Division and the Food Processing Division. The divisions specialise respectively in the construction and commissioning of production facilities either for pharmaceutical or for food-processing companies. The Pharmaceutical Division has experienced some problems in relation to an installation carried out during 2x01. As a result, the client involved is pursuing a claim against Target Engineering for costs and consequential loss. The key details relating to the claim are as follows:

Client A
Target Engineering was the sole building contractor on this project. The work, which involved the construction of a new manufacturing suite, was undertaken in the first quarter of 2x01 and the total value of the contract was €500,000. Since

the work was undertaken, Client A, a pharmaceutical company, has been unable to obtain suitable regulatory approval for the manufacturing suite as the test batches produced in the suite are showing signs of contamination. This contamination is attributed to the air conditioning system, installed by Target Engineering, importing dust particles into the suite. On 30 June 2x01 Client A instituted legal proceedings against Target Engineering for recovery of the full contract value plus a consequential loss claim of €250,000.

The legal case is still pending and the limit of Target Engineering's insurances in this respect totals €400,000. Solicitors and expert witnesses appointed by Target Engineering have privately advised that it is probable that Client A's action will be successful. Target Engineering's insurers have reviewed the circumstances in detail and have indicated in writing to Target Engineering that they will offer €400,000 in part-settlement of the claim and in full settlement of their liability as insurers under the policy.

Issue 4: Divisional Reorganisation

The Target Group continually evaluates the business performance of the group companies to ensure focus, effort and resources are concentrated on those areas that can generate maximum return for the Group. Experience and results over the last 18 months have clearly indicated that the Pharmaceutical Division of Target Engineering is proving to be less profitable than the Food Processing Division but is utilising the same resources and capital.

As a result, during November 2x01, a Divisional Reorganisation Plan was formulated to focus the future trading activities of Target Engineering exclusively on customers in the food processing sector. The Divisional Reorganisation Plan will have an impact on the staff, non-current assets and other resources which, to date, have been dedicated to the Pharmaceutical Division.

The details of the plan have already been discussed with, and communicated to, the relevant employees and their union representatives. It is widely known by the company's competitors, customers and suppliers that Target Engineering is no longer tendering for future contracts in the pharmaceutical sector. The timetable within the Divisional Reorganisation Plan assumes implementation commencing in February 2x02 with completion by June 2x02.

The key features of the Divisional Reorganisation Plan are as follows:

- 30 staff facing compulsory redundancy at a cost to the company of €500,000;
- 20 staff re-tasked to the Food Processing Division – re-training costs of €50,000;
- Investment in new systems to support expanded Food Processing Division €100,000.

None of the costs have been incurred yet, but Derek Rogers anticipates that he will create a restructuring provision in the financial statements of the coming year, i.e. 31 December 2x02, for €650,000 to cover, in full, the costs of implementing the plan.

In addition, Target Engineering has specialist tooling and plant and equipment which was previously utilised by the Pharmaceutical Division with a net book value in the draft financial statements of €1 million. Some of this equipment can be redeployed to the Food Processing Division but the remainder, which has a net book value of €250,000, can only be sold second-hand for an estimated €50,000. An agreement to sell the equipment at the estimated sale value has already been made with a prospective buyer.

Requirement:

Based on the accounting issues outlined above and the draft financial statements in Appendix I, prepare a memorandum to the audit manager in which you undertake the following:

Issue 1

(i) Review all the direct and associated costs involved in the construction of the Head Office building and identify which should be capitalised in the financial statements of Target Holdings.

5 marks

(ii) Set out the circumstances in which interest on borrowings may be capitalised and calculate the appropriate amount of interest that should be capitalised in the financial statements of Target Holdings in the year ended 31 December 2x01, together with any appropriate disclosures.

9 marks

(iii) What, if any, is the impact on the financial statements of Target Holdings of the contract for the construction and fitting out being awarded to Acorn.

6 marks

Issue 2

Set out how the disposal of the head office building should be reflected in the financial statements of Target Holdings for the year ended 31 December 2x01 together with any appropriate disclosures.

12 marks

Issue 3

Set out the impact, if any, of the third-party claim on the financial statements of Target Engineering for the year ended 31 December 2x01.

6 marks

Issue 4

Set out the impact, if any, of the Divisional Reorganisation Plan on the financial statements of Target Engineering for the year ended 31 December 2x01.

12 marks

Total 50 marks

Notes:

- **Re-drafted financial statements are not required. However, your report should include the journal entries in respect of any accounting adjustments required in respect of each accounting issue.**

- **Ignore any taxation implications of recommended accounting adjustments.**

FRS 102

Outline the key differences in accounting treatment if the financial statements were prepared in accordance with the requirements of FRS 102 *The Financial Reporting Standard applicable in the UK and Republic of Ireland.*

Appendix I

Draft Financial Statements for the year ended
31 December 2x01

Statement of Financial Position as at
31 December 2x01

	Target Holdings 31 December 2x01 €000	Target Engineering 31 December 2x01 €000
Non-current assets		
Tangible assets	8,500	27,000
Investments (TARGET ENGINEERING)	1,000	
	9,500	27,000
Current assets		
Inventory		3,000
Trade receivables	2,000	5,000
Inter-company	200	
Cash	100	200
	2,300	8,200
Total assets	11,800	35,200
Equity and liabilities		
Current liabilities		
Trade payables	200	7,000
Accruals/other payables	6,700	1,000
Inter-company	–	200
Overdraft	3,000	1,000
	9,900	9,200
Non-current liabilities		
Bank loans	500	3,000
Total liabilities	10,400	12,200
Equity		
Share capital	1,200	1,000
Retained earnings	200	22,000
Total equity and liabilities	11,800	35,200

Statement of Comprehensive Income for year ended 31 December 2x01

	Target Holdings €000	Target Engineering €000
Revenue	1,750	25,000
Cost of sales	100	12,500
Gross profit	1,650	12,500
Administration costs	1,200	4,000
Distribution costs		3,000
Finance costs	500	500
Profit/(loss) before tax	(50)	5,000
Tax		1,000
Profit/(loss) for the year	(50)	4,000

THE MAGNA GROUP*

Introduction

You are an audit senior in a firm of Chartered Accountants, Campbell Wilson & Co. It is March 2x07 and you are currently undertaking the audit in respect of the 2x06 financial statements of one of Campbell Wilson's largest clients, the Magna Group. The Magna Group of companies develops, manufactures and sells specialist scanning and imaging equipment for use in medical and security-related work.

Magna Holdings Ltd ('Magna Holdings') was formed over 30 years ago by two founders, Dr Patrick Bellamy and Dr Harry Shearer, who originally met while senior lecturers at the physics department of a renowned local university. The company was formed as part of a university-backed drive to realise the commercial applications of world-leading and unique research undertaken on campus. Since then the holding company has formed several new and very successful trading companies which have enjoyed worldwide commercial success. The share capital of Magna Holdings is held by the two founding partners, together with a colleague brought into the company to deliver sales and marketing expertise. Finally, a small amount of the share capital is held indirectly by the university.

*Based on 2003 Paper 2(i) in the Final Admitting Examination of the Institute of Chartered Accountants in Ireland.

The Magna Group is structured as follows:

Magna Holdings – holding company as 'umbrella' for other group activity.

- 100% subsidiary – Magna Security Ltd ('Magna Security') – develops and manufactures products for security applications.

- 100% subsidiary – Magna Medical Ltd ('Magna Medical') – develops and manufactures products for human medical applications.

- 80% subsidiary – Clear Scan Inc. ('Clear Scan') – a Ruritanian company which develops and manufactures scanning and imaging products for applications in the gaming and casino industries in Ruritania.

- 70% investment in Sureguard Ltd ('Sureguard') – operates security contracts in the public and private sectors.

A number of accounting issues have arisen in respect of the audit of the Group financial statements for the year ended 31 December 2x06. The senior partner of Campbell Wilson & Co., David Campbell, has requested that you review the various issues and prepare a report for the directors of the Magna Group which sets out the appropriate accounting treatment and disclosure in respect of each accounting issue, together with any necessary associated journal adjustments. The report is to be issued to the directors and discussed at a meeting to take place next week. The accounting issues and the draft financial statements are set out in Appendix I and Appendix II respectively.

Requirements:

Issue (a)

(i)   Explain how the investment in Sureguard should be treated and disclosed in the separate company financial statements of Magna Holdings and in the consolidated financial statements of the Magna Group for the year ended 31 December 2x06.

14 marks

(ii)   Set out the journal entries required to reflect your recommended accounting treatment under (i), together with any journal entries and disclosures arising from transactions between Magna Security and Sureguard during the year ended 31 December 2x06.

6 marks

Issue (b)

(i)   Set out how the investment in Clear Scan should be accounted for in the financial statements of Magna Holdings at the date of acquisition and calculate the goodwill arising on consolidation.

7 marks

(ii)   Set out what impact, if any, the reduction in actual and forecast profits of Clear Scan has on the carrying value of the investment and goodwill at 31 December 2x06.

8 marks

Issue (c)

Set out the impact, if any, of the withdrawal of the Canadian competitor on the carrying value of the 'mothballed' equipment in the financial statements of Magna Security for the year ended 31 December 2x06.

7 marks

Issue (d)

Set out how Projects A and B should be accounted for in the financial statements of Magna Medical for the year ended 31 December 2x06.

8 marks

Total 50 marks

Notes:

- **Re-drafted financial statements and consolidated financial statements are not required.**

- **Ignore any taxation implications of recommended accounting adjustments.**

- **It should be noted that, in their separate/individual financial statements, all companies within the Group account at cost for investments in subsidiaries, joint ventures and associates.**

- **It is Group policy to measure any non-controlling interest in subsidiaries at the non-controlling interest's proportionate share of the acquired company's identifiable net assets.**

FRS 102

Outline the key differences in accounting treatment if the financial statements were prepared in accordance with the requirements of FRS 102 *The Financial Reporting Standard applicable in the UK and Republic of Ireland.*

Appendix I

Accounting Issues Arising in Respect of the Audit of the Financial Statements of the Magna Group for the year ended 31 December 2x06

Issue (a) – Sureguard Ltd

As part of the commercial development of the group, Magna Holdings has been strategically seeking expansion into new but related business areas. On 1 January 2x06 Magna Holdings, together with another company, Standard Security, formed a new company, Sureguard Ltd ('Sureguard'), to bid for security contracts at ports, airports and other public and private buildings. Strategically, this is believed to represent a good 'fit', with Magna Holdings delivering the equipment, infrastructure and finance for the contracts whilst Standard Security sources the security manpower and day-to-day management to deliver the operational requirements of the contracts. During its first full year of trading Sureguard has successfully commenced a number of major contracts at retail stores and regional airports, and the initial performance of the company has been slightly ahead of expectations.

Magna Holdings holds 70% of the share capital of Sureguard with 30% held by Standard Security. Both Magna Holdings and Standard Security are fully involved in the strategic development of Sureguard and each company has two seats on the executive Board. Voting rights of the company are split equally between the two investors and, although not subject to any written agreement, it has been agreed and practised to date that either party can exercise a veto over key decisions. The intention is that in future years, if the company trades profitably, then the two investor companies will receive dividends from Sureguard.

From your audit work you are also aware that Magna Security has sold equipment to Sureguard, which is being utilised on the various security contracts. This equipment was invoiced to Sureguard in February 2x06 at €1.4 million sales value. The cost to Magna Security of these items was €1 million. A trade receivable remains in the books of Magna Security at 31 December 2x06 of €250,000 in respect of this transaction.

Issue (b) – Clear Scan Inc.

Magna Holdings purchased 80% of the share capital of Clear Scan on 1 January 2x06. Negotiations to purchase a stake in the company had commenced during the summer of 2x05 and had eventually been finalised in December 2x05 with the deal finally completing on 1 January 2x06. The purchase price of 18 million Ruritanian dollars was determined based on the estimates of the future profitability performance of Clear Scan over the next four years prepared by the directors of Magna Holdings and their advisers. During December 2x05 the directors of Magna Holdings estimated Clear Scan's trading profits before interest and tax over the next four years as follows:

Financial Year End	Profit Estimate R$000
31 December 2x06	3,750
31 December 2x07	3,750
31 December 2x08	7,500
31 December 2x09	7,500

Total profits over the four-year period were therefore estimated to be R$22.5 million; this was used to derive the purchase price of the company. At 31 December 2x05 the net assets of Clear Scan after fair value adjustment totalled R$10.5 million. The R$ rate has remained consistent throughout this period at 1.5:€1.

Unfortunately, as a result of adverse trading conditions during the first year's trading under the ownership of the Magna Group, the trading performance of Clear Scan has not matched the expectations prior to the takeover. Profit before interest and tax for the year to 31 December 2x06 was R$500,000 and the estimates for the next three years have been revised downwards as follows:

Financial Year End	Profit Estimate R$000
31 December 2x07	3,125
31 December 2x08	5,000
31 December 2x09	6,375

It may be assumed that the recoverable amount of Clear Scan varies in proportion to expected future profit. Ignore discounting.

Issue (c) – Portable Metal Detectors

Three years ago the majority of Magna Security's turnover and profits were derived from the manufacture and sale of portable metal detectors. However, in November 2x02 a rival Canadian company entered the market with cheaper, more easily portable equipment which utilised pioneering new technology capable of detecting a wider range of metals and materials even if present in smaller quantities. This 'new technology' effectively rendered Magna Security's products uncompetitive and virtually unsaleable. As a result of an impairment review prompted by the impact on trading of the Canadian competitor, Magna Security wrote down the value of its portable metal detector production line on the grounds of impairment and focused on other areas of its operations.

The equipment concerned comprised a production line and associated tooling purchased and first used in operation on 1 January 2x00 at a cost of €2 million. The equipment was depreciated straight-line over 10 years and with a full year's depreciation charged in the year of acquisition.

On 1 January 2x03, Magna Security took the decision to provide in full for the then NBV of the equipment, as the equipment was very specialised, had no value on the open market and could not be used in any other of the company's operations. The equipment was 'mothballed'.

In June 2x06 the Canadian company was forced to recall and withdraw its products from sale as a result of health scares experienced by operators of the equipment. Consequently, since June 2x06 Magna Security has been inundated with enquiries and orders for its original market leading product and production recommenced on 1 October 2x06, using the previously 'mothballed' production line.

Issue (d) – Development Projects

Magna Medical has a research facility dedicated to developing new technology for use in specialised imaging equipment with medical applications. The company has a consistently applied accounting policy for capitalising relevant development expenditure, which is then released over the life of the associated products. During the 2x06 financial year two major new projects have commenced.

Project A

During 2x06 Magna Medical commenced development of a new range of portable medical scanners which use mobile phone technology to link users (nurses and doctors) located in remote areas to consultants based in regional specialist centres. The potential applications and commercial returns are believed to be exceptional and are forecast to significantly exceed development costs.

Given the strategic importance of such a product, funds are available to complete the work. According to the detailed project plans and milestones the work will take a further 12 months to complete. Costs incurred to date total €450,000, with a further €1.2 million of investment required to complete the work during 2x07.

Project B

During 2x06 the company commenced contract development work for another medical product company, Star Monitors Ltd ('Star Monitors'), developing circuitry for use in human heart monitors. Costs incurred by Magna Medical, plus an agreed mark-up profit, will be paid in full by Star Monitors. Magna Medical has to date incurred €250,000 of costs in this project. Star Monitors made a payment on account of €100,000 in respect of this work in December 2x06, although Magna Medical has not yet invoiced any of this work to Star Monitors. Title to the intellectual property will transfer to Star Monitors on completion of the development work.

To date, the costs relating to both these products have been booked to deferred development expenditure in the statement of financial position of Magna Medical. The payment from Star Monitors has been accounted for by:

DR Bank €100,000

CR Capitalised Development Costs €100,000

Appendix II

Draft Financial Statements

	Magna Holdings Ltd	Magna Security Ltd	Magna Medical Ltd
	31 Dec 2x06 €000	31 Dec 2x06 €000	31 Dec 2x06 €000
Assets			
Non-current assets			
Property, plant and equipment	1,000	15,000	11,000
Intangible assets			2,000
Investments			
In Magna Security Ltd	1,000		
In Magna Medical Ltd	1,000		
In Clear Scan Inc.	12,000		
In Sureguard Ltd	140		
	15,140	15,000	13,000
Current assets			
Inventories		2,500	3,250
Trade receivables	200	5,000	4,000
Inter-company	300		300
Debt due from Sureguard	–	250	–
Cash	500		100
	1,000	7,750	7,650
Total assets	16,140	22,750	20,650
Equity and liabilities			
Share capital	1,000	1,000	1,000
Retained earnings	10,640	8,950	13,400
	11,640	9,950	14,400
Non-current liabilities			
Bank loans	3,000	1,000	1,250
Current liabilities			
Trade payables	1,000	4,000	3,000
Accruals	200	1,000	750
Inter-company	300	300	–
Overdraft	1,000	6,500	1,250
Total equity and liabilities	16,140	22,750	20,650

	Year Ended 31 Dec 2x06	Year Ended 31 Dec 2x06	Year Ended 31 Dec 2x06
	€000	€000	€000
Revenue	2,750	22,000	13,000
Cost of sales	300	12,000	8,000
Gross profit	2,450	10,000	5,000
Administration costs	300	4,000	1,000
Distribution costs	100	2,000	1,000
Finance costs	500	1,000	500
Profit before tax	1,550	3,000	2,500
Income tax expense	250	1,000	1,000
Profit for the year	1,300	2,000	1,500

Draft Financial Statements of Clear Scan Inc. – in Ruritanian Dollars

Statement of Financial Position

Clear Scan Inc.

31 December 2x06

	R$000
Non-current assets	8,500
Current assets	
Inventory	4,300
Trade receivables	
Cash	
Total assets	12,800
Equity and liabilities	
Share capital	2,000
Retained earnings	8,800
	10,800
Current liabilities	
Trade payables	1,500
Accruals	
Overdraft	500
Total equity and liabilities	12,800

Statement of Comprehensive Income

**Year Ended
31 December 2x06**

	R$000
Revenue	20,000
Cost of sales	17,750
Gross profit	2,250
Administration costs	1,000
Distribution costs	750
Finance costs	50
Profit before tax	450
Income tax expense	150
Profit for the year	300

Draft Financial Statements of Sureguard Ltd

Statement of Financial Position

Sureguard Ltd

31 December 2x06
€000

Non-current assets	9,100
Current assets	
Inventory	50
Trade receivables	1,700
Cash	150
Total assets	11,000
Equity and liabilities	
Share capital	200
Retained earnings	200
	400
Long-term liabilities	
Bank loans	10,000
Current liabilities	
Trade payables	100
Debt due to Magna Security	250
Accruals	50
Overdraft	200
Total equity and liabilities	11,000

Statement of Comprehensive Income

Year Ended
31 December 2x06

€000

Revenue	9,000
Cost of sales	7,000
Gross profit	2,000
Administration costs	400
Distribution costs	120
Interest	1,180
Profit before tax	300
Income tax expense	100
Profit for the year	200

HARRINGTON MOTORS LIMITED*

Introduction

Harrington Motors Ltd ('Harrington') is a successful Irish car dealership, which has grown rapidly over the last few years. The company acts primarily as an outlet for specific models of cars, but also has a repairs workshop. The company was founded by Mr Nick Harrington and has traded profitably for the last 30 years. Nick has recently retired and his son, Patrick, has taken over the business. Patrick is keen to expand the business and pursue new opportunities. He has asked you, as his newly appointed Financial Controller, to advise him on various accounting matters in the form of a memorandum. The financial year end of the company is 31 December.

The accounting issues are set out below and relevant financial information is set out in Appendix I.

---

*Based on 2004 Paper 2(i) in the Final Admitting Examination of the Institute of Chartered Accountants in Ireland.

Issue (a) – New Dealership

Harrington has been offered the opportunity to act as a dealer for a new make of environmentally friendly car, the Green Machine ('GM'). As the GM is relatively new to the Irish marketplace, Patrick Harrington has managed to negotiate favourable terms for the franchise in order to mitigate the risk to the company. Under the terms of the agreement, Harrington will take delivery of the cars without paying a deposit, and can return any or all of the cars to the manufacturer without penalty at any stage. This ensures that, if the vehicles are not popular with consumers, Harrington has a way of transferring the cars back to the manufacturer. Patrick Harrington feels that he has little to lose from a commercial viewpoint and is keen to pursue this arrangement.

The bookkeeper has included the cars purchased, at a total cost of €200,000, as purchases of inventory in the accounts. Two cars have been sold, at a total value of €40,000, and these have been included as revenue in the year. Each of the cars that has been sold had an original cost of €15,000 and the remainder of the cars are included in the year-end inventory figure.

Issue (b) – Premises

In the past Harrington operated from leased premises, and continued to do so from January to November 2x05, paying a monthly rental of €30,000. During December 2x05, the business re-located its entire operations to new purpose-built premises. The lease on the old premises runs until 31 December 2x07 and the lease does not permit re-letting the premises to another user. The former premises are now vacant and unused. Lease payments up to 31 December 2x05 have been charged as an expense in the statement of comprehensive income.

Patrick had spent several years trying to find alternative premises for the company without success. In the end he paid a business colleague, Mr Matthew Reid, a qualified architect, €50,000 to assist him in designing a purpose-built showroom and workshop. A site was eventually purchased in January 2x05 and the building was completed on 1 November 2x05.

The following costs have been capitalised in the accounts for year ended 31 December 2x05:

	€
Architect's fee	50,000
Lost revenue during two-week closure to facilitate move..................................	100,000
Purchase of land	980,000
Legal fees re: purchase of land	50,000
Building costs	500,000
Total costs	1,680,000

The bookkeeper has charged two months' depreciation on the total costs capitalised in the accounts. The depreciation policy for buildings in Harrington is to charge a full year's depreciation in the year of acquisition at 2% straight-line and none in the year of disposal.

On 31 December 2x05, Mr Reid advised Patrick that the showroom and workshop were worth €1,900,000 for their current purpose. However, due to new planning developments within the last year, the site is now worth in excess of this amount if developed for residential property. The current value on the open market for residential purposes would be around €2 million.

Patrick is keen to strengthen the statement of financial position of Harrington and would like your advice on how to incorporate these valuations in the financial statements.

Issue (c) – New Equipment

Patrick acquired new equipment for spraying cars at a cost of €200,000 in September 2x05. The equipment was tested by staff in September 2x05 to ensure that it would function correctly after implementation. As a result of the testing, various adjustments were made to the equipment, without which the equipment would not function correctly. The cost associated with this period was approximately €25,000. During the last three months of 2x05 the equipment was available for use but, due to a lack of marketing, it was only used intermittently. The monthly cost of running the equipment during that three-month period was €15,000.

Patrick is keen to capitalise the costs associated with this equipment, although his bookkeeper has expensed the costs to date as follows:

DR	Plant & equipment expenses	€70,000	
CR	Bank		€70,000

He would like your advice on the possibility of capitalising these costs and the journal entries required.

Issue (d) – New Customer

Patrick has been approached by a local firm, Smith Motors Ltd, which currently has an arrangement with one of Patrick's competitors, in relation to its fleet of 30 company cars. The cars are currently traded in every three years, with a once-off payment being made at the date of trade-in for each car. The owner of the local firm has decided to consider alternative methods of financing his fleet and would like to consider easing his cash flow burden by means of contract hire.

In order to provide this service, Patrick would need to purchase 30 new cars from the relevant manufacturers and to trade these in every three years. However, he feels that he should get a good deal on trade-ins due to his long-standing relationships with the relevant manufacturers.

The hire period would commence on 1 April 2x06 and run for three years. The schedule of inflows would be as follows:

1 April 2x06	€200,000
1 April 2x07	€100,000
1 April 2x08	€75,000

Patrick would like your advice regarding the accounting treatment and disclosure of these transactions.

Issue (e) – Potential Acquisition

Patrick Harrington has been approached by a businessman, John Coulter of Focus Ltd ('Focus'), who has asked him to consider investing in his business. Focus is a parts wholesaler and Patrick Harrington feels that this would be a useful investment and would add another dimension to his own business. The accounts of Focus are shown in Appendix I.

Included in the accounts of Focus is a property with a net book value of €1,675,500 which has a market value of €2,000,000.

Patrick has reviewed the accounts of Focus, and has discussed various alternative methods of investment with John Coulter. Both men feel that a 50:50

partnership would be unworkable, but have agreed to consider the following two options:

(1) Outright purchase of 100% of the share capital of Focus by Harrington for a consideration of €4,000,000. This would be financed by:

   (i)   the issue of 500,000 shares in Harrington at a price of €6.00 per share (nominal value = €1.00); and

   (ii) €1,000,000 from Harrington's cash resources.

(2) Purchase of an 18% stake in Focus by Harrington for €850,000 cash. Patrick Harrington would join the existing two directors on the Board of Focus and monthly Board meetings would be held to agree the strategic direction of the company.

Requirements:

Issue (a)

 (i) In relation to the potential new car dealership, explain the correct accounting treatment of the inventory with reference to relevant international accounting standards.

(ii) Set out the journal entries required to reflect your recommended accounting treatment under (a), together with the relevant disclosures.

6 marks

Issue (b)

 (i) Advise Patrick as to the recommended accounting treatment and disclosure of the vacant leased premises, setting out journal entries as appropriate.

(ii) Set out the costs that may be capitalised in the accounts in relation to the new building and any relevant adjusting journal entries.

(iii) Set out the journal entries required to incorporate the correct valuation into the financial statements, together with any relevant disclosures and requirements.

18 marks

Issue (c)

(i) Advise Patrick regarding the possibility of capitalising the costs incurred in relation to the installation of the new machinery. Provide relevant journal entries and disclosures.

4 marks

Issue (d)

(i) Advise Patrick as to the accounting treatment of the cars held for rental under the proposed contract hire arrangement.

4 marks

Issue (e)

(i) Explain to Patrick how each of the two options for investment in FOCUS would appear in the separate financial statements of HARRINGTON for the year ended 31 December 2x06. Provide journal entries for each scenario, incorporating the investment in the financial statements and advice as to the necessary disclosures.

8 marks

(ii) Regarding the proposed investment in FOCUS on 30 June 2x06, explain, using journal entries, the accounting treatment of each of the options in the consolidated accounts of HARRINGTON for the year ended 31 December 2x06.

10 marks

Total 50 marks

Notes:

• **Re-drafted financial statements and consolidated financial statements are NOT required.**

• **Ignore any taxation implications of recommended accounting adjustments.**

• **It should be noted that, in their separate financial statements, all companies within the Group account at cost for investments in subsidiaries, joint ventures and associates.**

FRS 102

Outline the key differences in accounting treatment if the financial statements were prepared in accordance with the requirements of FRS 102 *The Financial Reporting Standard applicable in the UK and Republic of Ireland.*

Appendix I

Focus Ltd
Statement of Comprehensive Income
for the year ended 30 June 2x06

	€
Revenue	6,235,367
Cost of sales	(3,990,635)
Gross profit	2,244,732
Administrative expenses	(1,425,235)
Finance costs	(66,538)
Profit before tax	752,959
Income tax expense	(185,235)
Profit for the year	567,724

Statement of Financial Position as at 30 June 2x06

	€
Assets	
Non-current assets	
- Premises, plant and equipment	2,542,698
Current assets	1,482,615
	4,025,313
Equity and liabilities	
Capital and reserves	
- Share capital	500,000
- Retained earnings	2,371,692
Total equity	2,871,692
Non-current liabilities	175,500
Current liabilities	978,121
Total equity and liabilities	4,025,313

THE O'NEILL GROUP*

Introduction

The O'Neill Group of companies is a successful wholesale and retail group. The owner, Mr David O'Neill, took over his father's department store several years ago, updated its image, restored its profitability and developed the business to its current status. In 2x00, Mr O'Neill decided to open an in-store restaurant for shoppers and other passing trade. The restaurant business (an incorporated entity) has proved to be a more difficult area for the Group due to changing trends and the performance of this company has been inconsistent over the years. The wholesale business, on the other hand, has developed in tandem with the retail outlet and has a steady trade with an established customer base. The group structure is straightforward, with O'Neill Enterprises Ltd ('O'Neill Enterprises') owning 100% of O'Neill Retail Ltd ('O'Neill Retail') and O'Neill Wholesale Ltd ('O'Neill Wholesale'), and 60% of O'Neill Restaurant Ltd ('O'Neill Restaurant').

Mr O'Neill is keen to further advance the business by making some changes in the group structure and would like your advice on the following issues in the form of a report. The accounting issues and relevant financial information are set out in Appendix I and Appendix II respectively.

*Based on 2005 Paper 2(i) in the Final Admitting Examination of the Institute of Chartered Accountants in Ireland.

Requirements:

Issue 1

Advise Mr O'Neill as to the recommended accounting treatment relating to the new refund policy of O'Neill Retail, setting out any journal entries required and all relevant disclosures relating to the financial statements for the year ended 31 December 2x05.

7 marks

Issue 2

(a) Set out how the part disposal of O'Neill Restaurant will impact on the financial statements of O'Neill Enterprises for the year ended 31 December 2x05 under international accounting standards. Provide relevant journal entries.

3 marks

(b) Explain how the part disposal of O'Neill Restaurant will be reflected in the consolidated financial statements of the Group for the year ended 31 December 2x05 under international accounting standards, providing relevant journal entries and disclosures.

8 marks

(c) Explain to Mr O'Neill, with reference to relevant international accounting standards, how O'Neill Restaurant will be treated in the Group financial statements from 1 January 2x06.

11 marks

Issue 3

(a) For each of the areas outlined under Issue 3 of Appendix I, compare the accounting policies adopted by Reid Enterprises and O'Neill Wholesale. Advise Mr O'Neill as to whether the policies of Reid Enterprises are in line with international accounting standards.

9 marks

(b) Compute the goodwill arising on the purchase of Reid Enterprises, based on the information available, and discuss the accounting treatment under international accounting standards.

6 marks

(c) Set out the journal entries that will be required to incorporate the trade, assets and liabilities of Reid Enterprises into O'Neill Wholesale on 1 January 2x06 under international accounting standards. Advise Mr O'Neill as to any disclosures required in the financial statements of O'Neill Wholesale for the year ended 31 December 2x05.

6 marks

Total 50 marks

Notes:

- **Re-drafted financial statements and consolidated financial statements are not required.**

- **It should be noted that, in their separate/individual financial statements, all companies within the Group account at cost for investments in subsidiaries, joint ventures and associates.**

- **It is Group policy to measure any non-controlling interest in subsidiaries at the non-controlling interest's proportionate share of the acquired company's identifiable net assets.**

FRS 102

Outline the key differences in accounting treatment if the financial statements were prepared in accordance with the requirements of FRS 102 *The Financial Reporting Standard applicable in the UK and Republic of Ireland.*

Appendix I

Issue 1 – O'Neill Retail

O'Neill Retail has introduced a new policy in 2x05 of refunding purchases by dissatisfied customers if goods are returned within one month with a proof of purchase. This facility is now well-known among the customer base and has proved popular with customers, prompting an increase in sales. It is anticipated that approximately 5% of goods sold in December 2x05 will be returned in January 2x06. The sales for December 2x05 were €550,000, with the average gross profit margin being 20%. All sales have been included in revenue. Mr O'Neill would like to know the correct accounting treatment and necessary disclosures for the new refunds policy.

Issue 2 – Part Disposal of O'Neill Restaurant

O'Neill Restaurant was incorporated seven years ago, funded by an investment in share capital by O'Neill Enterprises of €10,000. In its initial few years, the company traded well and built up an established clientele. However, it then entered a period of decline and its turnover and profitability suffered. A new restaurant manager was recruited four years ago, and he has worked very hard since then to develop the customer base and to increase the turnover and profitability of the company.

In 2x04 he was headhunted by a competitor and, in a bid to keep him, Mr O'Neill offered him an opportunity to purchase a stake in the company. At 31 December 2x04, the manager purchased 40% of the company at a price of €200,000. He is keen to purchase a further 30% of the company and a consideration of €175,000 has been negotiated with a completion date of 31 December 2x05. Mr O'Neill intends to retain the remaining 30% as he still wishes to continue his active involvement in the running of the restaurant and will still contribute to the management of the operation. No entries relating to the 30% purchase have been reflected in the statement of financial position (see Appendix II).

The fair value of the remaining investment in O'Neill Restaurant (i.e. 30%) at 31 December 2x05 was €154,000.

Mr O'Neill would like to understand the impact of this further sale on the financial statements of O'Neill Enterprises and on the consolidated financial statements for the year ended 31 December 2x05. He would also like to know how O'Neill Restaurant will be treated in the consolidated financial statements for the year ended 31 December 2x06.

Issue 3 – Potential acquisition of Reid Enterprises Ltd

O'Neill Wholesale is in negotiations to acquire the trade and net assets of a competitor, Reid Enterprises Ltd ('Reid Enterprises'). There are some differences in accounting policies between the two companies and Mr O'Neill would like to understand the main differences and their effect on the financial statements. He would also welcome comments on whether the policies of Reid Enterprises are in line with international accounting standards. The key areas meriting consideration are as follows:

Valuation of property
O'Neill Wholesale includes its non-specialised warehouse in its financial statements based on its depreciated cost, and discloses the open market value of the premises in the financial statements. Reid Enterprises, however, incorporates the market value of its premises into the financial statements. The market value of the premises owned by Reid Enterprises is €600,000 higher than the existing use value as there is a strong possibility of rezoning of the area in the future. The property owned by Reid Enterprises will be disposed of post-acquisition and new premises acquired to house the operation.

Furthermore, the financial statements of Reid Enterprises (Appendix II) include a deferred tax liability of €200,000 relating to the temporary difference created by the revaluation of the asset. Reid Enterprises has not yet entered into an agreement with a third party for sale of the premises.

Related party note
Mr O'Neill is aware that Reid Enterprises has several transactions with related companies, and the significance of these transactions is set out in the notes to the financial statements. He has noticed, however, that the names of the transacting companies have not been disclosed.

Acquisition of trade, assets and liabilities

It has been agreed in principle that the acquisition will take place as from 1 January 2x06. Only the trade, assets and liabilities of Reid Enterprises will be purchased and the calculation of the goodwill will follow the guidance for acquisition accounting under international accounting standards, with the consideration being €2,000,000 payable in cash by O'Neill Wholesale.

Appendix II

O'Neill Restaurant Ltd

Statement of Comprehensive Income for the year ended 31 December

	2x05	2x04
	€	€
Revenue	250,000	225,000
Cost of sales	(175,000)	(162,000)
Gross profit	75,000	63,000
Administrative expenses	(20,000)	(18,000)
Profit before tax	55,000	45,000
Income tax expense	(5,000)	–
Profit for the period	50,000	45,000

O'Neill Restaurant Ltd
Statement of Financial Position as at 31 December

	2x05	2x04
	€	€
Assets		
Non-current assets		
Property, plant and equipment	65,000	68,000
Current assets	80,000	60,000
Inter-company receivables	43,000	12,000
	188,000	140,000
Equity and liabilities		
Share capital	10,000	10,000
Retained earnings	146,000	96,000
	156,000	106,000
Current liabilities	32,000	34,000
Total equity and liabilities	188,000	140,000

The fair value of the net identifiable assets of O'Neill Restaurant at 31 December 2x05 was €180,000.

Reid Enterprises Ltd
Statement of Financial Position as at 31 December

	2x05 €	2x04 €
Assets		
Non-current assets		
Property, plant and equipment	2,100,000	2,203,000
Current assets	2,350,000	2,000,000
	4,450,000	4,203,000
Equity and liabilities		
Share capital	100,000	100,000
Reserves	749,850	458,000
	849,850	558,000
Non-current liabilities		
Long-term liabilities	1,100,000	1,300,000
Provisions	400,000	395,000
Current liabilities	2,100,150	1,950,000
Total equity and liabilities	4,450,000	4,203,000

FITZWILLIAM GROUP*

Introduction

Fitzwilliam Group Ltd ('Fitzwilliam Group') is a holding company and has 100% stake in each of the following companies. It is the policy of all Group companies to prepare financial statements under international accounting standards.

Fitzwilliam Construction Ltd ('Fitzwilliam Construction') is a company whose principal activity is the construction of buildings on behalf of third parties. Fitzwilliam Construction also acts as the principal contractor on development projects for buildings purchased by Fitzwilliam Rental Ltd ('Fitzwilliam Rental'). Fitzwilliam Rental is a property investment company which holds property for rental and also owns the Group headquarters building. Fitzwilliam Rental uses the fair value model when dealing with investment property and the revaluation model under IAS for all other completed properties. Fitzwilliam Retail Ltd ('Fitzwilliam Retail') is a company which owns several department stores. Fitzwilliam Group acts as a management company and is the entity through which the directors are remunerated.

*Based on 2006 Paper 2(i) in the Final Admitting Examination of the Institute of Chartered Accountants in Ireland.

DIAGRAM OF GROUP

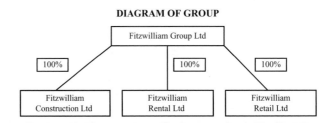

Various accounting issues have arisen within the group companies, and the financial controller has asked for your advice on a range of accounting issues which should be provided in the form of a memorandum. These issues are set out below.

(a) Fitzwilliam Construction

On 1 January 2x05 this company entered into a contract to develop a building for a third party. The contract price was €1,700,000 and the building work is well under way, with costs incurred to date and fully paid of €920,000 in respect of work certified at 31 December 2x05. The project has now run into difficulties and the project manager estimates that the costs to completion will be a further €850,000. Based on the contract agreement, the client is deemed to obtain control of work due when that work has been certified by the contract architect. The value of work certified at 31 December 2x05 was €880,000.

In addition, the building work on site has caused some contamination to the surrounding environment with an expected clean-up cost of €200,000. Fitzwilliam Construction has a widely published environmental policy in which it states it will make good all contamination caused by its actions; it has a record of honouring this policy.

(b) Fitzwilliam Rental

Fitzwilliam Rental purchased a disused building in the city docklands at a cost of €1,500,000 on 1 January 2x05. The intention at this time was to develop the property and subsequently to let the various floors to professional firms. A further €300,000 was spent over the next 11 months on renovations and improvements to the building prior to letting, with €200,000 of this being for work done at cost by Fitzwilliam Construction. The building was ready for tenant occupation on 1 December 2x05. The valuation of the completed property at 31 December 2x05 was €2,000,000.

Due to unforeseen difficulties in obtaining tenants, the building remained unoccupied.

In February 2x06, the docklands property was valued at €2,100,000 and the group then decided to immediately relocate its headquarters to this building. Fitzwilliam Rental managed to secure new tenants for the group's 'old' headquarters. The book value of those headquarters was €1,500,000 and the market value at the date of letting in February 2x06 was €1,800,000. The valuations of both properties were provided by independent qualified valuers. The financial controller would like your advice as to how to account for these property movements under international accounting standards.

Heating system in new headquarters

The Group moved into the new docklands property in February 2x06. The property has an estimated life of 50 years. However, it contains a sophisticated air conditioning and heating system, at a cost of €200,000, which is included in the value of the building of €2,100,000. The heating system will require replacement every 10 years and the company has entered into a contract with its supplier to replace the heating system at an agreed price of €200,000 every 10 years. The company plans to depreciate the building at €42,000 per annum and provide a further €20,000 each year to facilitate the replacement of the heating system. The policy of Fitzwilliam Rental is to depreciate assets on a monthly basis, and not to depreciate in the month of addition.

(c)   **Fitzwilliam Retail**

Fitzwilliam Retail entered into a transaction in March 2x05 whereby it agreed to enter into a sale of one of its department stores to a third party in order to raise capital for another project. At that time Fitzwilliam Retail also entered into a 10-year operating lease to lease back the store at a market rental. The sale price of the store was set at its market value of €2,500,000; the book value of the property in the books of Fitzwilliam Retail prior to the sale was €2,200,000.

(d) Fitzwilliam Group

As the Group has had a profitable trading year, the Board, at its meeting on 14 January 2x06, decided to propose a dividend of €750,000 in respect of the year ended 31 December 2x05. In addition, the Board agreed that, during the year ending 31 December 2x06, it would grant 50 share options to each of its 100 employees with a commencement date of 1 January 2x06. Each grant is conditional on the employee working for the Group for the next four years. The fair value of each share option at 1 January 2x06 was €20. It is likely that 25% of employees will leave during the four-year period, and thus forfeit their rights under the share option scheme. It is assumed that these departures will occur evenly over the four-year period.

Requirements:

Issue (a) – Fitzwilliam Construction

Advise the company as to the correct accounting treatment and disclosure for the contract under consideration with reference to relevant international accounting standards, together with supporting journal entries.

13 marks

Issue (b) – Fitzwilliam Rental

(i) Explain, with reference to international accounting standards, the accounting treatment which should be applied to the docklands property in the financial statements of Fitzwilliam Rental for the year ended 31 December 2x05. Journal entries are **not** required.

9 marks

(ii) Provide details of the relevant accounting treatment and disclosure in the financial statements of Fitzwilliam Rental for the year ending 31 December 2x06 for the docklands property and also for the old group headquarters. Journal entries are **not** required.

6 marks

(iii) Advise the financial controller, with reference to relevant international accounting standards, as to the correct accounting treatment for the air conditioning and heating system in the financial statements of Fitzwilliam Rental for the year ending 31 December 2x06. Journal entries are **not** required.

5 marks

Issue (c) – Fitzwilliam Retail

Explain, with reference to international accounting standards, the accounting treatment of the property transaction undertaken in the year ended 31 December 2x05 in the books of Fitzwilliam Retail. Provide relevant journal entries to reflect this transaction. Disclosures are **not** required.

6 marks

Issue (d) – Fitzwilliam Group

 (i) Explain, with reference to international accounting standards, how the proposed dividend will be reflected in the financial statements for the year ended 31 December 2x05.

4 marks

(ii) Advise the financial controller on how the share options will be reflected in the financial statements for the year ending 31 December 2x06, together with details of disclosures required by international accounting standards.

7 marks

Total 50 marks

Note:

• **Ignore all taxation implications.**

FRS 102

Outline the key differences in accounting treatment if the financial statements were prepared in accordance with the requirements of FRS 102 *The Financial Reporting Standard applicable in the UK and Republic of Ireland.*

HARDING GROUP*

Introduction

Harding plc ('Harding') is the holding company of a group of companies which prepares consolidated financial statements in accordance with international accounting standards. The principal activities of Harding are as a holding company and also as a property investment company. Throughout the year ended 31 December 2x06 the holding company owned 100% of two subsidiaries which are listed below:

Golf plc ('Golf')   A company whose principal activity is the sale of books through a website. The company has been underperforming in recent years and the sale of the company is currently being negotiated.

Holly plc ('Holly')   A company specialising in research and development in the chemical industry which was acquired during the year ended 31 December 2x05.

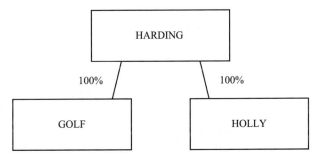

*Based on 2007 Paper 2(i) in the Final Admitting Examination of the Institute of Chartered Accountants in Ireland.

A further acquisition, Prospect plc ('Prospect'), is also being considered by the Board of Directors of Harding.

The Group Financial Director has approached you for advice in relation to various issues affecting the consolidated financial statements for the year ended 31 December 2x06 and he would like you to prepare a memorandum dealing with the matters listed below.

Requirements:

Prepare the memorandum for the Group Financial Director covering the following matters in respect of the year ended 31 December 2x06:

(a) (i) Advise the Group Financial Director as to the appropriateness of the costs included in 'Other operating expenses' in Golf with reference to relevant international accounting standards.

5 marks

(ii) Explain how Golf will be shown in the consolidated financial statements with reference to relevant international accounting standards. Disclosures are **not** required.

12 marks

(b) Advise the Group Financial Director as to the correct accounting treatment of the head office property and the investment property held in Harding. Provide relevant journal entries, ignoring any impact on the depreciation charge.

8 marks

(c) (i) Set out the correct accounting treatment to reflect the final net asset valuation of Holly, with reference to relevant international accounting standards. Journal entries are **not** required.

8 marks

(ii) Advise the Group Financial Director as to the correct accounting treatment of the development costs incurred in the years ended 31 December 2x05 and 31 December 2x06, with reference to relevant international accounting standards. Journal entries and disclosures are **not** required.

10 marks

(d) Explain the correct accounting treatment of the deferred tax issues in Prospect, and set out any relevant journal entries. Disclosures are **not** required.

7 marks

Total 50 marks

Notes:

- Ignore all taxation implications other than in relation to (d).

- It should be noted that, in their separate/individual financial statements, all companies within the Group account at cost for investments in subsidiaries, joint ventures and associates.

FRS 102

Outline the key differences in accounting treatment if the financial statements were prepared in accordance with the requirements of FRS 102 *The Financial Reporting Standard applicable in the UK and Republic of Ireland.*

Golf plc

Golf has been a loss-making subsidiary for many years and the Board agreed at a Board meeting in November 2x06 to sell Golf to a third party as a going concern. A price has been agreed, and final negotiations are currently under way with an anticipated completion date of September 2x07. Employees and customers were informed in December 2x06 of the pending sale. The Group Financial Director is keen to exclude Golf from the consolidated financial statements for the year ended 31 December 2x06 on the grounds that it is no longer part of continuing Group operations due to its impending sale. In previous years, Golf was included in the group results. Summary financial information for Golf is included below:

Golf plc – Statement of Comprehensive Income

	2x06 € million	2x05 € million
Revenue	80	50
Cost of sales	(50)	(70)
Gross profit/loss	30	(20)
Other operating expenses	(140)	(30)
Loss before tax	(110)	(50)

Included within 'Other operating expenses' in the financial statements of Golf for the year ended 31 December 2x06 were the following:

	€ million
Operating costs incurred	92
Provision for future operating losses	30
Impairment of assets	18
	140

The Group Financial Director would like to gain a fuller understanding of how the results of Golf will be shown in the consolidated financial statements for the year ended 31 December 2x06.

Harding plc

Harding owns two properties. One is used as the company's head office and is included in 'Property, plant and equipment' and the other is an investment property that is leased to a third party on a 10-year operating lease. In the past, Harding has revalued the head office building each year and transferred any movement to the revaluation reserve. The investment property was purchased during the year ended 31 December 2x05.

Relevant details of the cost and fair values of the properties are as follows:

	Head Office € million	Investment Property € million
Cost	20	19
Valuation 31 December 2x05	31	n/a
Valuation 31 December 2x06	29	23

The valuations at 31 December 2x06 have not yet been incorporated into the financial statements. The Board would like to apply the fair value model to its investment property for the current reporting period. Ignore any depreciation impact.

Holly plc

On 1 March 2x05 the group acquired a subsidiary company, Holly, for a consideration of €10 million. At the time of completion of the 2x05 financial statements a final valuation of net assets was not available, and goodwill was provisionally based on a net asset value of €8 million. The final valuation became available in December 2x06 and shows a net asset value of €7 million. The Group Financial Director has asked you to advise as to the effect of this information on the consolidated financial statements for the year ended 31 December 2x06.

Holly is currently engaged in a research and development project to develop a new chemical. The development costs in the year ended 31 December 2x05 of €5 million were written off as management felt they were not sufficiently confident of the ultimate profitability of the project. In the year ended 31 December 2x06, further development costs of €10 million have been incurred, with only an estimated €200,000 of costs to be incurred in the future. Production is expected to commence in the next few months.

The total trading profits from sales of the new product are now estimated at €20 million and the Board has decided to complete the project. The directors have again decided to write off the costs incurred in the year ended 31 December 2x06. The Group Financial Director has asked for your advice on whether this accounting treatment is in line with international accounting standards.

Prospect plc

The Group is currently considering a further acquisition, Prospect, a property investment company. The Financial Director has been reviewing the group deferred taxation provision and would like your advice on the impact of the following:

(1) Prospect has a portfolio of readily marketable government securities which are held as current assets at market value in the statement of financial position, with any increase or decrease being taken to the statement of comprehensive income. The gains on these investments are taxed when the investments are sold, and at present the securities are valued at €5 million above cost.

(2) Prospect intends to make an additional accrual for pension contributions of €1 million. This will not be allowable for tax purposes until it is paid.

Assume a corporation tax rate of 30%.

DARCY GROUP*

Introduction

Darcy plc ('Darcy') is the holding company of a group of companies which prepares individual and consolidated financial statements in accordance with international accounting standards (IFRS/IAS).

The principal activity of Darcy is as a holding company and throughout the year ended 31 December 2x07 Darcy owned 100% of Bingley plc ('Bingley') and Bennett plc ('Bennett').

Bingley is a company whose principal activity is commercial and residential property development. The company has been very profitable in recent years and its Board of Directors is hoping to expand the company further by forming relationships with similar companies.

Bingley is a company whose principal activity is the wholesale distribution of timber and other building supplies, some of which are also manufactured by the company.

Diagram of Group Structure

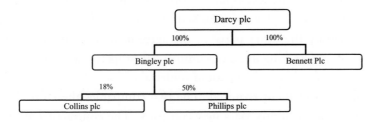

The Financial Director of the Group, Mr Fitzwilliam, has approached you for advice in relation to various issues which will affect the individual and consolidated

* Based on 2008 Paper 2(i) in the Final Admitting Examination of the Institute of Chartered Accountants in Ireland.

financial statements of the group for the year ended 31 December 2x07. He would like you to prepare a memorandum for him advising on how the matters detailed below should be treated.

It should be noted that in their separate/individual financial statements all companies within the Group account at cost for investments in subsidiaries, jointly controlled entities and associates.

It is Group policy to measure any non-controlling interest in subsidiaries at the non-controlling interest's proportionate share of the acquired company's identifiable net assets.

Bingley plc

Transactions with Collins plc

Bingley holds an 18% interest in another property development company, Collins. Collins has several other corporate shareholders. The majority of its shares are held by a property investment company unconnected with the Darcy Group. Bingley is represented on the Board of Directors of Collins and, via this representation, participates in all major decisions required to be taken in the management of the company. Bingley regularly supplies Collins with development land and, during the year ended 31 December 2x07, Bingley sold a development site to Collins at its open market value of €2,000,000. Bingley had purchased the site during the same year for €1,800,000.

Transactions with Phillips plc

During the year ended 31 December 2x07, Bingley entered into a contract with an unconnected property development company under which a new company, Phillips, was formed. Bingley owns 50% of the shares in Phillips, with the other 50% being held by the other party to the agreement. Phillips was formed for the purpose of undertaking a major commercial property development project, which neither of its shareholders could undertake alone due to its size and the working capital investment required. The two companies therefore decided to undertake the project jointly via a new company. The contractual arrangement between the two shareholders is such that Phillips will be managed by them jointly for the duration of the development project, and all profits or losses will be divided equally between them once the project is complete. It is anticipated that the project will take two to three years to complete.

Bennett plc

Acquisition of industrial saw

On 1 January 2x07 Bennett acquired an industrial saw from AB Finance Ltd on a finance lease. The lease payments are €5,000 per annum for four years, with an option to extend payments for a further two years at €500 per annum. The first payment was made upon delivery and subsequent payments are made annually in advance. The interest rate implicit in the lease is 12% per annum and the machine will have an estimated life of four years.

Shipment of timber products

On 19 December 2x07, Bennett delivered a large shipment of timber products to a potential new customer. Bennett had agreed with the customer that the goods would be sent subject to the customer's approval and could be returned, without cost to the customer, within 10 days of delivery. The customer agreed to speak with Bennett's sales representative within the 10-day period to advise him of whether the goods met with approval or not. The customer had not, however, contacted the company by the year-end of 31 December 2x07. The sales value of the shipment was €220,000 and this has not been included in the revenue of Bennett for the year.

Inventories

Bennett's inventories of building supplies include a great number of small products that cannot be specifically identified. Such items, referred to as "Category C" inventories, have always been included in the financial statements of the company on a last in first out (LIFO) basis. These inventories are valued at €640,000 at 31 December 2x07.

Mr Fitzwilliam had been content with this method of valuation of the inventories for a number of years, as the cost of the products did not tend to move significantly. However, in the current year (year ended 31 December 2x07), he has noted that the cost of some products has decreased considerably, with the effect that the inventories would be valued at €530,000 if a first in first out (FIFO) basis of valuation were used.

Mr Fitzwilliam has also noted that other inventories, included in the draft financial statements of Bennettt for the year ended 31 December 2x07 at a value of €130,000, could currently be sold for €280,000 as the product has become very popular with consumers. These inventories originally cost €190,000, but had been written down to €130,000 at 31 December 2x06.

Grant assistance

During the year ended 31 December 2x07, Bennett received a government grant to partially finance the purchase of some items of plant and machinery required for a planned expansion of the manufacturing side of the business. Expenditure of up to €1,500,000 of plant and machinery was approved by the government department involved, with the grant being approved for 60% of the total expenditure. The full amount of the grant had been received by 31 December 2x07.

The conditions on which the grant was approved were that the expenditure would relate to the purchase of specific items of plant and machinery and that an additional 10 members of staff would be hired.

At 31 December 2x07, Bennett had hired 12 extra staff members and had purchased €1,200,000 of the specified plant and machinery. It is the intention of the directors, if cash flow permits, to purchase a further €600,000 worth of plant and machinery in the year ended 31 December 2x08.

The plant and machinery purchased will be depreciated at 8% per annum on a straight-line basis. It is the company's policy to depreciate assets fully in the year of acquisition, regardless of the date of purchase.

The directors of Bennett feel that it is important to show grant assistance received separately in the financial statements. To date, the only accounting entry in relation to the grant received has been to record it as a separate item within deferred income in the draft financial statements of the company for the year.

Requirements:

(a) Bingley plc

(i) Advise Mr Fitzwilliam as to the correct accounting treatment and disclosure of the interest in Collins, and the sale of land to that company, in the consolidated financial statements of the Darcy Group for the year ended 31 December 2x07, with reference to international accounting standards (IAS/IFRS). Journal entries are **not** required.

14 marks

(ii) Explain, with reference to international accounting standards (IAS/IFRS), how the interest in Phillips should be accounted for in the consolidated financial statements of Darcy. Journal entries and disclosure notes are **not** required.

6 marks

(b) Bennett plc

(i) Advise Mr Fitzwilliam, with reference to international accounting standards (IAS/IFRS), of the correct accounting treatment of the finance lease in the financial statements of Bennett for the year ended 31 December 2x07. Show the relevant extracts in the statement of comprehensive income and statement of financial position. Disclosure notes are **not** required.

8 marks

(ii) Explain, with reference to international accounting standards (IAS/IFRS) the correct accounting treatment, together with supporting journal entries, of the shipment of timber products delivered to the potential new customer on 19 December 2x07 in the financial statements of Bennett for the year ended 31 December 2x07. Disclosure notes are **not** required.

4 marks

(iii) Advise Mr Fitzwilliam of the correct accounting treatment, under international accounting standards (IAS/IFRS) of the issues relating to the company's inventories in the financial statements of the company for the year ended 31 December 2x07. Set out any relevant journal entries. Disclosure notes are **not** required.

10 marks

(iv) Explain, with reference to international accounting standards (IAS/IFRS), the correct accounting treatment, including any relevant journal entries, of the government grant received by the company in the financial statements for the year ended 31 December 2x07. Draft the disclosure notes required.

8 marks

Total 50 marks

FRS 102

Outline the key differences in accounting treatment if the financial statements were prepared in accordance with the requirements of FRS 102 *The Financial Reporting Standard applicable in the UK and Republic of Ireland.*

Present Value Table

Present value of 1, i.e. $(1 + r)^{-n}$

where r = discount rate

n = number of periods until payment

Periods (n)	Discount rates (r)									
	1%	2%	3%	4%	5%	6%	7%	8%	9%	10%
1	0.990	0.980	0.971	0.962	0.952	0.943	0.935	0.926	0.917	0.909
2	0.980	0.961	0.943	0.925	0.907	0.890	0.873	0.857	0.842	0.826
3	0.971	0.942	0.915	0.889	0.864	0.840	0.816	0.794	0.772	0.751
4	0.961	0.924	0.888	0.855	0.823	0.792	0.763	0.735	0.708	0.683
5	0.951	0.906	0.863	0.822	0.784	0.747	0.713	0.681	0.650	0.621
6	0.942	0.888	0.837	0.790	0.746	0.705	0.666	0.630	0.596	0.564
7	0.933	0.871	0.813	0.760	0.711	0.665	0.623	0.583	0.547	0.513
8	0.923	0.853	0.789	0.731	0.677	0.627	0.582	0.540	0.502	0.467
9	0.914	0.837	0.766	0.703	0.645	0.592	0.544	0.500	0.460	0.424
10	0.905	0.820	0.744	0.676	0.614	0.558	0.508	0.463	0.422	0.386
11	0.896	0.804	0.722	0.650	0.585	0.527	0.475	0.429	0.388	0.350
12	0.887	0.788	0.701	0.625	0.557	0.497	0.444	0.397	0.356	0.319
13	0.879	0.773	0.681	0.601	0.530	0.469	0.415	0.368	0.326	0.290
14	0.870	0.758	0.661	0.577	0.505	0.442	0.388	0.340	0.299	0.263
15	0.861	0.743	0.642	0.555	0.481	0.417	0.362	0.315	0.275	0.239

	11%	12%	13%	14%	15%	16%	17%	18%	19%	20%
1	0.901	0.893	0.885	0.877	0.870	0.862	0.855	0.847	0.840	0.833
2	0.812	0.797	0.783	0.769	0.756	0.743	0.731	0.718	0.706	0.694
3	0.731	0.712	0.693	0.675	0.658	0.641	0.624	0.609	0.593	0.579
4	0.659	0.636	0.613	0.592	0.572	0.552	0.534	0.516	0.499	0.482
5	0.593	0.567	0.543	0.519	0.497	0.476	0.456	0.437	0.419	0.402
6	0.535	0.507	0.480	0.456	0.432	0.410	0.390	0.370	0.352	0.335
7	0.482	0.452	0.425	0.400	0.376	0.354	0.333	0.314	0.296	0.279
8	0.434	0.404	0.376	0.351	0.327	0.305	0.285	0.266	0.249	0.233
9	0.391	0.361	0.333	0.308	0.284	0.263	0.243	0.225	0.209	0.194
10	0.352	0.322	0.295	0.270	0.247	0.227	0.208	0.191	0.176	0.162
11	0.317	0.287	0.261	0.237	0.215	0.195	0.178	0.162	0.148	0.135
12	0.286	0.257	0.231	0.208	0.187	0.168	0.152	0.137	0.124	0.112
13	0.258	0.229	0.204	0.182	0.163	0.145	0.130	0.116	0.104	0.093
14	0.232	0.205	0.181	0.160	0.141	0.125	0.111	0.099	0.088	0.078
15	0.209	0.183	0.160	0.140	0.123	0.108	0.095	0.084	0.074	0.065

ROCKET GROUP

Introduction

Rocket plc ('Rocket') is the holding company of a group of companies which prepares their financial statements in accordance with international accounting standards. The principal activity of Rocket is to act as a holding company. Throughout the year ended 31 December 2x07 the holding company owned 100% of two subsidiaries which are listed below:

Launch plc ('Launch')   A company whose principal activity is the manufacture and sale of carpets to retail outlets.

Space plc ('Space')   A company specialising in developing and promoting a range of bathroom accessories.

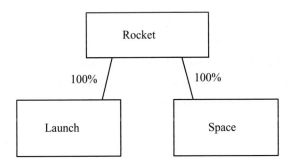

The Group Financial Director has approached you for advice in relation to various issues affecting the consolidated financial statements for the year ended 31 December 2x07 and she would like you to prepare a memorandum dealing with the matters listed below.

Requirements:

Prepare the memorandum for the Group Financial Director covering the following matters in respect of the year ended 31 December 2x07:

(a) (i) Advise the Group Financial Director as to the accounting treatment of the work in progress inventory of Launch at 31 December 2x07. Your advice should be based on the specialised carpet inventory only, and should take no account of the sale of surplus carpet materials in (a) (ii) below. Disclosures are **not** required.

14 marks

(ii) Explain how Launch should account for the surplus carpet materials, with reference to relevant international accounting standards. Provide relevant journal entries. Disclosures are **not** required.

5 marks

(iii) Advise the Group Financial Director as to the correct accounting treatment of the wool inventory of Launch at 31 December 2x07. Provide relevant journal entries. Disclosures are **not** required.

5 marks

(iv) Set out the correct accounting treatment in respect of the sale and leaseback of the factory and car park of Launch. Provide relevant journal entries. Disclosures are **not** required.

14 marks

(b) (i) Advise the Group Financial Director regarding the correct accounting treatment of the purchase and disposal of the building by Space. Provide relevant journal entries **and** disclosures.

12 marks

Total 50 marks

Notes:

- **Ignore all taxation implications.**
- **It should be noted that, in their separate/individual financial statements, all companies within the Group account at cost for investments in subsidiaries, joint ventures and associates.**

FRS 102

Outline the key differences in accounting treatment if the financial statements were prepared in accordance with the requirements of FRS 102 *The Financial Reporting Standard applicable in the UK and Republic of Ireland.*

Launch plc

(i) Work in progress inventory

Launch manufactures a range of specially designed carpets for the hotel and leisure industry, and a custom built factory was constructed for this purpose. Launch has achieved its target output of 10,000 customised carpets in each of the years 2x03–2x06. During 2x07 this production level was exceeded due to staff agreeing to work double shifts in order to meet an unexpected increase in demand during the summer season. Consequently, 12,000 finished carpets were produced in the year ended 31 December 2x07.

At 31 December 2x07, Launch had 200 carpets in inventory, which on average were 75% complete. Each completed carpet incurs the following costs:

	€
Materials	1,500
Labour	600
Distribution costs	100
Sales commissions	150
	2,350

The following additional costs were incurred in the year ended 31 December 2x07, in respect of the overall operation of the factory:

	€
Production supervisors' salaries	2,550,000
Depreciation of equipment	1,250,000
Administration costs	400,000
Interest relating to financing of inventory	90,000

One of the 75%-completed carpets was manufactured for the Regency, a family-run hotel, which, after a poor winter season, decided to close with immediate effect in early January 2x08. The general manager of the factory is confident that if Launch were to spend a total of €800 on promotion and distribution costs, that the carpet could be offloaded to another hotel group for €3,000.

(ii) Carpet ends and floor mats

During 2x07, Launch decided to market surplus carpet materials as carpet ends and floor mats. Previously, these materials had been dumped, but with spiralling waste disposal costs, it was decided to opt for an alternative use approach.

During 2x07 a cash surplus of €130,000 was generated from the sale of these products; it was estimated that inventories of surplus carpet materials at 31 December 2x07 could be sold in January for further net proceeds of €25,000.

(iii) Inventory of wool

Wool is the primary material used by Launch for the manufacture of specialised carpets. Wool inventory at 31 December 2x07 had cost €600,000 to purchase, but only had a net realisable value of €200,000. On the basis that Launch does not intend to dispose of the wool, the inventory has been included in the financial statements at a value of €450,000. It is believed that this partially reflects the fall in value of the wool, but also takes account of the intention to retain the inventory for use in the production process. It is expected that the finished carpets, into which the wool will be incorporated, can be sold at a reasonable profit margin.

(iv) Sale and Lease-back

On 1 January 2x07, the factory used for the manufacture of specialised carpets, along with its three-acre car park, was sold to an insurance company. Both assets were immediately leased back to Launch under a 50-year lease agreement.

The factory, which was completed in 2x02, had cost €6 million to construct. The car park had been purchased and developed alongside, at an additional cost of €4 million. Up to the time of their sale, both assets had been carried in the financial statements using the revaluation model of IAS 16 *Property, Plant and Equipment*. On the 31 December 2x06, the factory was included in the financial statements of Launch at its fair value of €10 million. The parking lot was included in the statement of financial position at €7 million on the same date.

Under the terms of the sale and lease-back agreement of 1 January 2x07, the factory was sold to the insurance company for €12 million, and the consideration agreed for the car park was €9 million, which was its fair value at the time of sale.

Launch agreed to pay 50 annual instalments, in advance, of €500,000 in respect of the factory. Launch has an option to extend the lease of the factory for a secondary period of 30 years by making further annual payments of €10,000.

Launch agreed to pay 50 annual instalments, in advance, of €400,000 in respect of the lease of the car park.

Launch charges depreciation of 2% per annum straight-line on the factory; no depreciation is charged in respect of the car park. It should be assumed that the interest rate implicit in the lease is 10%.

Space plc

Building
On 1 January 2x03, Space purchased a building for €6 million. The building was depreciated over 50 years on a straight-line basis. A full year's depreciation is charged in the year of purchase and no depreciation is charged in the year of sale.

On 1 January 2x05, the building was deemed to have suffered an impairment, and it was written down to €4 million. On 1 January 2x07, the building was revalued to €7 million. It was sold to Launch on 31 December 2x07 for €8 million, which was certified as its fair value by an independent auctioneer.

TELFER INDUSTRIAL GROUP

Introduction

Telfer Industrial Group comprises Telfer Holdings Limited and its subsidiary companies. In your capacity as Group Financial Accountant you are currently reviewing the draft consolidated financial statements of the group. The Finance Director has requested that you prepare a memorandum outlining any issues which may require amendment.

During your review of the financial statements, the following matters have been brought to your attention.

(1) Acquisition of Summit Limited

On 31 May 2x07 the parent company, Telfer Holdings Limited, purchased 25% of Summit Limited. Telfer Holdings Limited had Board representation in Summit Limited at that time, and was able to exercise significant influence over that company. Summit Limited is a producer and distributor of a high-margin industrial component, and Telfer's shareholding gives the Group a presence in an important and expanding market.

The 25% stake in Summit Limited was acquired for cash consideration of €2.5 million. The identifiable assets less liabilities of Summit Limited at that time were included in its statement of financial position at €7 million.

On 31 May 2x08, Telfer Holdings Limited acquired a further 65% of the shares in Summit Limited for a cash payment of €7.8 million. The identifiable assets less liabilities included in the statement of financial position of Summit Limited at that date amounted to €8 million. The fair value of these net assets was €9 million. At 31 May 2x08, the fair value of Telfer's previous 25% shareholding in Summit was €2.3 million.

Acquisition expenses of €200,000 were incurred by Telfer Holdings Limited in connection with the purchase of the controlling stake on 31 May 2x08.

On 28 February 2x09, Telfer Holdings Limited sold 20% of the shares in Summit Limited for cash proceeds of €3 million.

It is Group policy to value non-controlling interest at its proportionate share of the subsidiary's fair value of identifiable net assets.

In their separate/individual financial statements, companies within the Group account at cost for investments in subsidiaries, joint ventures and associates.

Ignore taxation.

(2) Property Asset

Rampton Limited is a wholly-owned subsidiary of Telfer Holdings Limited. On 1 June 2x06, Rampton Limited purchased a building at a cost of €2 million for use as an administrative office by company personnel. The property was revalued to €2.5 million at the 31 May 2x07.

The property proved to be surplus to requirements due to staff relocation, and in May 2x08 it was decided to dispose of it at the earliest opportunity. At 31 May 2x08, the property was classified as being held for sale. At that date, the market value was €3 million and selling costs were estimated at €100,000.

At 31 May 2x09, the property was valued at €1.8 million, net of selling costs, and it was withdrawn from sale at that date due to a scarcity of buyers. The value in use of the building at that time was estimated at €1.5 million.

Rampton Limited depreciates property over 50 years on a straight-line basis.

Ignore taxation.

(3) Intragroup Sales

During the year ended 31 May 2x09, Rampton purchased goods from Brink Limited, in which Telfer Holdings Limited held a 75% shareholding. These goods were supplied by Brink Limited at €12 million, inclusive of a mark-up of 25%.

One-third of these goods was held as inventory by Rampton Limited at 31 May 2x09. All companies in the Telfer Group pay corporation tax at 20%, six months after their year end.

(4) Sale of Goods

In May 2x09, Rampton Limited sold 10 units of its main product, an integrated waste management system. The selling price of each unit was €100,000, which included a profit margin of 20%. Two months' credit was allowed to purchasers of nine of the waste management systems, these terms being standard in the industry.

One customer was allowed a credit period of two years, on the basis that they would pay €121,000 at the date of settlement.

The draft financial statements of Summit Limited for the year ended 31 May 2x09 are included in Appendix I.

The Group financial statements have also been prepared in draft form in Appendix II.

Requirement:

You are required to draft a memorandum to the Finance Director of the Telfer Group, outlining your recommendations in respect of the following accounting issues.

(1) Acquisition and Disposal of Shares in Summit Limited

(i)   In respect of the 25% acquisition of shares on 31 May 2x07:

- Outline the appropriate accounting treatment and provide the necessary journal entries, in the financial statements of the Telfer Group.

(4 marks)

(ii) In respect of the 65% acquisition of shares on 31 May 2x08:

- Advise on the appropriate accounting treatment, provide the necessary journal entries and prepare the disclosure note for inclusion in the financial statements of the Telfer Group.

(15 marks)

(iii) *In respect of the disposal of 20% of the shares of Summit Limited on 28 February 2x09*

- Outline the appropriate accounting treatment and provide the necessary journal entries in the financial statements of the Telfer Group.

(5 marks)

(2) Property Asset

- Outline the recommended accounting treatment *and* provide the journal entries in the financial statements of Rampton Limited for the years ending 31 May 2x07, 2x08 and 2x09. Ignore taxation.

(11 marks)

(3) Intragroup Sales

(i)   Outline the appropriate accounting treatment and journal entries for this transaction in the financial statements of the Telfer Group at 31 May 2x09.

(4 marks)

(ii) Draft the relevant disclosure notes, if any, in the financial statements of the Group and the individual financial statements of Rampton Limited.

(4 marks)

(4) Sale of Goods

(i)   Outline the appropriate accounting treatment for the sale of goods by Rampton Limited.

(3 marks)

(ii) Provide the journal entries for these transactions in 2x09 and 2x10.

(4 marks)

FRS 102

Outline the key differences in accounting treatment if the financial statements were prepared in accordance with the requirements of FRS 102 *The Financial Reporting Standard applicable in the UK and Republic of Ireland.*

Appendix I

Draft Financial Statements of Summit Limited

Draft Statement of Comprehensive Income for the year ended 31 May 2x09

	2x09 €000	2x08 €000
Revenue	11,800	
Cost of sales	(7,950)	
Gross profit	3,850	
Distribution costs	(300)	
Administrative expenses	(500)	
Other expenses	(400)	
Finance costs	(400)	
Profit before tax	2,550	
Income tax expense	(1,370)	
Profit for the year from continuing operations	1,180	

Other comprehensive income:
Items that will not be reclassified to profit or loss:

Gains on property revaluation	250	
Total comprehensive income for the year	1430	

Draft Statement of Financial Position of Summit Limited at 31 May 2x09

	Notes	2x09 €000	2x08 €000
Assets			
Non-current assets			
Land and buildings		5,451	
Plant and equipment		4,645	
		10,096	
Current assets			
Inventories of finished goods		1,469	
Trade and other receivables		1,395	
Cash and cash equivalents		1,155	
		4,019	
Total assets		14,115	
Liabilities			
Current liabilities			
Trade and other payables		2,215	
Income tax payable		1,350	
		3,565	
Non-current liabilities			
Term loan		820	
Provisions		300	
		1,120	
Total liabilities		4,685	
Net assets		9,430	
Equity			
Equity attributable to owners of the parent			
Share capital		100	
Share premium account		250	
Revaluation surplus		1,000	
Retained earnings		8,080	
Total equity		9,430	

Appendix II

Draft Consolidated Financial Statements of the Telfer Group

Draft Consolidated Statement of Comprehensive Income for the year ended 31 May 2x09

	2x09	2x08
	€000	€000
Revenue	52,000	
Cost of sales	(27,950)	
Gross profit	24,050	
Distribution costs	(4,800)	
Administrative expenses	(10,500)	
Finance costs	(620)	
Profit before tax	8,130	
Income tax expense	(2,150)	
Profit for the year from continuing operations	5,980	
Other comprehensive income		
Items that will not be reclassified to profit or loss:		
Gains on property revaluation	1,400	
Total comprehensive income for the year	7,380	
Profit attributable to:		
Owners of the parent	5,550	
Non-controlling interests	430	
	5,980	
Total comprehensive income attributable to:		
Owners of the parent	6,950	
Non-controlling interests	430	
	7,380	

Draft Statement of Financial Position of the Telfer Group at 31 May 2x09

	Notes	2x09 €000	2x08 €000
Assets			
Non-current assets			
Property, plant and equipment		27,750	
Investment property		4,000	
Goodwill		3,800	
		35,550	
Current assets			
Inventories		3,444	
Investments		1,000	
Trade and other receivables		3,395	
Cash and cash equivalents		2,155	
		9,994	
Total assets		45,544	
Liabilities			
Current liabilities			
Trade and other payables		6,965	
Income tax payable		4,150	
		11,115	
Non-current liabilities			
Convertible debentures		1,600	
Term loan		2,120	
Provisions		3,400	
		7,120	
Total liabilities		18,235	
Net assets		27,309	

Equity
Equity attributable to owners of the parent

Share capital	1,000
Share premium account	1,700
Revaluation surplus	3,904
Other reserves	900
Retained earnings	17,205
	24,709
Non-controlling interests	2,600
Total equity	27,309

CAMPBELL GROUP

Introduction

You have recently been appointed as Financial Accountant for the Campbell Group of companies, which has a growing presence in the automobile and ancillary services sector. The Campbell Group, which is listed on the Dublin and London stock exchanges, is headed up by its parent company, Campbell Holdings Limited. There are also a number of subsidiary companies, most of which are wholly-owned by Campbell Holdings Limited. Group strategy has been to form a separate company for each main area of operation; currently there are individual subsidiaries responsible for car sales, car hire, valeting and repairs, leasing and hire purchase, and sales of motor accessories.

You have received a file from the Chief Accountant, Martin Mangan, which contains the following information:

- Matters arising from the 2x10 audit of the Group   (Appendix I below)
- Draft consolidated financial statements for the year
  ended 31 December 2x10.   (Appendix II below)

Requirements:

On the basis of the information provided by the Chief Accountant, draft a memorandum to Martin Mangan, outlining:

(1) The earnings per share figures of the Group for the year ended 31 December 2x10 (including the 2x09 comparative).

(2) The accounting treatment for employee benefits for the year ended 31 December 2x10. See detailed requirement in Appendix I. It should be assumed that the EPS computations in (1) above will not be affected by any adjustments required in this section.

(3) The additional disclosures required by international accounting standards, in view of the fact that the ordinary shares of the Campbell Group are listed on the Dublin and London stock exchanges.

FRS 102

Outline the key differences in accounting treatment if the financial statements were prepared in accordance with the requirements of FRS 102 *The Financial Reporting Standard applicable in the UK and Republic of Ireland*.

Appendix I

Matters Arising from the 2x10 Audit of the Campbell Group

(1) Share Capital

On the 31 December 2x09, the Campbell Group had 800 million issued ordinary shares of €1 par value. There were €200 million of 10% irredeemable preference shares in issue at the same date. The Campbell Group has no obligation to pay a dividend on the preference shares. However, an annual dividend is normally paid. There had been no change in issued share capital during the year ended 31 December 2x09.

The following additional ordinary shares were issued during the year ended 31 December 2x10:

(i)   On 1 January, the Group announced a one for four rights issue at €2 per share. The exercise date was the 1 February, and the market price immediately before the exercise date was €2.50.

(ii)   On 1 April, the Group issued 200 million ordinary shares for cash at full market price of €2.45.

(iii) On 1 July, the Group made a one for one bonus issue.

(iv)   On 1 October, the Group purchased 100 million treasury shares for cash of €2.50 per share. This was the market price at that date.

The following issues also relate to the ordinary shares of the Campbell Group:

–   On 1 April 2x10, share options were issued to 10 executives in the Campbell Group. Each executive had the option to purchase 20 million ordinary shares for an exercise price of €2 per share. The average market price of the ordinary shares during 2x10 was €2.50.

The exercise rights for each executive are dependent on completing three years of service with the Campbell Group up to 31 March 2x13.

- The 8% convertible debentures are convertible into ordinary shares in 2x12 at the rate of 50 shares per €100 of convertible loan stock.
- The Campbell Group pays corporation tax at 30%.

(2) Employee Benefits

(a) Short-term employee benefits

In December 2x10 a problem with the payroll system in one of the Campbell Group subsidiaries, Auto Limited, has meant that no record of payroll costs has been made for the entire month. Details of wages and salaries in that subsidiary for December are as follows:

	€ million
Wages and salaries (net)	10.4
PAYE	3.6
Employer's PRSI	1.1
Holiday pay	0.8
Medical insurance provided for staff	0.6
	16.5 (Note 1)

Note 1: €1.2 million relates to costs incurred in the construction of a new factory extension. With the exception of wages and salaries of €10.4 million, none of the above amounts were paid at 31 December 2x10.

The Campbell Group also pays an annual staff bonus of €2,000 to all employees who provide a minimum of ten months of service during the year, and who are employees of the Group at 31 December. Auto Limited had a total of 1,000 employees at 31 December 2x10, of whom 900 had worked 10 months or more during the year.

(b) Post-employment benefits

    (i) Defined contribution plan
The Campbell Group operates a defined contribution pension plan for employees who commenced employment with the Group on or after 1 January 2x07. Under the plan, post-employment benefits will be based on the returns on employer and employee contributions.

Required contributions for the Campbell Group for the year ended 31 December 2x10 amounted to €120 million, of which €25 million was outstanding at the year end. Employee contributions for the same period were €40 million, which have been paid in full.

No accounting entries have been made in respect of these contributions.

(ii)   Defined benefit plan

The Campbell Group operates a defined benefit pension plan for employees who commenced employment with the Group prior to the 1 January 2x07. The pension scheme is non-contributory.

At 31 December 2x09, the Campbell Group recorded a defined benefit liability of €600 million, comprising the following items:

	€ million
Present value of defined benefit obligation	1,680
Fair value of plan assets	1,080
Defined benefit liability	600

The following information relates to the year ended 31 December 2x10:

	€ million
Employer contributions paid on 31 December 2x10	400
Benefits paid on 31 December 2x10	150
Current service cost	390
Present value of defined benefit obligation at year end	2,300
Fair value of assets of plan at year end	1,650

The average yield on relevant corporate bonds was 4% on 1 January 2x10.

No accounting entries have been made in the year ended 31 December 2x10.

Requirements:

(i)   Defined contribution plan

Calculate the expense for the year ended 31 December 2x10, and the liability at 31 December 2x10.

(ii)   Defined benefit plan

Calculate the defined benefit expense for the year ended 31 December 2x10, and the defined benefit liability at 31 December 2x10.

Appendix II

Draft Statement of Financial Position of the Campbell Group
as at 31 December

	31 Dec 2X10 € million	31 Dec 2X09 € million
Non-current assets		
Tangible assets	8,620	6,000
Investments	1,000	
	9,620	6,000
Current assets		
Inventory	800	1,000
Trade receivables	2,200	2,000
Cash	300	200
	3,300	3,200
Total assets	12,920	9,200
Equity and Liabilities		
Current liabilities		
Trade and other payables	2,167	1,700
Bank overdraft	2,400	2,000
	4,567	3,700
Non-current liabilities		
Pension liability	600	600
8% convertible debentures	500	500
Total liabilities	5,667	4,800
Equity		
Share capital (Note 1)	2,600	1,000
Share premium	1,490	1,000
Equity reserve	33	–
Revaluation surplus	1,100	700
Retained earnings	1,230	1,500
	6,453	4,200
Non-controlling interests	800	200
Total equity (Note 2)	7,253	4,400
Total equity and liabilities	12,920	9,200

Note 1: share capital

	31 December 2x10 € million	31 December 2x09 € million
Ordinary shares of €1	2,400	800
10% irredeemable cumulative Preference shares	200	200
	2,600	1,000

Note 2: statement of changes in equity

	OSC	10% Pref. Shares	Share Premium	Equity Reserve	Retained Earnings	Revaluation Surplus	NCI	Total Equity
	€ million	€ million	€ million	€ million	€ million	€ million	€ million	€ million
Bal. @ 01/01/2x10	800	200	1,000	–	1,500	700	200	4,400
Rights issue	200		200					400
Issue at fair value	200		290					490
Bonus issue	1,200				(1,200)			
Treasury shares					(250)			(250)
Share option scheme				33				
Total comprehensive income					1,200	400	600	2,200
Preference dividend					(20)			(20)
Bal. @ 31/12/2x10	2,400	200	1,490	33	1,230	1,100	800	7,253

Draft Statement of Comprehensive Income of the Campbell Group
for the year ended 31 December

	2X10 € million	2X09 € million
Revenue	12,600	10,200
Cost of sales	7,880	6,800
Gross profit	4,720	3,400
Administration costs	1,200	1,000
Distribution costs	1,020	850
Finance costs	150	400
Profit before tax	2,350	1,150
Income tax expense	550	200
Profit for the year	1,800	950

Other comprehensive income:		
Items that will not be reclassified to profit or loss:		
Revaluation gains	400	250
Total comprehensive income for the year	2,200	1,200

	2x10 €million	2x09 €million
Profit attributable to:		
Owners of the parent	1,200	870
Non-controlling interests	600	80
	1,800	950
Total comprehensive income attributable to:		
Owners of parent	1,600	1,120
Non-controlling interests	600	80
	2,200	1,200

PART 2

SOLUTIONS

SOLUTION TO
BELLMOTH GROUP

(a) Goodman Hart and Co.

Memorandum

To: Yvonne Russell

From: Bill Baxter

Date: 3 February 2x06

Re: Bellmoth Group Financial Statements for the year ended 31 December 2x05

The following accounting issues have arisen as a result of the 2x05 audit:

(1) Caterpillar

 (i) Restructuring
  IAS 37 states that a provision for restructuring should only be recognised when the general recognition criteria for provisions are met. These criteria are outlined in paragraph 14 of IAS 37:

- An entity has a present obligation (legal or constructive) as a result of a past event.
- It is probable that an outflow of resources will be required to settle the obligation.
- A reliable estimate can be made of the amount of the obligation.

Additionally, IAS 37 states that a constructive obligation to restructure arises only when an entity:

- has a detailed formal plan for the restructuring; and
- has raised a valid expectation in those affected that it will carry out the restructuring by starting to implement that plan or announcing its main features to those affected by it (IAS 37, para 72).

These recognition criteria appear to have been satisfied in respect of Caterpillar's intention to downsize the provision of short-life foodstuffs. In identifying costs that can be recognised within a restructuring provision, IAS 37 states that ... 'a restructuring provision shall include only the direct expenditures arising from the restructuring, which are those that are both:

- necessarily entailed by the restructuring; and
- not associated with the ongoing activities of the entity' (IAS 37, para 80).

On the basis of the above requirements, the following amounts should be provided for by Caterpillar at 31 December 2x05:

	€000
Loss on disposal of non-current assets	650
Redundancy settlements	350
	1,000

IAS 37 states that 'provisions shall not be recognised for future operating losses' (para. 63).

IAS 37 also specifically excludes marketing costs from being included in a provision, on the basis that they:

- relate to the future conduct of the business and are not liabilities for restructuring at the end of the reporting period (IAS 37, para 81).

Warehouse re-design costs which will be incurred by Caterpillar are excluded on the same basis.

Thus, on the basis that Caterpillar is committed to the rationalisation of the short-life foodstuffs range, the following entry will be required in the 2x05 consolidated financial statements:

	DR €000	CR €000
Provision for loss on restructuring – SOCI P/L	1,000	
Provision for loss on restructuring – SOFP		1,000

(ii)   *Warranty provisions and refunds*

Warranty By offering a warranty, Caterpillar is effectively providing an assurance of quality. This warranty does not provide an additional good or service to Caterpillar's customers (i.e. there are no separate performance obligations). IFRS 15 requires that the estimated cost of satisfying the warranty obligation is provided for in accordance with the requirements of IAS 37.

Warranty provisions are specifically addressed in Appendix C of IAS 37. It is concluded that it is appropriate that a provision should be made for the best estimate of the costs of making good, under the warranty, those products sold before the end of the reporting period. Thus, a provision of €1.5 million should be set up in Caterpillar's 2x05 financial statements as follows:

	DR €000	CR €000
Warranty provision – P/L	1,500	
Warranty provision – SOFP		1,500

(Being warranty provision on goods sold in 2x05)

Customer Refunds Customers who purchased goods from Caterpillar during 2x05 have a right to return those goods. IFRS 15 requires that an entity should account as follows for products sold on this basis:

- recognise revenue for the amount of consideration to which the entity expects to be entitled (i.e. excluding consideration for the goods expected to be returned);
- recognise a refund liability; and
- recognise an asset (and corresponding adjustment to cost of sales) for the entity's right to recover products from customers).

Caterpillar has recognised the full amount of sales consideration in trade receivables and revenue. Therefore the following adjustment is required in respect of expected cash refunds:

	DR €000	CR €000
Revenue	800	
Provision for refunds – SOFP		800
(Being provision for cash refunds in 2x06 on 2x05 sales)		
Inventory – SOFP	400	
Cost of sales		400

(Being goods that are expected to be returned by customers, following cash refunds: €800,000 × $\frac{50}{100}$)

The exchange of goods sold in 2x05 will merely result in a change in inventory records, and they will have no effect on the company's recorded profit in2x05.

(iii) *Staff retraining costs*

Legislative changes at European level resulting in more stringent product design will result in staff retraining costs over the next three years. IAS 37 (Example 7 Appendix C), in respect of staff retraining, states that '… there is no obligation because no obligating event (retraining) has taken place'.

Therefore no provision should be made at 31 December 2x05 in respect of the future retraining costs that will be incurred due to European legislative changes.

(iv) *Joint venture*

IFRS 11 *Joint Arrangements* defines a joint venture as a joint arrangement whereby the parties that have joint control of the arrangement have rights to the net assets of the arrangement (IFRS 11, para 16).

Caterpillar's investment in Bumble Bee appears to qualify as a joint venture as defined by IFRS 11.

IFRS 11 requires that a joint venturer shall recognise its interest in a joint venture using the equity method (IFRS 11, para 24).

Thus, the following adjusting entries are required in relation to the draft consolidated financial statements of the group for the year ended 31 December 2x05:

	DR €000	CR €000
Investment in joint venture	1,000	
Bank		1,000

The loan raised by Caterpillar to finance the acquisition of Bumble Bee is a financial liability. In accordance with IFRS 9, it should be accounted for, net of transaction costs, at fair value. Thus, the following journal entry is required:

	DR €000	CR €000
Bank	955	
Loan		955

The profits of Bumble Bee for the year ended 31 December 2x05 should be recorded in the consolidated financial statements as follows:

	DR €000	CR €000
Investment in joint venture	700	
Share of profit of joint venture – P/L		700

(Being 50% of the after-tax profit of Bumble Bee for the period ended 31 December 2x05)

Where a joint venturer sells assets to a joint venture while the assets are retained by the joint venture, the joint venturer shall recognise only that portion of the gain or loss that is attributable to the interests of the other venturers (IAS 28, para 28).

As 50% of the goods sold by Caterpillar to Bumble Bee remain in the inventory of the joint venture at the year end, the following consolidation adjustment is required:

	DR €000	CR €000
Cost of sales	75	
Investment in joint venture		75

(Being elimination of Caterpillar's share of unrealised inter-company profit on inventory,

i.e. inter-company sales × profit margin × % held in inventory × Caterpillar's shareholding in Bumble Bee

i.e. (€1 million × 30% × 50% × 50%)

Bumble Bee's operating results are included in the consolidated financial statements of the Bellmoth Group on an equity basis. Thus, as the inventory of Bumble Bee is *not* included in the financial statements of the Group, there is no adjustment to inventory in the above journal entry.

Disclosure issues:

It will also be necessary to consider the disclosure requirements of IAS 24 *Related Party Disclosures*. As joint venturer and joint venture, Caterpillar and Bumble Bee are classified as related parties by the standard, thus requiring the following disclosures in the financial statements of Caterpillar and Bumble Bee and in the consolidated financial statements:

- Description of the relationship between them (joint venturer and joint venture).
- The amounts involved (sales of €1 million in the year ended 31 December 2x05).
- Any other elements of the transaction necessary for an understanding of its effect on the financial statements.
- The amounts due to or from the related parties, and provisions for doubtful debts due from such parties (IAS 24, para 18).

(v) *Tangible non-current assets*

(I) Sale of land

Land which was sold during 2x05 for €1.3 million continues to be included in the draft financial statements at 31 December 2x05. The following amending entries will therefore be required, in accordance with IAS 16 *Property, Plant and Equipment*, to record the disposal:

	DR €000	CR €000
Bank	1,300	
Land		800
Profit on disposal – P/L*		500
Revaluation surplus – SOFP	200	
Retained earnings – SOFP		200

*In accordance with IAS 1, subject to materiality, the profit on disposal should be separately disclosed in the statement of comprehensive income or in the notes (IAS 1, para 97).

(II) Investment property

IAS 40 *Investment Property* requires that an entity shall choose as its accounting policy either the fair value model or the cost model for all of its investment property (IAS 40, para 30). Caterpillar has opted for the fair value model; IAS 40 requires in this instance that changes in value be recorded in profit or loss for the period.

There has been an impairment of the investment property during 2x05 resulting from a rezoning decision. The following amending entry will therefore be required to the 2x05 draft financial statements:

	DR €000	CR €000
Impairment write-down – P/L	400	
Investment property		400

(Being impairment of investment property)

(2) Butterfly

(i) *Inventory*

The use of uniform accounting policies within a group is required by IFRS 10 *Consolidated Financial Statements* (IFRS 10, para 19). It should also be noted that IAS 2 *Inventories* requires that the costs for most inventories be assigned by using either FIFO or the weighted average cost formula (IAS 2, para 25).

It will therefore be necessary to change the LIFO valuation basis used by Butterfly for its wool inventories, so as to bring this into line with the FIFO basis used in the rest of the Bellmoth Group.

	$000
LIFO basis:	
8 tons at $50,000 per ton	400
7 tons at $60,000 per ton	420
2 tons at $70,000 per ton	140
	960
FIFO basis:	
9 tons at $70,000 per ton	630
8 tons at $60,000 per ton	480
	1,110

It will therefore be necessary to increase the value of raw material inventory by $150,000. This equates to an increase of €100,000 when translated into €s. Therefore, the following adjusting journal entry is required to the draft 2x05 consolidated financial statements:

	DR €000	CR €000
Inventory – SOFP	100	
Cost of sales		100*

In accordance with IAS 2 it is not necessary to reduce raw material inventory to its net realisable value, as long as the finished products into which it will be incorporated are expected to be sold at or above cost (IAS 2, para 32). Therefore no adjustment is necessary in respect of Butterfly's inventory of wool.

*At the end of the consolidated SOCI, profit for the year is divided between the owners of the parent and NCI. Non-controlling interests' share of Butterfly's profits will be increased by €20,000 at that point.

FRS 102

If the financial statements of the Bellmoth Group were prepared in accordance with FRS 102 *The Financial Reporting Standard applicable in the UK and Republic of Ireland*, the accounting treatment recommended in the forgoing case solution would apply. However, the following comments are relevant.

Jointly controlled entity (Issue (1) (iv) in this case solution)
FRS 102 identifies three types of investments in joint ventures. Caterpillar's investment in Bumble Bee would be regarded as a jointly controlled entity (FRS 102, para 15.8). A venturer is required to account for a jointly controlled entity using the equity method. IFRS 11 *Joint Arrangements* does not distinguish between different types of joint venture. However, the method of accounting required under FRS 102 is the same as that required by IFRS 11 *Joint Arrangements*, which is applied in this case solution.

Investment property (Issue (1) (v) (II) in this case solution)
FRS 102 requires that investment property is carried at fair value if its fair value can be measured reliably without undue cost or effort.

IAS 40 *Investment Property* permits a choice between the cost model and the fair value model. As Caterpillar has opted for the fair value model under IAS 40, the application of FRS 102 would not result in any change in accounting treatment.

SOLUTION TO CROMPTON PLANT AND FERTILISER GROUP

Memorandum

To: **Ms J. Smith, Finance Director**

From: **Ralph Thornton**

Date: **20 July 2x06**

Subject: (1) Accounting issues relating to Plant Life Limited
          (2) Accounting issues relating to other companies in the Group
          (3) Supplementary information

(1) Accounting Issues Relating to Plant Life Limited

(a) *Cost of acquisition of Plant Life Limited*

IFRS 3 *Business Combinations* requires that the consideration transferred in a business combination shall be measured at fair value, which shall be calculated as the sum of:

- the acquisition date fair value of assets transferred by the acquirer;
- liabilities incurred; and
- equity interests issued by the acquirer (IFRS 3, para 37).

(i) Equity shares issued

The 1 million shares issued by Crompton Holdings Limited should be recorded at fair value as follows (IFRS 3, para 37):

	DR €000	CR €000
Investment in Plant Life Limited	6,000	
Ordinary share capital		1,000
Share premium		5,000

(ii) Financial asset

The investment in Grafton Bank plc shares is a financial asset and should be regarded as being disposed of for a realised value of €1.35 million. IFRS 3 requires that any resulting gain or loss should be recognised by Crompton Holdings Limited in profit or loss as follows (IFRS 3, para 38):

	DR €000	CR €000
Investment in Plant Life Limited	1,350	
Financial asset		1,000
Profit on disposal of financial asset – P/L		350

Separate disclosure in the SOCI, or in the notes, should be considered, in accordance with IAS 1 *Presentation of Financial Statements*, subject to materiality (IAS 1, para 97).

(iii) Contingent consideration

The acquisition of Plant Life Limited also involves cash consideration of €400,000, contingent on certain profitability targets being achieved.

IFRS 3 requires that an acquirer shall recognise the acquisition-date fair value of contingent consideration as part of the consideration transferred in exchange for the acquiree (IFRS 3, para 39). At the acquisition date the fair value of the contingent consideration appeared to be zero, as the directors of Crompton Holdings Limited were confident that Plant Life would not achieve the necessary profitability targets.

IFRS 3 also states that *changes* in the fair value of contingent consideration resulting from events such as meeting profitability targets, are **not** measurement period adjustments, and must therefore be recognised in accordance with IFRS 9, IAS 37 or other IFRSs as appropriate (IFRS 3, para 58).

Payment of the cash consideration of €400,000 became probable on the 1 July 2x06 (before the financial statements were authorised for issue), as the awarding of a new contract to Plant Life meant that the required profitability targets were likely to be achieved.

This change constitutes an adjusting event after the reporting period, as defined by IAS 10 *Events After the Reporting Period*, and a provision for payment of the cash consideration should be recognised in the financial statements for the year ended 31 May 2x06.

IAS 37 states that, when the effect of the time value of money is material, the amount of a provision shall be the present value of the expenditure expected to be required to settle the obligation (IAS 37, para 45).

Therefore the following journal entry is required in respect of the deferred cash consideration:

	DR €000	CR €000
Acquisition costs – P/L	330	
Non-current liabilities		330

(Being fair value of deferred consideration of €400,000 discounted for 2 years @ 10% p.a.)

(iv) Acquisition expenses

The acquirer shall account for acquisition-related costs as expenses in the periods in which the costs are incurred (IFRS 3, para 53). The professional fees and general management expenses should therefore be charged to the profit or loss of Crompton Holdings Limited in the year ended 31 May 2x06.

	DR €000	CR €000
Acquisition costs – P/L	185	
Trade and other payables		100
Trade and other receivables		85

(b) *Allocation of the cost of the business combination to the assets and liabilities assumed*

(i) Inventories

The finished goods inventory of Plant Life Limited is included in its financial statements at €1.469 million, on a FIFO basis, at 31 May 2x06. However IFRS 3 states that an acquirer shall recognise an acquiree's identifiable assets at their acquisition date fair values (IFRS 3, para 18).

Fair value is defined as:

'…the price that would be received to sell an asset in an orderly transaction between market participants' (IFRS 13, Appendix A).

As the inventory of Plant Life Limited was sold for €200,000 less than its book value, the following adjusting journal entry is required:

	DR €000	CR €000
Retained earnings of Plant Life @ acquisition date	200	
Inventory		200

(ii) Reorganisation programme

IFRS 3 states that the acquirer shall recognise only the consideration transferred for the acquiree and the assets acquired and liabilities assumed in the exchange for the acquiree. Separate transactions should be accounted for in accordance with the relevant IFRSs (IFRS 3, para 51).

The fact that the Board of Directors of Plant Life Limited was already committed to the reorganisation programme prior to its acquisition by the Crompton Group, means that the costs of the programme should be regarded as a liability assumed at the acquisition date.

IFRS 3 also states that the acquirer shall measure an acquired non-current asset that is classified as held for sale at the acquisition date at fair value less costs to sell, in accordance with IFRS 5 (IFRS 3, para 31). Thus it will be necessary to write the value of machinery down by an amount of €100,000.

	DR €000	CR €000
Retained earnings of Plant Life @ acquisition date	350	
Machinery		100
Trade and other payables		250

(Being write-down of machine and liability for re-organisation costs at acquisition date)

The machinery should also be separately classified in the statement of financial position as 'assets held for sale' in accordance with IFRS 5, thus necessitating the following journal entry:

	DR €000	CR €000
Assets held for sale	300	
Machinery		300

(Being machinery re-classified at fair value less costs to sell)

(iii) Legal action

IFRS 3 states that, if the initial accounting for a business combination is incomplete by the end of the reporting period, the acquirer shall report provisional amounts for the items for which the accounting is incomplete (IFRS 3, para 45). IFRS 3 also requires that the acquirer should, during the measurement period, retrospectively adjust the provisional amounts to reflect new information obtained about facts and circumstances that existed at the acquisition date. The measurement period shall not exceed one year from the acquisition date (IFRS 3, para 45).

In the case of Plant Life Limited, a gain of €320,000 was realised on 20 June 2x06, prior to the date on which the financial statements of the Group were authorised for issue. This is an adjusting event after the reporting period, as defined by IAS 10, and it should replace the gain of €100,000 estimated at 31 May 2x06. The financial statements of Plant Life Limited should be adjusted as follows:

	DR €000	CR €000
Trade and other receivables	220	
Retained earnings of Plant Life @ acquisition date		220

(iv) Land and buildings

The land and buildings of Plant Life Limited should be restated to their fair value at 31 May 2x06 (IFRS 3, para 18). The following adjustment will be required:

	DR €000	CR €000
Land and buildings	202	
Revaluation surplus at acquisition date		202

IFRS 3 also requires that an acquirer should recognise and measure a deferred tax liability arising from an asset acquired in a business combination in accordance with IAS 12 *Income Taxes* (IFRS 3, para 24).

This will give rise to a temporary difference, as outlined in IAS 12, which will affect goodwill arising on acquisition (IAS 12, para 19). As the capital gains tax rate is 20%, this will necessitate the following journal entry:

	DR €000	CR €000
Revaluation surplus @ acquisition date	40.4	
Deferred tax liability – SOFP		40.4

(v) Dividend

In July 2x06, Plant Life Limited paid a dividend of €600,000 out of its profits of the year ended 31 May 2x06. IAS 27, *Separate Financial Statements*, requires that an entity should recognise a dividend from a subsidiary in profit or loss in its separate financial statements when its right to receive the dividend is established (IAS 27, para 12). Likewise, IAS 10 states that, if an entity declares a dividend after the reporting period, the dividend should not be recognised as a liability at the end of the reporting period (IAS 10, para 12).

Thus, the dividend will be recorded by Plant Life and Crompton Holdings as follows in the year ending 31 May 2x07:

	DR €000	CR €000
Retained earnings – SOFP	600	
Bank		600
(Being payment of dividend by Plant Life)		
Bank	600	
Dividend received – P/L		600
(Being receipt of dividend by Crompton Holdings Limited)		

Workings

(a) *Calculation of goodwill arising on the acquisition of Plant Life Limited*

Cost of control account in Plant Life Limited

	€000		€000
Investment in Plant Life Ltd	6,000	Ordinary share cap.	100
Investment in Plant Life Ltd	1,350	Share premium	250
Retained earnings (inventory)	200	Revaluation surplus	1,000
Retained earnings (reorg. costs)	350	Retained earnings	4,927
Revaluation surplus (def. tax)	40	Ret earnings (legal action)	220
		Revaluation surplus	202
		Goodwill*	1,241
	7,940		7,940

* Goodwill is computed as follows in accordance with IFRS 3 *Business Combinations* (IFRS 3, para 32):

	€
Consideration transferred at fair value (€6m + €1.35m)	7,350,000
Less, fair value of the acquisition-date amounts of the identifiable assets acquired and the liabilities assumed (€6.277m – €200,000 – €350,000 + €220,000 + €202,000 – €40,400)	(6,108,600)
Goodwill	1,241,400

(2) Accounting Issues Relating to Other Companies in the Group

(i)   Leisure centre

The leisure centre is *not* an asset of the group at 31 May 2x06. In substance the rights to future economic benefits will accrue almost exclusively to the employees' pension fund. The investment property should therefore be removed from Ingston's statement of financial position at 31 May 2x06.

Ingston, however, does have a different asset in the form of the five years' rental income from the leisure centre. On the assumption that the ultimate cash realisation can be assessed with reasonable certainty, the flow of rental inflows should be recognised in Ingston Limited's financial statements at 31 May 2x06, at their fair value. In order to determine the fair value it will be necessary to discount the rental inflows to present value at the Group's cost of borrowed funds of 10%. Using annuity tables, the present value of the rental inflows is €454,920 (€120,000 × 3.791).

The following adjustments will be required to the financial statements of the Group at 31 May 2x06:

	DR €000	CR €000
Revaluation of investment property – P/L	1,000*	
Provision for pension fund deficiency – SOFP	3,000**	
Investment property		4,000

*Being reversal of previous upward revaluation of investment property through profit or loss.

**Being re-classification of cost of investment property, as being offset against pension fund deficiency.

	DR €000	CR €000
Trade and other receivables	455	
Deferred income – SOFP		455

(Being recognition of future rental inflows from leisure centre)

FRS 102

If the financial statements of the Crompton Group were prepared in accordance with FRS 102 *The Financial Reporting Standard applicable in the UK and Republic of Ireland*, the accounting treatment recommended in this case solution would apply, except in relation to the following issues:

Contingent consideration in respect of the acquisition of Plant Life (Issue (1) (iii) in this case solution)

Contingent consideration would be included as part of the cost of acquiring Plant Life if it is probable that the consideration will be paid, i.e. more likely than not to be paid (FRS 102, para 19.12).

However, if the potential adjustment is not recognised at the acquisition date, but subsequently becomes probable, and can be measured reliably, the additional consideration should be treated as an adjustment to the cost of the combination (FRS 102, para 19.13).

Cash consideration of €400,000 was payable on 1 June 2x08, subject to certain profitability targets being achieved by Plant Life. Payment of this consideration was considered unlikely at the acquisition date, but subsequently payment became probable as Plant Life was awarded a new contract. Therefore the contingent consideration of €330,000 (discounted amount of the payment) should be included as part of the cost of the combination. Goodwill arising on acquisition would therefore be increased by €330,000.

Acquisition expenses relating to the acquisition of Plant Life (Issue (1) (iv) in this case solution)

FRS 102 states that the costs of a business combination will include any costs that are directly attributable to the business combination (FRS 102, para 19.11). Therefore the professional fees of €100,000 would be included as part of the consideration paid by the Crompton Group; consequently goodwill arising on acquisition would be increased by €100,000.

SOLUTION TO CURRENT ISSUES GROUP

Report

Subject: **Accounting issues relating to the financial statements for the
year ended 31 December 2x05**

Prepared for: **A. Dorgan, Finance Director**

Prepared by: **X. Erox**

Date: **1 March 2x06**

Contents

(1) Summary of Group Structure

As at 31 December 2x05, Current Issues Limited had the following subsidiary undertakings:

- Big Times Limited
- Blow the Whistle Limited
- Worthit Limited

At the same date Current Issues Limited also had an associate, Sometimes Limited.

(2) Accounting Treatment – Current Issues Group

Investments

(1) Acquisition of Big Times Limited

	Parent €	NCI €
Consideration	800,000	
Non-controlling interests		120,000
Less: fair value of identifiable net assets acquired	(400,000)	(100,000)
Goodwill	400,000	20,000

In accordance with IFRS 3 *Business Combinations,* goodwill should be recognised as an asset at the date of acquisition (IFRS 3, para 32).

(2) Investment in Sometimes Limited
Current Issues has significant influence in Sometimes Limited by virtue of its 25% shareholding. Sometimes Limited is therefore an associate of Current Issues Limited (IAS 28, para 3).

(3) Acquisition of Blow the Whistle Limited
Blow the Whistle Limited is a subsidiary of Current Issues following the acquisition of a 75% shareholding in that company. Intragroup sales which have taken place during the year of acquisition may have related party disclosure implications under IAS 24 *Related Party Disclosures*:

- Intragroup sales need not be disclosed in the *group financial statements,* as they will be cancelled on consolidation. The amount of sales that will be cancelled will be those that were made after acquisition (i.e. €600,000 × 70%)
- Disclosure of sales by Current Issues to Blow the Whistle after the 31 March 2x05 will be required in the separate financial statements of Current Issues and in the individual financial statements of Blow the Whistle as they are related parties from that date.

In accordance with IFRS 10 *Consolidated Financial Statements*, it will also be necessary to cancel any unrealised profit on inventory held at the reporting date, resulting from intragroup sales (IFRS 10, para B86(c)).

(4) Acquisition of Worthit Limited

Worthit Limited is a subsidiary of Current Issues Limited, following the acquisition of 80% of the equity shares in that company. The acquisition is regarded as a **bargain purchase** as the aggregate of the consideration transferred plus the amount of non-controlling interests is less than the fair value of identifiable net assets acquired:

	€000
Consideration transferred	450
Non-controlling interests* (€700,000 × 20%)	140
	590
Fair value of identifiable net assets acquired	(700)
	110

* IFRS 3 states that an acquirer shall measure any non-controlling interest in an acquiree either at fair value or at the non-controlling interest's share of the acquiree's identifiable net assets (IFRS 3, para 19). The latter method of measurement is adopted for this acquisition.

IFRS 3 states that an acquirer should recognise the resulting gain in profit or loss on the acquisition date (IFRS 3, para 34). However, before doing so, the acquirer should reassess whether it has correctly identified all of the assets acquired and all of the liabilities assumed. The acquirer is then required to review the measurement procedures used (IFRS 3, para 36). On the assumption that Current Issues has satisfied these requirements, the following journal entry is required in the consolidated financial statements:

	DR €000	CR €000
Net assets	700	
Gain on bargain purchase – P/L		110
Bank		450
Non-controlling interests		140

(a) *Related party issues*

(i) Loan

Mr Smith, being a director of Current Issues, is regarded as part of the company's key management personnel by IAS 24 *Related Party Disclosures*, and is therefore identified as a related party by the standard (IAS 24, para 9). Subject to materiality, details relating to the loan to Mr Smith should be disclosed in the financial statements of Current Issues, and of the Group. The following disclosures will be required:

- Description of the relationship between the related parties (director of Current Issues).
- The amounts involved (loan of €1 million).
- Any other elements of the transaction necessary for an understanding of the financial statements.
- The amounts due to or from the related parties at the end of the reporting period, and provisions for doubtful debts due from such parties at that date (IAS 24, para 18).

(ii) Sale of printing press

- *Sale of printing press by Current Issues to Big Times*
  As Big Times and Current Issues are subsidiary and parent respectively, they are defined as related parties (IAS 24, para 9(b)). Subject to its materiality, details of this sale should therefore be disclosed in the individual/separate financial statements of both companies.

  As the inter-company sale will be cancelled on consolidation, disclosure in the group financial statements is not required.

- *Gift of printing press by Sometimes to Big Times*
  Sometimes and Big Times are related parties. This transaction will therefore need to be disclosed, subject to its materiality, as follows:

        – the individual financial statement of Big Times;

        – the individual financial statements of Sometimes; and

        – the consolidated financial statements of the Current Issues Group.

(iii)   **Purchase of dye by Sometimes from Fine Tune**
Neither Sometimes nor Fine Tune is a member of the Current Issues Group. Therefore, no disclosure issues arise which are relevant to the Group.

    As Sometimes and Fine Tune are subject to common control, they are deemed to be related parties (IAS 24, para 9(a)). Therefore, details of the purchase of dye should be disclosed in the financial statements of both companies.

(b)   *Sale of assets*

(i)   **Sale of freehold land by Current Issues to Money Limited**
The IASB Conceptual Framework requires that financial statements should reflect the substance of transactions – not necessarily their legal form (Chapter 4.6). In substance, the monies received by Current Issues from Money Limited represent a loan arrangement rather than a sale. This is so because Current Issues continues to incur the risks of ownership of the asset, and to derive the potential benefits therefrom. The put and call options which are in place have the effect of ensuring that the land will again become the legal property of Current Issues after two years have elapsed.

    The following entry should be made to record the amounts received from Money Limited:

	DR €000	CR €000
Bank	700	
Loan		700

(ii)   **Purchase and sale of freehold buildings by Current Issues**
The accounting treatment employed in respect of these buildings since the date of purchase should be as follows:

	DR €000	CR €000
Freehold buildings	300	
Bank		300
(Being purchase of asset 1 Jan 2x02)		
Depreciation expense	6	
Accumulated depreciation		6
(Being depr. charge for 2x02)		
Depreciation expense	6	
Accumulated depreciation		6
(Being depr. charge for 2x03)		
Accumulated depreciation	12	
Freehold buildings		12
(Being cancellation of accumulated depreciation)		
Freehold buildings	212	
Revaluation surplus – OCI		212
(Being reval. of bldg at 31 Dec. 2x03 – deferred tax is ignored as per instruction in question)		
Depreciation expense	10.4	
Accumulated depreciation		10.4
(Being depr. charge for 2x04: €500,000/48)		
Revaluation surplus – SOFP	4.4	
Retained earnings – SOFP		4.4
(Being amortisation of revaluation surplus to retained earnings for 2x04: i.e. €212,000/48)*		
Bank	600	
Accumulated depr.	10.4	
Profit on disposal – P/L		110.4**
Freehold buildings		500
(Being disposal of bldg in 2x05)		

Revaluation surplus – SOFP	207.6	
Retained earnings – SOFP		207.6

(Being transfer of balance on
Revaluation surplus to Retained
Earnings on disposal in 2x05)

*This annual transfer is optional, in accordance with IAS 16, para 41.
**Subject to materiality considerations, separate disclosure may
be required in the statement of comprehensive income or in the
notes (IAS 1, para 97).

(c)   Financing

(i)   Incorporation of Fudgeit Limited

Although the setting up of Fudgeit Limited has the form of a joint
arrangement there is a lack of joint control, which is a required
component of a joint arrangement (IFRS 11, para 4). Thus, it
appears in substance to be an attempt to exclude a loan of €500,000
from the Group financial statements of Current Issues. Under the
equity method, the loan obtained by Fudgeit is totally excluded
from the statement of financial position of the Group.

IFRS 10 *Consolidated Financial Statements* states that an investor controls an investee when the investor is exposed to, or has
rights to, variable returns … and has the ability to affect those
returns through its power over the investee (IFRS 10, para 7).
Through its control of the Board of Directors of Fudgeit, Current
Issues has the ability to affect its variable returns from its investment in that company.

Fudgeit should therefore be regarded as a subsidiary of Current
Issues and its financial statements should be consolidated as part
of the group.

(ii)   Arrangement with Advance Factors

The agreement with Advance Factors is primarily a non-recourse
factoring agreement, with Current Issues only being liable for the first €10,000 of bad debts. The normal level of
bad debts incurred by Current Issues is 3% of gross debtors,
which at the time of the factoring agreement amounted to

€1 million. Therefore the risks and rewards of ownership relating to the debtors appear to have substantially passed to Advance Factors.

The following amounts should therefore be included in the group statement of financial position in relation to the debtors factored by Current Issues:

	€000
Current Assets	
Trade receivables	250
Current Liabilities	
Trade and other payables	59.5*

*Trade and other payables include the following:	
Accrued interest & fees	€49,500
Provision for Factor's recourse to Current Issues	€10,000
	€59,500

(d)   Titles

(i)   Internally generated titles

IAS 38 states that: 'Internally generated brands, mastheads, publishing titles, customer lists and items similar in substance shall not be recognised as intangible assets' (IAS 38, para 63).

Therefore the sums expended by Current Issues in promoting the Group's titles should not be capitalised, but should be expensed to profit or loss as they are incurred.

The fact that expenditure of €450,000 on internal titles was included as an asset in the statement of financial position of Current Issues at 31 December 2x04 constitutes a prior period error. If this error were deemed to be material, IAS 8 requires a retrospective restatement of items affected in an entity's financial statements:

• restating the comparative amounts for the prior period(s) presented in which the error occurred; *or*

- if the error occurred before the earliest prior period presented, restating the opening balances of assets, liabilities, and equity for the earliest prior period presented (IAS 8, para 42).

In the case of retrospective restatement, IAS 1 *Presentation of Financial Statements* also requires that a statement of financial position be presented at the beginning of the earliest comparative period (IAS 1, para 10(f)).

The following journal entry will reflect the net effect of correcting the error in the financial statements of Current Issues and those of the Group:

	DR €000	CR €000
Retained earnings	450	
Intangible assets		450

(ii) Titles purchased from No Time Limited

These titles represent an intangible asset obtained by means of separate acquisition. Such assets are always considered to give rise to probable future economic benefits that will accrue to an entity (IAS 38, para 25). As the cost can also be reliably measured, the titles purchased from No Time Limited fully satisfy the criteria to be recognised as an asset (IAS 38, para 21).

These titles, like all intangible assets, should be measured initially at cost (IAS 38, para 24). Subsequently, an entity is required to choose either the cost model or the revaluation model as its accounting policy. If the revaluation model is chosen, all other assets in the same class should be accounted for similarly, unless there is no active market for those assets (IAS 38, para 72). It is not usually appropriate to revalue intangible assets as there is rarely an active market for such assets.

Current Issues appears to have adopted the cost model for the titles acquired from No Time Limited. Thus the titles should be carried at their cost of €100,000, less any accumulated amortisation and any accumulated impairment losses (IAS 38, para 74).

(e)   *Impairment of assets*

IAS 36 *Impairment of Assets*, requires an impairment review to be carried out where indicators of impairment suggest that a company's assets may not be fully recoverable (IAS 36, para 9). For this purpose, the e-learning division is identified as a cash-generating unit, and the impairment review process requires the following procedures to be employed:

- As the fair value less costs to sell (€500,000) of the assets of the division are less than the assets' net book value in the statement of financial position (€1.2m), a value in use computation is required.

- **Value in use computation:**

Terminal value of net assets of division (based on pre-tax and pre-finance costs as required by IAS 36, para 50)	€1.43 million*
Discount factor for year 5 using a discount rate of 16%	0.4761
Present value of cash flows of cash generating unit	€680,000

*IAS 36 does not permit the inclusion of estimated future cash flows that are expected to arise from improving or enhancing an asset's performance. Thus, cash inflows of €1,400,000 resulting from planned development expenditure are not included (IAS 36, para 44). Software development costs are excluded on a similar basis.

The recoverable amount of the net assets of the e-learning division is the *higher* of:

- fair value less costs to sell of €500,000; and
- value in use €680,000.

Thus, the recoverable amount is €680,000. As this is less than the value of the net assets (€1,200,000) in the statement of financial position, the value of the assets of the division should be reduced. The required reduction of €520,000 should be accounted for, in accordance with IAS 36, para 104, as follows:

(i) goodwill of €300,000 should be eliminated;
(ii) the balance of €220,000 should be written off against the other assets of the division, pro-rata on the basis of the carrying amount of each asset.

Therefore the following journal entry is required:

	DR €000	CR €000
Impairment write-off – P/L	520	
Goodwill		300
Intangible non-current assets (€220,000 × (400,000/900,000))		98
Tangible non-current assets (€220,000 × (500,000/900,000))		122

These write-downs should be included in profit or loss for the year ended 31 December 2x05, and if material they should be separately disclosed in accordance with IAS 1, para 97.

(f) Miscellaneous impairment issues

(i) Printing presses

As the reasons for the impairment write-downs of 2x03 have now been reversed, the printing presses should be restored to their recoverable amount (IAS 36, para 114). The extent to which depreciation has been reduced, due to the previous impairment write-down, must however be taken into account at the time of the reversal (IAS 36, para 117).

The amount of the impairment reversal must therefore be calculated as follows:

	€	€
Original impairment write-down (€200,000 – €60,000)		140,000
Depreciation in 2x04 if based on original cost (€400,000/10)	40,000	
Actual depreciation in 2x04 (€60,000/5)	(12,000)	
Under-depr. in 2x04 due to impairment write-down in 20x3		(28,000)
Impairment reversal in 2x05 (restricted)		112,000

This will restore the printing press to €160,000 (i.e. €112,000 + (€60,000 – €12,000)) at 31 December 2x04, which is equivalent to what its NBV would have been (i.e. €400,000 × 40%) had the original impairment not been recorded.

The following journal entry is required to effect this adjustment:

	DR €	CR €
Tangible non-current assets	112,000	
Impairment write-back – P/L		112,000

(Being write-back in 2x05 of previous impairment reversal)

The above write-back should be included in profit or loss in 2x05, and disclosed separately if material. The revised book value of €160,000 should be written off at 25% per annum on a straight-line basis, commencing in 2x05.

(ii) Land
The revision of consumer preferences in 2x05 has meant that the amount at which the land was valued in 2x02 should now be reinstated as a conservative estimate of the asset's current value. The following journal entry will be required to effect the reversal:

	DR €	CR €
Land	300,000	
Impairment write-back – P/L		100,000*
Revaluation surplus – OCI		200,000**

*Disclose separately if material.

**Deferred tax is ignored, as per instruction in question.

(iii)   Titles

IAS 36 *Impairment of Assets* requires that an impairment loss recognised in prior periods (for an asset other than goodwill) shall be reversed if, and only if, there has been a change in the estimates used to determine the asset's recoverable amount since the last impairment loss was recognised (IAS 36, para 114). Clearly, improved content that has led to the revision of consumer preferences falls into this category. Therefore the previous impairment loss should be reversed as follows:

	DR €	CR €
Intangible assets – SOFP	250,000	
Reversal of impairment loss – P/L		250,000*

*Disclose separately if material.

(g)   *Miscellaneous provisions and contingency issues*

(i)   Legal action

In accordance with IAS 37 *Provisions, Contingent Liabilities and Contingent Assets*, in respect of the action taken by the celebrity plaintiff in November 2x05, it was clear on 31 December 2x05 that Current Issues had a present obligation resulting from a past event. On this basis, a provision should be recognised (IAS 37, para 14).

On 31 March 2x06, the date on which the financial statements are authorised for issue, legal opinion was that the plaintiff was likely to be awarded €100,000. This provides further evidence relating to a condition existing at the end of the reporting period, and it therefore constitutes an adjusting event after the reporting period date (IAS 10, para 3).

Therefore, a provision of €100,000 should be recognised at 31 December 2x05 in relation to the action being taken by the celebrity plaintiff. Provision should also be made for whatever legal costs may ensue if the action goes to court.

	DR €000	CR €000
Legal claim – P/L	100	
Provision for legal claim – SOFP		100

- A contingent liability of €100,000 should be disclosed by way of note in the financial statements, in respect of the additional amount which might be awarded by the court (IAS 37, para 28). There is a risk of a transfer of economic benefits which, at a 25% level of probability, must be considered as being more than remote.

- The counter-claim made against a publicity group is a contingent asset (IAS 37, para 10). It is possible (but not virtually certain) that a cash settlement of €20,000 may be agreed. As an inflow of economic benefits is probable, details of the counter-claim should be disclosed by way of note in the financial statements (IAS 37, para 34).

(ii)   Review of provisions

- Restructuring costs should only be recognised as a provision when an entity has an *obligation* to carry out the restructuring (IAS 37, para 71). The preparation of a detailed formal plan which has begun to be implemented, or at least has been discussed with parties likely to be affected, is evidence of such an obligation (IAS 37, para 72).

  As yet, only an outline plan for the restructuring has been prepared by Current Issues, and there is little evidence that the company is committed to proceeding with it. The provision of €250,000 should therefore be reversed as follows:

	DR €000	CR €000
Provision – SOFP	250	
Decrease in provision – P/L		250

This represents the correction of an error in the previous year. The adjustment is made in the 2x05 financial statements. If the error is deemed to be material, however, it would have to be corrected retrospectively in accordance with IAS 8 *Accounting Policies, Changes in Accounting Estimates and Errors.*

- Ongoing repairs should be charged to expense as they are incurred (IAS 16, para 12). The fact that a provision of €300,000 was set up by Current Issues for the ongoing repair of printing presses constitutes an error. If the error is considered material, the provision should be eliminated in accordance with IAS 8, para 41, as follows:

  - €50,000 to be added back to profit for the year ended 31 December 2x05
  - €250,000 to be reversed retrospectively.

Should the error **not** be deemed material, it should be reversed in its entirety in the 2x05 financial statements.

The fact that a significant proportion of the provision will be required during 2x06 suggests that there may be grounds for carrying out an impairment review of the printing presses, as required by IAS 36 *Impairment of Assets.*

- IAS 16 *Property, Plant and Equipment,* requires that the initial estimate of the costs of dismantling and removing an asset be included in the asset's cost (IAS 16, para 16). On the basis that there is a present obligation to decommission the printing presses, resulting from a past event (i.e. their purchase), a decommissioning liability should be recognised, in accordance with IAS 37 *Provisions, Contingent Liabilities and Contingent Assets.*

The estimated decommissioning expenses of €300,000 will therefore be recorded as follows:

	DR €000	CR €000
Plant and equipment – SOFP	300	
Provision for decommissioning costs – SOFP		300

This will result in an increase in the depreciation charge in respect of plant and equipment.

(iii) Payments to retired employees

The commitment to pay pensions to retired employees is a past service cost under IAS 19 *Employee Benefits*.

A provision should be made for the present value of the pension payments to the retired employees as this represents an increase in the obligation of the fund. The company's pre-tax WACC is considered an appropriate discount rate for this purpose (IAS 37, para 47).

	€	Disc. factor @ 12%*	PV
2x06	150,000	.893	133,950
2x07	200,000	.797	159,400
2x08	250,000	.712	178,000
2x09	280,000	.636	178,080
2x10	320,000	.567	181,440
2x11	350,000	.507	177,450
	1,550,000		1,008,320

*It is assumed that the obligation to make pension payments will arise on the last day of each year.

This obligation would also be regarded as an onerous contract, as defined in IAS 37 (IAS 37, para 10). A contract is onerous when the unavoidable costs of meeting the obligations under it exceed the economic benefits expected to be received under it.

A provision of €1.008 million should be recognised in the financial statements at 31 December 2x05. If material, it will be disclosed separately in the statement of comprehensive income or the notes, in accordance with IAS 1.

The following journal entry will be required:

	DR € million	CR € million
Pension costs – P/L	1.008	
Provision for pension costs – SOFP		1.008

(h)   Tangible non-current assets

(i)   Capitalisation of costs
The following should be capitalised as part of the construction cost of the mini-printing press, in accordance with IAS 16 *Property, Plant and Equipment*:

	€
• Machine part components (net of trade discount)	19,000
• Option premium (the construction of the printing press was probable when this cost was incurred)	3,000
• External labour costs	10,000
• Labour costs of own employees	13,000
• Safety procedure costs	2,000
• Trial print runs	2,000
• Financing costs	3,000
• Estimated dismantling costs	1,500
Total costs capitalised	53,500

Lecture note:

– The cost of correcting *design errors* is not capitalised as this is considered an 'abnormal cost' by IAS 16, para 22
– *Marketing costs* are not capitalised as they are not necessary to bring the printing press into working condition
– Financing costs are capitalised, as required by IAS 23 *Borrowing Costs*
– The cost of the trial print runs is capitalised on the assumption that the printing press could not otherwise operate at normal levels

Applying a rate of 10% straight-line, depreciation of €4,850 ((€53,500 – €5,000) × 10%) will be charged for the year ended 31 December 2x05. This will reduce the net book value of the printing press to €48,650.

At 31 December 2x05 it had become apparent that the carrying value of the printing press may be in excess of its recoverable amount. The following estimated values apply at that date:

- net selling price €40,000
- value in use €42,000

Thus the printing press has a recoverable amount of €42,000 (i.e. the higher of its net selling price and its value in use). This is less than the asset's net book value, thus necessitating an impairment write down of €6,650.

The following journal entries will be required during the year ended 31 December 2x05:

	DR €	CR €
Plant and equipment	53,500	
Bank		52,000
Provision for dismantling – SOFP		1,500
(Being capitalisation of the costs of constructing the mini-printing press)		
Depreciation expense – P/L	4,850	
Accum. depr. plant and machinery		4,850
(Being depreciation charge for year)		
Impairment write-down – P/L	6,650	
Plant and equipment		6,650
(Being impairment write-down)		

(ii) Subsequent expenditure

The amounts capitalised by Current Issues Limited are analysed as follows:

- *Annual overhaul of printing presses*
  - An entity should not recognise the costs of an asset's day-to-day servicing as an asset (IAS 16, para 12). The costs incurred must therefore be expensed to the profit or loss. A case for capitalisation could have been made if it related to a major overhaul, but the annual nature of the work does not suggest that the work is at the requisite level.

- *Removal of partitioning in factory*
  - Costs shall be recognised as part of a non-current asset if, and only if:

    (i) it is probable that future economic benefits associated with the item will flow to the entity; and

    (ii) the cost of the item can be measured reliably (IAS 16, para 7).

  - IAS 16, para 20 also states that the costs of relocating or reorganising part or all of an entity's operations should not be included in the carrying amount of an item of property, plant and equipment.

  - The removal of the partitioning is expected to increase worker productivity, which means that it is probable that future economic benefits will flow to the entity. However, as the removal of partitioning is likely to be construed as the reorganisation of Current Issue Limited's operations, the cost incurred should **not** be capitalised.

  - A valuation of the factory will provide the ultimate test as to whether the removal of the partitioning has increased the asset's value. Should this be the case, then, subject to the company's accounting policy, a revaluation surplus can be recorded.

- *Replacement of lifts*
  - IAS 16, para 13 states that such expenditure should be capitalised where it complies with the recognition criteria of IAS 16, para 7 (see above). On the assumption that it does, the cost of replacing the lifts should be capitalised.

  - IAS 16 also requires that the carrying amount of the lift that is replaced should be derecognised (IAS 16, para 13). The gain or loss should be included in profit or loss. Gains should not be classified as revenue (IAS 16, para 68).

- *Relocation of printing presses*
  - The costs of reorganising an entity's activities should *not* be capitalised (IAS 16, para 20(c)).

- *Extension of warehouse*
  - This expenditure clearly results in an improvement in the non-current asset, with a consequent enhancement of economic benefits. The costs of the extension should therefore be capitalised.

The following journal entry is required to reverse the treatment of amounts which have incorrectly been capitalised:

	DR €	CR €
Expenses – P/L	330,000	
Non-current assets		330,000

(Being reversal of amounts capitalised relating to the annual overhaul of printing presses, the removal of factory partitioning and the relocation of printing presses)

(iii) Revaluation gains

(I) *Office building*
The net book value of the building at 31 December 2x05 was €920,000. The revaluation at 31 December 2x05 will be effected as follows:

	DR €	CR €
Accumulated depreciation	80,000	
Buildings		80,000
Buildings	580,000	
Revaluation surplus – OCI		580,000*

*Deferred tax is ignored, as per instruction in question.

(II) *Factory building*

This represents the reversal in 2x05 of a previously recognised loss. The following journal entries are appropriate (years prior to 2x05 are provided for illustration purposes):

	DR €000	CR €000
Buildings	500	
Bank		500
(Being purchase of factory in 2x03)		
Depr. expense – P/L	10	
Accumulated depr. buildings		10
(Being depr. on factory for 2x03)		
Depr. expense – P/L	10	
Accumulated depr. buildings		10
(Being depr. on factory for 2x04)		
Write-down of building – P/L	180	
Buildings		180
(Being write-down of building to €300,000 at 31 December 2x04)		

The building now has a carrying value of €300,000

Depr. expense – P/L	6.25	
Accumulated depr. buildings		6.25
(Being depr. on factory for 2x05, based on a carrying value of €300,000 and a remaining useful life of 48 years)		

Accumulated depr. buildings	6.25	
Buildings		6.25

(Being elimination of accumulated depreciation at time of revaluation of building)

Buildings	196.25	
Revaluation surplus – OCI		20
Reversal of previous write-down – P/L		176.25

(Being reversal of previous write-down)

Thus, the revaluation gain is recognised in profit or loss only to the extent of the previous impairment loss, as reduced by an adjustment relating to subsequent depreciation (required by IAS 36, para 117).

i.e. previous impairment loss – depreciation adjustment = gain to be recognised in current yr profit or loss.

€180,000 – €3,750** = €176,250

**This is the amount by which depreciation fell subsequently (i.e. was not expensed in profit or loss in 2x05) as a result of the write-down in 2x04. This amount is computed as €10,000 (i.e. depreciation that would have been charged in 2x05 if the asset had not been written down in value) – €6,250 (i.e. actual depr. for 2x05).

(iv) Revaluation losses

(I) Land site

The fall in value of the land site at 31 December 2x05 relates to an impairment in the asset as its recoverable amount has fallen. This loss in value should be charged to profit or loss for the year ended 31 December 2x05 as follows:

	DR €000	CR €000
Impairment write-down – P/L	100	
Land & buildings		100

(II) *Property*

Loss in 2x05 following a previous upward revaluation:
The following journal entries are required (pre-2x05 entries included for illustration purposes):

	DR €000	CR €000
Buildings	750	
Bank		750
(Being purchase of property in 2x03)		
Depreciation expense	15	
Accumulated depreciation buildings		15
(Being depreciation of property for 2x03)		
Depreciation expense	15	
Accumulated depreciation buildings		15
(Being depreciation of property for 2x04)		
Accumulated depreciation buildings	30	
Buildings		30
(Being elimination of accumulated depreciation at time of revaluation of building)		
Buildings	280	
Revaluation surplus – OCI		280*
(Being revaluation of building at 31 December 2x04)		
Depreciation expense	20.8	
Accumulated depreciation buildings		20.8
(Being depreciation of property for 2x05: i.e. €1m × 1/48)		
Accumulated depreciation buildings	20.8	
Buildings		20.8
(Being elimination of accumulated depreciation at time of revaluation of building)		

Revaluation surplus – OCI	280	
Buildings		280

(Being set-off of loss against
  revaluation surplus on same
  asset in 20x5)

Buildings write-down – P/L	99.2	
Buildings		99.2

(Being portion of impairment write
  down charged to profit or loss in
  20x5 – i.e. excess of write down over
  revaluation surplus on the same asset)

* Deferred tax is ignored, as per instruction in question.

(v) Disposal of land

The following journal entries are required to effect the disposal of the land. Pre-2x05 entries are included for illustration purposes:

	DR €000	CR €000
Land	200	
Bank		200
(Being purchase of land in 2x02)		
Land	110	
Revaluation surplus – OCI		110*
(Being revaluation of land in 2x04)		
Bank	370	
Land		310
Profit on disposal – P/L		60
(Being profit on disposal in 2x05)		
Revaluation surplus – SOFP	110	
Retained earnings – SOFP		110
(Being realisation of revaluation surplus on disposal of land)		

* Deferred tax is ignored, as per instruction in question.

(i)   Accounting policy issues

   (i)   Research and development

The Directors have decided that, commencing in 2x05, development costs should be amortised by reference to the expected time horizon of future sales (previously amortised in accordance with expected future sales revenue), as new information indicates that this would better reflect the consumption of the future economic benefits of the development costs.

The question arises as to whether the revised write-off procedure in respect of development costs represents a change in accounting policy.

IAS 8 *Accounting Policies, Changes in Accounting Estimates and Errors* states that the expected pattern of consumption of the future economic benefits embodied in depreciable assets is an accounting estimate (IAS 8, para 32). IAS 8 also states that changes in accounting estimates result from new information or new developments, and are therefore not corrections of errors (IAS 8, para 5).

The decision to amortise development costs over the expected time horizon of future sales is being taken as it would better reflect the consumption of the asset's future economic benefits. This decision is being taken in light of new information based on past experience. Hence, the change in respect of the amortisation of development costs is a change in accounting estimate.

IAS 8 requires that the effect of a change in accounting estimate shall be recognised prospectively by including it in profit or loss in:

- the period of the change, if the change affects that period only; *or*
- the period of the change and future periods, if the change affects both (IAS 8, para 36).

   (ii)   Investment property

The premises should be reclassified as investment property at 31 December 2x05, and it should be stated at fair value.

The question arises as to whether the revised treatment represents a change in accounting policy. This issue is addressed by

IAS 8, which states that the following is **not** a change in accounting policy:

'The application of an accounting policy for transactions, other events or conditions that differ in substance from those previously occurring' (IAS 8, para 16(a)).

In the case of the investment property of Current Issues, there is no change in the method of presentation of assets that satisfy the qualifying criteria of IAS 40. Had the premises in question previously satisfied the conditions set by IAS 40, presumably it would have been included in the financial statements as an investment property.

The revised treatment in the 2x05 financial statements results from a condition that differs in substance (i.e. the nature of the asset has changed), rather than from a change in Current Issues' accounting policy. Thus, it does **not** represent a change in accounting policy and retrospective application does not apply.

The failure to depreciate the premises in 2x03 and 2x04 was, however, an error. If this error is deemed to have been material it should be corrected retrospectively, in accordance with IAS 8. If not material, no adjustment is required as the additional depreciation will be offset by the gain on revaluation of the investment property in 2x05.

FRS 102

If the financial statements of the Current Issues Group were prepared in accordance with FRS 102 *The Financial Reporting Standard applicable in the UK and Republic of Ireland*, the accounting treatment recommended in this case solution would apply, except in relation to the following issues.

Non-controlling interest (Issue (2) (1) in this case solution)
FRS 102 requires that, at the acquisition date, non-controlling interest should be measured at NCI's share of the subsidiary's identifiable net assets. Thus, the IFRS 3 option of measuring NCI at its date-of-acquisition fair value is not allowed under FRS 102.

Consequently, NCI would be computed as follows at the date of acquisition of Big Times by the Current Issues Group:

identifiable net assets of Big Times at acquisition date × 20%

$$= €500,000 × 20\%$$

Therefore, NCI at the date of acquisition of Big Times

$$= €100,000$$

Goodwill arising on acquisition, all of which would relate to the owners of the parent, would then amount to €400,000.

Goodwill (Issue (2) (1) in this case solution)

FRS 102 states that goodwill shall be considered to have a finite life, and it should be amortised on a systematic basis over its life. If an entity is unable to make a reliable estimate of the useful life of goodwill, the life shall not exceed five years (FRS 102, para 19.23).

Goodwill of €400,000 (adjusted as above to comply with FRS 102) arose on 1 January 2x02 as a result of the acquisition of Big Times Limited by Current Issues. On the assumption that goodwill is being amortised over five years, the following journal entry will be required in the consolidated financial statements for the year ended 31 December 2x05:

	DR	CR
	€000	€000
Consolidated retained earnings	320	
Goodwill		320

(Being amortisation of goodwill from 1 January 2x02–31 December 2x05, i.e. €400,000 × 4/5)

Goodwill amortisation of €80,000 will be charged to the profit or loss of the Current Issues Group for the year ended 31 December 2x05.

Negative goodwill (Issue (2) (4) in this case solution)

Negative goodwill (called a bargain purchase in IFRS 3) should, at the acquisition date, be included in the consolidated SOFP, immediately below goodwill, and followed by a subtotal of the net amount of goodwill (FRS 102, para 19.24).

Subsequently, the negative goodwill should be credited to profit or loss in the periods in which non-monetary assets acquired are recovered (e.g. for PPE, this would be the periods in which PPE is depreciated).

The above treatment will apply in the case of negative goodwill of €110,000 relating to the acquisition of Worthit Limited.

SOLUTION TO FRONTPAGE GROUP

Rockwell Spate & Co. Chartered Accountants

Memorandum

To: **Patrick Queally**

From: **A. Senior**

Date: **20 February 2x06**

Re: **Frontpage Group**

Further to your recent e-mail I have now had the opportunity to review the issues arising in respect of the audit of the Frontpage Group for the year ended 31 December 2x05. I will deal with each issue in turn.

(1) Inventory in Frontpage Limited

(i) *Publishing delay*
The delay in publication of the history book gives rise to a possible NRV issue as a rival publication is now likely to hit the market before Frontpage Limited.
   This can be evaluated as follows:

	€000
Cost	
Materials	100
Production salaries*	120
Depreciation of equipment	20
	240

*The loss of the illustrations, which had to be re-done in January 2x06, constitutes an abnormal conversion cost, and should be excluded from inventorised costs (IAS 2, para 16(a)).

General administration and selling and distribution costs should be written off as incurred, and should not be included in the inventory valuation.

	€000
NRV	
Estimated sales proceeds of history publication	450
Less: completion costs and selling and distribution costs:	
Production salaries	(90)
Selling and distribution costs	(220)
Net realisable value	140

The work on the history book, which represents work in progress at 31 December 2x05, should be valued at the lower of cost and net realisable value (IAS 2, para 9). A journal adjustment is required to re-state inventory to its correct valuation, and this is outlined in Appendix I below.

(ii) *Printing stationery*

Although it may seem reasonable to use LIFO as a method of computing the cost of Frontpage Limited's stationery inventory, its use is not permitted by IAS 2. Thus, it will be necessary to re-state inventory on a FIFO basis (weighted average cost is also permitted by IAS 2).

The old inventory of printing paper should be reviewed for the possibility of physical deterioration, though this seems unlikely as 2x05 is the first year that stationery inventories have been carried, and the reams of paper are kept in a sealed warehouse.

	€000
LIFO valuation basis	
10,000 reams @ €11.40	114
5,000 reams @ €11.40 × (1.05)	60
	174
FIFO valuation basis	
10,000 reams @ €11.40 × $(1.05)^4$ (note 1)	139
5,000 reams @ €11.40 × $(1.05)^3$ (note 1)	66
	205

Note 1: in accordance with IAS 2, inventory should be valued *after* deducting the 5% trade discount (IAS 2, para 11 and IFRIC November 2004).

Inventories of printing stationery have been included in the financial statements at €174,000 on a LIFO valuation basis. However, the use of LIFO is not permitted by IAS 2. It is necessary therefore to employ a FIFO valuation basis, which would give an inventory value of €205,000. Thus a journal adjustment is necessary to increase the inventory value at 31 December 2x05, and this is included in Appendix I below.

(iii)   *Excess dye*
The excess dye which results from Frontpage Limited's printing process represents a minor by-product, one whose cost is not separable from the company's main product. In accordance with IAS 2, the inventories of such by-products, when immaterial, may be measured at net realisable value, and this value is deducted from the cost of the main product (IAS 2, para 14).

This treatment results in the carrying value of the main product not differing materially from its cost. The following journal entry is required:

	DR €000	CR €000
Materials inventory – SOFP	50	
Cost of sales		50

(Being inclusion of excess dye as inventory at NRV. An equivalent amount is offset against the production costs of Frontpage Limited's main product.)

(2) Financing Arrangements

*   *Bad debt*
The insolvency of a debtor after the year end is an adjusting event after the reporting period, as outlined in IAS 10, para 9(b).

In this case, a debtor owing the company €500,000 at the year end has gone into liquidation. Frontpage Limited is liable for this entire bad debt, as the factor is in a position to recover its advance of €8 million from the remaining collectible debtors of €9.8 million (€10.3m – €.5m). This is included in the journal adjustments in Appendix I below.

It may also be necessary to reassess the bad debts provision at 31 December 2x05 in view of the liquidation in January 2x06.

- *Presentation in statement of financial position*
  The non-recourse funds of €7m advanced by the factor are non-refundable and, therefore, trade receivables can be reduced by that amount.

  The amount of with-recourse funds received from the factor should continue to be included as a liability in the statement of financial position.

  On the assumption that the bad debts provision will remain at 5% of gross debtors, the presentation in the statement of financial position at 31 December 2x05 can be summarised as follows:

	€000
Current assets	
Trade and other receivables	2,310*
Current liabilities	
Trade and other payables	7,200**

*Gross amount in statement of financial position – bad debt borne by Frontpage – non-recourse funds from factor – bad debts provision

i.e. €10.3m – €.5m – €7m – €.49m (i.e. €9.8 million × 5%)
    = €2.31 million

**Amount per statement of financial position at 31 December 2x05 of €14.2 million, less non-recourse funds advanced by factor of €7 million.

Disclosure
The bad debt write-off of €500,000, subject to its materiality, should be separately disclosed in the notes to the financial statements, in accordance with IAS 1 (IAS 1, para 97).

(3) Disposal of Shares in Sideissue Limited and Related Issues

(a) *Disposal of shares*

Frontpage Limited acquired 30% of the equity shares of Sideissue in 2x02 at a cost of €5 million. Frontpage had representation on the Board of Directors of Sideissue from that date until the disposal of the shares in September 2x05.

As Frontpage held 30% of the shares of Sideissue, it appears to have been in a position to exercise significant influence over that company's financial policies. Sideissue was therefore correctly classified as an associate of Frontpage (IAS 28, para 5). On this basis it was accounted for under the equity basis of accounting in the consolidated financial statements of the Frontpage Group.

The profit/loss on disposal of the shares in Sideissue will be recorded as follows:

(I) Separate financial statements of Frontpage Limited

The profit or loss on disposal of the shares held in Sideissue should be computed as follows:

	€000
Proceeds of sale	9,000
Cost of shares	(5,000)
Profit on disposal	4,000

As this amount is material, it should be disclosed separately, either in the statement of comprehensive income or the notes of Frontpage Limited, in accordance with IAS 1 *Presentation of Financial Statements* (IAS 1, para 97).

The following journal entry will be required in the financial statements of Frontpage Limited to record the disposal:

	DR €000	CR €000
Bank	9,000	
Investment in Sideissue		5,000
Profit on disposal – P/L		4,000

(II)   Group financial statements
The profit or loss on disposal of the shares held in Sideissue should be computed as follows:

	€000	€000
Proceeds of sale		9,000
Less: carrying amount of Sideissue at date of disposal (IAS 28, para 22(b))		
Acquisition cost of shares	5,000	
Frontpage Limited's share of post-acquisition profits brought forward at 1 January 2x05 (€7 million – €4 million) × 30%	900	
Frontpage Limited's share of profits of Sideissue for the 9 months ended 30 September 2x05 (€2 million – €600,000) × 30%	420	
		(6,320)
Profit on disposal		2,680

As the profit on disposal is a material amount it should be separately disclosed in the consolidated statement of comprehensive income of the Frontpage Group, or in the notes, in accordance with IAS 1 *Presentation of Financial Statements* (IAS 1, para 97).

The following journal entry will be required in the financial statements of the Group to record the disposal:

	DR €000	CR €000
Bank	9,000	
Investment in Sideissue		6,320
Profit on disposal – P/L		2,680

(b)   *Profit for nine months ended 30 September 2x05.*
The Group share of Sideissue's profit after tax should be recorded as follows in the financial statements for the year ended 31 December 2x05.

	DR €000	CR €000
Investment in Sideissue	420	
Share of profit of associate – P/L		420

(c)   *Inter-company sales*

In the nine months ended 30 September 2x05, Backpage Limited recorded sales of €900,000 to Sideissue. Backpage Limited is a subsidiary of Frontpage Limited, and Sideissue was an associate of Frontpage up to the time of its disposal.

Backpage and Frontpage are defined as related parties by IAS 24. As the amount of inter-company sales is material, details should be disclosed as follows:

- Description of the relationship between them (subsidiary and associate of Frontpage).
- The amounts involved (sales for the nine months ended 30 September 2x05).
- Any other elements of the transaction necessary for an understanding of the financial statements.
- The amounts due to or from the related parties at end of the reporting period, and provisions for doubtful debts due from such parties at that date (IAS 24, para 17).

Disclosure will be required in the following financial statements:

(i)   *Group financial statements*
Disclosure is required as a subsidiary and an associate are defined as related parties by IAS 24.

(ii)   *Financial statements of Sideissue Limited*
Disclosure is required.

(iii)   *Financial statements of Backpage Limited*
Disclosure is required.

(4)   Construction of office building

(i)   *Reinstatement of costs written off*
Where assets, other than goodwill, suffer an impairment in value, IAS 36 *Impairment of Assets* requires the impairment write-down to be reversed if there has been a change in the estimates used to determine the asset's recoverable amount since the last impairment loss was recognised (IAS 36, para 114).

It is a requirement of IAS 36, however, that the carrying amount of an asset attributable to a reversal of an impairment loss shall not exceed the carrying amount that would have been determined (net of depreciation) had no impairment loss been recognised for the asset in previous years (IAS 36, para 117).

This applies in the case of Backpage Limited, as the building was available for use in November 2x03. IAS 16 states that depreciation should be charged during periods that an asset is idle (IAS 16, para 55). Thus, depreciation would have been higher had the impairment loss not been written off to profit or loss.

Depreciation which would otherwise have been charged is calculated as follows:

€000

Years ended 31 December 2x03, and
31 December 2x04 (€1 million × 2% × 2 years)   40

IAS 36 also states that any increase in the carrying value of an asset above the carrying amount that would have been determined (net of depreciation) had no impairment loss been recognised for the asset in prior years is a revaluation (IAS 36, para 118).

Thus, the impairment write-back to profit or loss in 2x05 is restricted and is limited to €960,000. An adjusting journal entry is required, as Backpage credited the entire reversal of €1 million to profit or loss. This adjustment is outlined in Appendix I below.

(ii) *Capitalisation of borrowing costs*
The Board of Backpage capitalised borrowing costs incurred in respect of the construction of the office building. IAS 23 *Borrowing Costs* restricts the capitalisation of borrowing costs to amounts incurred during the period of construction. Thus, only the interest incurred between the commencement of construction (1 January 2x03) and the point of completion (30 November 2x03) can be capitalised.

A journal adjustment is required to reverse the amount capitalised in 2x05 relating to the period after 30 November 2x03 (i.e. €200,000). This adjustment is outlined in Appendix I below.

It will also be necessary to allow for depreciation on the amount of borrowing costs capitalised relating to the 2x03 construction period. This is computed as €6,000 (i.e. €100,000 × 2% × 3 years). See journal adjustment in Appendix I.

(5) Legal and Miscellaneous Issues

(i) *Legal action*

As there has been no further development of the legal action threatened by the rival publishing group it may be only a remote possibility that legal action will be taken against Frontpage Limited. This viewpoint would seem to be supported by the fact that there has been no evidence in writing that the publishing group intends to proceed with its claim. Legal advice could, if necessary, be sought to confirm that John Walker is correct in this regard.

Should it transpire that there is more than a remote possibility of a claim against Frontpage being successful, details of the contingent loss should be disclosed by way of a note in the financial statements, in accordance with IAS 37 *Provisions, Contingent Liabilities and Contingent Assets* (IAS 37, para 28). If it is probable that a claim against the company would be likely to succeed, provision should be made for any probable loss (IAS 37, para 14).

On the basis of the available evidence, it would not seem appropriate to recognise a provision or to make any disclosures relating to the threat of legal action, at this stage.

The possible counter-claim mentioned by John Walker should be separately assessed. At this stage it does not seem likely to arise, as such it should not be recognised or disclosed in the financial statements.

(ii) *Artistic work*

IAS 16 *Property, Plant and Equipment* permits entities to use either the cost model or the revaluation model. It is clear that Frontpage has used the cost model in accounting for the painting. The net book value of €8,000 at 31 December is therefore a correct valuation, and no adjustment is required in the 2x05 financial statements.

Thomas Walker, who has a controlling interest in Margin Limited, is a close relative of John Walker, who is a member of the key management personnel of Frontpage. Margin Limited is therefore a related party of Frontpage.

The sale of the painting would therefore be identified by IAS 24 *Related Party Disclosures* as being a related party transaction

(IAS 24, para 9). Thus, details of the transaction should be disclosed as follows:

- Description of the relationship between the parties (company controlled by close family member of key management personnel in Frontpage).
- The amounts involved (sale of painting for €350,000, which had a market value of €700,000).
- Any other elements of the transaction necessary for an understanding of the financial statements.
- The amounts due to or from the related parties at the end of the reporting period, and provisions for doubtful debts due from such parties at that date (IAS 24, para 17).

Disclosure should be made in the 2x06 Group financial statements, as the transaction involving the painting took place between a member of the Group (i.e. Frontpage Limited) and a party to whom the group is related (i.e. Margin Limited).

Disclosure is also required in the financial statements of Frontpage Limited.

The following journal entry will be required in the 2x06 financial statements of the Frontpage Group:

	DR €000	CR €000
Bank	350	
Property, plant and equipment		8
Profit on disposal of asset – P/L		342

(6) Deferred Tax

Deferred tax liability required at 31 December 2x05:

	€000
Accelerated capital allowances (Note 1)	500
Pension costs accrued (Note 2)	(300)
Deposit interest prepayment (Note 3)	80
Development costs (Note 4)	250
Net temporary taxable difference requiring a deferred tax liability	530

Deferred tax liability required at 25%

  (i.e. at the tax rate currently enacted)   133

Add: deferred tax liability on land (note 5)   100

Deferred tax liability required at 31 December 2x05   233

Less: deferred tax liability at 31 December 2x04   (100)

Increase in deferred tax liability at 31 December 2x05   133

Note 1: NBV of plant and machinery €1.4 million, less tax base of €900,000. This is a taxable temporary difference of €500,000.

Note 2: Pension costs are allowed for taxation when paid. Therefore the €300,000, which has already been charged in Frontpage Limited's statement of comprehensive income, will be allowed for taxation purposes when it is paid. The accrual therefore represents a deductible temporary difference, as the carrying value of the accrual at 31 December 2x05 was €300,000 and its tax base was zero.

Note 3: Deposit interest is taxed on receipt. The deposit interest prepayment therefore represents a taxable temporary difference. Its carrying value at 31 December 2x05 was €80,000 and its tax base was zero.

Note 4: Development costs are tax deductible when paid. There is a taxable temporary difference at 31 December 2x05, as the carrying value of the asset is €250,000 at that date, and its tax base is zero.

Note 5: Taxable temporary difference on land: Frontpage Limited has land which has been revalued by €500,000. At a capital gains tax rate of 20% this will give rise to an expected capital gains tax liability of €100,000 (i.e. €500,000 @ 20%). This was a taxable temporary difference at 31 December 2x05 as the carrying value of the asset was €500,000 more than its tax base.

Appendix I

Journal Entries in Group Financial Statements:

	DR €000	CR €000
Cost of sales	250	
Inventory – SOFP		250
(Being adjustment to reduce work in progress at 31 December 2x05 to net realisable value)		

Inventory – SOFP	31	
Cost of sales		31
(Being adjustment to restate inventories of printing stationery to a FIFO valuation basis at 31 December 2x05)		
Materials inventory – SOFP	50	
Cost of sales		50
(Being inclusion of excess dye as inventory at NRV. An equivalent amount is offset against the production costs of Frontpage Ltd's main product.)		
Bad debts expense – P/L	500	
Trade receivables		500
(Being liquidation of customer in January 2x06, all of which is borne by Frontpage Ltd)		
Increase in prov. for bad debts – P/L	240	
Provision for bad debts – SOFP		240
(Being increase in bad debts provision at 31 December 2x05)		
Impairment loss reversal – P/L	40	
Revaluation surplus – OCI		40
(Being restriction of impairment write-back by Backpage in 2x05)		
Finance costs – P/L	200	
Buildings		200
(Being restriction of capitalisation of borrowing costs to the period of construction of the office building by Backpage Ltd)		
Depreciation expense	6	
Accumulated depreciation of buildings		6
(Being depreciation on amount of finance costs capitalised: €100,000 × 2% × 3 years)		

Revaluation surplus – OCI	100*	
Deferred tax – P/L	33	
Deferred tax liability – SOFP		133
(Being increase in deferred tax liability		
at 31 December 2x05)		

*It should be noted that, as the revaluation surplus is recorded in other comprehensive income, so also should the deferred tax that relates to that surplus.

FRS 102

If the financial statements of the Frontpage Group were prepared in accordance with FRS 102 *The Financial Reporting Standard applicable in the UK and Republic of Ireland*, the accounting treatment recommended in this case solution would apply, except in relation to the following issue:

Borrowing costs (Issue (4) (ii) in this case solution)
In respect of borrowing costs that are directly attributable to the acquisition, production or construction of a qualifying asset, FRS 102 permits an entity to:

- capitalise these costs as part of the cost of the asset; or
- recognise these costs as an expense in profit or loss in the period in which they are incurred (FRS 102, para 25.2).

In this case solution, under IAS 23 Backpage Limited was required to capitalise costs of €100,000 relating to the construction of a new office building.

FRS 102 would alternatively permit Backpage to write off the borrowing costs of €100,000 to profit or loss in the period in which they are incurred. If this policy is adopted by the Frontpage Group, the original write-off of the borrowing costs in 2x03 should not have been reversed in 2x05. A journal adjustment to restore the group's original accounting treatment would therefore be required. This would also include the reversal of depreciation charged on borrowing costs capitalised.

	DR €000	CR €000
Finance costs – P/L	100	
Buildings		100
Accumulated depreciation	6	
Depreciation expense		6

SOLUTION TO HARDCOURT GROUP

Comerford Lane & Co. Chartered Accountants

Memorandum

To: **Beatrice Lambe**

From: **A. Senior**

Date: **26 February 2x06**

Re: **Hardcourt Group**

Further to your recent e-mail I have now had the opportunity to review the issues arising in respect of the audit of the Hardcourt Group for the year ended 31 December 2x05. I will deal with each issue in turn.

(1) Acquisition of Claycourt Limited

IFRS 3 *Business Combinations* requires that an acquirer shall recognise an acquiree's identifiable assets at their acquisition-date fair values (IFRS 3, para 18).

Fair value is defined as "… the price that would be received to sell an asset in an orderly transaction between market participants" (IFRS 13, Appendix A).

(i) Inventory
Prior to the work in progress inventory of Claycourt Limited being available for sale, it will be necessary to deduct the completion costs. The fair value is therefore calculated as follows:

	€000
Selling price	400
Less: completion costs	(70)
Fair value as per IFRS 3	330

It will therefore be necessary to reduce the value of Claycourt Limited's inventory from its book value of €500,000 to its fair value of €330,000.

(ii)   *Due diligence costs*
IFRS 3 requires that the acquirer shall account for acquisition-related costs as expenses in the periods in which the costs are incurred (IFRS 3, para 53). The due diligence costs therefore have been correctly charged to profit or loss of Hardcourt Limited in the year ended 31 December 2x05.

(iii)   *Quoted investments*
Quoted investments should be valued at market price, which in this case is €800,000.

(iv)   *Intragroup sales*
IFRS 10 requires that intragroup transactions be eliminated in full (IFRS 10, para B86). Profits and losses resulting from intragroup transactions that are recognised in assets, such as inventory, should also be eliminated in full (IFRS 10, para B86).

(v)   *Goodwill arising on the acquisition of Claycourt Limited:*

	€000	€000
Consideration paid		8,500
Non-controlling interest* (€7,230k × 15%)		1,085
		9,585
Less: fair value of identifiable net assets acquired:		
Book value	7,000	
Reduction in value of inventory	(170)	
Fair value premium of quoted investments	500	
Deferred tax on premium @ 20%	(100)	
		(7,230)
Goodwill arising on acquisition		2,355

*IFRS 3 states that an acquirer shall measure any non-controlling interest in an acquiree either at fair value or at the non-controlling interest's proportionate share of the acquiree's identifiable net assets (IFRS 3, para 19). The latter method of measurement is adopted in this solution, in accordance with the Group's policy.

(vi)   *Journal entries*

Financial statements of the Group:

	DR €000	CR €000
Net assets	7,230	
Goodwill on acquisition	2,355	
Bank		8,500
Non-controlling interest (15%)		1,085
(Being acquisition of Claycourt Limited)		
Cost of sales*	40	
Inventory		40
(Being elimination of unrealised intragroup profit on inventory: i.e. €200k × 1/5)		
Deferred tax asset – SOFP	12	
Deferred tax credit – P/L*		12
(Being deferred tax impact on elimination of unrealised intragroup profit on inventory: deductible difference of €40,000 × 30%)		
Revenue	1,200	
Cost of sales		1,200
(Being cancellation of intragroup sales, following the acquisition of Claycourt on 1 July 2x05; €200,000 × 6)		

*NCI will be charged/credited with their share of these adjustments when profit for the year in the consolidated SOCI is divided between owners of the parent and NCI.

Financial statements of Hardcourt Limited:

	DR €000	CR €000
Investment at cost	8,500	
Bank		8,500
(Being consideration paid for acquisition of Claycourt Limited)		

(vii)   *Disclosure issues*

Group financial statements – general disclosures

IFRS 3 requires that an acquirer shall disclose information that enables users of its financial statements to evaluate the nature and financial effect of a business combination that occurs during the current reporting period (IFRS 3, para 59).

Related party disclosures

Group financial statements

IAS 24 classifies a parent company and its subsidiary as being related parties (IAS 24, para 9). Inter-company sales in the post-acquisition period will be cancelled in the Group financial statements, and therefore no disclosure issues arise.

Financial statements of Hardcourt Limited

Hardcourt Limited will be required to provide details of transactions with Claycourt for the six months ended 31 December 2x05.

Financial statements of Claycourt Limited

The financial statements of Claycourt Limited should disclose the following information:

- The fact that Hardcourt Limited is the parent company of Claycourt Limited.
- Sales to Hardcourt Limited for the six months ended 31 December 2x05.
- The amount of outstanding balances.

(2) Revaluation of Land

The following journal entries would have been made at the time of the previous revaluation:

	DR €000	CR €000
Land	500	
Revaluation surplus – OCI		500

(Being revaluation of land from €1m to €1.5m)

	DR €000	CR €000
Revaluation surplus – OCI	100	
Deferred tax liability – SOFP		100

(Being deferred tax on revaluation surplus)

The subsequent loss in value of the land, resulting from the rezoning decision, is an impairment as defined by IAS 36 *Impairment of Assets*. It should first be offset against the previous revaluation surplus on the land, with the excess being charged in profit or loss for the year ended 31 December 2x05 (IAS 36, para 60).

	DR €000	CR €000
Revaluation surplus – OCI	400	
Deferred tax liability – SOFP	100	
Impairment write-down – P/L	300	
Land		800

(Being impairment write-down of land)

A deferred tax asset may possibly arise in respect of the impairment write-down of land. This would occur if the impairment write-down of €300,000 can be offset against capital gains arising on other assets within the Hardcourt Group. The maximum amount of the deferred tax asset would be €60,000 (i.e. €300,000 × 20%).

(3) Restructuring

A detailed restructuring plan has been drawn up in respect of the closure of the timberland division and details have been announced to the staff.

Consequently certain restructuring costs should be recognised as a provision in accordance with IAS 37 *Provisions, Contingent Liabilities and Contingent Assets.*

(i)   Redundancy costs

A provision should be made, in accordance with IAS 37, for redundancy costs that are likely to be incurred in the restructuring.

It is certain that redundancy costs of €800,000 will be incurred. This amount should be provided for at 31 December 2x05.

Additionally, it is possible that further redundancy settlements of €200,000 may have to be paid. This will be classified as a contingent liability under IAS 37, and details should be disclosed (IAS 37, para 28).

(ii)   Operating losses

Operating losses of €600,000 are expected to be incurred by the timberland division in the five months ending 31 May 2x06. IAS 37 states that provisions should **not** be recognised for future operating losses (IAS 37, para 63). This treatment is stipulated as future operating losses do not meet the definition of a liability, which requires a present obligation arising from past events.

However, IAS 37 also states that where an entity has an onerous contract the present obligation under the contract should be recognised and measured as a provision (IAS 37, para 66). Although the timberland division is closing, contractual commitments are in place to continue to service customers until 31 May 2x06. On the assumption that this commitment can be verified, it appears to constitute an onerous contract; the costs of fulfilling it should be provided as it gives rise to a present obligation arising from past events. Thus, to the extent that the operating losses for the first five months of 2x06 relate to contractual commitments to customers, a provision should be made for this amount at 31 December 2x05.

Alternatively, should the costs of breaching the contractual commitments with customers be less than the operating losses that will be incurred in fulfilling the contract, the former should instead be provided in accordance with IAS 37.

(iii)   *Discontinued operation*

IFRS 5 defines a discontinued operation as "a component of an entity that either has been disposed of, or is classified as held for sale and:

- represents a separate major line of business or geographical area of operations
- is part of a single co-ordinated plan to dispose of a separate major line of business or geographical area of operations, *or*
- is a subsidiary acquired exclusively with a view to resale" (IFRS 5, para 32).

The timerberland division clearly has not been disposed of as yet. Consequently, to be classified as a discontinued operation, the assets of the division would have to be classified as held for sale. For this to be the case, an asset or disposal group must be available for immediate sale in its present condition (IFRS 5, para 7). As operating activities must continue until 31 May 2x06, clearly this condition is not satisfied at 31 December 2x05. The timberland division must therefore be classified as a continuing operation for the year ended 31 December 2x05.

The decision to close the timberland division should be disclosed in the financial statements.

(4)   Land

IFRS 5 *Non-current Assets Held for Sale and Discontinued Operations* states that an entity shall classify an asset as held for sale if its carrying amount will be recovered principally through a sale transaction rather than through continuing use (IFRS 5, para 6).

For this to be the case:

- the asset must be available for immediate sale in its present condition;
- the sale must be highly probable;
- the transfer is to be completed within one year (IFRS 5, para 7 and 8).

The land site that is surplus to requirements appears to satisfy the above criteria, it should therefore be regarded as a non-current asset held for sale. The land should:

- be shown separately in the statement of financial position as an asset held for sale; and
- be valued at the lower of either the carrying value or fair value less costs to sell.

If the land were a depreciable asset, it should not be depreciated any further after it has been classified as held for sale.

The following information is available in respect of the land:

- Fair value   €2 million
- Carrying value   €1.7 million
- Selling costs   €30,000
- Cost   €800,000

The following journal entries are applicable:

	DR €000	CR €000
Property, plant and equipment	800	
Bank		800
(Being original purchase of land)		
Property, plant and equipment	900	
Revaluation surplus – OCI		900
(Being revaluation of land to €1.7m under the revaluation model of IAS 16)		
Revaluation surplus – OCI	180	
Deferred tax liability – SOFP		180
(Being tax @ 20% on revaluation surplus)		
Property, plant and equipment	300	
Revaluation surplus – OCI		300
(Being revaluation of land by €300,000 under the revaluation model of IAS 16,		

prior to being re-classified as held for
sale, in accordance with IFRS 5, para 18)

Revaluation surplus – OCI	60	
Deferred tax provision – SOFP		60
(Being tax @ 20% on revaluation surplus)		

Non-current asset held for sale	2,000	
Property, plant and equipment		2,000
(Being transfer of asset in accordance with IFRS 5)		

At the point the asset is transferred to non-current assets held for sale, a further adjustment is necessary as the fair value less costs to sell (€1.97m) is less than the asset's carrying value of €2m (IFRS 5, para 15).

Selling expenses – P/L	30	
Asset held for sale		30
(Being selling expenses of asset held for sale)		

Deferred tax liability – SOFP	6	
Revaluation surplus – OCI		6

(Being reduction of deferred tax liability, on the assumption that the selling expenses are deductible in computing the chargeable gain on disposal of the land)

The balance on revaluation surplus will remain until the asset is sold, at which point it will be transferred to retained earnings (IAS 16, para 41).

(5) Capital Grants

Government grants should not be recognised until there is reasonable assurance that:

- the entity will comply with the grant conditions; and
- the grant will be received (IAS 20, para 7).

This clearly implies that government grants should be recognised once the above conditions are satisfied. This view is supported in the IASB's Conceptual Framework document, which states that income should be recognised when an increase in future economic benefits, related to an increase in an asset, has arisen and can be reliably measured (Paragraph 4.47).

It is not permissible therefore to account for capital grants on a cash receipts basis. Thus, the change to an accruals basis for recognising the grants in the financial statements is the correction of an error. If it is considered to be a *material* error, IAS 8 requires that a retrospective correction be made (IAS 8, para 42). Otherwise, the correction will be made in the current period only.

In respect of the grant commitments in place at 31 December 2x05, on the assumption that there is reasonable assurance of the grant conditions being complied with, the following journal adjustment will be required:

	DR €000	CR €000
Receivables	200	
Deferred income – SOFP		200

Disclosure issues
Machinery was sold by Hardcourt Limited to Claycourt Limited in November 2x05. As these companies are related parties (Claycourt is a subsidiary of Hardcourt), IAS 24 requires the following disclosure:

Financial statements of the Group
No disclosure will be required in the Group financial statements, as this transaction will be cancelled on consolidation.

Individual financial statements of Claycourt Limited and separate financial statements of Hardcourt Limited
The following information should be disclosed in the financial statements of Claycourt Limited and Hardcourt Limited:

- Description of the relationship between the related parties (parent and subsidiary).
- Description of the transactions (sale of machinery).
- The amounts involved (value of machinery sold).
- The amount of any outstanding balances and provisions for doubtful debts relating thereto.
- Any other elements of the transaction necessary for an understanding of the financial statements (IAS 24, para 17).

FRS 102

If the financial statements of the Hardcourt Group were prepared in accordance with FRS 102 *The Financial Reporting Standard applicable in the UK and Republic of Ireland*, the accounting treatment recommended in this case solution would apply, except in relation to the following issues.

Acquisition expenses

FRS 102 states that the costs of a business combination will include any costs that are directly attributable to the business combination (FRS 102, paragraph 19.11). Therefore the due diligence costs of €400,000 would be included as part of the consideration paid by Hardcourt, and consequently:

- goodwill arising on the acquisition of Claycourt would be increased by €400,000; and
- profit of the Hardcourt Group for the year ended 31 December 2x05 would be increased by €400,000.

Goodwill (Issue (1) (v) in this case solution)

FRS 102 states that goodwill shall be considered to have a finite life, and that it should be amortised on a systematic basis over its life. If an entity is unable to make a reliable estimate of the useful life of goodwill, the life shall not exceed five years (FRS 102, para 19.23).

Goodwill of €2,755,000 (adjusted for the above amendment relating to acquisition expenses) arose on 1 July 2x05 as a result of the acquisition of Claycourt Limited by Hardcourt. Assuming that goodwill is being amortised over five years, and that a full year's amortisation is charged in the year of acquisition, the following journal entry will be required in the consolidated financial statements for the year ended 31 December 2x05:

	DR €000	CR €000
Amortisation of goodwill – P/L	551	
Goodwill		551

(Being amortisation of goodwill for year ended 31 December 2x05, i.e. €2,755,000 × 1/5)

Goodwill amortisation of €551,000 will be charged to the profit or loss of the Hardcourt Group for the year ended 31 December 2x05.

Non-controlling interest (Issue (1) (v) in this case solution)
FRS 102 requires that, at the acquisition date, non-controlling interest should be measured at NCI's share of the subsidiary's identifiable net assets. Thus, the IFRS 3 option adopted in this case solution is consistent with FRS 102.

Non-current assets held for sale (Issue (4) in this case solution)
The concept of a non-current asset held for sale is not considered in FRS 102. Therefore, the reclassification of the land site in this case solution would not occur if the Hardcourt Group was preparing its financial statements in accordance with FRS 102.

Government grants (Issue (5) in this case solution)
FRS 102 requires government grants to be recognised either based on the performance model or the accrual model (FRS 102, para 24.4). The use of the latter model is required by IAS 20.

The performance model requires an entity to recognise grants in income when performance-related conditions (if any) are satisfied, and when the grant proceeds are received or receivable.

In respect of the grant commitments received at 31 December 2x05, Hardcourt Limited has the option, under FRS 102, of using the accrual model, which has been employed in this case solution.

Alternatively, Hardcourt could use the performance model. On the assumption that all performance-related conditions have been complied with at 31 December 2x05, the performance model would result in the following journal entry in Hardcourt Limited's 2x05 financial statements:

	DR €000	CR €000
Receivables	200	
Grant income – P/L		200

SOLUTION TO
HEALTHFIRST GROUP

Lantry Mansfield & Co.

Memorandum

To: **Susan Gilmartin**

From: **A. Senior**

Date: **24 February 2x06**

Re: **Healthfirst Group**

Further to our recent meeting I have now had the opportunity to review the issues arising in respect of the audit of the Healthfirst Group for the year ended 31 December 2x05. I will deal with each issue in turn.

(1)   Goodwill Arising on the Acquisition of Scanright Limited

Goodwill on acquisition will be computed as follows at 1 April 2x05:

	€000	Parent €000	NCI €000
Cost of investment		6,500	
Non-controlling interests			1,147
Book value of identifiable net assets acquired at 1 April 2x05	4,800		
Premium on valuation of land holdings	800		

Deferred tax liability			
on premium @ 20%	(160)		
Reduction in value of inventory	(95)		
	(5,345)	(4,543)	(802)
Goodwill arising on consolidation		1,957	345

Total goodwill arising on the acquisition of Scanright is €2,302,000. Of this amount, €1,957,000 relates to the owners of Healthfirst, and €345,000 relates to NCI.

(2) Intragroup Sales

IFRS 10 *Consolidated Financial Statements* requires that intragroup transactions should be eliminated in full (IFRS 10, para B86). Profits and losses resulting from intragroup transactions that are recognised in assets, such as inventory, should also be eliminated in full (IFRS 10, para B86).

In respect of the intragroup sales by Scanright to Healthfirst, the profit should be eliminated to the extent that the goods have not been resold outside of the Group. Thus the amount of profit that should be eliminated can be computed as follows:

€960,000 × 20% (percentage of goods still held by Healthfirst)
× 20% (margin of profit) = €38,400.

The following journal entry will be required in the Group financial statements to effect this elimination of profit:

	DR €000	CR €000
Cost of sales	38.4*	
Inventory (SOFP)		38.4
Deferred tax asset – SOFP	9.6	
Deferred tax credit – P/L		9.6*
(Being deferred tax asset arising – i.e. €38,400 × 25%)		
Revenue	720	
Cost of sales		720
(Being intragroup sales for nine months ended		

31 December 2x05; €960,000 × 9/12)

*NCI will be charged/credited with 15% of these amounts when the Group profit for the year (in the consolidated SOCI) is divided between the owners of Healthfirst and the NCI.

IAS 24 *Related Party Disclosures* requires that disclosure be made of related party transactions. As there is a parent–subsidiary relationship, Healthfirst Limited is deemed to be a related party of Scanright Limited (IAS 24, para 9). Disclosure of intragroup sales will be required as follows:

(i)   *Group financial statements*

Inter-company sales between Healthfirst and Scanright that occurred in the post-acquisition period will be cancelled on consolidation, and therefore disclosure will not be required in the Group financial statements.

(ii) *Financial statements of Healthfirst and Scanright*

Both companies will be required to provide details of inter-company sales, in accordance with IAS 24, para 17, as follows:

- the nature of the relationship between the parties;
- a description of the transactions;
- the amounts involved;
- amounts of outstanding balances;
- provisions for doubtful debts.

(3) Deferred Taxation

IAS 12 requires that deferred tax be provided on almost all temporary differences. Thus the amount of deferred tax that should be provided by the Healthfirst Group at 31 December 2x05 can be computed as follows:

		€000
Deposit interest		
Carrying value in financial statements	€50,000	
Tax base	–	
Taxable temporary difference at 31 December 2x05		50
Plant and machinery		
NBV of plant and machinery at 31 Dec. 2x05	€2m	
Tax WDV of plant and machinery at 31 Dec. 2x05	€1.4m	
Taxable temporary difference at 31 December 2x05		600
Development costs		
Carrying value in financial statements	€800,000	

Tax base	–	
Taxable temporary difference		800
Intragroup sales (see 2 above)		
Carrying value of inventory in financial statements	–	
Tax base	38,400	
Deductible temporary difference		(38.4)
Net taxable temporary differences		1,411.6
Deferred tax @ 25%		352.9
Deferred tax on revaluation gain @ 20%		80
Deferred tax liability required @ 31 December 2x05		432.9
Less: existing liability		(100.0)
Increase in deferred tax liability at 31 December 2x05		332.9

The following journal entries will be required in the financial statements of the Healthfirst Group at 31 December 2x05.

	DR €000	CR €000
Deferred tax charge – P/L	252.9	
Deferred tax liability – SOFP		252.9

(Being increase in deferred tax liability on items subject to income tax @ 25%)

	DR €000	CR €000
Deferred tax charge – OCI	80	
Deferred tax liability – SOFP		80

(Being deferred tax liability in respect of the revaluation of land & buildings)

Disclosures

- Major components of the tax expense.
- Aggregate current and deferred tax relating to items taken to equity.
- Explanation of the relation between tax expense and accounting profit/loss.
- Explanation of changes in tax rates.
- Amount (and dates) of any deductible temporary differences unrecognised.
- Aggregate of temporary differences relating to investments for which no deferred tax liability is recognised.

- For each type of temporary difference, deferred tax assets and liabilities recognised, not recognised, and the movement recognised in the income statement (IAS 12, para 79–12, para 81).

(4) Investment Property

IAS 40 *Investment Property* requires that if a building is to qualify as investment property it must not be occupied by the owner (IAS 40, para 9(c)). Thus, this building must be re-classified as land and buildings with effect from 1 January 2x05, and the asset transferred out of investment property at its fair value (IAS 40, para 60).

While this is a change in presentation of the building in the financial statements, it relates to an alteration in the nature of the asset rather than a change in accounting policy of the Healthfirst Group. Thus, this is *not* a change in accounting policy (as defined by IAS 8) and retrospective application is not required.

The following journal entry will be required at 31 December 2x05:

	DR €000	CR €000
Land and buildings	1,300	
Investment property		1,300

(Being re-classification of the investment property in 2x05)

Depreciation expense – P/L	26	
Accumulated depreciation buildings		26

(Being depreciation on the building @ 2% p.a. straight line for y/e 31 December 2x05)

(5) Sale of Franchise

IAS 38 *Intangible Assets* requires that an intangible asset should be derecognised on disposal, and that the gain or loss should be determined as the difference between the net disposal proceeds and the carrying amount of the asset (IAS 38, para 113).

IAS 38 also states that the gain/loss should be recognised in profit or loss, but should not be classified as revenue (IAS 38, para 113).

Thus, the following journal entry will be required in respect of the sale of the franchise on 1 November 2x05:

	DR €000	CR €000
Revenue – P/L	2,273	
Trade receivables		2,273
(Being reversal of sales entry made by Suretime Ltd – i.e. $2.5m/1.1)		
Trade receivables	2,273	
Franchise – SOFP		1,000
Profit on disposal of franchise – P/L		1,273
(Being disposal of franchise on 1 November 2x05)		
Bank/financial asset	2,381	
Trade receivables		2,273
Foreign currency gain – P/L		108
(Being receipt of sales proceeds on 20 December 2x05 – i.e. $2.5m/1.05)		

The profit on sale will, subject to materiality, be disclosed separately in the statement of comprehensive income or the notes of Suretime Limited, and in the consolidated financial statements of the Healthfirst Group (IAS 1.97).

At 31 December 2x05, the $2.5 million held on deposit is a monetary asset, and it should be translated into euro at the exchange rate prevailing at the end of the reporting period (IAS 21, para 23). Thus the following journal entry will be required:

	DR €000	CR €000
Bank/financial asset	119	
Foreign currency gain – P/L		119

(Being gain on translation of funds held in $ bank a/c on 31 December 2x05: i.e. (2.5m/1) – (2.5m/1.05))

The exchange rate prevailing on 15 February 2x06 is a non-adjusting event after the reporting period, as defined by IAS 10, and it should not be included in the financial statements for the year ended 31 December 2x05.

FRS 102

If the financial statements of the Healthfirst Group were prepared in accordance with FRS 102 *The Financial Reporting Standard applicable in the UK and Republic of Ireland*, the accounting treatment recommended in this case solution would apply, except in relation to the following issues.

Non-controlling interest (Issue (1) in this case solution)
FRS 102 requires that, at the acquisition date, non-controlling interest should be measured at NCI's share of the subsidiary's identifiable net assets. Thus, the IFRS 3 option of measuring NCI at its date-of-acquisition fair value is not allowed under FRS 102.

Consequently, NCI would be computed as follows at the date of acquisition of Scanright by the Healthfirst Group:

Identifiable net assets of Scanright at acquisition date × 15%
$$= €5,345,000 × 15\%$$
Therefore NCI at the date of acquisition of Scanright
$$= €802,000 \text{ (rounded)}$$

Goodwill arising on acquisition, all of which would relate to the owners of the parent, would then amount to €1,957,000.

Goodwill (Issue (1) in this case solution)
FRS 102 states that goodwill shall be considered to have a finite life, and that it should be amortised on a systematic basis over its life. If an entity is unable to make a reliable estimate of the useful life of goodwill, the life shall not exceed five years (FRS 102, para 19.23).

Goodwill of €1,957,000 (adjusted as above to comply with FRS 102) arose on 1 April 2x05 as a result of the acquisition of Scanright Limited by the Healthfirst Group. On the assumption that goodwill is being amortised over five years, and that a full year's amortisation is charged in the year of acquisition, the following journal entry would be required in the consolidated financial statements for the year ended 31 December 2x05:

	DR €000	CR €000
Amortisation of goodwill – P/L	391.4	
Goodwill		391.4

(Being amortisation of goodwill for year ended 31 December 2x05, i.e. €1,957,000 × 1/5)

Goodwill amortisation of €391,400 will be charged to the profit or loss of the Healthfirst Group for the year ended 31 December 2x05.

SOLUTION TO MAINPART GROUP

Mr Patrick Hartson   28 February 2x06
Chairman
Mainpart Holdings Limited
Main Street
Maintown

Report on Accounting Issues in Respect of 2x05 Audit

Dear Mr Hartson,

Further to our recent discussions, we enclose a copy of our report for the Board, which sets out the appropriate accounting treatment and disclosure requirements regarding various matters which have arisen in respect of the 2x05 audit of the Mainpart Group companies.

We look forward to discussing these issues with you in detail.

Yours sincerely,

A. Bitpart
Witherspoon, Holt & Co., Chartered Accountants

(1) Construction of Building

(a) *Costs to be capitalised*

IAS 16 *Property, Plant and Equipment* requires that property, plant and equipment should initially be measured at cost (IAS 16, para 15). Cost comprises an asset's:

- purchase price;
- any costs directly attributable* to bringing the asset to the location and condition necessary for it to be capable of operating in the manner intended by management;
- the initial estimate of dismantling and removing the item (IAS 16.16).

*Directly attributable costs are the incremental costs that would have been avoided if the asset had not been constructed or acquired.

The following costs should be capitalised in respect of the construction of the new factory premises:

		€000
Site preparation costs		100
External labour costs (excluding 'abnormal' costs caused by the industrial dispute)		600
Materials (exclusive of VAT and trade discount)		1,295.45
Production overheads		
– Staff recruited for project	100	
– Salary of safety officers	140	
– Other variable overheads	80	
		320
Interest costs (Note 1)		240
Total cost of building		2,555.45

The amount of costs capitalised must therefore be reduced by €774,550, necessitating the following journal adjustment:

	DR €000	CR €000
Expenses – SOCI P/L	774.55	
Buildings		774.55

The following journal entry is required in respect of depreciation on the building for the year ended 31 December 2x05.

	DR €000	CR €000
Depreciation expense	51.11	
Accumulated depreciation		51.11
(€2,555,450 × 2%)		

Note 1: interest costs

Restrict to exclude strike period during which the interest cost was a holding cost and not a cost of production (IAS 23, para 20).

$$\text{Interest to be capitalised} = €300,000 \times \frac{8 \text{ months}}{10 \text{ months}}$$

$$= €240,000$$

The investment income of €12,000 earned during the strike period should be included in profit or loss for the period.

Note 2: excluded costs

IAS 16 does not permit the capitalisation of the following costs:

	€000
General management	
– not directly attributable	100
Re-design costs	
– 'abnormal' cost	170
Location map & brochure	
– not a production cost	10
Security personnel recruitment	
– occurs after construction period	20
Official opening luncheon	
– not a production cost	30

(b) *Related party disclosure*

IAS 24 *Related Party Disclosures* requires the disclosure of transactions with related parties. The standard identifies an investor and associate as related parties (IAS 24, para 9). Mainpart Limited holds 22% of the shares in Small Part Limited who supplied the labour for the construction of the building. Should Mainpart be in a position to exercise significant influence over Small Part Limited, the two companies would therefore be related parties under IAS 24. On the assumption that this is the case, the following disclosures are required in the Group financial statements and financial statements of Mainpart Limited and Small Part Limited:

- Description of the relationship between the parties (investing company and associate).

- Description of the transaction (provision of external labour for construction of factory premises).

- The amounts involved (cost of labour supplied).

- The amount of outstanding balances and provisions for doubtful debts related thereto.

- Any other elements of the transaction necessary for an understanding of the financial statements (IAS 24, para 17).

(2) Disposal of Subsidiary

(a) Profit on disposal

(i) Separate financial statements of Mainpart Limited
The profit on disposal of an asset is the difference between net sales proceeds and the carrying amount at the time of disposal. This can be computed as follows:

	€000
Net sales proceeds	32,000
Carrying amount (i.e. cost × 90%)	(19,800)
Profit on disposal	12,200

The draft financial statements of Mainpart Limited have incorrectly computed the profit on disposal as being €10 million (i.e. €32 million – €22 million). This error is due to the fact that the entire investment has been eliminated from the statement of financial positions, even though a 10% shareholding is still retained. The following journal adjustment will therefore be required:

	€000	€000
Investment @ cost	2,200	
Profit on disposal – SOCI P/L		2,200

(ii) Group financial statements

If a parent loses control of a subsidiary, in accordance with IFRS 10, it should:

- derecognise the assets and liabilities of the former subsidiary from the consolidated statement of financial position;

- recognise any investment retained in the former subsidiary at its fair value at the date when control is lost; and

- recognise the gain or loss associated with the loss of control (IFRS 10, para 25).

In respect of the disposal of 90% of Subpart Limited, this is represented as follows:

	€000
Consideration received	32,000
Investment retained at fair value	3,500
	35,500

Less:

Goodwill at 1 July 2x05 relating to the acquisition of Subpart	2,000
Assets less liabilities of the subsidiary at their carrying amounts at the date that control is lost	26,000
Profit on disposal of Subpart Limited – consolidated SOCI P/L	7,500

Subpart Limited's results should be included in the Group financial statements up to the date of disposal, i.e. 1 July 2x05, (IFRS 10, para 20). In accordance with IAS 1, the profit on disposal should be separately disclosed in the current year's statement of comprehensive income or in the notes of Mainpart Limited **and** of the Group (IAS 1, para 97).

(b) *Disclosure issues*

(i) Disposal

- A component of an entity is defined as: 'Operations and cash flows that can be clearly distinguished, operationally and for financial reporting purposes, from the rest of the entity' (IFRS 5 Appendix A). It is clear that Subpart Limited, being a separate legal entity, qualifies as a component of the Mainpart Group.

- A discontinued operation is a *component of an entity* that meets the conditions outlined in IFRS 5, para 32. To be classified as a discontinued operation, a component of an entity must be held for sale, or already disposed of, and meet one of the following criteria:

  – It must represent a major line of business or geographical area of operations.
  – It must be part of a single co-ordinated plan to dispose of a separate major line of business or geographical area of operations.
  – It must be a subsidiary acquired exclusively with a view to resale.

The net assets of Subpart were €26 million on the date that Mainpart lost control of the subsidiary. The total net assets of the Mainpart Group amounted to €62.25 million in the draft financial statements at 31 December 2x05. It is clear therefore that Subpart Limited represents a major line of business in the context of the group, and the disposal of 90% of that company constitutes a discontinued operation.

Disclosures required:
- *On the face of the statement of comprehensive income:*
  A single amount, being the total of the after-tax profit or loss of the discontinued operation, and the after-tax gain or loss from disposing of the assets comprising the discontinued operation (IFRS 5, para 33(a)).

- *In the notes or on the face of the statement of comprehensive income:*

  – The revenue, expenses and pre-tax profit or loss and the income tax expense of the discontinued operation.
  – The gain or loss on disposal of the subsidiary.

- The net cash flows attributable to the operating, investing and financing activities of the subsidiary (IFRS 5, para 33(b)).

- *Additional disclosures in the notes for assets that have been sold in the current period*

  - A description of the non-current asset.
  - A description of the facts and circumstances of the sale.
  - The gain or loss recognised and, if not separately presented on the face of the statement of comprehensive income, the caption in the statement of comprehensive income that includes that gain or loss (IFRS 5, para 41).

(ii) Related party issues

Should there be any intragroup transactions involving Mainpart Limited and Subpart Limited from 1 January–1 July 2x05, these will be cancelled on consolidation. In accordance with IAS 24, disclosure requirements would, however, apply in the financial statements of the *separate/individual* companies as Mainpart and Subpart were related by virtue of one party exercising control over the other (IAS 24, para 9).

Transactions in the period after the date of disposal (2 July–31 December 2x05) will also need to be considered in the context of IAS 24. Mainpart Limited's remaining interest during this period is 10%. As this level of shareholding does not normally constitute a related party relationship, no disclosure requirements arise.

(3) Restructuring

IAS 37 states that a provision should be recognised when:

- An entity has a present obligation (legal or constructive) as a result of a past event.
- It is probable that an outflow of resources will be required to settle the obligation.
- A reliable estimate can be made of the amount of the obligation (IAS 37, para 14).

A provision for restructuring costs is recognised only when the general recognition criteria, outlined above, are met (IAS 37, para 71). Clearly, as Mainpart Limited has already begun to implement the restructuring of its gardening division it has a present obligation to do so, and it is probable that an outflow of resources will be required, which can be reliably estimated.

Thus, the following provision should be made in respect of the restructuring plan for Mainpart Limited's gardening division:

	€000
Redundancy amounts paid early in 2x06	800
Costs of retraining programme*	100
Enhanced staff pensions	1,526.4
– discounted to present value at the Group's WACC of 12%	
= €220,000 + (€220,000 × annuity factor for 11 years)	
= €220,000 + (€220,000 × 5.938)	
Lease provision (Note 1)	306.2
Total provision required at 31 December 2x05	2,732.6

*IAS 37 (Appendix C, Example 7) states that no provision should be made for training costs, on the basis that there is no obligation as no obligating event (i.e. training) has taken place. In the case of Mainpart Limited, however, a provision of €100,000 is appropriate as this is the extent to which redundancy costs cannot (even with retraining) be avoided.

A provision for future operating losses is not permitted by IAS 37 as they do not meet the definition of a liability, which requires that there is a present obligation arising from past events (IAS 37, para 63).

Note 1: lease provision

This represents an onerous contract in the context of IAS 37, para 10. Thus, provision should be made for the four remaining annual instalments, i.e. €90,000 × 4 = €360,000. When discounted to present value at 12%, this will amount to €306,180 (i.e. €90,000 × 3.402).

Mainpart Limited is confident that half of this amount can be recouped by sub-letting the premises to another tenant. At this point, however, this is a contingent asset, whose recognition is not permitted (IAS 37, para 31). Details of this probable inflow of economic benefits should, however, be disclosed by way of note where an inflow of economic benefits is regarded as being probable (IAS 37, para 34).

Journal adjustment

The journal adjustment required in respect of the restructuring of the gardening division can now be put through as follows:

	DR €000	CR €000
Increase in provision for restructuring – P/L	2,732.6	
Provision for restructuring – SOFP		2,732.6
(Being provision for restructuring of gardening division of Mainpart Limited)		

Disclosure issues:

- On the basis of its materiality, the restructuring provision should be disclosed separately in Mainpart Limited's statement of comprehensive income (and that of the Group), or in the notes, in accordance with IAS 1, para 87.

- Disclosures should be provided in accordance with IAS 37, para 84–92.

(4) Disposal of Land

The IASB's Conceptual Framework requires that an entity's financial statements should reflect the substance of a transaction. It is apparent that the land in question has not, in substance, been disposed of by Rent Part Limited. This conclusion is evidenced by its transfer back to the company on 12 January 2x06. The land should therefore continue to be recognised by Rent Part Limited as an asset at 31 December 2x05, and the following journal adjustment is required:

	DR €000	CR €000
Land	800	
Profit on disposal – P/L	1,200	
Trade and other receivables		2,000

FRS 102

If the financial statements of the Mainpart Group were prepared in accordance with FRS 102 *The Financial Reporting Standard applicable in the UK and Republic of Ireland*, the accounting treatment recommended in this case solution would apply, except in relation to the following issues.

Disposal of subsidiary (Issue (2) (a) (ii) of this case solution)
FRS 102 states that goodwill shall be considered to have a finite life, and that it should be amortised on a systematic basis over its life. If an entity is unable to make a reliable estimate of the useful life of goodwill, the life shall not exceed five years (FRS 102, para 19.23).

Subpart Limited had been acquired by Mainpart Limited on 1 January 2x03. Assuming goodwill has not suffered any impairment since that date, goodwill of €2 million would have arisen at the date of acquisition of Subpart Limited. In accordance with FRS 102, this goodwill would be considered to have a finite life. Assuming the Mainpart Group has not decided to use an alternative useful life, the maximum period of five years is applied in this case.

Therefore, under the requirements of FRS 102, goodwill would have been amortised by €400,000 in 2x03 and in 2x04. Consequently, on the date on which Mainpart disposed of 90% of its interest in Subpart, the group profit on disposal of €7.5 million (computed under IFRS), would be increased to €8.3 million.

SOLUTION TO
MILLENNIUM GROUP

(a) Adjustments to Draft Financial Statements

(1) Sale of Land

It is questionable whether a contract exists for the sale of the land in this instance. IFRS 15 states that " ... a contract does not exist if each party to the contract has the unilateral right to terminate a wholly unperformed contract without compensating the other party" (IFRS 15, para 12).

Millennium Plc has not yet transfered the land to the customer. Nor has Millenium Plc received, and is not yet entitled to receive, any consideration. Completion of the contract may depend on the customer's planning application being successful. It is not probable therefore, that Millenium Plc will collect the consideration of €1.5 million that has been agreed. Consequently, the sale of the land should not be recognised in the 2x05 financial statements.

The journal entry required to reverse the sale of the land is outlined in Appendix I below – see journal entry (i).

The question also arises as to whether the land should, at 31 December 2x05, be classified as being held for sale. For this treatment to apply, the sale must be highly probable (IFRS 5, para 7). As this is not the case, the land should not be re-classified in the financial statements at 31 December 2x05.

(2) Purchase of Building

In accordance with IAS 16 *Property, Plant and Equipment*, there are a number of points to consider in relation to the purchase of the building on 1 January 2x05:

- The useful life of an asset is defined by IAS 16 in terms of the present owner (i.e. the period over which an asset is expected to be available for use by an entity (IAS 16, para 6)). Thus, 10 years rather than 50 years is the relevant life in this case.

- Residual value is defined by IAS 16, para 6 as being based on current prices, thus excluding the effects of future inflation (IAS 16, para 6).

On this basis, the depreciable amount of the building is €100,000 (i.e. €1.6m – €1.5m), and the useful life of the building is 10 years. Thus the depreciation charge for the year ended 31 December 2x05 is €10,000. See journal entry (ii) in Appendix I below.

(3) Sale of Subsidiary

- As the operations and cash flows of Leading Edge Limited can be clearly distinguished, it is defined as a component of the Group (IFRS 5, Appendix A).

- A discontinued operation is a component of an entity that either has been disposed of or is classified as held for sale, and

    - represents a major line of business or geographical area of operations; *or*
    - is part of a single co-ordinated plan to dispose of a separate major line of business or geographical area of operations; *or*
    - is a subsidiary acquired exclusively with a view to resale.

Leading Edge had contributed 50% of the Group's data backup sales, with a turnover of €3 million and operating profit of €1 million for the six months ended 30 June 2x05. The Millennium Group's turnover and operating profit for the year ended 31 December 2x05 were €16.8 million and €7.6 million respectively. Thus, it can be concluded that Leading Edge is a major line of business within the Group, and its disposal is classified as a discontinued operation.

Disclosures required:
(i)   On the face of the statement of comprehensive income:

A single amount, being the total of the after-tax profit or loss of the discontinued operation, and the after-tax gain or loss from disposing of the assets comprising the discontinued operation (IFRS 5, para 33(a)).

(ii) In the notes or on the face of the statement of comprehensive income:

–   The revenue, expenses and pre-tax profit or loss and the income tax expense of the discontinued operation.
–   The gain or loss on disposal of the subsidiary.
–   The net cash flows attributable to the operating, investing and financing activities of the subsidiary (IFRS 5, para 33(b) and (c)).

(iii) Additional disclosures in the notes for non-current assets that have been sold in the current period:

–   A description of the non-current asset.
–   A description of the facts and circumstances of the sale;
–   The gain or loss recognised and, if not separately presented on the face of the statement of comprehensive income, the caption in the statement of comprehensive income that includes that gain or loss.
–   The segment in which Leading Edge is reported under IFRS 8 *Operating Segments*.

(4) Software costs

(a) *External purchase of software*

Computer software is generally regarded as an intangible asset (IAS 38, para 9).

An intangible asset should be recognised if:

(i)   it is probable that the expected future economic benefits that are attributable to the asset will flow to the entity; *and*

(ii)   the cost of the asset can be measured reliably (IAS 38, para 21).

Intangible assets that are acquired separately are assumed to satisfy the probability requirement in (i) above (IAS 38, para 25).

- Therefore, €700,000 of the purchased software should be capitalised as an intangible asset as its cost can be reliably measured and its future economic benefits will flow to Millennium Plc (IAS 38, para 21).

- The other software (€100,000) is an essential component of Millennium Plc's mainframe computer and should be treated as part of that tangible asset (IAS 38, para 4).

- The software should be depreciated using an expected useful life of five years, with the exception of the software for the mainframe computer which should be depreciated over three years.

- See journal entries in section (iii) of Appendix I below.

(b) Software development

In order to assess whether an internally generated intangible asset meets the criteria for recognition, IAS 38 requires that an entity should classify the generation of the asset into:

- a research phase, and
- a development phase (IAS 38, para 52).

Assets arising from the **research** phase of an internal project shall **not** be recognised (IAS 38, para 54).

An intangible asset arising from the **development** phase of an internal project shall be recognised if an entity can demonstrate all of the following (IAS 38, para 57):

– technical feasibility;

– intention to complete the intangible asset and use or sell it;

– how the intangible asset will generate probable future economic benefits;

– the availability of adequate resources to complete the development; and

– its ability to measure reliably the expenditure attributable to the intangible asset during its development.

On the basis that these prerequisite conditions are complied with, the expenditure of €500,000 relating to the employment of additional programmers should be recognised as an intangible asset.

(c) Software acquired for development work

Software costing €400,000 was acquired to assist in the development of a new product costing system, which is currently at the development phase. On the assumption that it satisfies the six criteria in paragraph IAS 38, para 57, the software costs should be recognised as an intangible asset.

IAS 38 requires that amortisation of intangible assets should commence when the asset is available for use, and that the asset should then be amortised over its useful life (IAS 38, para 97). See journal entry (iv) in Appendix I below.

(5) Investment in Future Developments Limited

(i) Classification

IFRS 11 *Joint Arrangements* defines a joint venture as a joint arrangement whereby the parties that have joint control of the arrangement have rights to the net assets of the arrangement (IFRS 11, para 16).

The purchase of the 50% stake in Future Developments Limited appears to satisfy the definition of a joint venture in IFRS 11.

IFRS 11 requires that a joint venturer shall recognise its interest in a joint venture using the equity method (IFRS 11, para 24).

(ii) Sale of land plot by Future Developments Limited to Millennium Plc

When a joint venturer purchases an asset from a joint venture, the joint venturer shall not recognise its share of the profits of the joint venture from the transaction until it re-sells the asset to an independent party.

The profit on sale of the land by Future Developments Limited should therefore be eliminated to the extent of the joint venturer's share in that company (IAS 31, para 49). Thus, €150,000 (i.e. €300,000 × 50%) of the profit on sale should be eliminated in preparing the consolidated financial statements of the

Millennium Group. See journal entry (v) in Appendix I below for details of this adjustment.

Future Developments Limited and Millennium Plc are defined as related parties (IAS 24, para 9(c)). Thus, subject to its materiality, details of the sale should be disclosed as follows:

– in the Group financial statements; and
– in the individual/separate financial statements of Future Developments Limited and Millenium Plc.

The disclosures should outline:
– Nature of relationship between Future Developments and Millennium.
– The amounts involved in the transaction.
– Amounts of any outstanding balances (IAS 24, para 17).

(iii) Sale of inventory by a subsidiary of the Group to Future Developments Limited

• IFRS 11 requires that the joint venturer shall recognise only that portion of the gain or loss that is attributable to the interests of the other joint venturers.

• Thus, an adjustment should be made in the Group financial statements eliminating half of the profit of €250,000. See journal entry (v) in Appendix 1 below.

• There are also implications for related party disclosures in accordance with IAS 24:

Subject to its materiality, disclosure of the transaction will be required in the Group financial statements, as the transaction has taken place between a subsidiary of the Group (Century Limited) and a joint venture of the Group (Future Developments Limited).

(iv) Consolidation adjustment in respect of joint venture

As the joint venture is included in the Group financial statements on an *equity basis,* it will be necessary to include a consolidation adjustment in respect of the investing group's share of the post-acquisition retained profit of Future Developments Limited. See journal entry (vi) in Appendix I below.

Appendix I

(b) Journal Entries in Group Financial Statements

	DR €000	CR €000
(i) Reversal of sale of land:		
Land	1,200	
Profit on disposal – P/L	300	
Trade and other receivables		1,500
(Being cancellation of sale of land)		
Retained earnings – SOFP	200	
Revaluation surplus – SOFP		200
(Being reversal of transfer of revaluation surplus to realised reserves)		
(ii) Depreciation of building		
Depreciation charge – P/L	10	
Accumulated depreciation		10
(Being depreciation on building for 20x5)		
(iii) Externally-purchased software		
Equipment	100	
Intangible assets		100
(Being re-classification of software as property, plant and equipment)		
Amortisation of intangible assets		
Amortisation – P/L	140	
Intangible asset		140

(Being amortisation of software for 20x5:
€700,000/5)

Depreciation expense – P/L	33	
Accumulated depreciation		33

(Being depr. charge on software acquired for
mainframe computer for 20x5: €100,000/3)

(iv) Software acquired for development work

Development costs	400	
R&D costs – P/L		400

(Being capitalisation of software costs
incurred as part of development work)

(v)

Cost of sales – P/L	125	
Investment in joint venture		125

(Being adjustment in the Group accounts
on an **equity basis**)

(vi) Investment in Future Developments Ltd

- **Sale of land to Millennium Plc**

Share of profit of joint venture – P/L	150	
Land		150

(Being cancellation of Millennium's share of profit on inter-company
sale of land by JV)

- **Consolidation adjustment**

Investment in Future Developments Ltd	407	
Consolidated retained earnings		407

(Being investing group's share of post-acq. retained profit of joint
venture: i.e. (€4,347,000* − €3,533,000) × 50%)

*As per statement of financial position of Future Developments
Limited at 31 December 2x05.

FRS 102

If the financial statements of the Millennium Group were prepared in accordance with FRS 102 *The Financial Reporting Standard applicable in the UK and Republic of Ireland*, the accounting treatment recommended in this case solution would apply. The following is worth noting however.

Jointly controlled entity (Issue (5) in this case solution)
FRS 102 identifies three types of investments in joint ventures. Millennium's investment in Future Developments would be regarded as a jointly controlled entity (FRS 102, section 15.8). A venturer is required to account for a jointly controlled entity using the equity method. Therefore the method of accounting required under FRS 102 is the same as that required by IFRS 11 *Joint Arrangements*, which has been applied in this case solution.

SOLUTION TO
NORMAN EPSTOW LIMITED

(a) Adjustments to Draft Financial Statements

(i)   Termination of toy soldier item sales

Appendix A of IFRS 5 *Non-current Assets Held for Sale and Discontinued Operations* defines a component of an entity as '...operations and cash flows that can be clearly distinguished, operationally and for financial reporting purposes, from the rest of the entity.'

Toy soldier item sales would constitute a component under this definition. For a component to be classified as a discontinued operation it must be held for sale, or already disposed of, and meet one of the following criteria:

– Represent a major line of business or geographical area of operations.

– Be part of a single co-ordinated plan to dispose of a separate major line of business or geographical area of operations.

– Be a subsidiary acquired exclusively with a view to resale (IFRS 5, para 32).

Because the toy soldier item sales are part of a larger product group (in 2x05 they comprised approximately 13% of total item sales and 2.6% of total sales) they fail to meet the qualifying conditions in paragraph 32 of the standard, and would not therefore be regarded as a discontinued operation.

To the extent that assets at 31 December 2x05 of the toy soldier item category are retained, it is likely that these assets are required to fill occasional orders from important customers. As such assets are not available for immediate sale, they do not qualify as assets held for sale (IFRS 5, para 7).

(ii)   *Research and development*

IAS 38 requires that an intangible asset arising from development shall be recognised if six prerequisite criteria are satisfied (IAS 38, para 57).

The research into developing an alternative to the existing lead-based compound has had positive results. It is probable that Norman Epstow Limited will soon have a substantially improved process for the manufacture of kit sales products. On the assumption that the expenditure satisfies the criteria referred to above, the following accounting treatment will be appropriate:

- IAS 38 states that expenditure on an intangible item that was initially recognised as an expense shall not be recognised as part of the cost of an intangible asset at a later date (IAS 38, para 71). Thus, it is not permissible to write back the R&D expenditure incurred in 2x04, even though the project now appears to be commercially viable. The write-back in the 2x05 financial statements will therefore need to be reversed.

  See journal entry (i) in Appendix I below.

- It seems reasonable that the expenditure in 2x05 should be treated as development costs. It is therefore correct that no charge should be made in the statement of comprehensive income. It will be necessary, however, to reclassify as development costs the €70,000 currently included under trade and other receivables.

  See journal entry (i) in Appendix I below.

- In accordance with IAS 16 *Property, Plant and Equipment*, it will be necessary to provide for depreciation on the machine purchased in February 2x05. As the machine is being used for development work, however, its future economic benefits are being absorbed by a research project that qualifies as an intangible asset. The depreciation on the machine should therefore be included in development costs as an asset, rather than being charged to profit or loss (IAS 16, para 49).

  See journal entry (i) in Appendix I below.

(iii)   *Sale of production rights*

The purchase of production rights in relation to miniature figures associated with the Muhammad Ali film can be regarded as the acquisition of an intangible asset. IAS 38 requires that an intangible asset should be derecognised on disposal, and that the gain or loss should be determined as the difference between the net disposal proceeds and the carrying amount of the asset (IAS 38, para 112–113).

IAS 38 also states that the gain/loss should be recognised in profit or loss, but should not be classified as revenue (IAS 38, para 113).

Subject to materiality, the profit on disposal should be separately disclosed in the statement of comprehensive income or in the notes, in accordance with IAS 1, para 97.

See journal entry (ii) in Appendix I below.

(iv)   *Sale of premises*

The disposal proceeds of the premises should be reduced by a provision for repairs. This relates to a condition of sale that the purchaser be compensated for dry rot repairs. Thus, a present obligation exists as a result of a past event, and a provision is required at 31 December 2x05 (IAS 37, para 14).

A settlement of €20,000 was agreed in February 2x06 that constitutes an adjusting event after the reporting period (IAS 10, para 9(a)). This should be provided for at 31 December 20x5 (IAS 10, para 8).

Consideration should also be given to the separate disclosure of the profit on disposal, either in the statement of comprehensive income or in the notes (IAS 1, para 97).

It will also be appropriate to transfer the unrealised surplus on revaluation of the premises of €84,800 to realised reserves.

Details relating to the purchase and disposal of the premises are outlined below, and the adjustment to the 2x05 financial statements is provided as journal entry (iii) in Appendix I.

	DR €000	CR €000
Buildings	120	
Bank		120
(Being purchase of building in 2x02)		

Depreciation expense – P/L	2.4	
Accumulated depreciation		2.4
(Being depreciation charge for 2x02)		
Depreciation expense – P/L	2.4	
Accumulated depreciation		2.4
(Being depreciation charge for 2x03)		
Accumulated depreciation	4.8	
Buildings		4.8
(Being offset of accumulated depr. on reval. of bldg at 31 December 2x03)		
Buildings	84.8	
Revaluation surplus – OCI		84.8
(Being revaluation of building to €200,000 at 31 December 2x03)		
Depreciation expense – P/L	4.2	
Accumulated depreciation		4.2
(Being depreciation charge for 2x04: €200,000/48)		
Bank	300	
Accumulated depreciation	4.2	
Building		200
Provision for repairs – SOFP		20
Profit on disposal – P/L		84.2
(Being disposal of building in 2x05)		
Revaluation surplus – SOFP	84.8	
Retained earnings – SOFP		84.8
(Being transfer of unrealised surplus to realised reserves)		

(v) *Joint venture arrangement with Checkmate Limited*

This is a joint operation, which involves the use of the assets and other resources of Norman Epstow and Checkmate, rather than the establishment of another entity that is separate from the joint operators themselves.

IFRS 11 states that in respect of its interests in a joint operation, a joint operator shall recognise in its financial statements:

- its assets, including its share of any assets held jointly;

- its liabilities, including its share of any liabilities incurred jointly;

- its revenue from the sale of its share of the output arising from the joint operation;

- its share of the revenue from the sale of the output by the joint operation; and

- its expenses, including its share of any expenses incurred jointly. (IFRS 11, para 20)

Thus, the following accounting treatment will apply in relation to Norman Epstow's financial statements:

- The machinery purchased in connection with the manufacture of the chess sets should be included as an asset.

- Manufacturing and selling costs of €250,000 should be included in cost of sales.

- Cash sales of €360,000 should be recognised as revenue (i.e. 60% of total cash sales).

- Inventories of €100,000 should be included as an asset at 31 December 2x05. This is appropriate, as all of the manufacturing costs have been incurred by Norman Epstow.

- IAS 2 requires that inventory be valued at the lower of either cost or net realisable value (IAS 2, para 29). Cost in this case amounts to €100,000 and NRV can be estimated at €377,000 (Note 1). Thus, the closing inventory of chess sets should be included in Norman Epstow's statement of financial position at its cost to date of €100,000.

Note 1: NRV

	€	
Estimated selling price	480,000*	(assuming a mark up of 300% on manufacturing costs, as earned on chess sets already sold, and adjusted for Norman Epstow's share of revenue)
Less: completion costs	(100,000)	
Less: selling costs	(3,000)	
NRV	377,000	

See journal entry (iv) in Appendix I below

*Estimated selling price

	€
Cost of inventory when completed	200,000
Add profit margin @ 300%	600,000
Selling price	800,000
Norman Epstow's share @ 60%	480,000

(vi)   *Jointly-owned property*

This property is a joint operation, as defined by IFRS 11 *Joint Arrangements.*

The property jointly owned by Norman Epstow is investment property, and should be classified as such, rather than being included under property, plant and equipment.

IAS 40 *Investment Property* permits entities to choose either a fair value model or a cost model for all of its investment properties (IAS 40, para 30). On the assumption that Norman Epstow Limited opts for the fair value model, its share of the gain arising during the six months ended 31 December 2x05 should be included in profit or loss for that period.

Also, Norman Epstow's share of rental income should be included in profit or loss.

See journal entry (v) in Appendix I below.

Appendix I

Journal Entries

	DR €000	CR €000
(i) R&D		
Net operating expenses – P/L	50	
Trade and other receivables		50
(Being reversal of reinstatement of 2x04 development costs)		
Development costs – SOFP	70	
Trade and other receivables		70
(Being reclassification of 2x05 development expenditure)		
Development costs – SOFP	6	
Accumulated depreciation		6
(Being depreciation for 2x05 on machine acquired for development work)		
(ii) Sale of production rights		
Revenue	550	
Intangible assets		250
Profit on disposal of intangible asset – P/L		300
(Being disposal of production rights)		
(iii) Disposal of premises		
Bank	300	
Accumulated depreciation	4.2	
Building		200
Liability for repair costs – SOFP		20
Profit on disposal of premises – P/L		84.2
(Being disposal of building in 2x05)		
Revaluation surplus – SOFP	84.8	
Retained earnings – SOFP		84.8
(Being transfer of unrealised surplus to realised reserves)		

(iv) Joint operation – manufacture of chess sets

Machinery	200	
Bank		200
(Being purchase of machinery)		

Cost of sales	40	
Accumulated depreciation machinery		40
(Being depreciation of machinery for 2x05)		

Cost of sales	210	
Bank		210
(Being cost of sales – excluding depreciation)		

Bank	360	
Revenue		360
(Being Norman Epstow's agreed share of revenue)		

Inventory	100	
Cost of sales		100
(Being partly completed chess sets at 31 December 2x05 valued at cost)		

(v) Joint operation – investment property

Investment property	350	
Property, plant and equipment		350
(Being reclassification of property as an investment property)		

Investment property	100	
Gain on revaluation – P/L		100
(Being Norman Epstow's share of gain on revaluation of investment property)		

Bank	10	
Rental income – P/L		10
(Being Norman Epstow's share of rental income)		

FRS 102

If the financial statements of Norman Epstow were prepared in accordance with FRS 102 *The Financial Reporting Standard applicable in the UK and Republic of Ireland*, the accounting treatment recommended in this case solution would apply, except in relation to the following issues.

Development costs (Issue (a) (ii) in this case solution)
The capitalisation of development expenditure that satisfies the qualifying criteria is optional under FRS 102 (FRS 102, para 18.8H).

The capitalisation of €70,000, in accordance with IAS 38, is therefore a permissible treatment under FRS 102. This is the treatment applied in this case solution.

Alternatively, under FRS 102, Norman Epstow could opt to write-off the €70,000 development costs to profit or loss. In this event the expenditure, which is currently recorded as trade and other receivables, would be reclassified as follows:

	DR €000	CR €000
Research and development costs – P/L	70	
Trade and other receivables		70

Joint operation (Issue (a) (v) in this case solution)
FRS 102 identifies three types of investments in joint ventures. Norman Epstow's arrangement with Checkmate Limited would be regarded as a jointly controlled operation (FRS 102, para 15.4). A venturer is required to account for a jointly controlled operation by recognising:

- the assets it controls and the liabilities that it incurs; and
- the expenses it incurs and its share of income.

The method of accounting required under FRS 102 is the same as that required by IFRS 11 *Joint Arrangements*, which has been employed in this case solution.

Jointly controlled asset (Issue (a) (vi) in this case solution)
The property that is jointly controlled with Telstar Limited would be defined as a jointly controlled asset by FRS 102 (FRS 102, para 15.6). FRS

102 requires that a venturer should recognise a jointly controlled asset in its financial statement as follows:

- its share of the jointly controlled asset;
- any liabilities that it has incurred;
- its share of any liabilities incurred jointly;
- its share of income and expenses from the jointly controlled asset; and
- any expenses it has incurred in respect of its interest in the jointly controlled asset.

The method of accounting required under FRS 102 is the same as that required by IFRS 11 *Joint Arrangements*, which has been employed in this case solution.

SOLUTION TO RIGHT TYPE GROUP

Dartry Maunsell & Co.

Memorandum

To: **Martina O'Sullivan**

From: **A. Senior**
Date: **24 February 2x06**

Re: **Right Type Group**

Further to our recent meeting I have now had the opportunity to review the issues arising in respect of the audit of the Right Type Group for the year ended 31 December 2x05. I will deal with each issue in turn.

(1) Establishment of Side Type Limited

IFRS 11 *Joint Arrangements* defines a joint venture as a joint arrangement whereby the parties have rights to the net assets of the arrangement (IFRS 11 Appendix A).

The establishment of Side Type Limited qualifies as a joint venture.
IFRS 11 requires that a joint venturer shall recognise its interest in a joint venture using the equity method (IFRS 11, para 24).

Equity method
Under the equity method, the investment is initially recognised at cost and adjusted thereafter for the post-acquisition change in the investor's share of net assets of the investee. The profit or loss of the investor includes the investor's share of the profit or loss of the investee (IAS 28, para 3).

The following journal entries will apply in the Group financial statements, under the equity method:

	DR €000	CR €000
Investment in joint venture	1,500	
Bank		1,500

(Being Right Type's share of cost of setting up Side Type Limited)

Expenses – P/L	750	
Bank		750

(Being fee paid by Right Type to Milton Property Care for 9 months ended 31 December 2x05)

Investment in joint venture	150	
Share of profit – Consolidated P/L		150

(Being share of profit of Side Type Limited for
9 months ended 31 December 2x05)

Disclosure issues

Right Type Limited is classified as a related party of Side Type Limited, on the basis that it has joint control over it (IAS 24, para 9). Subject to materiality, details of transactions between the companies will need to be disclosed as follows:

- In the individual financial statements of Side Type Limited, details of transactions with Right Type;
- Disclosure will be required in the individual financial statements of Right Type Limited of transactions with Side Type Limited;
- Transactions between Right Type and Side Type will also require disclosure in the financial statements of the Right Type Group.

(2) Intangible Assets

(a) Right Type brand name

IAS 38 states that: 'Internally generated brands, mastheads, publishing titles, customer lists and items similar in substance shall not be recognised as intangible assets' (IAS 38, para 63).

Thus, the sums expended by the Right Type Group in promoting the quality of its brand name should not have been capitalised, but should instead have been expensed to profit or loss as they were incurred. This constitutes a material prior-period error, and should be corrected retrospectively in the first set of financial statements authorised for issue after its discovery (IAS 8, para 42).

The Right Type Group's statement of changes in equity will be required to adjust the opening balance of each affected component of equity (i.e. retained earnings), and comparative amounts presented in the financial statements should be adjusted.

Extract from Statement of Changes in Equity for the year ended 31 December 2x05

	Share Capital	Retained Earnings	Total
Balance at 31 December 2x03 as re-stated	X	Y*	X + Y
Profit for the year ended 31 December 2x04 as re-stated		(€0.24m)	(€0.24m)
Restated balance at 1 January 2x05			X + Y − €0.24m
Changes in equity for 2x05			
Balance at 31 December 2x05			

*Original balance less €1.2m

The following journal entries will be required:

	DR €000	CR €000
Retained earnings	1,440	
Intangible asset		1,440

(Being write-off of Right Type brand up to 31 December 2x04)

	DR €000	CR €000
Expenses – P/L	288	
Intangible asset		288

(Being write-off of expenditure on Right Type brand capitalised in year ending 31 December 2x05)

IAS 8 requires the following disclosure in respect of prior-period errors:

- the nature of the prior-period error;
- for each prior period presented, to the extent practicable, the amount of the correction;
- the amount of the correction at the beginning of the earliest prior period presented;
- if retrospective restatement is impracticable for a particular prior period, the circumstances that led to the existence of that condition and a description of how and from when the error has been corrected (IAS 8, para 49).

Additionally, IAS 1 requires that a statement of financial position be presented at the beginning of the earliest comparative period (i.e. 1 January 2x04) when an entity makes a retrospective restatement of items in its financial statements (IAS 1, para 10(f)).

(b)   Well Build brand

Recognition

IAS 38 states that an intangible asset shall be recognised if:

(i)   it is probable that the expected future economic benefits that are attributable to the asset will flow to the entity; *and*

(ii)   the cost of the asset can be measured reliably (IAS 38, para 21).

IAS 38, para 25 states that intangible assets which are separately acquired are always considered to satisfy the probability recognition criterion in (i) above. Clearly, the acquisition cost of the Well Build brand can also be measured reliably. Therefore, in accordance with IAS 38, the Well Build brand should be recognised as an intangible asset.

IAS 38 also requires that an intangible asset should be measured initially at its cost (IAS 38, para 24). It is thus necessary to eliminate the premium above cost attributed to the Well Build brand. The following journal entry will be required:

	DR €000	CR €000
Gain on a bargain purchase – SOFP*	1,000	
Intangible assets – Well Build brand		1,000

(Being re-statement of Well Build brand to cost price)

*It was incorrect, in any event, to record this gain in the SOFP. IFRS 3 requires that a gain on a bargain purchase (i.e. negative goodwill) should be recorded in profit or loss by the acquirer (IFRS 3, para 34).

Measurement after recognition

IAS 38 requires that an entity should choose either the cost model or the revaluation model as its accounting policy, with a similar policy being applied to all assets in the same class (IAS 38, para 72).

Fair value, for the purposes of revaluations under IAS 38, should be determined by reference to an active market (IAS 38, para 75). However IAS 38 states that an active market cannot exist for brands, on the basis that each such asset is unique (IAS 38, para 78).

Thus, it would not be appropriate to revalue the Well Build brand as clearly there is no active market for this type of asset.

Amortisation

IAS 38 states that, where intangible assets are regarded as having indefinite useful lives, they should not be amortised (IAS 38, para 107). The decision of the Right Type Group not to amortise the Well Build brand is therefore in accordance with the standard.

In accordance with IAS 36 *Impairment of Assets,* however, an entity is required to test an intangible asset with an indefinite life for impairment, by comparing its recoverable amount with its carrying amount:

- annually, *and*
- whenever there is an indication that the intangible asset may be impaired (IAS 36, para 9 and 10).

Disclosure

The following disclosures are required by IAS 38 for each class of intangible assets:

- Whether the useful lives are indefinite or finite and, if finite, the useful lives or the amortisation rates used.
- The amortisation methods used for intangible assets with finite useful lives.
- The gross carrying amount and any accumulated amortisation at the beginning and end of the period.
- The line item(s) of the statement of comprehensive income in which any amortisation of intangible assets is included.
- A reconciliation of the carrying amount at the beginning and end of the period (IAS 38, para 118).

(3) Expenditure on assets

(i) Replacement of lift

IAS 16 states that parts of property, plant and equipment requiring replacement should be included as part of the cost of the related asset if the expenditure satisfies the recognition criteria in paragraph 7 of the standard (IAS 16, para 13).

IAS 16, para 7 states that an asset should be recognised if:

- it is probable that future economic benefits associated with the item will flow to the entity, and
- the cost of the item can be measured reliably.

These prerequisites appear to be satisfied in this case – the replacement lift will therefore be classified as capital expenditure. The lift should be included as part of the head office building.

IAS 16 requires that each part of an item of property, plant and equipment with a cost that is significant in relation to the total cost of the item shall be depreciated separately (IAS 16, para 43). Thus, unlike the Group's buildings, which are depreciated over 50 years, the lift should be depreciated over its useful life of 10 years.

In computing the depreciable amount of the lift, the asset's estimated residual value should be deducted from its cost. The residual value should be calculated based on current prices, and not on those expected to prevail in 10 years' time (IAS 16, para 6).

IAS 16 requires that the carrying amount of those parts that are replaced is derecognised, with the gain or loss being included in profit or loss. Gains should not be classified as revenue (IAS 16, para 13 and 68).

IAS 16 also states that the initial estimate of the costs of dismantling and removing an asset be included in the asset's cost (IAS 16, para 16). Thus, a corresponding asset will be set up on the basis that the expenditure provides access to future economic benefits. Thus, the estimated present value of the decommissioning expenses (i.e. €30,000) will be provided for and included as part of the cost of the lift. As the decommissioning costs will be a year closer (at 31 December 2x05) to being paid, it will be necessary to unwind the discount by one year during 2x05.

The following journal entries will be required:

	DR €000	CR €000
Land and buildings	30	
Provision for decommissioning – SOFP		30
(Being provision for costs of decommissioning the lift)		
Depreciation expense – P/L	31	
Accumulated depreciation land and buildings		31

(Being depreciation charge on lift for 2x05, based on a depreciable amount of €310,000*, and an estimated useful life of 10 years)

*Cost + decommissioning provision – residual value
  i.e. €300,000 + €30,000 – €20,000

	DR €000	CR €000
Finance costs – P/L	3	
Provision for decommissioning costs – SOFP		3

(Being unwinding of discount during 2x05 @ 10%. This is computed as €30,000 × 10%.)

(ii) *Compliance with fire regulations*
Certain items of property, plant and equipment may be necessary for an entity to obtain the future economic benefits from its other assets. Such items qualify for recognition as assets (IAS 16, para 11).

Fire safety equipment is an example of this type of asset, and capital expenditure on such an asset should be capitalised.

IAS 16 also states that the costs of day-to-day servicing of an asset should be recognised in profit or loss as incurred. The purpose of these expenditures is often described as being for the repair and maintenance of the item of property, plant and equipment (IAS 16, para 12).

On the basis of the above requirements of IAS 16, the following treatment is recommended in respect of expenditure incurred in connection with fire regulation compliance:

- The repair of fire doors is part of the repair and maintenance of the company's buildings, and this expenditure should be expensed in profit or loss.
- The installation of fire escapes appears to satisfy the requirements of paragraph 11 of IAS 16, and this expenditure should be capitalised as part of land and buildings.
- The purchase of fire safety equipment similarly represents capital expenditure; this amount should be capitalised as part of fixtures and fittings.

The following journal entries will be required:

	DR €000	CR €000
Repairs and maintenance – P/L	50	
Fixtures and fittings		50
(Being re-classification of fire door repairs as revenue expenditure)		
Accumulated depreciation fixtures and fittings	40	
Depreciation expense – P/L		40
(Being reversal of original depreciation charge)		
Depreciation expense – P/L	5	
Accumulated depreciation land and buildings		5

(Being depreciation on fire escapes
  for 2x05, on the basis that a full year's
  depreciation @ 2% p.a.
  SL is charged in the year of purchase)

	DR	CR
Depreciation expense – P/L	10	
Accumulated depreciation fixtures and fittings		10

(Being depreciation on safety
  equipment for 2x05, on the basis that
  a full year's depreciation @ 10% p.a.
  RB is charged in the year of purchase)

(4) Revenue Issues

(i) *Sale of residential homes*

In respect of the completed sales of 12 houses, these should be
recorded as revenue in accordance with IFRS 15, para 31. The customers have obtained control of the houses and Right Type Limited
has satisfied its performance obligation. The following journal entries
are required:

	DR €000	CR €000
Bank/trade receivables	3,600	
Revenue		3,600
(Being the sale of 12 houses)		
Cost of sales	2,040	
Inventory (SOFP)		2,040
(Being cost of 12 houses)		

A deposit has been received on a further four houses, the sale being
dependent on an engineer's report, and on the purchaser being able to
raise finance. As these customers have not yet obtained control of the
houses, no sale should be recognised by the Right Type Group. The
deposits received should be recorded as a liability.

	DR €000	CR €000
Bank	80	
Trade and other payables		80

These four houses should be included in inventory and recorded at the lower of cost and net realisable value.

In respect of the remaining eight houses in the development, the lease agreements which have been signed constitute operating leases, as defined by IAS 17, para 4. These will be recorded as income, on a straight-line basis over the lease term (IAS 17, para 50).

Two of the lessees have, however, signed unconditional contracts to purchase a house, with the December lease instalment being offset against the purchase price. The following journal entries will be required:

	DR €000	CR €000
Bank	24	
Lease income – P/L		24
(Being instalments received on operating leases)		
Lease income – P/L	2	
Revenue		2
(Being lease instalments offset against buyers' purchase price of houses)		

The signing of unconditional purchase contracts by two customers on 2 December means that the criteria of IFRS 15, para 31, have been complied with – the customers have obtained control of their houses and Right Type Limited has satisfied its performance obligation. The following journal entry will be required at 31 December 2x05:

	DR €000	CR €000
Trade receivables	598	
Revenue		598
(Being the sale of two houses, net of offsetting lease instalments)		
Cost of sales	340	
Inventory (SOFP)		340
(Being the cost of the two houses sold)		

The remaining six houses, which are let under operating leases, should be included in inventory and recorded at the lower of cost and net realisable value.

(ii) *Provision of security service*

Property Sites receives and consumes the benefits provided by Right Type's performance as the latter company performs its obligations.

In accordance with IFRS 15, this constitutes a performance obligation satisfied over time. Therefore revenue from this contract should be recognised over time (IFRS 15, para 35).

As the result of a security breach in November 2x05, however, Property Sites Limited is entitled to a partial refund/reduction of amounts paid/payable. In accordance with IAS 37, para 14, this represents a present obligation as the result of a past event, and a provision should be recorded at 31 December 2x05.

The following entries are required:

	DR €	CR €
Bank	2,400	
Income from security service – P/L		2,400
(Being income from security contract for Oct and Nov 2x05)		
Income from security service – P/L	600	
Provision for customer refund – SOFP		600

(Being provision for refund of November security fee of €1,200 less income of €600 for December 2x05)

(5) Land

The land acquired for building purposes would be more in the nature of inventory were the company to proceed with its diversification plans. As such it should be valued at the lower of either cost or net realisable value (IAS 2, para 28).

The land bank was acquired for a cost of €1 million, and there is a possibility of planning permission being withdrawn, in which case the net realisable value of the land would be €400,000.

Thus, the land should be restated to its cost figure of €1 million. The possible withdrawal of planning permission is akin to a contingent liability, as defined in IAS 37, para 10. Details should be disclosed in the financial statements (IAS 37, para 28).

The following journal adjustment will be required at 31 December 2x05:

	DR €000	CR €000
Revaluation surplus – OCI	500	
Inventory (i.e. land bank) – SOFP	1,000	
Land		1,500

(Being reclassification of land as a current asset)

The land should also be reclassified as inventory in the financial statements of previous years.

(6) Village Living Concept

This project would appear to satisfy the criteria of IAS 38 *Intangible Assets* to be classified as development phase research expenditure (IAS 38, para 57). This was clarified by the success of the rights issue in January 2x06 which provides funding for the completion of the project.

The mobile information office was acquired through a finance lease (as defined in IAS 17, para 4) so should be included in property, plant and equipment, with the corresponding leasing liability also being shown in the financial statements. The mobile information office should be capitalised at its fair value (€600,000) or, if lower, at the present value of the minimum lease payments (€600,000), each determined at the inception of the lease (IAS 17, para 20).

IAS 17 requires that the finance charge in a finance lease should be allocated to each period during the lease term so as to produce a constant periodic rate of interest on the remaining balance of the liability (IAS 17, para 25). A lessee may, however, use some form of approximation to simplify the calculation (IAS 17, para 26). In accordance with Group policy the sum of digits method is employed to allocate the finance charge relating to the lease of the mobile information office.

In respect of the depreciation of the mobile information office, the annual charge constitutes part of the development cost, and it should be included in the carrying value of that asset (IAS 16, para 49).

The rights issue is a non-adjusting event after the reporting period (IAS 10, para 3). As such it should be disclosed in the financial statements.

In order to reflect the above requirements, the following journal adjustments should be made:

		€000	€000
(i)	Development costs – SOFP	300	
	Labour costs – P/L		300
	(Being deferral of labour costs incurred in respect of Village Living concept)		
(ii)	Equipment	600	
	Lease obligation – SOFP		600
	(Being capitalisation of mobile office acquired through finance lease)		
(iii)	Lease obligation	100	
	Lease charges – P/L		100
	(Being reversal of leasing charge to profit or loss)		
(iv)	Development costs – SOFP	120	
	Accumulated depreciation		120
	(Being depreciation for 2x05 on mobile office)		
(v)	Development costs – SOFP	50	
	Accrued interest – SOFP		50
	(Being lease interest charge for 2x05 capitalised as part of development costs – see note 1)		

Note 1: amortisation of lease interest

The sum of digits method is used to approximate a constant periodic rate of interest on the remaining balance of the liability.

Periods	Interest for period(Rounded)	Relevant period
7	€200,000 × 7/28 = 50,000	6 M/E 31/12/2x05
6	€200,000 × 6/28 = 43,000	6 M/E 30/06/2x06
5	€200,000 × 5/28 = 36,000	6 M/E 31/12/2x06
4	€200,000 × 4/28 = 29,000	6 M/E 30/06/2x07
3	€200,000 × 3/28 = 21,000	6 M/E 31/12/2x07
2	€200,000 × 2/28 = 14,000	6 M/E 30/06/2x08

1	€200,000 × 1/28 =	7,000	6 M/E 31/12/2x08
–	(Note 2)		
28		200,000	

Note 2: No interest is allocated to the final period as the lease instalments are payable in advance. Thus, no capital will be outstanding for the final six months of the lease term.

Note 3: At 31 December 2x05, the outstanding lease liability in the statement of financial position will be computed as follows:

	€000
Current liability (€200,000 less interest of €93,000)	107
Non-current liability (€500,000 less interest of €107,000)	393
	500

Lease interest accrued of €50,000 will also be included in current liabilities.

FRS 102

If the financial statements of the Right Type Group were prepared in accordance with FRS 102 *The Financial Reporting Standard applicable in the UK and Republic of Ireland*, the accounting treatment recommended in this case solution would apply, except in relation to the following issues.

Jointly controlled entity (Issue (1) in this case solution)
FRS 102 identifies three types of investments in joint ventures. Right Type's investment in Side Type would be regarded as a jointly controlled entity (FRS 102, para 15.8). A venturer is required to account for a jointly controlled entity using the equity method. Therefore the method of accounting required under FRS 102 is the same as that required by IFRS 11 *Joint Arrangements*, which has been applied in this case solution.

Amortisation of intangible assets (Issue (2) (b) in this case solution)
FRS 102 regards all intangible assets as having a finite useful life (FRS 102, para 18.19). If an entity is unable to make a reliable estimate of the useful life of an intangible asset, the life shall not exceed five years (FRS 102, para 18.20).

The Right Type Group must therefore determine the useful life of the Well Build brand name, and amortise the asset over that period. Alternatively, if no reliable estimate of its useful life can be made, the Well Build brand should be amortised over five years. In the latter case the following journal entry would be required in the 2x05 financial statements.

	DR €000	CR €000
Amortisation of intangible asset – P/L	600	
Intangible asset		600

(Being amortisation of Well Build brand name over an assumed useful life of five years, i.e. €3m/5 = €600,000, on the assumption that a full year's amortisation is charged in the year of purchase)

SOLUTION TO
TRACER GROUP

Clarke, Scriven & Co.

Memorandum

To: **Julie Crimson**

From: **A. Senior**
Date: **24 March 2x06**

Re: **Tracer Group**

Further to our recent meeting I have now had the opportunity to review the issues arising in respect of the audit of the Tracer Group for the year ended 31 December 2x05. I will deal with each issue in turn.

Issue (a) – Construction of Head Office Building

(i)   *Initial cost of head office building*

     The head office building was included in the non-current assets of Tracer Limited at 30 September 2x05 at a total cost of €4.17 million.

     Property, plant and equipment should initially be measured at cost (IAS 16, para 15). IAS 16 states that *cost* comprises an asset's purchase price together with any costs directly attributable to bringing the asset into working condition for its intended use.

Directly attributable costs include the following:

- costs of site preparation
- professional fees (IAS 16, para 17).

The overriding requirement in capitalising directly attributable costs is that they must be *incremental,* and would therefore have been avoided if the asset had not been constructed or acquired.

Costs that are **not** incremental costs of an item of property, plant and equipment include administration and other general overhead costs (IAS 16, para 19).

Thus, the head office building of Tracer Limited should have been capitalised, exclusive of general administrative overheads of €400,000. Consequently, the following correcting journal entry is required:

	DR €000	CR €000
Administrative expenses – P/L	400	
Property, plant and equipment		400

(ii) Borrowing costs

Borrowing costs that are directly attributable to the construction of a qualifying asset should be capitalised as part of the cost of that asset (IAS 23, para 9).

Capitalisation should commence when expenditures are being incurred, borrowing costs are being incurred and activities that are necessary to prepare the asset for its intended use or sale are in progress (IAS 23, para 17).

Capitalisation should however be suspended during periods in which active development is interrupted (IAS 23, para 20). In the case of Tracer Limited therefore, no costs should be capitalised that relate to the period of work stoppage, 1 April–30 June 2x05. Capitalisation should cease when substantially all of the activities necessary to prepare the asset for its intended use or sale are complete, which in Tracer Limited's case is 30 September 2x05 (IAS 23, para 22).

The amount of borrowing costs to be capitalised should therefore be computed as follows:

Item	Cost €000	Timescale from commencement on 1 January to date of completion on 30 September (excluding work stoppage period of 3 months)	Annual equivalent €000
Site clearance	200	6 months	100
Legal fees	70	6 months	35
April Certificate	1,600	3 months	400
Sept. Certificate	1,900	0 months	
Total	3,770		535

To the extent that an entity borrows funds generally and uses them for the purpose of obtaining a qualifying asset, the entity shall determine the amount of borrowing costs eligible for capitalisation by applying a capitalisation rate to the expenditures on the asset (IAS 23, para 14). The capitalisation rate should be the weighted average of the borrowing costs that are outstanding during the period (IAS 23, para 14).

The interest rate was 8% from 1 January to 31 March, and 9% from 1 July to 30 September. Therefore the weighted average rate for the relevant period under review (excluding 3 months' work stoppage) was 8.5%.

When this is applied to the relevant annualised costs of €535,000, the borrowing costs to be capitalised amount to €45,475. The following journal entry is therefore required:

	DR €000	CR €000
Property, plant and equipment	45.5	
Bank		45.5

(iii) *Depreciation*

Depreciation begins when an asset is available for use (IAS 16, para 55), which in the case of the new head office building is 30 September. Three months' depreciation is therefore charged as follows:

	DR €000	CR €000
Depreciation expense – P/L	19.1	
Accumulated depreciation		19.1

(Being depreciation on head office building as follows: ((€4,170,000 – €400,000 + €45,500) × 2% × 3/12)

(iv) Revaluation at 31 December 2x05

It is normal practice that accumulated depreciation on buildings is offset against the gross carrying value when property assets are being revalued (IAS 16, para 35). The following entry will therefore be required at 31 December 2x05, to revalue the head office building to €6 million:

	DR €000	CR €000
Accumulated depreciation	19.1	
Property, plant & equipment		19.1
Property, plant & equipment	2,203.6	
Revaluation surplus – OCI		2,203.6

(Being revaluation of building at 31 December 2x05:
€6,000,000 –(€3,770,000 + €45,500 – €19,100))

	DR	CR
Revaluation surplus – OCI	446	
Deferred tax liability – SOFP		446

(Being deferred tax on revaluation surplus @ 20%)*

*Deferred tax is levied on the amount by which the asset is revalued in excess of its original cost. Borrowing costs are excluded from cost for this purpose as it is assumed that they will not be deductible in computing the chargeable gain. Therefore the amount of deferred tax is computed as: (€6m – €3.77m) × 20%.

(v) Accounting policy note

Borrowing costs incurred in respect of the construction of qualifying assets are treated as part of the cost of those assets. Capitalisation commences when expenditures are being incurred, borrowing costs are being incurred, and activities that are necessary to prepare the asset for its intended use are in progress. Capitalisation of borrowing costs is suspended during extended periods in which active development is interrupted.

Issue (b) – Government Grant

Government grants should be recognised when there is reasonable assurance that:

- an entity will comply with any conditions attached to the grants, *and*
- the grants will be received (IAS 20, para 7).

Comps Limited made an error in 2x04 by offsetting the grant against the cost of the related asset. This is unlikely to have been a material error, particularly as the error did not affect profit for the year ended 31 December 2x04. Therefore retrospective correction of the error is not required.

Comps Limited may also have been incorrect in recognising the government grant of €100,000 if there was not reasonable assurance of the conditions relating to employment targets being met.

On 31 December 2x05 it will be necessary to provide for the repayment of the grant, following the government inspection in July of that year. This provision is necessary, in accordance with IAS 37 *Provisions, Contingent Liabilities and Contingent Assets,* as there is a 60% probability that the grant will have to be repaid.

IAS 20 states that a government grant which becomes repayable shall be accounted for as a revision to an accounting estimate (IAS 20, para 32).

Comps Limited has also failed to capitalise the decommissioning costs of the machine, which is a requirement of IAS 16 (IAS 16, para 6(c)). This does not constitute a material error, however, and retrospective adjustment is not required under IAS 8.

The following correcting journal entries are required:

	DR €000	CR €000
Plant and machinery	100	
Liability for grant repayment – SOFP		100
(Being reinstatement of asset to gross cost, and creation of provision for repayment of grant)		
Depreciation expense – P/L	19	
Accumulated depreciation		19
(Being two years' depreciation originally avoided due to deduction of grant from the asset in 2x04)		

Plant and machinery	10	
Provision for decommissioning – SOFP		10*
(Being provision for decommissioning of machine)		
Depreciation expense – P/L	1.9	
Accumulated depreciation		1.9
(Being two years' depreciation on capitalised decommissioning costs)		

*This provision has not been discounted to present value on the basis that the effect of the time value of money is not material.

It should also be noted that Comps Limited should not have offset the government grant against the asset cost in 2x04. Although this treatment is permitted by IAS 20, it is prohibited by company law. This does not constitute a material error however, and a prior-period adjustment is not required.

Issue (c) – Share Options

The increase in the rights to an entity's shares requires an increase in a component of equity. When the payment for goods or services does not represent an asset, IFRS 2 *Share-based Payment* requires the offsetting entry to be expensed.

Tracer Limited issued share options on 31 December 2x03 to its key executives, with the exercise of the options conditional on the completion of two years' service from that date. The issue of these options is considered to relate to the services the employees will provide over the vesting period. Therefore the fair value of the share-based payment, determined at the grant date, should be expensed over the two years commencing on 1 January 2x04.

Each of the options issued to the 10 executives of Tracer Limited has a fair value of €0.80 at 31 December 2x03, the date of grant of the options. On the basis that one executive does not qualify for the options, the total expense is therefore €720,000 (100,000 × 9 × €0.80). In accordance with IFRS 2, this should be accounted for as follows:

	DR €000	CR €000
Share option expense – P/L	400	
Equity reserve – SOFP		400

(Being estimated cost of share option scheme for year ended 31 December 2x04, based on the allocation of the fair value at option grant date over the vesting period (10 × 100,000 × €0.80/2) as all 10 executives were expected to qualify as at that date)

	DR	CR
Share option expense – P/L	320	
Equity reserve – SOFP		320

(Being estimated cost of share option scheme for year ended 31 December 2x05, based on the allocation of the fair value at option grant date over the vesting period ((9 × 100,000 × €0.80) − €400,000))

Eight executives exercised their options on 31 December 2x05 and they each paid a total of €100,000 for their shares. This should be recorded by Tracer Limited as follows:

	DR €000	CR €000
Bank	800	
Equity reserve – SOFP	640	
Ordinary share capital		400
Share premium		1,040

In respect of the remaining executive, a balance of €80,000 will be held in reserves pending a decision on the exercise rights of Patrick Cudmore, the executive dismissed by Tracer Limited.

Mr Cudmore, who was dismissed in April 2x05, immediately instigated legal proceedings against the company. In February 2x06, when the financial statements were authorised for issue, it was likely that he would be awarded €500,000 in compensation. It was also possible that he would be awarded an additional €400,000.

As there was a present obligation at 31 December 2x05, resulting from a past event, a provision of €500,000 should be recognised in the financial statements (IAS 37, para 14). There was also a contingent liability of €400,000, which should be disclosed by way of note (IAS 37, para 28).

The following journal entry is required in respect of the financial statements of Tracer Limited for the year ended 31 December 2x05:

	DR €000	CR €000
Compensation expense – P/L	500	
Provision for compensation – SOFP		500

(Being provision for compensation award)

Issue (d) – Disposal of Shares

(i)   *Separate financial statements of Tracer Limited*
The profit or loss on disposal will be computed as the difference between the disposal proceeds of the shares and their cost.

	€000
Disposal proceeds	12,000
Less:	
Cost of shares (€9 million × 6/9)	(6,000)
Profit on disposal	6,000

The following journal entry will be required in the separate financial statements of Tracer Limited in respect of the disposal:

	DR €000	CR €000
Bank	12,000	
Investment in Airlight Limited		6,000
Profit on disposal – P/L		6,000*

*If this is considered a material amount its separate disclosure is required by IAS 1 *Presentation of Financial Statements,* either on the face of the statement of comprehensive income or in the notes (IAS 1, para 97).

(ii) *Group financial statements*
If a parent loses control of a subsidiary, in accordance with IFRS 10, it should:

- derecognise the assets (including any goodwill) and liabilities of the subsidiary at their carrying amounts at the date that control is lost;
- derecognise the carrying amount of any non-controlling interests in the former subsidiary at the date when control is lost;
- recognise any investment retained in the former subsidiary at its fair value at the date when control is lost;
- recognise the fair value of the consideration received; and
- recognise any resulting difference as a gain or loss in profit or loss attributable to the parent (IFRS 10, para 98).

From the perspective of the financial statements of the Group, the disposal of a controlling interest in Airlight Limited is represented as follows:

	€000	€000
Consideration received		12,000
Investment retained at fair value (€10.5m × 30%)		3,150
Non-controlling interests at date of disposal (€10.5m × 10%; based on % of net assets)		1,050
		16,200

Less:

Assets less liabilities of the subsidiary at their carrying amounts at the date that control is lost (Note 1)	(10,500)	
Goodwill eliminated on disposal/loss of control (Note 2)	(4,500)	
Profit on disposal of Airlight Limited – consolidated SOCI P/L	1,200	

Note 1: the amount of identifiable net assets at 30 September 2x05 is computed as follows:

identifiable net assets when 90% stake in Airlight was acquired (i.e. €5m) + post-acquisition retained earnings of Airlight up to 30 September 2x05 of €5.5m (i.e. (€7m + (€2m × 9/12)) – €3m).

Note 2: goodwill eliminated on disposal/loss of control.
This is the goodwill that arose when Airlight Limited was acquired:

	€000
Consideration paid	9,000
Share of identifiable net assets acquired (i.e. €5 million × 90%)	(4,500)
Goodwill arising on the acquisition of Airlight Limited	4,500

Airlight Limited ceases to be consolidated as a subsidiary of the Tracer Group on 30 September 2x05, and its income and expenses are included in the consolidated financial statements until that date (IFRS 10, para 20). At that date, by virtue of Tracer Limited being able to exercise significant influence over Airlight Limited, it will become an associate of the Group (IAS 28, para 2). The remaining investment in Airlight Limited will be carried at its fair value of €3.15m, at the date when control is lost (IFRS 10, para 25).

The following journal entry will be required in the Group financial statements in respect of the disposal, and the recognition of the retained investment in Airlight Limited as an investment in an associate:

	DR €000	CR €000
Bank	12,000	
Non-controlling interests	1,050	
Investment in associate	3,150	
Goodwill		4,500
Identifiable net assets		10,500
Profit on disposal – P/L		1,200

The results of Airlight, after disposal, will be included in the Group accounts using equity accounting. Therefore the following journal entry will be required in the year ended 31 December 2x05:

	DR €000	CR €000
Investment in associate	150	
Share of profit of associate – P/L		150

(Being group share of associate's profit for the three months ended 31 December 2x05: €2m × 30% × 3/12)

(iii) Disclosure requirements relating to the disposal of shares in Airlight Limited
The disposal of the shares in Airlight Limited constitutes a discontinued operation, as defined by IFRS 5. The *Group* financial statements should disclose:

(I) A single amount on the face of the statement of comprehensive income comprising the total of:

- the post-tax profit or loss of discontinued operations; and
- the post-tax gain or loss on disposal (IFRS 5, para 33(a)).

(II) An analysis of the single amount in (a) into:

- the revenue, expenses and pre-tax profit or loss of discontinued operations;
- the related income tax expense as required by IAS 12; and
- the gain or loss on disposal and the related income tax expense as required by IAS 12.

The analysis may be presented in the notes or on the face of the statement of comprehensive income (IFRS 5, para 33(b)).

(III) The net cash flows attributable to the operating, investing and financing activities of discontinued operations (IFRS 5, para 33(c)).

The Tracer Group will be required to re-present the above disclosures for prior periods presented in the financial statements (IFRS 5, para 34).

FRS 102

If the financial statements of the Tracer Group were prepared in accordance with FRS 102 *The Financial Reporting Standard applicable in the UK and Republic of Ireland*, the accounting treatment recommended in this case solution would apply, except in relation to the following issues.

Borrowing costs (Issue (a) (ii) in this case solution)
In respect of borrowing costs that are directly attributable to the acquisition, production or construction of a qualifying asset, FRS 102 permits an entity to:

- capitalise these costs as part of the cost of the asset; or
- recognise these costs as an expense in profit or loss in the period in which they are incurred (FRS 102, para 25.2).

In this case solution, under IAS 23, Tracer Limited was required to capitalise costs of €45,500 relating to the construction of a new office building.

FRS 102 would alternatively permit Tracer to write off the borrowing costs of €45,500 to profit or loss in the period in which they are incurred. If this policy is adopted by the Tracer Group, the following journal adjustment will be required to write off the interest costs.

	DR €000	CR €000
Finance costs – P/L	45.5	
Bank		45.5

The depreciation charge for the period would then be based on an asset cost that does not include capitalised borrowing costs. The following journal entry would therefore be required.

	DR €000	CR €000
Depreciation expense – P/L	18.9	
Accumulated depreciation		18.9

(Being depreciation on head office building as follows:

(€4.17m – €400k) × 2% × 3/12))

Government grants (Issue (b) in this case solution)

FRS 102 requires government grants to be recognised according to either the performance model or the accrual model (FRS 102, para 24.4). The use of the latter model is required by IAS 20. Additionally, FRS 102 does not permit a government grant to be offset against the cost of a related asset.

The performance model requires an entity to recognise grants in income when performance-related conditions (if any) are satisfied, and when the grant proceeds are received or receivable.

If Comps Limited had used the accrual model, as permitted by FRS 102, the accounting treatment would be the same as that outlined in this case solution.

However, if Comps Limited had recognised the grant in 2x04 in accordance with the performance model of FRS 102, the following entry would be required in July 2x05 when the grant becomes repayable.

	DR €000	CR €000
Cost of grant repayment – P/L	100	
Grant repayment liability – SOFP		100

Disposal of shares (Issue (d) in this case solution)

FRS 102 states that goodwill shall be considered to have a finite life, and that it should be amortised on a systematic basis over its life. If an entity is unable to make a reliable estimate of the useful life of goodwill, the life shall not exceed five years (FRS 102, para 19.23).

Airlight Limited had been acquired by Tracer Limited on 1 January 2x02, with goodwill of €4.5 million arising on the acquisition. In accordance with FRS 102, this goodwill would be considered to have a finite life. On the assumption that the Tracer Group has not decided to use an alternative useful life, the maximum period of five years is assumed to apply in this case.

Therefore, under the requirements of FRS 102, goodwill would have been amortised by €900,000 in 2x02, 2x03 and 2x04.* Consequently, in 2x05, when Tracer disposed of 60% of Airlight Limited's shares, the group profit on disposal of €1.2 million (computed under IFRS), would be increased to €3.9 million.

* It is assumed that goodwill is not amortised in the year that the group loses control over a subsidiary.

SOLUTION TO VERSATILE GROUP

Turnbull Bramston & Co.

Memorandum

To: **Frank DeCourcey**

From: **A. Senior**
Date: **24 February 2x06**

Re: **Versatile Group**

Further to our recent meeting I have now had the opportunity to review the issues arising in respect of the audit of the Versatile Group for the year ended 31 December 2x05. I will deal with each issue in turn.

Issue (a) – Disposal of Excess Limited

(i) *Separate financial statements of Versatile Limited*
Excess Limited will have been recorded at cost as a financial asset in the financial statements of Versatile Limited. Subsequent adjustments will have been made only in respect of dividends received/receivable from Excess Limited.

The profit on disposal will be computed as the net disposal proceeds, less the original cost of investment – see the journal entry in (iii) below.

IAS 37 *Provisions, Contingent Liabilities and Contingent Assets,* requires a provision to be recognised when:

- an entity has a present obligation as a result of a past event;
- it is probable that an outflow of resources will be required to settle the obligation; *and*
- a reliable estimate can be made of the amount of the obligation (IAS 37, para 14).

As a result of the sale of Excess Limited, Versatile has an obligation to repay any unrecorded liabilities to the purchaser. Thus, it will be necessary to provide for unrecorded liabilities of €10 million in respect of the indemnity provided by Versatile Limited.

(ii) *Group financial statements*

In accordance with IFRS 3 *Business Combinations,* goodwill arising on the acquisition of Excess Limited will have been calculated as the future economic benefits arising from assets acquired that are not individually identified and separately recognised (IFRS 3, Appendix A).

IFRS 10 *Consolidated Financial Statements* requires that a subsidiary be consolidated up to the date that a parent ceases to exercise control over it (IFRS 10, para 20). On 30 September 2x05, Versatile Limited disposed of its entire shareholding in Excess Limited, and therefore ceased to exercise control over it from that date.

If a parent loses control over a subsidiary, in accordance with IFRS 10, it should (IFRS 10, para 25):

- derecognise the assets and liabilities of the former subsidiary from the consolidated SOFP;
- recognise any investment retained in the former subsidiary at its fair value when control is lost; and
- recognise the gain or loss associated with the loss of control.

In respect of the disposal of Excess Limited, this is represented as follows:

	€000
Consideration received	250,000
Non-controlling interests at date of disposal (€115m × 20%)	23,000
	273,000

Less:

Assets less liabilities of the subsidiary at their carrying amounts at the date that control is lost (€40m + (€100m – €25m))	(115,000)
Unrecorded liabilities (Note 1)	(10,000)
Goodwill (€62m – (€40m × 80%))	(30,000)
Profit on disposal of Versatile Limited – consolidated SOCI P/L	118,000

Note 1: this is an adjusting event, in accordance with IAS 10 *Events after the Reporting period.*

The journal entries to effect the above are outlined in (iii) below.

Group revenue will be reduced by €187.5 million (€200 million × 125% × 9/12) in respect of goods sold by Mercer Limited to Excess Limited from 1 January 2x05 to the date of disposal. Group cost of sales will be reduced by an equivalent amount. No adjustment will be required in respect of intra-group profit on inventory, as Excess Limited is no longer a subsidiary of the Group at 31 December 2x05.

See the journal entries in (iii) below.

(iii) Journal entries

	DR € million	CR € million
Separate Financial Statements of Versatile Limited		
Investment in Excess Limited	62	
Bank		62
(Being purchase of shares in Excess Limited several years ago)		
Bank	250	
Investment in Excess Limited – P/L		62
Indemnity provision – SOFP		10
Profit on disposal of Excess Limited – P/L		178
(Being profit on disposal of Excess Limited on 30 September 2x05)		
Group Financial Statements		
Identifiable net assets	40	
Goodwill (€62m – (€40m × 80%))	30	

Bank		62
Non-controlling interests – SOFP		8

(Being purchase of shares in Excess Limited several years ago)

Revenue	187.5	
Cost of Sales		187.5

(Being elimination of intragroup sales for
9 months ended 30 September 2x05
i.e. €200m × 125% × 9/12)

Net assets	75	
Consolidated retained earnings		60
Non-controlling interests – SOFP		15

(Being post-acquisition retained profit of
Excess Limited)

Bank	250	
Non-controlling interests – SOFP	23	
Net assets		115
Goodwill		30
Indemnity provision – SOFP		10
Profit on disposal – P/L		118

(Being disposal of Excess Limited)

(iv) *Disclosure requirements*

In the financial statements of Versatile Limited, the profit on disposal of €178 million will be disclosed separately in the statement of comprehensive income or in the notes, in accordance with IAS 1 *Presentation of Financial Statements* (IAS 1, para 97). A similar disclosure will be required in the Group financial statements in respect of the Group's profit on disposal of €118 million.

The disposal of Excess Limited is a discontinued operation, as defined by IFRS 5 *Non-current Assets Held for Sale and Discontinued Operations* (IFRS 5, Appendix A). This is based on the fact that Excess was a **component** of the group (i.e. its operations and cash flows were clearly distinguishable), and it was a separate major line of business. The following disclosures are required:

- The sum of the post-tax profit or loss of the discontinued operation and the post-tax gain on disposal should be presented as a single amount on the face of the statement of comprehensive income (IFRS 5, para 33(a)).

- Detailed disclosure of revenue, expenses, pre-tax profit or loss, and related income taxes is required either in the notes, or on the face of the statement of comprehensive income in a section distinct from continuing operations (IFRS 5, para 33(b)).
- The net cash flows attributable to the operating, investing and financing activities of the discontinued operation. These disclosures may be presented either in the notes or on the face of the financial statements (IFRS 5, para 33(c)).

IAS 24 *Related Party Disclosures* regards fellow subsidiaries, Mercer and Excess, as being related parties, because they are members of the same group (IAS 24, para 9). Intragroup sales in the period 1 January 2x05–30 September 2x05 will be cancelled on consolidation, therefore no disclosure requirement arises in respect of the Group financial statements.

Disclosure will be required, however, in the individual financial statements of Mercer Limited and Excess Limited of sales of €187.5 million by Mercer to Excess arising in the nine months ended 30 September 2x05.

Issue (b) – Revaluation of Land

The accounting treatment of this asset will be determined in accordance with IAS 16 *Property, Plant and Equipment.*

At 31 December 2x04 the land was revalued to €80 million, reflecting its development potential. This treatment was fully in accordance with IAS 16, which permits companies to adopt a revaluation policy as long as it applies to all assets in the same class (IAS 16, para 29).

Due to the local council's decision not to allow the shopping centre to proceed, the asset suffered an impairment as there was a reduction in its future economic benefits, and it was reduced to a valuation of €30 million at 31 December 2x05. In accordance with IAS 36 *Impairment of Assets,* this write-down should be offset against a previous surplus on the same asset, any excess being charged to profit or loss (IAS 36, para 60).

It will be necessary to provide for deferred tax on the remaining revaluation surplus (IAS 12, para 15). The fact that deferred tax was not provided previously constitutes an error. It is unlikely, however, to be considered a material error in view of the group's size and the fact that the gain on the asset was unrealised and therefore not recognised in profit or loss. Thus, retrospective restatement is **not** required.

Journal entries

	DR € million	CR € million
Land	15	
Bank		15
(Being purchase of land in 2x03)		
Land	65	
Revaluation surplus – OCI		65
(Being revaluation of land at 31 December 2x04)		
Revaluation surplus – OCI	50	
Land		50
(Being impairment loss at 31 December 2x05)		
Revaluation surplus – OCI	3	
Deferred tax liability – SOFP		3
(Being deferred tax on remaining revaluation surplus of €15 million @ CGT rate of 20%)		

Issue (c) – Work in Progress/Development Site

The site acquired by Minstrel Limited would be regarded as a current asset, as it will be used by the company for the construction of retail units, is therefore akin to inventory. IAS 2 requires that inventories be valued at the lower of either cost or net realisable value; the site should not therefore have been revalued (IAS 2, para 28). It will be necessary to reverse the revaluation as follows:

	DR € million	CR € million
Revaluation surplus – OCI	15	
Land		15

(Being reversal of previous revaluation)

The following journal entries are required in respect of Contract 6211Y:

	DR € million	CR € million
Contract a/c	15.5	
Bank/trade payables		15.5
(Being production costs to date at 31 December 2x05)		
Cost of sales	12.2	
Contract a/c		12.2
(Being production costs of work certified at 31 December 2x05)		
Contract a/c	15	
Revenue		15
(Being value of work certified at 31 December 2x05)		
Trade receivables	8.8	
Contract a/c		8.8

(Being amounts invoiced on
  contract for the year ended
  31 December 2x05)		

Bank	6.3	
Trade receivables		6.3
(Being amounts received from client)		

Extracts from Financial Statements of Minstrel Limited

Statement of Comprehensive Income for the year ended 31 December 2x05

	€ million
Revenue	15
Less: cost of sales	(12.2)
Gross profit on Contract 6211Y	2.8

The profit recognised on Contract 6211Y at 31 December 2x05 cannot exceed the ultimate profit on the contract. It is necessary therefore to calculate the over-all expected outcome of the contract as follows:

	€ million	€ million
Contract price		28.5
Less:		
Costs to date	15.5	
Costs to complete	7.7	
		23.2
Estimated final profit on Contract 6211Y		5.3

As the contract is expected to provide an eventual profit of €5.3 million, it is appropriate to recognise profit of €2.8 million (i.e. value of work certified of €15 million less cost of work certified of €12.2 million) at 31 December 2x05.

Statement of Financial Position of Minstrel Limited at 31 December 2x05

	€ million
Current assets	
Amount recoverable on contracts (Note 1)	9.5
Trade and other receivables	2.5

Note 1: amount recoverable on contracts

Item	Contract 6211Y
	€ million
Costs to date	15.5
Add: recognised profits	2.8
	18.3
Less: amounts billed	(8.8)
Net amount	9.5

Issue (d) – Research & Development

(i) Expenditure incurred in connection with the 'wizmo' must satisfy the six prerequisite conditions of IAS 38 *Intangible Assets* to be classified as development costs (IAS 38, para 57). On the assumption that it does comply with these criteria, expenditure in relation to the 'wizmo' should be capitalised.

IAS 16 *Property, Plant and Equipment* states that on some occasions the future economic benefits embodied in an asset are absorbed in producing other assets. In this case the depreciation charge constitutes part of the other asset, and is included in its carrying amount (IAS 16, para 49).

As the machine purchased on 1 January 2x05 is being utilised for the 'wizmo' project, the related depreciation should therefore be capitalised as part of development costs.

(ii) Journal entries

	DR € million	CR € million
Development costs – SOFP	6.5	
Bank/trade and other payables		6.5
(Being the capitalisation of development costs in accordance with IAS 38)		
Machinery	2.5	
Bank/trade and other payables		2.5
(Being purchase of machine for development)		
Development costs – SOFP	0.5	
Accumulated depreciation		0.5
(Being depreciation for 2x05, capitalised in accordance with IAS 16)		

FRS 102

If the financial statements of the Versatile Group were prepared in accordance with FRS 102 *The Financial Reporting Standard applicable in the UK and Republic of Ireland*, the accounting treatment recommended in this case solution would apply, except in relation to the following issues.

Development costs (Issue (d) in this case solution)
The capitalisation of development expenditure that satisfies the qualifying criteria is optional under FRS 102 (FRS 102, para 18.8H).

€6.5 million development costs, incurred in connection with the 'wizmo', have been capitalised in this case solution in accordance with IAS 38. Additionally, depreciation of €500,000 on machinery being used in connection with the 'wizmo' has been capitalised as part of development costs. This accounting treatment is also permissible under FRS 102.

Alternatively, under FRS 102, Versatile Limited could opt to write-off the €6.5 million development costs to profit or loss. In this event, the €500,000 depreciation for 2x05 would also be expensed to profit or loss. The following journal entries would be required:

	DR € million	CR € million
Research and development costs – P/L	6.5	
Bank/trade and other payables		6.5
Machinery	2.5	
Bank/trade and other payables		2.5
(Being purchase of machine for development work)		
Depreciation expense – P/L	0.5	
Accumulated depreciation		0.5
(Being depreciation for 2x05)		

Sale of subsidiary (Issue (a) (ii) in this case solution)
FRS 102 states that goodwill shall be considered to have a finite life, and that it should be amortised on a systematic basis over its life. If an entity is unable to make a reliable estimate of the useful life of goodwill, the life shall not exceed five years (FRS 102, para 19.23).

Excess Limited had been acquired by Versatile Limited in 2x00, with goodwill of €30 million arising on the acquisition. In accordance with FRS 102, this goodwill would be considered to have a finite life. On the assumption that the Versatile Group has not decided to use an alternative useful life, the maximum period of five years is assumed to apply in this case.

Therefore, under FRS 102 requirements, goodwill would have been fully amortised by 31 December 2x04. Consequently, in 2x05, when Versatile Limited disposed of its entire shareholding in Excess Limited, the group profit on disposal of €118 million (computed under IFRS), would be increased to €148 million.

SOLUTION TO VORSTER GROUP

(1) General

(a) *Motor Factors Limited*

A subsidiary is defined by IFRS 10 *Consolidated Financial Statements* as 'an entity that is controlled by another entity' (IFRS 10, Appendix A). As Vorster Limited holds a majority (80%) of the voting rights in Motor Factors Limited, the latter company is therefore a subsidiary of Vorster Limited. It should be accounted for using the acquisition method, and the acquisition cost and the assets and liabilities of Motor Factors at acquisition date should be measured at fair value.

As it is impracticable to prepare interim financial statements for Motor Factors up to 31 December 2x05, the financial statements for the year ended 31 October 2x05 may be used for the purpose of preparing consolidated financial statements as these do not differ by more than three months from those used by the Group (IFRS 10, Appendix B92). The financial statements of Motor Factors should however be adjusted for the effects of significant items or events that occur between 31 October 2x05 and 31 December 20x5.

(b) *Auto Parts Limited*

A joint venture is a joint arrangement whereby the parties that have joint control of the arrangement have rights to the net assets (IFRS 11, Appendix A). Auto Parts was set up by Vorster Limited and Magnus Limited to buy scrapped cars and store the parts for sale. Vorster Limited and Magnus Limited exercise joint control over Auto Parts Limited for their mutual benefit.

Thus, Auto Parts is a joint venture and it should be accounted for using the equity method in accordance with IAS 28 *Investments in Associates and Joint Ventures*.

(c)   *Cycle Accessories Limited*

IFRS 10 *Consolidated Financial Statements* states that consolidation of an investee should cease when the investor loses control of the investee. Vorster Limited sold this subsidiary on 30 September and, in accordance with IFRS 10, it should be included in the Group financial statements as a subsidiary until that date.

Cycle Accessories constitutes a discontinued operation under IFRS 5. A single amount (€270,000) is disclosed on the face of the statement of comprehensive income, comprising the total of:

– the post-tax profit of Cycle Accessories (€188,000); and
– the post-tax gain on disposal of the disposal group constituting the discontinued operation (€82,000) (IFRS 5, para 33(a)).

See Appendix I below.

The results of Cycle Accessories will also be classified as a discontinued operation in the 2x04 comparative statement of comprehensive income.

An analysis of the results of Cycle Accessories is required, either in the notes or on the face of the statement of comprehensive income. If presented on the face of the statement of comprehensive income, it should be presented separately in a section identified as relating to discontinued operations (IFRS 5, para 33(b)).

2.   Consolidated Statement of Financial Position

Consolidated Statement of Financial Position of the Vorster Group as at 31 December 2x05*

	€000	€000
Assets		
Non-current assets		
Freehold land and bldgs @ NBV		1,200
Plant and mach. @ NBV		1,200

Goodwill	647
Investment in joint venture ((780 × 50%) − 30)	360
	3,407
Current assets	
Inventory	1,550
Trade receivables	1,500
Bank	950
	4,000
Total assets	7,407
Equity and liabilities	
Equity attributable to equity-holders	
of the parent	
Ordinary share capital	450
Capital reserves	200
Retained earnings (See Appendix I (d)(ii))	3,215
	3,865
Non-controlling interest (See Appendix I (d)(i))	207
Total equity	4,072
Non-current liabilities	
Deferred tax	25
Long-term loans	970
	995
Current liabilities	
Trade payables	1,560
Taxation	780
Total current liabilities	2,340
Total equity and liabilities	7,407

* The consolidated statement of financial position contains 100% of the assets and liabilities of Vorster Limited and Motor Factors Limited.

(3) Consolidated Statement of Comprehensive Income

Consolidated Statement of Comprehensive Income
for the year ended 31 December 2x05
(See Appendix I(a) below)

	2x05 €000	2x04 €000
Continuing Operations		
Revenue	4,000	
Cost of sales	(2,530)	
Gross profit	1,470	
Other income	330	
Distribution costs	(350)	
Administrative expenses	(475)	
Share of profit of joint venture	(210)	
Finance costs	200	
Profit before tax	985	
Income tax expense	(400)	
Profit for the period from continuing operations	585	
Profit for the period from discontinued operations	270	
Profit for the period	855	
Attributable to:		
Owners of the parent	855	

Lecture Note:

Motor Factors was acquired on 31 October 2x05, and has prepared its financial statements for the year ended 31 October 2x05. Thus, as none of its results relate to the post-acquisition period, they are not included in the consolidated statement of comprehensive income for 2x05.

Appendix I – Workings

(a) Consolidated Statement of Comprehensive Income for the year ended 31 December 2x05

	Vorster Limited	Cycle Accessories (9/12)	Total
	€000	€000	€000
Revenue	4,000	750	4,750
Cost of sales	(2,500)	(225)	(2,725)
Adjustment – inventory profit	(30)		(30)
Gross profit	1,470	525	1,995
Other income	330	–	330
Distribution costs	(350)	(90)	(440)
Administrative expenses	(475)*	(60)	(535)
Finance costs	(200)	(75)	(275)
Profit on disposal of Cycle Accessories		82**	82
Share of profit of joint venture	210		210
Profit before tax	985	382	1,367
Income tax expense	(400)	(112)	(512)
Profit for the period	375	270	855
Ret. profit @ 01/01/05	1,755	430	2,185
Ret. profit @ 31/12/05	2,130	700	3,040

*Includes write-off of professional fees relating to the acquisition of Motor Factors Limited.

** Group profit of €82,000 (rounded – see (b) (ii) below), relating to the disposal of Cycle Accessories is shown in that company's column, so as to obtain a single amount of €270,000 as the profit for the period from discontinued operations.

This amount is separately disclosed in the group statement of comprehensive income, as required by IFRS 5, para 33. It represents the sum of:

– post-tax profit of the discontinued operation of €188,000; and
– post-tax gain of €82,000 recognised on the disposal of the assets constituting the discontinued operation.

(b) Profit on Disposal of Cycle Accessories Limited

(i) *Separate financial statements of Vorster Limited*
The profit on disposal of Cycle Accessories Limited recognised in the separate financial statements of Vorster Limited is €700,000. This represents the excess of consideration received over the cost of the investment.

(ii) *Financial statements of the Vorster Group*
When a parent loses control over a subsidiary, in accordance with IFRS 10, it should:

- derecognise the assets and liabilities of the former subsidiary;

- recognise any investment retained at its fair value when control is lost; and

- recognise the gain or loss associated with the loss of control attributable to the former controlling interest (IFRS 10, para 25).

This is represented as follows:

	€000
Consideration received	900
Less:	
Assets less liabilities of the subsidiary at their carrying amounts at the date that control is lost (€1,230,000 + (€250,000 × ¾)) — €600,000	817.5
Group profit on disposal of Cycle Accessories	82.5

(c) Journal Entries

(i) *Relating to the acquisition of Motor Factors*

In accordance with IFRS 3, the following consolidation adjustments are required:

	DR €000	CR €000
Acquisition expenses – P/L Vorster Ltd	25	
Investment in Motor Factor		25
(Being professional fees previously included as cost of investment – now written off to profit or loss)		
Land & buildings	100	
Revaluation surplus – Motor Factors		75
Deferred tax liability – SOFP		25
(Being revaluation of non-current assets of Motor Factors at acquisition date)		
Revaluation surplus – Motor Factors	75	
Cost of control		60
Non-controlling interests		15
(Being allocation of revaluation surplus at acquisition date)		
Cost of control in Motor Factors	144	
Non-controlling interests	36	
Current tax payable		180
(Being accrual for income tax at acquisition date)		
Provision for reorganisation costs – SOFP	90	
Cost of control		72
Non-controlling interests		18

(Being reversal of reorganisation costs provided for in the 2x05 financial statements of Motor Factors. These are costs which the acquirer expects but is not obliged to incur in the future, and are not liabilities at the acquisition date (IFRS 3, para 11).

(ii) *Relating to the joint venture in Auto Parts*

The following consolidation adjustment is required in accordance with IAS 28:

	DR €000	CR €000
Investment in joint venture	385	
Consolidated retained earnings		385

(Being joint venturer's share of post-acquisition retained earnings of joint venture, i.e. €770,000 × 50%)

	DR	CR
Consolidated retained earnings	30	
Investment in joint venture		30

(Being elimination of Vorster Limited's share of inter-company profit on inventory: €300,000 × 1/5 × 50%)

(d) General ledger accounts

(i) *Acquisition of Motor Factors*

Cost of Control a/c in Motor Factors

	€000		€000
Investment in Mot Fact. (€1,500,000 – €25,000)	1,475	OSC	160
		Retained earnings	680
Current tax payable (€180,000 × 80%)	144	Reval. surplus (€75,000 × 80%)	60
		Reversal of provision for reorganisation expenses (€90,000 × 80%)	72
		Goodwill (Note (I))	647
	1,619		1,619

Non-controlling Interests in Motor Factors

	€000		€000
Income tax payable	36	OSC	40
		Retained earnings	
Bal. to consolidated SOFP	207	(€850,000 × 20%)	170
		Revaluation surplus	15
		Reversal of provision for	
		reorganisation expenses	18
	243		243

Retained Earnings of Motor Factors

	€000		€000
Cost of control		Balance from SOFP	850
(€850,000 × 80%)	680		
Non-controlling interests			
(€850,000 × 20%)	170		
	850		850

Note (I)

In accordance with IFRS 3, goodwill arising on acquisition is computed as follows (IFRS 3, para 32):

	€000
Fair value of consideration paid (€1,500k – €25k)	1,475
Non-controlling interests (1,035 × 20%)	207
	1,682
Less: fair value of identifiable net assets acquired	
(1,050k + €75,000* – €180,000 + €90,000)	(1,035)
Goodwill	647

*The fair value adjustment is €100,000 less a deferred tax liability of €25,000.

(ii)   Consolidated retained earnings

Consolidated Retained Earnings

	€000		€000
Elim. of intragroup profit			
on inventory	30	From SOFP of Vorster	2,885
Professional fees	25	50% of post-acq. retained	
		earnings of Auto Parts	385
Bal. to consolidated			
SOFP	3,215		
	3,270		3,270

FRS 102

If the financial statements of the Vorster Group were prepared in accordance with FRS 102 *The Financial Reporting Standard applicable in the UK and Republic of Ireland*, the accounting treatment recommended in this case solution would apply, except in relation to the following issues.

Acquisition expenses relating to the acquisition of Motor Factors Limited
(Issue 1(a) in this case solution)
FRS 102 states that the costs of a business combination will include any costs that are directly attributable to the business combination (FRS 102, para 19.11). Therefore, the professional fees of €25,000 would be included as part of the consideration paid by the Vorster Group and consequently:

*   goodwill arising on the acquisition of Motor Factors would be increased by €25,000; and
*   profit of the Vorster Group for the year ended 31 December 2x05 would be increased by €25,000.

Acquisition of Motor Factors Limited (Issue 1 (a) in this case solution)
FRS 102 states that goodwill shall be considered to have a finite life, and that it should be amortised on a systematic basis over its life. If an entity is unable to make a reliable estimate of the useful life of goodwill, the life shall not exceed five years (FRS 102, para 19.23).

Goodwill of €672,000 (as adjusted to include acquisition expenses) arose on 31 October 2x05 as a result of the acquisition of Motor Factors Limited by the Vorster Group. Assuming that goodwill is to be amortised over five years and that a full year's amortisation is charged in the year of acquisition, the following journal entry would be required in the consolidated financial statements for the year ended 31 December 2x05.

	DR €000	CR €000
Amortisation of goodwill – P/L	134.4	
Goodwill		134.4

(Being amortisation of goodwill for year ended 31 December 2x05, i.e. €672,000 × 1/5)

Joint venture (Issue 1(b) in this case solution)

FRS 102 identifies three types of investments in joint ventures. Vorster's investment in Auto Parts would be regarded as a jointly controlled entity (FRS 102, para 15.8). A venturer is required, under FRS 102, to account for a jointly controlled entity using the equity method. Therefore the method of accounting required under FRS 102 is the same as that required by IFRS 11 *Joint Arrangements*, which has been applied in this case solution.

SOLUTION TO
WEBSTER GROUP

Craughwell James & Co.

Memorandum

To: **Pamela Deane**

From: **A. Senior**

Date: **28 February 2x07**

Re: **Webster Group**

Further to our recent meeting I have now had the opportunity to review the issues arising in respect of the audit of the Webster Group for the year ended 31 December 2x06. I will deal with each issue in turn.

Issue (a) – Deferred Tax

Computation of deferred tax balance at 31 December 2x06

	€ million
(i) Temporary differences relating to the 12.5% corporation tax rate	

• **Deposit interest**
Taxable temporary difference in respect of
interest receivable at 31 December 2x06 — 2.4

• **Intragroup inventory profit**
Deductible temporary difference in
respect of intragroup profit on
inventory (€36m × 0.25 × 0.5) — (4.5)

• **Capital allowances**

Net book value at 31 December 2x06	€4,820m	
Tax written down value at 31 December 2x06	(€4,420m)	
Taxable temporary difference at 31 December 2x06		400
Net taxable temporary differences at 31 December 2x06		397.9

(ii) Temporary differences relating to the 20% capital gains tax rate

	€ million
• **Land site** Taxable temporary difference at 31 December 2x06	150
• **Investment property** Taxable temporary difference at 31 December 2x06	15
Total taxable temporary differences at 31 December 2x06	165

(iii) Deferred tax computation

Taxable temporary differences of €397.9m @ 12.5%	49.7
Taxable temporary differences of €165m @ 20%	33.0

Deferred tax liability required at 31 December 2x06	82.7
Deferred tax liability at 31 December 2x05	(20.0)
Increase in deferred tax liability at 31 December 2x06	62.7

€32.7 million of this increase in deferred tax liability will be charged to the profit or loss of the Group for the year ended 31 December 2x06. An exception, however, will be that part of the increased liability which relates to the revaluation of the land site. The revaluation surplus on the land site in 2x06 was not recorded in profit or loss, but was instead reflected in other comprehensive income. Thus, the deferred tax charge on the revaluation surplus will similarly be recorded in other comprehensive income.

The amount of the deferred tax liability relating to the land site revaluation is computed as the revaluation surplus × CGT rate, i.e. €150m × 20% = €30m.

The journal entry to reflect the increase in deferred tax liability at 31 December 2x06 is as follows:

	DR € million	CR € million
Deferred tax charge – P/L	32.7	
Deferred tax charge – OCI	30.0	
Deferred tax liability – SOFP		62.7

Issue (b) – Closure of Division

Disposal group held for sale
IFRS 5 states that an entity shall classify a non-current asset (or disposal group) as held for sale if its carrying amount will be recovered principally through a sale transaction rather than through continuing use (IFRS 5, para 6). The export division appears to qualify under this requirement, as the assets are available for immediate sale, and it is highly probable that their sale will be completed early in 2x07.

The net assets of the export division of First Limited constitute a disposal group and, as they include a non-current asset (i.e. buildings), they should be accounted for under the rules of IFRS 5 (IFRS 5, para 4).

At the 30 November 2x06 (i.e. the date on which the disposal group is classified as held for sale), the carrying amount of all the assets and liabilities in the disposal group should be measured in accordance with applicable

IFRSs. Thus, inventory should be written down from its cost of €30 million to its net realisable value of €26 million, in accordance with IAS 2 (IAS 2, para 28).

	DR € million	CR € million
Cost of sales	4	
Inventory – SOFP		4

(Being reduction of inventory to NRV @ 30 Nov 2x06)

The carrying value of the assets of the export division should not exceed their recoverable amount (IAS 36, para 59). The carrying value of the division's net assets at 30 November (after the inventory adjustment above) amounts to €68.6 million. Their recoverable amount is €63.9 million, thus necessitating the following journal adjustment:

	DR € million	CR € million
Impairment loss – P/L	4.7	
Net assets – SOFP		4.7

(Being remeasurement of net assets of export division to fair value less costs to sell – it is assumed that all of the assets of the export division fall within the scope of IAS 36)

The net assets of the division should now be classified as a disposal group held for sale (IFRS 5, para 6):

	DR € million	CR € million
Disposal group held for sale – current asset	63.9	
Net assets of export division		63.9

(Being classification of net assets of the export division as a disposal group held for sale)

The assets of the export division should be presented separately from other current assets in the consolidated statement of financial position at 31 December 2x06 (IFRS 5, para 38). It will be appropriate to classify the assets of the export division held for sale under current assets (IFRS 5, para 3).

The liabilities of the export division should be presented separately from other liabilities in the consolidated statement of financial position (IFRS 5, para 38).

The assets and liabilities of the export division should *not* be offset and presented as a single amount (IFRS 5, para 38).

Discontinued operation

IFRS 5 defines a discontinued operation as a component of an entity that has either been disposed of or is classified as held for sale. The export division of First Limited is classified as held for sale on 30 November 2x06 and is therefore a discontinued operation in the 2x06 financial statements.

The following should be presented as a single amount on the face of the consolidated statement of comprehensive income:

- €88 million, being the sum of the post-tax loss of the export division (i.e. €96m – €12m + €4m inventory write down) *plus*

- €4.7 million, being the post-tax loss recognised on the remeasurement of the export division at fair value less costs to sell (IFRS 5, para 33).

Issue (c) – Interest Costs

IAS 23 requires that costs that are directly attributable to the acquisition, construction or production of a qualifying asset shall be capitalised as part of the cost of that asset (IAS 23, para 11).

Second Limited has previously written off all interest costs to the statement of comprehensive income. In 2x06, however, it has decided to treat interest costs incurred on the construction of a new factory building as part of the cost of the asset.

Second Limited's failure to capitalise interest costs incurred during 2x05 constitutes an error. Should the error be considered material, retrospective amendment will be required in accordance with IAS 8 *Accounting Policies, Changes in Accounting Estimates and Errors.*

In accordance with IAS 23, capitalisation should commence when expenditures are being incurred, borrowing costs are being incurred and activities that are necessary to prepare the asset for its intended use or sale are in progress (IAS 23, para 20). In the case of Second Limited, this date is 1 January 2x05.

IAS 23 also requires that borrowing costs should **not** be capitalised when construction is interrupted as such costs are costs of holding partially completed assets and do not qualify for capitalisation (IAS 23, para 24). In respect of Second

Limited, therefore, interest costs incurred between 1 April 2x06 and 30 June 2x06 should be expensed to profit or loss.

Capitalisation should cease when substantially all of the activities necessary to prepare the asset for its intended use or sale are complete, which in Second Limited's case is 30 September 2x06 (IAS 23, para 25).

General overheads are **not** a directly attributable cost relating to the construction of the factory building by Second Limited, and therefore related borrowing costs should not be capitalised.

Borrowing costs that should have been capitalised in 2x05

Item	Cost € million	Timescale from commencement on 1 January 2x05 to 31 December 2x05	Annual equivalent € million
Site clearance*	46	12 months	46
Building materials	120	9 months	90
Direct labour and production overheads	60	7 months	35
Total			171

*Although site clearance is completed by 31 March 2x05, the site is not suitable for its intended use until construction work is completed on 30 September 2x06. Therefore, borrowing costs relating to the site clearance work should continue to be capitalised until 30 September 2x06 (IAS 23, para 27).

The interest rate was 7% (bank base rate + 2%) from 1 January to 31 December 2x05. When this is applied to the eligible costs of €171 million, the borrowing costs to be capitalised amount to €12 million.

As the financial statements of the Webster Group are not provided for the year ended 31 December 2x05, it is not possible to determine if this error would be regarded as being material. If it is treated as a material error, then the following adjustment would be required in the 2x06 financial statements:

	DR € million	CR € million
Land and buildings	12	
Retained earnings		12

(Being correction of interest costs expensed in 2x05, which are now capitalised by means of retrospective adjustment)

If the error is not regarded as material, the 2x06 financial statements would be adjusted as follows:

	DR € million	CR € million
Land and buildings	12	
Finance costs – P/L		12

Borrowing costs to be capitalised in 2x06

Item	Cost € million	Timescale from 1 January 2x06 to 30 September 2x06 (excluding 3-month suspension period)	Annual equivalent € million
Site clearance	46	6 months	23
Bldg mats (20x5)	120	6 months	60
Bldg mats (2x06)	140	3 months	35
Direct lab. & prod. o/h's (2x05)	60	6 months	30
Direct lab. & prod. o/h's (2x06)	100	3 months	25
Total			173

The interest rate was 8% (bank base rate + 2%) from 1 January to 30 September 2x06. When this is applied to the relevant costs of €173 million, the borrowing costs to be capitalised amount to €13.84 million (i.e. €173 million × 8%).

The following journal entry is therefore required:

	DR € million	CR € million
Land and buildings	13.84	
Finance costs – P/L		13.84

(Being correction of interest costs expensed in 2x06, which are now capitalised)

Accounting policy note

During 2x06, Second Limited changed its accounting policy for the treatment of borrowing costs that are directly attributable to the construction of a new factory building. In previous periods, Second Limited had written off such costs as an expense. Second Limited has now decided to include these costs as part of qualifying assets, as this treatment is required in accordance with the revised rules of IAS 23 *Borrowing Costs*.

Issue (d) – Revenue

The existence of a significant financing component in a contract

IFRS 15 *Revenue from Contracts with Customers* requires that, in determining the transaction price, an entity shall adjust the promised amount of consideration for the effects of the time value of money if the timing of payments provides the customer with a significant benefit (IFRS15, para 60). An entity need not adjust the promised amount of consideration, however, if the credit period is not expected to exceed one year (IFRS 15, para 63).

As the credit period allowed by First Limited does not exceed one year, the deferred payment sales will therefore be recorded as follows by First Limited in its 2x06 financial statements:

	DR € million	CR € million
Trade receivables	340	
Revenue		340

The customers who purchased goods from First Limited during 2x06 have a right to return the goods. IFRS 15 requires that an entity should account for products sold on this basis as follows:

- recognise revenue for the amount of consideration to which the entity expects to be entitled (i.e. excluding consideration for the goods expected to be returned); and
- recognise an asset (and corresponding adjustment to cost of sales) for the entity's right to recover products from customers.

Additionally, IAS 37 *Provisions, Contingent Liabilities and Contingent Assets* requires that a provision be recognised for the best estimate of the costs of refunds. The sale of the goods is an obligating event as it gives customers the right to return goods purchased, and the refund involves a probable outflow of economic resources.

Therefore, First Limited's deferred payment sales for 2x06 should be recorded as follows:

	DR € million	CR € million
Trade receivables	340	
Revenue €340m × 96%		326.4
Provision – SOFP €340m × 4%		13.6
(Being deferred payment sales for 2x06)		

	DR € million	CR € million
Inventory – SOFP €340m × 4% × $\frac{75}{100}$ × 90%	9.2	
Cost of sales		9.2
(Being goods that can be resold, following their return by customers)		

Issue (e) – Financial instruments

(i) *Loan stock*

IFRS 9 *Financial Instruments* states that, after initial recognition, financial assets should be measured at fair value or amortised cost (IFRS 9, para 5.2.1). A financial asset should be measured at amortised cost if both of the following conditions are met:

(a) the asset is held in order to collect contractual cash flows; and

(b) the cash flows are solely payments of principal and interest.

The loan stock purchased by Second Limited satisfies these conditions, and should be accounted for at amortised cost as follows:

	DR €000	CR €000
Financial asset	10,000	
Bank		10,000
(Being purchase of loan stock on 1 January 2x06)		

Financial asset	1,000	
Interest receivable – P/L		1,000
(Being interest @ 10% for y/e 31 December 2x06)		

Financial asset	1,100	
Interest receivable – P/L		1,100
(Being interest @ 10% for y/e 31 December 2x07 i.e. (€10m + €1m) × 10%)		

Financial asset	1,210	
Interest receivable – P/L		1,210
(Being interest @ 10% for y/e 31 December 2x08 i.e. (10m + €1m + €1.1m) × 10%)		

Bank	13,310	
Financial asset		13,310
(Being encashment of loan stock at maturity)		

(ii) *Purchase and disposal of shares*

IFRS 9 *Financial Instruments* states that a financial asset should be measured at fair value unless it is measured at amortised cost (IFRS 9, para 4.1.4). IFRS 9 also requires that a gain or loss should be recognised in profit or loss for most financial assets measured at fair value (IFRS 9, para 5.7.1).

Therefore the purchase and disposal by Second Limited of shares in Smile Plc should be accounted for as follows:

	DR €000	CR €000
Financial asset	85,000	
Bank		85,000
(Being purchase of equity shares on 1 January 2x06)		
Investment income receivable – SOFP	3,000	
Investment income – P/L		3,000
(Being dividend income due from Smile Plc at 31 December 2x06)		

Financial asset	12,000	
Revaluation gain – P/L		12,000

(Being remeasurement of equity shares at
  fair value at 31 December 2x06)

Bank	103,000	
Financial asset		97,000
Gain on disposal of shares – P/L		6,000

(Being gain on disposal of shares in
  February 2x07)

FRS 102

If the financial statements of the Webster Group were prepared in accordance with FRS 102 *The Financial Reporting Standard applicable in the UK and Republic of Ireland,* the accounting treatment recommended in this case solution would apply, except in relation to the following issues.

Closure of division (Issue (b) in this case solution)
The concept of a disposal group held for sale is not considered in FRS 102. Therefore the reclassification of the export division of First Limited would not occur if the Webster Group was preparing its financial statements in accordance with FRS 102.

The accounting treatment relating to the impairment of the export division's assets would, however, be the same as that outlined in this case solution.

Borrowing costs (Issue (c) in this case solution)
In respect of borrowing costs that are directly attributable to the acquisition, production or construction of a qualifying asset, FRS 102 permits an entity to:

- capitalise these costs as part of the cost of the asset; or
- recognise these costs as an expense in profit or loss in the period in which they are incurred (FRS 102, para 25.2).

The accounting treatment in this case solution would be consistent with the requirements of FRS 102 if the Webster Group had a policy, under FRS 102, of capitalising interest costs incurred in relation to the construction of the new factory building.

Alternatively, FRS 102 would permit Second Limited to write-off the borrowing costs to profit or loss in the period in which they are incurred. If this policy is adopted by the Webster Group, no adjustment will be required as borrowing costs have already been expensed in the consolidated financial statements.

SOLUTION TO
THE HAYWARD GROUP

Parker Russell & Co. Chartered Accountants

Accounting Issues Relating to the Hayward Holdings Group

Report dated 31 March 2x10

(a) **Business Rationalisation**

(b) **Head Office Building**

(c) **Flexible Packaging**

(d) **New Opportunity**

Mr Jim Hayward
Chairman
Hayward Holdings Limited
Any Street
ANYTOWN
31 March 2x10

Report on accounting issues in respect of 2x09 audit

Dear Mr Hayward,

Further to our recent discussions, please find enclosed a copy of our report which sets out the appropriate accounting treatment and disclosure requirements regarding various matters which have arisen in respect of the 2x09 audit of the various Hayward Group companies.

I look forward to discussing these issues with you in detail when we meet next week.

Yours sincerely,

A. N. Auditor

Issue (a) – Business Rationalisation

(i) *Restructuring provision*
In accordance with IAS 37 *Provisions, Contingent Liabilities and Contingent Assets,* a provision should only be recognised when:

- an entity has a present obligation (legal or constructive) as a result of a past event;
- it is probable that an outflow of resources embodying economic benefits will be required to settle the obligation; *and*
- a reliable estimate can be made of the amount of the obligation (IAS 37, para 14).

In terms of restructuring, a constructive obligation to restructure arises only when an entity (IAS 37, para 72):

- has a detailed formal plan for the restructuring, *and*
- has raised a valid expectation in those affected that it will carry out the restructuring by starting to implement that plan, or by announcing its main features to those affected by it.

The standard goes on to state that a management or Board decision to restructure does **not** give rise to a constructive obligation unless the entity has (before the end of the reporting period):

- started to implement the restructuring plan; or
- announced the main features of the plan to those affected by it in a sufficiently specific manner to raise a valid expectation to them that the entity will carry out the restructuring (IAS 37, para 75).

In this case, although Hayward Adhesives has developed a plan that has been approved in principle by the Board of Directors, the plan remains confidential and has neither been announced publicly nor discussed with those who may be affected by it. Consequently, in accordance with IAS 37, no provision should be made in the 2x09 financial statements for the costs of implementation of the exit plan.

(ii) *Non-current assets (or disposal groups) classified as held for sale, in accordance with IFRS 5*
A non-current asset (or disposal group) should be classified as held for sale if its carrying amount will be recovered principally through a sale transaction rather than through continuing use (IFRS 5, para 6).

For this to be the case, the asset (or disposal group) must be available for immediate sale in its present condition, and its sale must be highly probable (IFRS 5, para 7). A sale is highly probable if management is committed to a plan to sell the asset (or disposal group), and an active programme to locate a buyer and complete the plan has been initiated. Further, the asset (or disposal group) must be actively marketed for sale at a price that is reasonable in relation to its current fair value. In addition, the sale completion should normally be expected within one year from the date of classification (IFRS 5, para 8).

The above conditions appear to be satisfied in respect of the continuous printing equipment used by Hayward Adhesives, which constitutes a disposal group under IFRS 5 (i.e. a group of assets to be disposed of together). The equipment is available for sale, management is committed to a plan to sell (Board Decision in October 2x09), a buyer has been located (in the Far East), the price is reasonable in relation to the current fair value of the equipment, and the sale is expected to be completed within one year (the exit plan is expected to take six months to complete).

Thus, in accordance with IFRS 5, the equipment should be reclassified as a disposal group held for sale. IFRS 5 requires that, immediately before its initial classification as held for sale, the carrying amounts of a disposal group should be measured in accordance with applicable IFRSs (IFRS 5, para 18).

Applying the requirements of IAS 16 *Property, Plant and Equipment*, in respect of assets being measured under the cost model of IAS 16, such assets should be carried at cost less any accumulated depreciation and any accumulated impairment losses. To ascertain if an impairment loss has occurred in respect of the equipment of Hayward Adhesives, it will be necessary to compare its carrying value and its recoverable amount:

- Carrying value €2 million
- Value in use – very limited value, not stated
- Fair value less costs to sell €900,000.

The equipment has a recoverable amount (the higher of either the value in use or the fair value less costs to sell, as per IAS 16, para 6) of €900,000, which is less than its carrying value of €2 million. Consequently, an impairment write-down is required, and the equipment should then be reclassified as a disposal group held for sale. The following journal entries are required:

	DR €000	CR €000
Impairment write-down – P/L	1,100	
Plant and equipment		1,100
(Being impairment write-down of equipment to its recoverable amount)		
Disposal group held for sale – SOFP	900	
Plant and equipment		900
(Being reclassification of equipment as a non-current asset held for sale)		

(iii)   *Discontinued operation*

Definition
IFRS 5 defines a discontinued operation as a component of an entity that has either been disposed of or is classified as held for sale, and:

- represents a separate major line of business or geographical area of operations;
- is part of a single co-ordinated plan to dispose of a separate major line of business or geographical area of operations; *or*
- is a subsidiary acquired exclusively with a view to resale (IFRS Appendix A).

Hayward Adhesives is a component of the Hayward Group, being a separate major line of business. The net assets of this division represent a disposal group held for sale (see (ii) above), and Hayward Adhesives therefore qualifies as a discontinued operation in accordance with Appendix A of IFRS 5.

Presentation
The following should be presented as a single amount on the face of the statement of comprehensive income of Hayward Forms, and that of the Group (IFRS 5, para 33):

- The sum of the post-tax profit or loss of the discontinued adhesives operation

- The post-tax gain or loss recognised on the measurement of the equipment at fair value less costs to sell (i.e. €1.1m adjusted for tax).

Disclosure

Detailed disclosure of the following information must be provided in the financial statements of Hayward Forms Limited, and those of the Group:

– Revenue, expenses, pre-tax profit or loss and related income taxes. This can be provided either in the notes or on the face of the statement of comprehensive income, in a separate section from continuing operations. Such disclosure must cover the current and all prior periods presented in the financial statements (IFRS 5, para 33).

Issue (b) – Head Office Building

On 31 December 2x09, Hayward Holdings entered into a binding agreement to sell its head office building to Alpha Investments Ltd for €2 million. The agreement includes back-to-back put-and-call options for transfer of title to the building back to Hayward Holdings at a price calculated on the basis of €2 million plus indexation at the bank base lending rate. This option will automatically activate at the end of five years. Hayward will pay a rent to Alpha Investments based on the average daily bank rate +5%.

In accounting for this, and other transactions, the IASB *Framework Document* requires Hayward Holdings to reflect the substance of the transactions into which it has entered. The substance of this transaction may be determined by considering the position of both buyer and seller, together with their motives for agreeing to its various terms. Ownership of an asset will generally confer the following risks and benefits:

Benefits
- the benefit of any expected increase in the value of the asset; and
- benefits arising from use or development of the asset

Risks
- the risk of unexpected variation in the value of the asset; and
- the risk of obsolescence.

In this case, following the transfer of the building to Alpha Investments Ltd on 31 December 2x09, it would appear that the risks and rewards of ownership continue to be vested in Hayward Holdings. They continue to bear any obsolescence risk, and it is they who will benefit from any increase in the value of the building. It is also apparent that Alpha Investments Ltd is getting a lender's return from the funds advanced to Hayward Holdings. This return is linked to the bank interest rate rather than to any change in the value of the building.

Consequently, the substance of this transaction is that Hayward Holdings has obtained a secured loan from Alpha Investments Ltd. Hayward should continue to recognise the building in its financial statements and record the proceeds received from Alpha Investments as a liability. Interest should be accrued over the period of the advance. The building should continue to be depreciated and assessed annually for any indication of impairment.

The transaction should be reflected as follows in the financial statements of Hayward Holdings (and of the Group) at 31 December 2x09.

	DR €000	CR €000
Bank	2,000	
Loan		2,000

(Being proceeds received in respect of securitised loan)

Related party implications

Hayward Holdings and Alpha Investments Ltd are both controlled by Jim Hayward, they are therefore deemed to be related parties by IAS 24. The following information should be disclosed in the financial statements of Hayward Holdings and those of the Group (IAS 24, para 17):

- The nature of the related party relationship (subject to common control).
- Details of the transaction (securitised loan from Alpha Investments).
- Outstanding balances (amount of €2 million loan + interest which remains outstanding).
- Any other information necessary for an understanding of the potential effect of the relationship on the financial statements.

Issue (c) – Flexible Packaging

(i) *Danish customer*

Hayward Flexo has included in its sales for the year an item that was not physically despatched until after the year end.

Although a contract exists for the sale of goods by Hayward Flexo to Danobuy, the goods were not despatched until late January 2x10. The despatch of the goods represents a performance obligation that Hayward Flesco must fulfil in order for Danobuy to obtain control of the goods. Revenue cannot be recognised until this performance obligation is satisfied.

Therefore, in accordance with IFRS 15, the correct treatment is to retain the product in finished goods inventory, and to invoice the goods when they are dispatched in January 2x10.

IAS 2 states that inventory should be held at the lower of cost and net realisable value (IAS 2, para 9). In this instance cost will be lower, and should be calculated as follows:

	€000
Selling price	400
Less: profit content @ 70%	(280)
Material cost	120
Add: production overhead @ 15%	18
Inventory @ cost	138

The following journal entries are required:

	DR €000	CR €000
Revenue – P/L	400	
Trade receivables		400
(Being reversal of initial transaction)		
Inventory – SOFP	138	
Cost of sales		138
(Being inclusion of goods in inventory @ 31 December 2x09)		

(ii) *French customer*

During the year Hayward Flexo has sold product to a customer in France which has, prior to the year-end, proved to be defective.

It has been determined that Hayward Flexo will have to issue a credit note to the customer and, in addition, pay damages of €100,000. The following journal entry will be required in the 2X09 financial statements of Hayward Flexo:

	DR €000	CR €000
Revenue	500	
Compensation claim – P/L	100	
Trade and other payables		600
(Being amount payable to French customer)		

The ink supplier has indicated that it will cover part of the costs incurred by Hayward Flexo as it was partly responsible for the problems that have arisen. IAS 37 states that, where some or all of the expenditure required to settle a provision is expected to be reimbursed by another party, the reimbursement should be recognised only when it is virtually certain to be received if the entity (Hayward Flexo) settles the obligation (IAS 37, para 53). In this case, the ink supplier has offered in writing to reimburse Hayward Flexo for 50% of the costs of settling the matter.

Per IAS 37, the amount recognised for the reimbursement should be treated as a separate asset (IAS 37, para 53).

The following journal entry is required in respect of the 2x09 financial statements of Hayward Flexo:

	DR €000	CR €000
Trade and other receivables – SOFP	300	
Compensation claim – P/L		300
(Being amount of compensation receivable from ink supplier)		

Issue (d) – New Opportunity

From an accounting perspective, the key question is how should the investment in Virtual Inc. Ltd be presented in the Group financial statements. There are a number of alternatives:

- a trade investment
- an associate
- a joint venture
- a subsidiary.

A trade investment implies a limited interest, which does not give the investor significant influence. The 25% stake purchased by Hayward Holdings appears to provide the Group with significant influence over the policies of Virtual Inc., particularly as the Hayward Group has two members on that company's Board.

For the investment to qualify as a subsidiary, the investor has to control the investee (IFRS 10) – in this case the other shareholder retains a 75% stake, and therefore Hayward Holdings could not be said to control Virtual Inc.

It is clear, therefore, that Virtual Inc. is either an associate or a joint venture of the Hayward Group. An associate is defined as an entity over which the investor has significant influence, and that is neither a subsidiary nor an interest in a joint venture (IAS 28, para 3). A joint venture is a joint arrangement whereby the parties that have joint control of the arrangement have rights to the net assets.

A distinction between an associate and a joint venture is that in a joint venture no party can control the investee company on its own. In this case, there does not appear to be any contractual agreement as to control, and control has been retained by Dave Foster, who still retains 75% of the share capital of Virtual Inc.

On the basis of the above analysis, Virtual Inc. is an associate of the Hayward Group.

Accounting for Virtual Inc.

(i) *Separate financial statements of Hayward Holdings Limited*
The shares purchased in Virtual Inc. will initially be recorded as an investment at cost. Subsequently, Hayward Holdings Limited will record dividends received from Virtual Inc., along with any impairment in that company's value. The following entry, which has already been made by Hayward Holdings Limited, accurately reflects the purchase of its shares in Virtual Inc.

	DR €000	CR €000
Investment in Virtual Inc. Ltd	7,300	
Bank		7,300

(ii) *Group financial statements*
In accordance with IAS 28 *Investments in Associates and Joint Ventures,* Virtual Inc. should be accounted for in the financial statements of the Hay-

ward Group using the equity method (IAS 28, para 16). It should initially be recognised at cost, and adjusted thereafter for the post-acquisition change in the investor's share of net assets of the investee. The profit or loss of the investor should include the investor's share of the profit or loss of the investee (IAS 28, para 10). Investments in associates accounted for using the equity method should be classified as non-current assets (IAS 28, para 15).

Thus, in the financial statements of the Hayward Group, the following journal entries are required in respect of the investment in Virtual Inc.:

	DR €000	CR €000
Investment in associate	7,300	
Investments		7,300
(Being re-classification of investment)		
Investment in associate	37.5	
Share of profit of associate – consolidated P/L		37.5
(Being group share of post-acquisition earnings of Virtual Inc. – see Note 1)		

Note 1: on the assumption that the profits of Virtual Inc. are earned evenly over the year, profit earned in the period 1 October – 31 December 2x09 is €37,500 (i.e. €600,000 × 3/12 × 25%).

FRS 102

If the financial statements of the Hayward Group were prepared in accordance with FRS 102 *The Financial Reporting Standard applicable in the UK and Republic of Ireland*, the accounting treatment recommended in this case solution would apply, except in relation to the following issues.

Disposal group classified as held for sale (Issue (a) (ii) in this case solution)
The concept of a disposal group held for sale is not considered in FRS 102. Therefore the reclassification of the printing equipment of the Hayward Adhesives division in this case solution would not occur if the Hayward Group was preparing its financial statements in accordance with FRS 102.

Discontinued operation (Issue (a) (iii) in this case solution)

The FRS 102 definition of a discontinued operation does not include a disposal group held for sale. Therefore, Hayward Adhesives would not be classified as a discontinued operation in the financial statements of the Hayward Group for the year ended 31 December 2x09.

SOLUTION TO
BLACK BAY BOATS

ABC & Co. Chartered Accountants

Memorandum

To: **D. Bosse**

From: **A. Senior**

Date: **20 March 2x13**

Re: **Black Bay Boats Limited**

Further to your recent e-mail I have now had the opportunity to review the issues arising in respect of the audit of Black Bay Boats Limited for the year ended 31 December 2x12. I will deal with each issue in turn.

(1) Investment in Pleasure Craft Inc.

There are a number of accounting and disclosure issues linked to the investment in Pleasure Craft Inc. These include:

(a) How should the investment be accounted for?

(b) What value/cost should be placed on the investment, and what fair value adjustments are required to determine the net assets of Pleasure Craft Inc.?

(c) What is the value of goodwill arising on acquisition?

(d) Disclosures required.

(a) *How should the investment be accounted for?*

IFRS 10 *Consolidated Financial Statements,* defines a subsidiary as an entity that is controlled by another entity (IFRS 10, Appendix A). An investor controls an investee when the investor is exposed to, or has rights to, variable returns, and has the ability to affect those returns through its power over the investee (IFRS 10, Appendix A).

In this case therefore, at the time of the first investment of 10%, Pleasure Craft Inc. would *not* have been treated as a subsidiary. At 30 September 2x12 the total investment has increased to 50%, although a majority of the voting rights are still not controlled as the company's equity is split 50:50 between Black Bay Boats and Bill & Ted Powers. In this case Jim Kennedy has been appointed MD, and the Pleasure Craft operation is being managed as part of Black Bay Boats through the same management structures and using the same systems. It is also noteworthy that Bill and Ted Powers have withdrawn from the management of the business. Clearly, therefore, Black Bay Boats had rights, on 30 September 2x12, that gave it the ability to direct the relevant activities of Pleasure Craft Inc.

One can conclude that Black Bay Boats exercises control over Pleasure Craft Inc., and that the latter company became a subsidiary at 30 September 2x12.

(b) *What value should be placed on the investment?*

The cost of each investment was as follows:

31 March 2x12 – 10% of share capital for $1 million

30 September 2x12 – 40% of the share capital for $5 million.

At each date the $:€ rate was 1.60:1, which means that the total cost in € was €3.75 million. This is correctly accounted for in the draft financial statements of Black Bay Boats Limited.

Fair value adjustments

IFRS 3 requires that the consideration transferred in a business combination shall be measured at fair value, which shall be calculated as the sum of:

- the acquisition date fair value of assets transferred by the acquirer;
- liabilities incurred; and
- equity interests issued by the acquirer (IFRS 3, para 37).

I note the following from the background papers supplied:

- A property valuation report dated 1 January 2x12. This had been undertaken by professional valuers acting on behalf of Pleasure Craft Inc. and indicated that the company's primary property has increased by $1m in value compared to its carrying amount in the financial statements of Pleasure Craft Inc. The previous valuation was carried out in 2x07.

- A major customer of Pleasure Craft Inc. filed for bankruptcy on 1 September 2x12. At that time he owed the company $200,000. It is believed that nothing will be recovered from the bad debt.

The net assets of Pleasure Craft Inc. must be adjusted to reflect these items.

	1 January '12 $000	31 March '12 $000	30 Sept '12 $000	31 December '12 $000
Net assets per accounts	9,000	9,280	9,840	10,120
Fair value adjustments	+1,000	+1,000	+1,000 −200	+1,000 −200
Adjusted net assets	10,000	10,280	10,640	10,920

IFRS 3 also requires that where a business combination is achieved in stages, the acquirer must remeasure its previously held equity interest at acquisition date fair value (IFRS 3, para 42). The resulting gain or loss, if any, should be recognised in profit or loss (IFRS 3, para 42).

As the adjusted net asset amounts represent fair value, the value of Pleasure Craft Inc. will have increased to $10,640,000 between Black Bay Boats' initial investment of 10% on 31 March 2x12 and its additional investment of 40% on 30 September 2x12.

Thus, remeasuring the 10% stake acquired by Black Bay Boats on the 31 March 2x12 will give rise to a fair value of $1,064,000 at acquisition date (i.e. 30 September 2x12). At an exchange rate of €1 = $1.6, this amounts to €665,000. This represents a gain of €40,000 on the initial cost of investment (i.e. €625,000), and it will be recorded as follows in the Group financial statements of Black Bay Boats:

	DR €000	CR €000
Investment in Pleasure Craft	40	
Gain on restatement of investment – P/L		40

(c) *Goodwill*

IFRS 3 requires that goodwill is measured as the excess of (1) over (2) (IFRS 3, para 32):

(1) the aggregate of:

(i) the consideration transferred (€3,125,000) — i.e. $5m/1.6

(ii) the amount of any non-controlling interest in the acquiree (€3,325,000) – i.e. ($10,640,000/1.6) × 50%

(iii) in a business combination achieved in stages, the acquisition date fair value of the acquirer's previously held equity interest in the acquiree (€665,000) – i.e. ($10,640,000/1.6) × 10%

(2) the net of the acquisition-date amounts of the identifiable assets acquired and the liabilities assumed (measured in accordance with IFRS 3) (€6,650,000) – i.e. $10,640,000/1.6

Thus, goodwill = (€3,125,000 + €3,325,000 + €665,000) – €6,650,000

= €465,000

(d) *Accounting record of acquisition of shares in Pleasure Craft Inc.*

(i) Separate financial statements of Black Bay Boats

	DR €000	CR €000
Investment in Pleasure Craft Inc.	625	
Bank		625
(Being purchase of 10% of Pleasure Craft)		
Investment in Pleasure Craft Inc.	3,125	
Bank		3,125
(Being purchase of 40% of Pleasure Craft)		

(ii) Group financial statements of Black Bay Boats

	DR €000	CR €000
Investment in Pleasure Craft	625	
Bank		625
(Being purchase of 10% stake in Pleasure Craft Inc.)		
Investment in Pleasure Craft	40	
Gain on restatement of investment – P/L		40
(Being remeasurement of previously held equity interest at acquisition date fair value)		
Net assets ($10,640/1.6)	6,650	
Goodwill	465	
Bank		3,125
Non-controlling interests (€6,650,000 x 50%)		3,325
Investment in Pleasure Craft (€625,000 + €40,000)		665
(Being purchase of 40% stake in Pleasure Craft Inc.)		

(e) *Disclosure*

Appendix B of IFRS 3 requires that an acquirer shall disclose specific information for each business combination that occurs during the reporting period (IFRS 3, Appendix B.64).

The following disclosure note, relating to the acquisition of Pleasure Craft Inc., is based on the illustrative examples in IFRS 3:

Para. ref.		€000
B64 (a-d)	On 31 March 2x12 Black Bay Boats acquired 10% of the outstanding ordinary shares of Pleasure Craft. On 30 September Black Bay Boats acquired 40% of Pleasure Craft and obtained control of that company by virtue of its control over policy and decision making. As a result of the acquisition, Black Bay Boats has achieved penetration into the lucrative US market.	
B64 (e)	The goodwill of €465,000 arising from the acquisition, consists largely of the increased market opportunities from combining the operations of Black Bay Boats and Pleasure Craft.	
B64 (k)	The following table summarises the consideration paid for Pleasure Craft and the amounts of the assets acquired and liabilities assumed at the acquisition date, as well as the fair value at the acquisition date of the non-controlling interest in Pleasure Craft:	
	At 30 September 2x12 **Consideration**	
B64 (f)(i)	Cash	3,125
B64 p (i)	Fair value of Black Bay Boat's equity interest in Pleasure Craft before the business combination	665
		3,790
B64 (i)	Recognised amounts of identifiable assets acquired and liabilities assumed	6,650
B64 (o)(i)	Non-controlling interest in Pleasure Craft	(3,325)
	Goodwill	465
		3,790

(2)   Foreign Currency Loan

A foreign currency loan is a monetary liability, as defined by IAS 21 *The Effects of Changes in Foreign Exchange Rates*. Under the procedures set out in IAS 21, exchange gains or losses on foreign currency borrowings would normally be reported as part of a company's profit or loss, and would flow through into the consolidated statement of comprehensive income.

Separate financial statements of Black Bay Boats
IAS 21 however states that the rules of IFRS 9 apply to hedge accounting for foreign currency items (IAS 21, para 27). The foreign currency loan may, in the case of Black Bay Boats, be regarded as a hedge against exchange rate movements in respect of its investment in Pleasure Craft Inc.

IFRS 9 defines a cash flow hedge as ". . . a hedge of the exposure to variability in cash flows that:

(i)   is attributable to a particular risk associated with . . . a recognised asset or liability . . . or a highly probable forecast transaction, *and*

(ii)   could affect profit or loss."   (IFRS 9, para 6.5.2)

The $ loan taken out by Black Bay Boats to finance its acquisition of shares in Pleasure Craft Inc. appears to qualify as a cash flow hedge. IFRS 9 stipulates that a cash flow hedge that meets the qualifying conditions should be accounted for as follows (IFRS 9, para 6.5.11):

The separate component of equity associated with the hedged item is adjusted to the lower of the following:

- the cumulative gain or loss on the hedging instrument (i.e. the $ loan) from inception of the hedge; *and*
- the cumulative change in fair value of the hedged item (i.e. investment in Pleasure Craft Inc.) from the inception of the hedge.

The gain or loss on the hedging instrument that is determined to be an effective hedge is recognised in other comprehensive income.

Any remaining gain or loss on the hedging instrument (that is not an effective hedge) is recognised in profit or loss.

Therefore, Black Bay Boats should denominate its investment in Pleasure Inc. in US dollars and compute the exchange gain/loss at the end of each accounting period, and the exchange gains or losses on the borrowings should then be offset, as other comprehensive income, against these exchange differences.

This treatment can be reflected as follows:

	$US	Rate @ acq'n	€000	Rate @ y/e	€'000
Investment	6,000	1.6	3,750	2.0	3,000
Borrowings	3,000	1.6	1,875	2.0	1,500

This means that the reduction in the fair value of the investment can be off-set against the reduction in the carrying value of the loan. The adjustment is restricted to the amount of the gain on the loan of €375,000.

	DR €000	CR €000
Loss on translation of investment – OCI	375	
Investment		375
Foreign currency loan	375	
Gain on translation of loan – OCI		375
(Being $ loan used as cash flow hedge to cover $ investment)		

Group financial statements
Hedges of a net investment in a foreign operation should be accounted for in a similar way to cash flow hedges.

(3) Revaluation of Showroom

IAS 16 permits a choice between the cost model and the revaluation model in respect of property, plant and equipment (IAS 16, para 29). It is clear that, in respect of its showroom property, Black Bay Boats has opted for the revaluation model.

Revaluation gains should be recognised in profit or loss only to the extent (after adjusting for subsequent depreciation) that they reverse revaluation losses that were previously recognised in profit or loss in respect of the same asset. All other revaluation gains should be recognised in other comprehensive income and accumulated in equity under the heading of revaluation surplus (IAS 16, para 39).

Where a revaluation gain reverses a revaluation loss that was previously recognised in profit or loss, the gain recognised in profit or loss is reduced by the amount of depreciation that would have been charged had the loss previously taken to the statement of comprehensive income not been recognised in the first place. This is to achieve the same overall effect that would have been reached had the original downward revaluation not occurred.

In this situation it is necessary to consider the following information:

- The company has been trading for 13 years, and the showroom would have been bought at the date of inception. It is assumed therefore that the year of purchase was 2x00.
- The cost of the showroom was €6.25 million.
- A full year's depreciation is charged in the year of purchase.

On the basis that the showroom was depreciated at 2% per annum on a straight-line basis, the following journal entries would have been made up to the time of the first revaluation:

	DR €000	CR €000
Depreciation expense – P/L	125	
Accumulated depreciation		125
(Being annual depreciation from 2x00–2x09 inclusive)		

A total of €1.25 million (10 years at €125,000 per year) would have been charged. Consequently, the NBV of the showroom at 31 December 2x09, prior to the first revaluation, was €5 million (€6.25m − €1.25m).

The following is a summary of subsequent events:

		€000
2x09:	Net book value at 31 December 2x09	5,000
2x10:	Asset write-down	(2,000)
		3,000
	Depreciation for year (€3 million/40 years)	(75)
	NBV at 31 December 2x10	2,925
2x11:	Depreciation for year	(75)
	NBV at 31 December 2x11	2,850
2x12:	Depreciation for year	(75)
		2,775
	Revaluation gain	3,225
	Valuation at 31 December 2x12	6,000

The above amendments 2x10–2x12 will require the following journal entries:

		DR €000	CR €000
2x10:	Impairment loss – P/L	2,000	
	PPE		2,000
	(Being write down of showroom to €3 million)		
	Depreciation expense – P/L	75	
	Accumulated depreciation		75
	(Being depreciation on showroom for 2x10)		
2x11:	Depreciation expense – P/L	75	
	Accumulated depreciation		75
	(Being depreciation on showroom for 2x11)		
2x12:	Depreciation expense – P/L	75	
	Accumulated depreciation		75
	(Being depreciation on showroom for 2x12)		
	Accumulated depreciation	225	
	PPE		225
	(Being reversal of accumulated depreciation on revaluation of showroom)		
	PPE	3,225	
	Reversal of previous impairment loss – P/L*		1,850
	Revaluation surplus – OCI		1,375
	(Being revaluation of showroom)		

* Reversal of previous impairment loss

The reversal of the previous impairment loss is restricted as follows:

	€000
Previous impairment loss charged to profit or loss	2,000
Less: additional depreciation that would have been charged had the impairment write-down not taken place: i.e. (3 years × (€125,000 – €75,000))	(150)
	1,850

Disclosure

If items of property, plant and equipment have been revalued, the following information should be disclosed (IAS 16.77):

(i) the effective date of the revaluation;

(ii) whether an independent valuer was involved;

(iii) for each revalued class of property, plant and equipment, the carrying amount that would have been recognised had the assets been carried under the cost model;

(iv) the revaluation surplus, indicating the change for the period and any restrictions on the distribution of the balance to shareholders.

(4) Black Bay Boats: Motor Craft

IFRS 15 states that when an entity (e.g. Baggio Boats) delivers a product to another party (e.g. Black Bay Boats), one must consider whether that other party has obtained control of the product (IFRS 15, Appendix B, para 77). A product that has been delivered to another party may be held in a consignment arrangement if that other party has not obtained control of the product. In this event, the other party (i.e. Black Bay Boats) would not include the goods as inventory or recognise a corresponding liability.

Indications that an arrangement is a consignment arrangement include the following (IFRS 15, Appendix B, para 78):

(i) The product is controlled by the supplying entity until a specified event occurs, such as the sale of the product to a customer.

(ii) The supplying entity is able to require the return of the product, or transfer of the product to a third party. In this case, Baggio Boats has already exercised its rights in this way.

(iii) The dealer (i.e. Black Bay Boats) does not have an unconditional obligation to pay for the product (although it may be required to pay a deposit).

It is clear, having considered these criteria of IFRS 15, that the relationship between Black Bay Boats and Baggio Boats involves consignment arrangements. Therefore Black Bay Boats should not recognise the craft held as inventory, nor should a corresponding liability be included in its financial statements. Therefore the following journal entry is required to amend Black Bay Boats' record of the deposit paid to Baggio:

	DR €000	CR €000
Trade and other receivables	100	
Trade payables		100
(Being correction of entry made for payment of deposit to Baggio Boats)		

FRS 102

If the financial statements of the Black Bay Boats Group were prepared in accordance with FRS 102 *The Financial Reporting Standard applicable in the UK and Republic of Ireland*, the accounting treatment recommended in this case solution would apply, except in relation to the following issue.

Acquisition of Pleasure Craft Inc. (Issue 1 in this case solution)
FRS 102 states that goodwill shall be considered to have a finite life and that it should be amortised on a systematic basis over its life. If an entity is unable to make a reliable estimate of the useful life of goodwill, the life shall not exceed five years (FRS 102, para 19.23).

Goodwill of €465,000 arose on 30 September 2x12 as a result of the acquisition of Pleasure Craft Inc. by Black Bay Boats Limited. Assuming that goodwill is to be amortised over five years and that a full year's amortisation is charged in the year of acquisition, the following journal entry would be required in the consolidated financial statements for the year ended 31 December 2x12.

	DR €000	CR €000
Amortisation of goodwill – P/L	93	
Goodwill		93
(Being amortisation of goodwill for year ended 31 December 2x05, i.e. €465,000 × 1/5)		

SOLUTION TO TARGET GROUP

Memorandum

To: **An Audit Manager**

From: **An Audit Senior**

Date: **14 April 2x02**

Re: **Audit of Target group**

Further to your recent request I have now undertaken a review of the various matters arising in respect of the audit of the Target Group for the year ended 31 December 2x01.

My conclusions as to the recommended accounting treatment, together with the relevant draft journal entries to adjust the financial statements, are noted in the attached schedules.

A. Senior

New Head Office Building

Using a site which the company purchased during the previous financial year, Target Holdings has constructed a new head office building. This has raised a number of accounting issues:

    (i)   Which elements of cost involved in the construction and fitting out of the premises should be capitalised in the books of Target Holdings?

    (ii)   How should the interest charges and arrangement fees incurred in relation to the premises be treated in the books of Target Holdings?

    (iii) What are the implications of part of the contract work on the fitting out of the premises being undertaken by a company in which a co-owner and director of Target Holdings is also involved?

    (iv) How should the disposal of the property to Fitzpatrick Properties be reflected in the financial statements of Target Holdings Limited for the year ended 31 December 2x01, and how should the subsequent lease be disclosed?

Issue 1 (i) – Calculation of Cost of New Head Office Building

In the non-current assets of Target Holdings at 31 December 2x01 the building has been capitalised at a total cost of €4,820,000 comprised as follows:

    (i)   Acquisition of site €2,700,000
    (ii)   Site clearance and preparation €240,000
    (iii) Construction and fitting out €1,680,000
    (iv) General administration overhead allocation capitalised €200,000.

In accordance with IAS 16, property, plant and equipment should initially be measured at its cost (IAS 16, para 15). Only those costs that are directly attributable to bringing the asset into working condition for its intended use should be included in its measurement (IAS 16, para 16). The cost of a non-current asset (whether acquired or self-constructed) comprises its purchase price and any costs directly attributable to bringing it into working condition for its intended use.

Administration and other general overhead costs that are not directly attributable should be excluded from the cost of a non-current asset. Therefore the general administrative overhead of €200,000 which has been capitalised should be excluded as follows:

	DR €000	CR €000
Administrative costs – P/L	200	
Land and buildings		200

(Being write-off of amounts previously capitalised)

IAS 16 also sets out examples of directly attributable costs which include the following (IAS 16, para 17):

    (i)   acquisition costs (such as import duties and non-refundable purchase taxes);

    (ii)   cost of site preparation;

    (iii)   initial delivery and handling costs;

    (iv)   installation costs; and

    (v)   professional fees (such as legal, architects' and engineers' fees).

Therefore, the legal fees and the architect's fees which were previously expensed to profit or loss should be capitalised.

The journal entries required are as follows:

	DR €000	CR €000
Land and buildings	90 + 220	
Legal and prof. fees – P/L		90 + 220

(Being capitalisation of amounts previously written off)

This means that the adjusted cost of the land and buildings is €4,820,000 – €200,000 + €90,000 + €220,000: i.e. €4,930,000.

Issue 1 (ii) – Capitalisation of Interest

Derek Rogers has requested that we consider whether there is any opportunity to capitalise the interest charges incurred during the development phase of the property prior to occupation.

IAS 23 *Borrowing Costs* states that borrowing costs which are directly attributable to the acquisition, construction or production of a qualifying asset shall be capitalised as part of the cost of that asset (IAS 23, para 8). A qualifying asset is an asset that necessarily takes a substantial period of time to get ready for its intended use or sale (IAS 23, para 5). Clearly the head office building of Target Holdings would be classified as a qualifying asset under IAS 23.

Where the entity has borrowed specific funds for the purpose of financing the construction of a qualifying asset, eligible costs are the actual costs incurred, less any income earned on the temporary investment of such borrowings (IAS 23.12). As Target Holdings has arranged an extension to its overdraft facility, specifically to finance the construction of the head office building, the actual borrowing costs incurred should be used in this instance.

Where borrowing costs are capitalised, the following rules apply in respect of commencement, suspension and cessation (IAS 23, para 17–25).

The commencement date for capitalisation is the date on which the entity first meets all of the following conditions:

(a)   expenditures are being incurred; *and*

(b)   borrowing costs are being incurred; *and*

(c)   activities that are necessary to prepare the asset for its intended use are in progress.

Capitalisation of finance costs should be suspended during periods in which active development is interrupted, and cease when substantially all the activities that are necessary to prepare the asset for its intended use or sale are complete. Therefore any capitalisation must cease when the building was occupied on 1 October 2x01.

Calculation of Interest to be Capitalised
Excluding the overhead allocation and including the legal and architect's fees, the eligible costs and the timescales involved are summarised below:

Item	Eligible borrowing period and interest rate	Interest to be capitalised
January 1 Certificate: Acquisition of site and legal and architect's fees €2.89 million	1 Jan–31 March @ 9% 1 April–30 Sept @ 9.75%	€65,025 €140,888

Item	Eligible borrowing period and interest rate	Interest to be capitalised
January 31 Certificate: Architect's fees and site clearance and preparation of €300,000	1 February–31 March @ 9% 1 April–30 Sept @ 9.75%	€4,500 €14,625
31 March Certificate: Construction and fitting out of €480,000	1 April–30 Sept @ 9.75%	€23,400
Total		**€248,438**

	DR	CR
	€000	**€000**
Land and buildings	248.4	
Interest charges – P/L		248.4

(Being capitalisation of interest in respect of construction costs)

In addition, it is also appropriate to include the arrangement fees of €28,700 associated with the extension of the bank overdraft, which are an attributable cost. These fees were incurred on 1 January 2x01, and would have incurred interest charges of €2,050 ((€28,700 × 9% × 3 months) + (€28,700 × 9.75% × 6 months)). This results in a total cost of €30,750, which should be capitalised as follows:

	DR	CR
	€000	**€000**
Land and buildings	30.75	
Bank charges – P/L		30.75

(Being capitalisation of bank charges in respect of construction costs)

This brings the total adjusted cost of the building at 30 September 2x01 to €5,209,150 (i.e. €4,930,000 + €248,400 + €30,750).

Depreciation
Depreciation should be charged from the time the asset is brought into use. In this case the policy is to write-off land and buildings on a straight-line over 50

years. Based on a cost of €5,209,150, the annual charge would be €104,183 and the monthly charge €8,682.

	DR	CR
	€000	€000
Depreciation – P/L	26	
Accumulated depreciation		26

(Being depreciation on the property for three months from 1 Oct to 31 Dec 2x01).

Disclosure

The financial statements should disclose:

(a)   the amount of borrowing costs capitalised during the period; and

(b)   the capitalisation rate used to determine the amount of borrowing costs eligible for capitalisation (IAS 23, para 26)

Issue 1 (iii) – Related Party Transaction

The construction and fitting out of the head office building was undertaken by Acorn Developments Ltd, which is 40%-owned by Steve Rogers, who also owns 50% of Target Holdings Limited.

Acorn and Target are not subject to joint control. In fact, Steve Rogers does not appear to control either entity. Neither is there a direct shareholding interest by one company in the other. Given his equity stake, however, it is likely that Steve Rogers exercises significant influence over both companies. Acorn Developments and Target Holdings are therefore defined as related parties (IAS 24, para 9).

Evidence of this influence is that Target has accepted a tender significantly higher than another tender, despite the fact that all three attained the required quality threshold. This would appear to indicate that through Steve Roger's interest in both companies, Acorn has been in a position to exert significant influence over Target.

The financial statements of Target Holdings, and the Group financial statements, should disclose the following information in accordance with IAS 24, para 18:

(a)   a description of the relationship between the related parties (subject to significant influence);

(b)   a description of the transactions (tender undertaken);

(c)   the amounts involved (amount of the tender);

(d)   any other information about the transaction necessary for an under-standing of the potential effect of the relationship on the financial statements (e.g. other tenders at lower amount).

Issue 2 – Disposal of Building

On 31 December 2x01 Target Holdings disposed of the property to Fitzpatrick Properties Limited for €6.5 million.

The first issue to be determined here is whether, in substance, the property has actually been sold to Fitzpatrick Properties Limited. In this case the risks and rewards of the asset have been transferred to the property company, and Target has no continuing rights, bar the tenancy under the lease. There is no obliga-tion or option to repurchase the property, and future increases in the value of the property will accrue to Fitzpatrick, not Target. The asset has therefore been disposed of by Target Holdings.

It follows therefore that the arrangement between Target Holdings and Fitz-patrick Properties constitutes a sale and lease-back agreement, and it should be accounted for under the rules of IAS 17 *Leases*. In accordance with IAS 17, a **finance lease** is a lease that transfers substantially all the risks and rewards of ownership of an asset to the lessee. An **operating lease** is a lease other than a finance lease (IAS 17, para 4).

In this case the lease period is five years and the total amount payable under the lease will be 5 × €575,000, which is only a small part of the fair value of the leased asset. The lease is clearly therefore an operating lease.

In a sale and lease-back transaction which results in an operating lease:

(i)   any profit or loss should be recognised immediately, provided it is clear that the transaction is established at fair value (IAS 17, para 61);

(ii)   if the sale price is above fair value, the excess should be deferred and amortised over the period for which the asset is expected to be used (IAS 17, para 61).

In this case, the difference between the fair value (€5.5 million) and the net book value (€5.183 million) of the recently completed head office building should be taken to profit or loss during the year ended 31 December 2x01. The excess (€1 million) should be deferred and released over the period of the lease i.e. at €200,000 per annum.

The following journal entries will be required in respect of the disposal of the property:

	DR €000	CR €000
Other payables	6,500	
Disposal account		6,500
Disposal account	5,209	
Land and buildings		5,209
Accumulated depreciation	26	
Disposal account		26
Disposal account	1,317	
Deferred income (SOFP)*		1,000
Gain on disposal – P/L		317

(Being entries necessary to reflect disposal of property)

*Excess of disposal proceeds over fair value of asset. This element of the profit is deferred, and will be amortised over the period for which the asset is expected to be used (IAS 17.61).

This means that the net effect of the disposal on profit or loss is a gain of €317,000. Subject to materiality, this should be disclosed separately in accordance with IAS 1 *Presentation of Financial Statements*.

Issue 3 – Third-party Claim

Client A
In accordance with IAS 37 *Provisions, Contingent Liabilities and Contingent Assets*, a provision should be recognised when an entity has a present obligation as a

result of a past event, when payment is probable and when a reasonable estimate can be made of the amount of the obligation (IAS 37, para 14).

Applying the definitions of IAS 37 to this instance:

- *present obligation* – this exists where it is more likely than not that a past event gives rise to a present obligation. Target Engineering has undertaken work during the period under review which has been found by its own expert witnesses to be defective. It appears almost certain that Target Engineering will have to make a financial settlement to compensate its customer.

- *payment is probable* – in order to settle the matter Target Engineering is likely to have to refund the €500,000 in respect of the original sale, as well as meeting the consequential losses incurred by Client A as a result of its defective work.

In the case of Target Engineering, it is likely that a present obligation exists and the recognition criteria are met. Therefore a provision of €750,000 should be made.

The company's insurers, however, have indicated that they will cover part of the costs required to settle the claim. Per IAS 37, where some or all of the expenditure required to settle a provision is expected to be reimbursed by another party, the reimbursement should be recognised only when it is virtually certain that reimbursement will be received if the entity (Target Engineering) settles the obligation (IAS 37, para 53). In this case the insurer has indicated in writing that it will make a settlement at up to €400,000, the limit on the insurance policy.

The following journal entries will be required:

	DR €000	CR €000
Legal claim – P/L	350	
Trade and other receivables	400	
Provision – SOFP		750
(Being provision in respect of Client A)		

This may also fall to be separately disclosed in accordance with IAS 1 *Presentation of Financial Statements*.

Issue 4 – Restructuring

IAS 37 *Provisions, Contingent Liabilities and Contingent Assets* permits a restructuring provision to be made when an entity has:

(a) A detailed formal plan for the restructuring, identifying at least:

   (i) the business or part of a business concerned;

   (ii) the principal locations affected;

   (iii) the location, function, and approximate number of employees who will be compensated for terminating their services;

   (iv) the expenditures that will be undertaken;

   (v) when the plan will be implemented; **and**

(b) has raised a valid expectation in those affected that it will carry out the restructuring by starting to implement that plan or announcing its main features to those affected by it (IAS 37, para 72).

In this instance, a plan was formulated during November 2x01 to withdraw from the pharmaceutical element of the business. The plan has already been discussed with, and communicated to, the relevant employees and their union representatives, and it is publicly known. The timetable within the plan assumes implementation commencing in February 2x02, with completion by June 2x02.

The key features of the plan are as follows:

   (i) 30 staff facing compulsory redundancy at a cost to the company of €500,000;

   (ii) 20 staff re-tasked to the Food Processing Division – re-training costs of €50,000;

   (iii) investment in new systems to support expanded Food Processing Division of €100,000.

The plan would therefore appear to fit the conditions of restructuring provisions under IAS 37. Some of the costs (i.e. the training and the system investment costs) are specifically identified by IAS 37 as not being eligible for inclusion within the restructuring provision (IAS 37, para 81). The provision for the balance of €500,000 should be created in the financial statements for the year ended 31 December 2x01.

A journal entry will be required as follows:

	DR €000	CR €000
Restructuring provision – P/L	500	
Provision – SOFP		500
(Being provision for restructuring)		

Disclosure
An entity should disclose the following for each class of provision:

(a) the carrying amount at the beginning and end of the period;

(b) additional provisions made in the period, including increases to existing provisions;

(c) amounts used (i.e. incurred and charged against the provision) during the period;

(d) unused amounts reversed during the period; and

(e) the increase during the period in the discounted amount arising from the passage of time and the effect of any change in the discount rate (IAS 37, para 84).

Impairment
In addition, Target Engineering has specialist tooling and plant and equipment which was previously utilised by the Pharmaceutical Division with a net book value of €1 million. Some of this can be redeployed to the Food Processing Division, but the remainder, which has a net book value of €250,000, can only be sold on the second-hand market for an estimated €50,000. An outline agreement to sell the equipment has already been made with a prospective buyer.

Under IAS 36 *Impairment of Assets*, all assets should be reviewed at the end of each reporting period for indications of impairment (IAS 36, para 9). Impairment is measured by comparing the carrying value of the asset with its recoverable amount. The recoverable amount is the higher of an asset's:

(i)   fair value less costs of disposal *or*

(ii) its value in use.

Fair value less costs of disposal is the amount obtainable from the sale of an asset or cash-generating unit, less the costs of disposal. Value in use is the present value of the future cash flows expected to be derived from an asset or cash-generating unit.

In this case, therefore, the fair value less costs of disposal is the value on the second-hand market i.e. €50,000. This will be higher than the value in use, which is depressed by the fact that the division will be shortly closed down, and the equipment cannot be used in another group activity.

Journal entry required:

	DR €000	CR €000
Impairment write down of equipment – P/L	200	
Plant and equipment		200
(Being write down in respect of impairment)		

IFRS 5, *Non-Current Assets Held for Sale and Discontinued Operations,* states that a non-current asset should be classified as held for sale if its carrying amount will be recovered principally through a sale transaction (IFRS 5, para 6). Thus, the specialist equipment in the Pharmaceutical Division should be reclassified as follows:

	DR €000	CR €000
Asset held for sale	50	
Plant and equipment		50

FRS 102

If the financial statements of the Target Group were prepared in accordance with FRS 102 *The Financial Reporting Standard applicable in the UK and Republic of Ireland*, the accounting treatment recommended in this case solution would apply, except in relation to the following issues.

Borrowing costs (Issue 1 (ii) in this case solution)
In respect of borrowing costs that are directly attributable to the acquisition, production or construction of a qualifying asset, FRS 102 permits an entity to:

- capitalise these costs as part of the costs of the asset; or
- recognise these costs as an expense in profit or loss in the period in which they are incurred (FRS 102, para 25.2).

In this case solution, under IAS 23, Target Holdings was required to capitalise borrowing costs of €250,450, i.e. €248,400 + €2,050, relating to the construction of a new head office building. This accounting treatment is permitted by FRS 102.

Alternatively, FRS 102 would permit Target Holdings to write-off the borrowing costs of €250,450 to profit or loss in the period in which they are incurred. If this policy is adopted, no adjustment will be required in respect of borrowing costs as Target Holdings has already charged all interest costs to profit or loss.

The depreciation charge for the period would then be based on an asset cost that does not include capitalised borrowing costs. The following journal entry would therefore be required, rather than the one that is included in this case solution.

	DR €000	CR €000
Depreciation expense – P/L	24.8	
Accumulated depreciation		24.8

(Being depreciation on head office building as follows: (€5,209,150 − €250,450) × 2% × 3/12)

Non-current asset held for sale (Issue 4 in this case solution)
The concept of a non-current asset held for sale is not considered in FRS 102. Therefore, the re-classification of the specialist tooling and plant in this case solution would not occur if the Target Group was preparing its financial statements in accordance with FRS 102.

SOLUTION TO
THE MAGNA GROUP

3 March 2x07

The Board of Directors
Magna Holdings Group
Riverview Drive
Pembroke Rd
Dublin 4

Dear Board Members,

Further to our recent meeting regarding the financial statements for the year ending 31 December 2x06, I am enclosing a report for your attention.

I will contact you shortly to arrange an appointment to discuss the matters raised in greater detail.

Yours sincerely,

Ian Cartright
Campbell Wilson & Co. Chartered Accountants

Draft Financial Statements of the Magna Group
for the year ended 31 December 2x06

Report Dated 3 March 2x07

Campbell Wilson & Co.

Chartered Accountants

Contents

(a)   Accounting treatment of investment in Sureguard Limited

(b)   Accounting treatment of investment in Clear Scan Limited

(c)   Impact of withdrawal of Canadian competitor on the financial statements of Magna Security Limited

(d)   Accounting treatment of development projects

Issue (a) Treatment of Investment in Sureguard

You have requested that we explain how the investment should be treated in the separate financial statements of Magna Holdings Limited and in the consolidated financial statements of the Group.

(i) *Separate financial statements of Magna Holdings Limited*
     The shares purchased in Sureguard will initially be recorded as an investment at cost. Subsequently, Magna Holdings Limited will record dividends received from Sureguard, along with any impairment in that company's value. The following entry, which has already been made by Magna Holdings Limited, accurately reflects the purchase of its shares in Sureguard Limited.

| | DR | CR |
	€	€
Investment in Sureguard Ltd	140,000	
Bank		140,000

(ii) *Group financial statements*
      As regards the Group financial statements, there are a number of ways in which the investment could possibly be treated. I will analyse each of these in turn:

Is it a subsidiary?
A subsidiary is an entity over which another entity (the parent) has control. Control over an investee exists when the investor is exposed to, or has rights to, variable returns and has the ability to affect those returns through its power over the investee (IFRS 10, Appendix A). In this case, although Magna holds the majority of the ordinary share capital of Sureguard, it does not have control. It must exercise control in conjunction with Standard Security Limited, and Standard Security has the power of veto over key decisions. It should therefore **not** be treated as a subsidiary.

Is it an associate?
An associate is defined as an entity over which the investor has significant influence (IAS 28, para 3). In this situation, although Magna

Holdings has the opportunity to exercise significant influence, the company is managed jointly and therefore the investment should **not** be treated as an associate.

Is it a joint venture?

A joint venture is a joint arrangement whereby the parties that have joint control of an arrangement have rights to the net assets of the arrangement (IFRS 11, Appendix A).

Joint control exists only when decisions require the unanimous consent of the parties sharing control (IFRS 11, Appendix A).

In this case, although Magna Holdings Limited owns a majority of the shares, contractual arrangements with the other shareholder, Standard Security, mean that in practice the shareholders share control over their investee. Sureguard Limited therefore should be treated as a joint venture.

The effect of the requirement in the definition, for unanimous consent, is to give each joint venturer a veto on such decisions. This veto is what distinguishes a joint venturer from a non-controlling holder of the shares in a company, because the latter, having no veto, is subject to the policies of the majority.

In this case, therefore, despite the fact that a 70% shareholding is held by Magna Holdings Limited, the investment should be treated as a joint venture and not a subsidiary.

Accounting for joint ventures

In the consolidated financial statements, an investor should include a joint venture using the equity method of accounting (IFRS 11, para 24).

The *equity method of accounting* means that the investment is initially recognised at cost, and adjusted thereafter for the post-acquisition change in the venturer's share of the joint venture's net assets (IAS 28, para 3).

The following journal entry should therefore be made to record Sureguard Limited at its cost, plus a share of its post-acquisition retained profits:

	DR €	CR €
Investment in joint venture	140,000	
Consolidated retained earnings (€200,000 @ 70%)		140,000

Transactions between a joint venturer and a joint venture

Where a joint venturer sells assets to a joint venture, and the assets are retained by the joint venture, the joint venturer shall recognise only that portion of the gain or loss that is attributable to the interests of the other venturers (IAS 28, para 28).

Therefore it will be necessary to eliminate the profit on sale of start-up equipment by Magna Security (a 100% subsidiary of Magna Holdings) to Sureguard Limited as follows:

	DR €	CR €
Profit on disposal – consolidated P/L	280,000	
Investment in joint venture		280,000
(Being elimination of investing group's share of profit on sale of equipment €400,000 @ 70%)		

Inter-company balances and transactions

Because joint ventures are not part of the Group, balances between the investor and its associates or joint ventures are **not** eliminated, and therefore unsettled normal trading transactions should be included as current assets or liabilities.

In this case, therefore, it is necessary to eliminate the Group's share of the inter-company profit arising on the sale of equipment from Magna Security to Safeguard, but it is **not** necessary to eliminate the trading balance which exists between the two companies at the end of the year, which should remain in current assets and current liabilities.

Disclosures

Inter-company transactions

Magna Security Limited (a 100% subsidiary of Magna Holdings) and Sureguard Limited (a joint venture of Magna Holdings) are related parties, as defined by IAS 24. The sale of equipment by Magna Security to Sureguard constitutes a related party transaction.

Subject to materiality, the following information should be disclosed in the financial statements of Magna Security and of the Magna Group.

- The nature of the related party relationship
- Details of the transaction (sale of equipment to Sureguard) and outstanding balances (amount due by Sureguard to the Magna Group)
- Any other information that is necessary for an understanding of the potential effect of the relationship on the financial statements (IAS 24, para 17).

Issue (b) Clear Scan Inc.

(i) Computation and recognition of goodwill

The Magna Group should recognise as an asset, goodwill acquired on its acquisition of shares in Clear Scan Inc. The goodwill should be measured as the excess of (I) over (II) below (IFRS 3, para 32):

(I) The aggregate of:
   - the consideration transferred, measured at acquisition-date fair value;
   - the amount of any non-controlling interest in the acquiree.

(II) The net of the acquisition-date amounts of the identifiable assets acquired and the liabilities assumed, measured in accordance with IFRS 3.

Thus, goodwill is computed as follows:

Consideration transferred	R $18m	
Translate @ 1.5		€12m
Net assets per accounts on 1 January 2x06	R $10.5m	
Amount of non-controlling interests in Clear Scan (20%)	R $2.1m	
Translate @ 1.5		€1.4m
Total		**€13.4m**
Identifiable net assets acquired and liabilities assumed	R $10.5m	
Translate @ 1.5		**€7m**
Goodwill (€13.4m – €7m)		**€6.4m**

IAS 36 *Impairment of Assets* requires that goodwill should, for the purpose of impairment testing, be allocated from the acquisition date to each of the acquirer's cash-generating units that is expected to benefit from the synergies of the business combination (IAS 36, para 80). In this instance it is assumed that goodwill arising on the acquisition of Clear Scan is allocated in its entirety to a single cash-generating unit (i.e. Clear Scan Inc.).

A cash-generating unit to which goodwill has been allocated must be tested for impairment annually (IAS 36, para 90). As Clear Scan was acquired one year ago, it will be necessary to review goodwill relating to its acquisition. It would, in any event, be necessary to carry out the review, as changes in circumstances would indicate that the value of goodwill may have become impaired.

The next question to consider is whether in fact goodwill has been impaired as a result of poor trading performance, both realised and anticipated.

(ii) *Impairment review*
Impairment reviews should be performed in accordance with the requirements of IAS 36 *Impairment of Assets*.

The impairment review should comprise a comparison of the carrying amount of the goodwill, with its recoverable amount (the higher of fair value less costs of disposal or value in use) (IAS 36, para 10). To the extent that the carrying amount exceeds the recoverable amount, goodwill is impaired and should be written down. The impairment loss should be recognised in profits or loss (IAS 36, para 60).

In this instance, it is assumed that the initial cost of investment of €12 million was determined, based on the projected profits of Clear Scan over the first four years, post-takeover. These were estimated to total R$22.5 million, which, converted at 1.5:1, equals €15 million **(€12 million for an 80% shareholding)**.

However, based on the first year's trading and the revised estimate of trading profits for the next three years, total profits over the four-year period are likely to be R$15 million. This would then translate to €10 million **(€8 million for an 80% shareholding)**. This constitutes the value-in-use* of the cash-generating unit, and (in the absence of fair value less costs of disposal) also its recoverable amount.

Consequently, the goodwill figure should be reduced by €4 million, from €6.4 million to €2.4 million.

This will require the following journal entry in the **financial statements of the Magna Holdings Group**.

	DR	CR
	€000	**€000**
Impairment write down – P/L	4,000	
Goodwill		4,000

As the investment in Clear Scan has suffered an impairment, an adjustment will also be necessary to the **separate financial statements of Magna Holdings Limited**, as follows:

	DR	CR
	€000	**€000**
Impairment write down – P/L	4,000	
Investment in Clear Scan Limited		4,000

This write down should be separately disclosed in both sets of financial statements, in accordance with the requirements of IAS 1 *Presentation of Financial Statements*.

---

*It is assumed that the profits of the first four years provide an estimate of the present value of the future cash flows of Clear Scan.

Issue (c) Portable Metal Detectors – Reversal of Past Impairment

IAS 36 *Impairment of Assets* requires that an entity should assess at each reporting date whether there is any indication that an impairment loss recognised in prior periods, for an asset other than goodwill, may no longer be required or may have decreased. If any such indication exists, the entity should estimate the recoverable amount of that asset (IAS 36, para 110).

A reversal of an impairment loss for an asset (other than goodwill) should be recognised immediately in profit or loss, to the extent that the original impairment was charged to profit or loss. The reversal in the statement of comprehensive income is however restricted by the amount of any depreciation/amortisation that would have been charged had no impairment loss been written off in previous periods. Any remaining balance of an impairment reversal should be regarded as a revaluation (IAS 36, para 117–121).

IAS 36 also states that a reversal of an impairment loss for a cash-generating unit should be allocated to the assets of the unit, except for goodwill, pro rata with the carrying amounts of those assets (IAS 36, para 122). These increases in carrying amounts should be treated as reversals of impairment losses for individual assets, as outlined in the previous paragraph.

Events and circumstances, such as the withdrawal of a major competitor, act as triggers for an impairment review and may indicate that the recoverable amount of an asset has increased. This is the case in respect of Magna Security's equipment, whose recoverable amount appears to have increased in value as the result of a major competitor having to withdraw its products from sale.

The equipment was brought into use by Magna Security on 1 January 2x00, as part of a cash-generating unit, comprising a production line and associated tooling. Therefore, three years' depreciation had been charged at €200,000 per annum at the time of the impairment on 1 January 2x03. This resulted in a net book value of €1.4 million, which was written off in its entirety as an impairment write-down.

Subsequent depreciation which would have been charged between 1 January 2x03 and 1 October 2x06 (3 years and 9 months) amounts to €750,000. Therefore, the equipment should be reinstated at €650,000 (i.e. €1,400,000 less €750,000).

Thus, the previous impairment should be reversed as follows:

	DR €	CR €
Plant and equipment	650,000	
Reversal of impairment loss – P/L		650,000
(Being reversal of previous impairment loss)		
Depreciation expense – P/L	50,000	
Accumulated depreciation		50,000

(Being depreciation for 3 months from 1 October 2x06 – 31 December 2x06

$$= \quad €650,000 \times \frac{3 \text{ months}}{39 \text{ months}})$$

Should the equipment be increased to a higher amount than €650,000, any excess will be regarded as a revaluation, and will therefore not be credited to profit or loss.

Issue (d) – Development Projects

The recognition of an item as an intangible asset requires an entity to demonstrate that the item meets (IAS 38, para 18):

(i) the definition of an intangible asset
(ii) the recognition criteria of IAS 38, para 21, require that the expected future economic benefits that are attributable to the asset will flow to the entity, and that the cost of the asset can be measured reliably.

Project A
Project A, which is development phase research, appears to meet the criteria for deferment under IAS 38, para 57, which requires that an entity can demonstrate all of the following:

– technical feasibility;
– intention to complete the intangible asset and use or sell it;
– its ability to use or sell the intangible asset;
– how the intangible asset will generate future economic benefits;
– the availability of adequate resources to complete and use or sell the intangible asset; and
– its ability to measure reliably the expenditure attributable to the intangible asset during its development.

On the assumption that Project A satisfies the foregoing conditions, Magna Medical must capitalise the expenditure relating to the development of Project A. The accounting treatment that has been adopted is correct and no further adjustments are necessary.

Project B

During 2x06 the company commenced contract development work for another medical product company (Star Monitors Limited), developing circuitry for use in human heart monitors. Title to the intellectual property will transfer to Star Monitors on completion of the development work. Costs incurred plus an agreed mark-up profit will be paid in full by Star Monitors. Magna Medical has to date incurred €250,000 of costs on this project. Star Monitors made a payment on account of €100,000 in respect of this work in December 2x06.

On 31 December 2x06, control over the asset has yet to pass to Star Monitors and Magna Medical has still to satisfy its performance obligations under the contract. Therefore no revenue is recognised, in accordance with the requirements of IFRS 15 *Revenue from Contracts with Customers*.

However, work that Magna Medical has done on behalf of Star Monitors is fully recoverable. It is therefore an asset, in the form of work in progress, and it should be included as an asset at 31 December 2x06, to the extent that Magna has not yet been reimbursed by Star Monitors.

It should be accounted for as follows:

	DR €	CR €
Work in progress – SOFP	250,000	
Capitalised development costs – SOFP		250,000
(Being research costs incurred by Magna Medical – reclassified as work in progress)		
Capitalised development costs – SOFP	100,000	
Work in progress – SOFP		100,000
(Being reclassification of costs reimbursed to Magna Medical)		

FRS 102

If the financial statements of the Magna Group were prepared in accordance with FRS 102 *The Financial Reporting Standard applicable in the UK and Republic of Ireland*, the accounting treatment recommended in this case solution would apply, except in relation to the following issues.

Joint venture (Issue (a) in this case solution)
FRS 102 identifies three types of investments in joint ventures. Magna Holdings' investment in Sureguard Limited would be regarded as a jointly controlled entity (FRS 102, para 15.8). A venturer is required to account for a jointly controlled entity using the equity method. Therefore, the method of accounting required under FRS 102 is the same as that required by IFRS 11 *Joint Arrangements*, which has been applied in this case solution.

Development costs (Issue (d) in this case solution)
The capitalisation of development expenditure that satisfies the qualifying criteria is optional under FRS 102 (FRS 102, para 18.8H).

The capitalisation of €450,000 in this case solution, relating to **Project A** (in accordance with IAS 38), is a permissible treatment under FRS 102.

Alternatively, under FRS 102, Magna Medical could opt to write off the €450,000 development costs to profit or loss. In this event, the expenditure, which is currently recorded as development costs, would be reclassified as follows.

	DR €000	CR €000
Research and development costs – P/L	450	
Development costs		450

The accounting treatment of **Project B** in this case solution is consistent with the requirements of FRS 102.

SOLUTION TO HARRINGTON MOTORS LIMITED

Memorandum

To:	**Patrick Harrington**
From:	**A. N. Accountant**
Subject:	**Accounting Issues re Expansion**
Date:	**February 2x06**

Further to our recent meeting, I have set out below my recommendations regarding the accounting treatment and disclosure of the accounting issues relating to the proposed business expansion.

Issue (a) New Dealership – Consignment Inventory

IFRS 15 states that a product that has been delivered to another party may be held in a consignment arrangement if that other party has not obtained control of the product, in which case the goods should not be recognised as inventory by the party holding them, nor should a corresponding liability be recognised.

Harrington Motors can return any or all of the cars to the manufacturer at any stage without incurring a penalty. Consequently, the manufacturer continues to bear the risk of obsolescence and other commercial risks. This can therefore be regarded as a consignment arrangement.

Therefore the inventory is not an asset of Harrington Motors Limited, and it should not be included in the statement of financial position until control has been transferred. The notes to the financial statements should explain the nature of the arrangement, the amount of consignment inventory held at the year end and the main terms under which it is held.

Journal entries required:

	DR €000	CR €000
Trade payables	170	
Purchases		170
(Being reversal of purchases in respect of goods acquired on a sale or return basis)		
Cost of sales	170	
Inventory – SOFP		170
(Being removal of goods in respect of which control has not passed to Harrington Motors)		

Issue (b) Premises

(i) *Lease*

This type of lease is dealt with by IAS 37 *Provisions, Contingent Liabilities and Contingent Assets*, which states that:

> "If an entity has a contract that is onerous, the present obligation under the contract shall be recognised and measured as a provision (IAS 37, para 66)."

In this instance:

- Harrington Motors is committed to making payments on a leased premises, which it is not occupying and which can not be re-let to another user.
- There is a present obligation as a result of a past obligating event, i.e. the signing of a lease contract, giving rise to a legal obligation.
- The transfer of economic benefits is probable.
- The amount of the liability can be estimated with reasonable certainty.

Thus, the amounts payable under the lease satisfy the conditions for a provision, and the best estimate of the unavoidable lease payments should be recognised as a liability.

Journal entry required:

	DR €000	CR €000
Rental charge – P/L	720	
Provision – SOFP		720

(Being provision for amounts payable under onerous lease contract)

If the effect of the time value of money is material, IAS 37 requires that the amount of a provision shall be its present value (IAS 37, para 45). Thus, consideration should be given to discounting the above provision to its present value.

The following details should be disclosed in the financial statements for the year ended 31 December 2x05 (IAS 37, paras 84–85):

(I)   A brief description of the nature of the obligation, and expected timing of payment, together with an indication of any uncertainties.
(II) Details of the movement in the provision (increase of €720,000) and the closing balance (€720,000).

Subject to its materiality, the provision charged to profit or loss should also be separately disclosed, in accordance with IAS 1 *Presentation of Financial Statements*.

(ii) Costs to be capitalised in respect of new building

IAS 16 *Property, Plant and Equipment* states that, at recognition, an asset shall be measured at its cost (IAS 16, para 15).

IAS 16 also states that the cost of an item of property, plant and equipment comprises (IAS 16, para 16):

- its purchase price
- any directly attributable costs
- the initial estimate of the cost of dismantling and removing the asset.

In the case of Harrington Motors, costs amounting to €1.68 million have been capitalised in respect of the construction of a new purpose-built showroom and workshop. It may, however, not be appropriate to capitalise certain of these costs:

• Harrington Motors has capitalised €100,000 of revenue lost during relocation as part of the premises' cost. IAS 16 excludes the *costs of opening a new facility*, and the *costs of conducting business in a new location* from being capitalised as part of an item of property, plant and equipment (IAS 16, para 19).

This amount should therefore be excluded from the cost of the new premises, and the following journal entry is required:

	DR €000	CR €000
Lost revenue – P/L	100	
Premises		100

(Being reversal of amounts capitalised)

Depreciation has not been charged on a correct basis by the bookkeeper, who has charged two months' depreciation on the total costs capitalised in the financial statements (i.e. €1,680,000 × 2/12 × 2%) = €5,600.

The accounting policy of Harris Motors is to charge a full year's depreciation in the year of acquisition. Therefore the correct charge is a full year's depreciation at 2%, based on the correct capitalised figure of €1,580,000, excluding land of €1,030,000. This amounts to €11,000.

Journal entry required:

	DR €000	CR €000
Depreciation expense – P/L	5.4	
Accumulated depreciation		5.4

(Being correction of depreciation charge on new premises for the year ended 31 December 2x05)

(iii) Valuation of premises

IAS 16 states that an entity has the choice of using the cost model or the revaluation model in respect of each entire class of property, plant and equipment (IAS 16, para 29).

As Patrick Harrington is anxious to strengthen the statement of financial position of Harrington Motors, it seems likely that the revaluation policy will be adopted in respect of the new custom-built showroom. In this event, the premises should be carried at its fair value at the date of revaluation, less any subsequent accumulated depreciation and subsequent impairment losses (IAS 16, para 31).

IFRS 13 *Fair Value Measurement* states that the highest and best use of a non-financial asset (to market participants) might be obtained through its use in combination with other assets as a group. It is likely, in the case of Harrington Motors, that the highest and best use of the premises would be achieved by combining it with the other assets of the business as a going concern. On that basis, its existing use value of €1.9 million should be used as the fair value of the premises in the financial statements.

Journal entry required:

	DR €000	CR €000
Accumulated depreciation	11	
Premises		11
(Being elimination of accumulated depreciation at the time of revaluation)		
Premises	331	
Revaluation surplus – OCI		331
(Being revaluation of premises to fair value €1.9 million – €1.58 million + €11,000)		

The following information should be disclosed where assets are stated at revalued amounts (IAS 16, para 77):

- Effective date of valuation.
- Whether an independent valuer was involved.
- Methods and assumptions applied in estimating fair value.
- Extent to which fair value was determined with reference to observable prices in an active market, or using other valuation techniques.
- The carrying amount that would have been recognised under the cost model.
- The revaluation surplus, indicating the change for the period and any restrictions on the distribution of the balance to shareholders.

Lecture note: The question states that the tax implications of adjustments should be ignored. If this were not the case, Harrington Motors would be required to provide for deferred tax in respect of the revaluation surplus, in accordance with IAS 12 *Income Taxes*.

Issue (c) – New Equipment

IAS 16 states that the costs of testing whether an asset is functioning properly should be regarded as directly attributable costs (IAS 16, para 17).

Additionally, IAS 16 states that costs incurred, while an item capable of operating in the manner intended by management has yet to be brought into use (or is operated at less than full capacity), should be expensed (IAS 16, para 20).

Applying these requirements to the new equipment of Harrington Motors:

- The various essential costs (totalling €25,000) incurred during the commissioning period should be capitalised.
- Costs of €45,000 were incurred during the initial operating period as, due to slack demand, the equipment was used only intermittently. These costs must be expensed, in accordance with IAS 16, and cannot be capitalised as part of the cost of the equipment.

Journal entry required:

	DR €000	CR €000
Plant and equipment	25	
Expenses – P/L		25

(Being the capitalisation of essential commissioning costs, which had been expensed to profit or loss)

Issue (d) – New Customer

The lease of cars to the local firm over three years constitutes an operating lease, as defined by IAS 17 *Leases* (IAS 17, para 4). This standard requires that any asset held for use in operating leases by a lessor should be carried in the statement of financial position of the lessor (IAS 17, para 49). In this case, the cars should be recorded as a non-current asset by Harrington Motors.

In accordance with IAS 17, the depreciation policy for leased assets should be consistent with the lessor's normal depreciation policy for similar assets, and depreciation should be calculated in accordance with IAS 16 (IAS 17, para 53). As the cars are expected to be traded in every three years by Harrington Motors, they should be depreciated over this period net of their expected residual value.

In the case of an operating lease, no selling profit should be recognised by a dealer lessor (such as Harrington Motors), as the transaction is not the equivalent of a sale (IAS 17, para 55).

IAS 17 states that *rental income* receivable by a lessor from an operating lease should normally be recognised as income on a straight-line basis over the lease period (IAS 17, para 50). In the case of Harrington Motors, however, it will be appropriate to recognise income in accordance with the payment schedule (€200,000 in year 1, €100,000 in year 2, and €75,000 in year 3). This treatment is justified where "… another systematic basis is more representative of the time pattern in which use benefit derived from the leased asset is diminished" (IAS 17, para 50). In the case of car rental, it can be assumed that the quality of use from the asset diminishes in line with age. Alternatively, the rental income could be recognised on a straight-line basis.

Note: accounting by lessors is beyond the scope of this book.

Issue (e) – Potential Acquisition

(1)   Separate financial statements of Harrington Motors Limited

(i)   Outright purchase of 100% of the share capital of Focus Ltd
The investment in Focus Limited will be shown either at *cost* or in accordance with IFRS 9 (IAS 27, para 10). In accordance with company policy, the former basis will apply and the following journal entry would be required:

	DR €000	CR €000
Investment in Focus Ltd	4,000	
Bank		1,000
Share capital		500
Share premium		2,500

(Being purchase of 100% of shares in Focus Limited)

(ii)   Purchase of an 18% stake in Focus Limited
An associate is defined as an entity over which the investor has significant influence (IAS 28, para 3).

Significant influence is defined as the power to participate in the financial and operating policy decisions of the investee, but is not control or joint control of these policies (IAS 28, para 3). If an investor holds 20% or more of the voting power of the investee, it is presumed that the investor has significant influence, unless it can be clearly demonstrated that this is not the case. Conversely, if the investor holds less than 20% of the voting power, it is presumed that the investor does not have significant influence, unless such influence can be clearly demonstrated (IAS 28, para 5).

IAS 28 identifies representation on the board of directors as providing evidence of significant influence (IAS 28, para 6). Thus, although only 18% of the shares in Focus Limited are held by Harrington Motors, it is probable that significant influence is still exercised through board representation.

An investment in an associate shall be accounted for in an investor's separate financial statements either at cost, in accordance with IFRS 9, or using the equity method as described in IAS 28 (IAS 27, para 10). In accordance with company policy, the former basis will apply and the following journal entry would be required:

	DR €000	CR €000
Investment in Focus Limited	850	
Bank		850
(Being purchase of 18% of Focus Limited)		

(2)   *Consolidated financial statements*

(a)   Accounting treatment

- **100% purchase – subsidiary**
  IFRS 10 *Consolidated Financial Statements* defines a subsidiary as an entity that is controlled by another entity (IFRS 10, Appendix A). Focus Limited will be a subsidiary undertaking of Harrington Motors Limited, and IFRS 3 stipulates the following requirements in relation to the preparation of consolidated financial statements:

(i) All business combinations to be accounted for by the acquisition method (IFRS 3, para 4).

(ii) The consideration transferred should be measured at fair value, which should be calculated as the sum of the acquisition-date fair values of the assets transferred by the acquirer, the liabilities incurred by the acquirer to the former owners of the acquiree and the equity interests issued by the acquirer (IFRS 3, para 37).

(iii) The acquirer shall measure the identifiable assets acquired and the liabilities assumed at their acquisition-date fair values (IFRS 3, para 18).

(iv) The acquirer shall recognise goodwill as (ii) above plus the amount of any non-controlling interest in the acquiree less (iii) above (IFRS 3, para 32).

The following consolidation adjustments will be necessary when incorporating Focus Limited into the consolidated financial statements:

	DR €	CR €
Net assets	3,196,192*	
Goodwill	803,808	
Investment in Focus Limited		4,000,000

*(Non-current assets €2,867,198** + Current assets €1,482,615) –
(Current liabilities €978,121 + L. T. liabilities €175,500)
**Including revaluation of property

- **18% purchase – associate**
  In the consolidated financial statements, IAS 28 *Investments in Associates and Joint Ventures* requires that all associates be accounted for using the equity method.

The cost of investing in Focus Limited will already have been recorded in the separate financial statements of Harrington Motors at 30 June 2x06. No further adjustment will be necessary, at that date, in order to incorporate Focus Limited into the consolidated financial statements.

- **Subsequent profits**

  For a 100% purchase

  – The profit/loss of Focus Limited arising between 1 July 2x06 and 31 December 2x06 will be included under the relevant headings in the statement of comprehensive income of the Group.
  – Intragroup trading should be eliminated.

  For an 18% purchase

  – The profit or loss of the Harrington Motors Group will include the Group's share of the profit or loss of Focus Limited from 1 July 2x06.

FRS 102

If the financial statements of Harrington Motors were prepared in accordance with FRS 102 *The Financial Reporting Standard applicable in the UK and Republic of Ireland*, the accounting treatment recommended in this case solution would apply, except in relation to the following issue.

Purchase of a subsidiary (Issue (2) (a) in this case solution)
The implications for Harrington Motors of a 100% acquisition of Focus Limited are set out above in this case solution.

Additionally, FRS 102 states that goodwill shall be considered to have a finite life, and that it should be amortised on a systematic basis over its life. If an entity is unable to make a reliable estimate of the useful life of goodwill, the life shall not exceed five years (FRS 102, para 19.23).

Goodwill of €803,808 would arise as a result of the purchase of 100% of Focus Limited. Assuming that goodwill is to be amortised over five years, and that a full year's amortisation is charged in the year of acquisition, annual amortisation of goodwill would be recorded as follows in the consolidated financial statement of Harrington Motors.

	DR €000	CR €000
Amortisation of goodwill – P/L	160.8	
Goodwill		160.8

(Being annual amortisation of goodwill, i.e. €803,808 × 1/5)

SOLUTION TO
THE O'NEILL GROUP

Grimbsy, Holt & Co.

Accounting Issues Relating to the 2x05 Financial Statements of the O'Neill Group of Companies

Report dated 16 February 2x06

Contents

Mr David O'Neill
Managing Director
The O'Neill Group
Central Road
Ballindown

16 February 2x06

Report on accounting issues in respect of 2x05 financial statements

Dear Mr O'Neill,

Further to our recent discussions, we enclose a copy of our report which sets out the appropriate accounting treatment and disclosure requirements regarding various matters which have arisen in respect of the 2x05 financial statements of the O'Neill Group.

I look forward to discussing these issues with you in detail when we meet next week.

Yours sincerely,

A. N. Accountant
Grimbsy, Holt & Co.

Issue 1 – O'Neill Retail Ltd

IFRS 15 *Revenue from Contracts with Customers* requires the following accounting treatment when customers have a right to return goods:

- recognise revenue for the amount of consideration to which the entity expects to be entitled (i.e. excluding consideration for the goods expected to be returned); and
- recognise an asset (and a corresponding adjustment to cost of sales) for the entity's right to recover products from customers.

Additionally, IAS 37 *Provisions, Contingent Liabilities and Contingent Assets* requires that a provision be recognised for the best estimate of the cost of refunds. In this regard, the sale of the goods is an obligating event as it gives customers the right to return goods purchased, and the refund involves a probable outflow of economic resources.

As O'Neill Retail has already recorded all goods sold as revenue, the following journal adjustments will be required:

	DR €	CR €
Revenue	27,500	
Provision – SOFP		27,500
(Being best estimate of return of goods purchased; €550,000 × 5%)		
Inventory – SOFP	22,000	
Cost of sales		22,000
(Being best estimate of goods, at cost, that will be recovered from customers; €27,500 × 80/100)		

If the expected level of goods is returned in January 2x06, the following journal entry will be required in 2x06:

	DR €	CR €
Provision – SOFP	27,500	
Trade receivables – SOFP		27,500
(Being return of goods in January 2x06)		

Issue 2 – Sale of O'Neill Restaurant Ltd

(a) *Treatment in Parent Company's Separate Financial Statements*

The cash received on disposal of the investment and the gain on that disposal will be recorded in the parent company's separate financial statements. The gain will be the difference between the consideration received and the carrying value of the investment.

	€
Disposal proceeds	175,000
Cost of investment	(3,000)
Profit on disposal	172,000

The following journal entry is required in respect of the disposal:

	DR €	CR €
Cash/bank	175,000	
Investment at cost		3,000
Profit on disposal – P/L		172,000

Given its materiality, the profit on disposal should be separately disclosed, in accordance with IAS 1 *Presentation of Financial Statements*.

(b) *Treatment in Group Financial Statements*

If a parent loses control over a subsidiary, in accordance with IFRS 10, it should:

- derecognise the assets and liabilities of the former subsidiary;
- recognise any investment retained in the former subsidiary at its fair value at the date when control is lost; and
- recognise the gain or loss associated with the loss of control (IFRS 10, para 25).

O'Neill Restaurant will cease to be consolidated as a subsidiary of the O'Neill Group on 31 December 2x05, and its income and expenses are included in the consolidated financial statements until that date (IFRS 10, para 20). At that date, by virtue of O'Neill Enterprises being able to exercise significant influence over O'Neill Restaurant, it will become an associate of the Group (IAS 28, para 3).

The following journal entry will be required in the Group financial statements in respect of the disposal, and the reclassification of O'Neill Restaurant as an associate:

	DR €	CR €
Bank	175,000	
Non-controlling int.* (€156,000 × 40%)	62,400	
Investment in associate**	154,000	
Net assets		156,000
Profit on disposal – P/L		235,400

   *Non-controlling interest: (net assets of O'Neill Restaurant @ 31/12/2x05 × 40%)

   **Investment in associate (fair value of retained 30% interest on date of disposal as given in question)

Presentation and Disclosure

- O'Neill Restaurant was a subsidiary of the O'Neill Group up to 31 December 2x05. Its operations and cash flows were clearly distinguishable from the rest of the group, and it was therefore a component of the group, in accordance with IFRS 5 *Non-current Assets Held for Sale and Discontinued Operations* (IFRS 5 Appendix A).

- A discontinued operation is a component of an entity that meets the conditions outlined in paragraph 32 of IFRS 5. For a component to be classified as a discontinued operation it must be held for sale, or already disposed of, and meet one of the following criteria:

> – It must represent a major line of business or geographical area of operations.
> – It must be part of a single co-ordinated plan to dispose of a separate major line of business or geographical area of operations.
> – It must be a subsidiary acquired exclusively with a view to resale.

As O'Neill Restaurant was a major line of business in the O'Neill Group, the disposal of a controlling interest in that company constitutes a discontinued operation, in accordance with IFRS 5.

Disclosures required

(i) In the statement of comprehensive income:
A single amount, being the total of the after-tax profit or loss of the discontinued operation, and the after-tax gain or loss from disposing of the assets comprising the discontinued operation (IFRS 5, para 33). This disclosure is also required for prior periods presented in the financial statements (IFRS 5, para 34).

(ii) In the notes or on the face of the statement of comprehensive income (IFRS 5, para 33):

> – The revenue, expenses and pre-tax profit or loss and the income tax expense of the discontinued operation.
> – The gain or loss on disposal of the subsidiary.
> – The net cash flows attributable to the operating, investing and financing activities of the subsidiary.

This disclosure is also required for prior periods presented in the financial statements (IFRS 5, para 34).

(iii) Additional disclosures in the notes for assets that have been sold in the current period (IFRS 5, para 41):

> – A description of the non-current asset.
> – A description of the facts and circumstances of the sale.
> – The gain or loss recognised and, if not separately presented on the face of the statement of comprehensive income, the caption in the comprehensive income statement that includes that gain or loss.

(c) Treatment in 2x06 Consolidated Financial Statements

As and from 31 December 2x05, O'Neill Restaurant meets the definition of an associate under IAS 28 *Investment in Associates and Joint Ventures,* on the basis that the O'Neill Group exercises significant influence and O'Neill Restaurant is neither a subsidiary nor a joint venture of the group (IAS 28, para 3).

In accordance with IAS 28, O'Neill Restaurant should be accounted for in the consolidated financial statements of the O'Neill Group in 2x06 using the equity method (IAS 28, para 16). The investment should initially be recognised at cost (in this case, the fair value at 31 December 2x05 represents deemed cost), and adjusted thereafter for the investor's share of the post-acquisition change in the investee's net assets.

The profit or loss of the investor should include the investor's share of the profit or loss of the investee (IAS 28, para 3). Investments in associates should be classified as a non-current asset (IAS 28, para 15).

Issue 3 – Potential Acquisition of Reid Enterprises Ltd

(a) Accounting policies

Valuation of property
IAS 16 *Property, Plant and Equipment* requires that an entity should apply either the cost model or the revaluation model to an entire class of property, plant and equipment (IAS 16, para 29).

Reid Enterprises applies the revaluation model in respects of its premises. Where the revaluation model is chosen, IAS 16 requires that assets be carried at their fair value at the date of the revaluation, less any subsequent accumulated depreciation and subsequent impairment losses (IAS 16, para 31).

Deferred tax
IAS 12 *Income Taxes* requires that full provision be made for almost all temporary differences. Thus, in providing for deferred tax in respect of the temporary difference arising on the revaluation of its premises, Reid Enterprises is in full compliance with IAS 12. Although no agreement has been entered into for the sale of the premises, it is still necessary to provide for deferred tax on the revaluation of the building. Further, IAS 12 does not permit a deferred tax liability to be discounted.

Related parties
Except for the identity of an entity's parent, IAS 24 *Related Party Disclosures* does not require the disclosure of the names of related parties. Thus, Reid Enterprises is not required to disclose the names of related companies with whom transactions have taken place. The nature of the related party relationship must, however, be disclosed.

(b) Goodwill arising on the purchase of Reid Enterprises

	€
Consideration	2,000,000
Net assets at fair value*	(849,850)
Goodwill	1,150,150

*As the non-current assets of Reid Enterprises are at market value, and as a deferred tax liability has been recognised in respect of the revalued premises, no further fair value adjustments are required.

(c) *Journal entry required to incorporate the trade and assets of Reid Enterprises Ltd into the books at 1 January 2x06*

	DR €	CR €
Goodwill	1,150,150	
Non-current assets	2,100,000	
Current assets	2,350,000	
Current liabilities		2,100,150
Long-term liabilities		1,100,000
Provisions		400,000
Bank		2,000,000

The acquisition of Reid Enterprises will require disclosure as a non-adjusting event after the reporting period, in accordance with IAS 10 *Events after the Reporting Period*. Disclosure of the nature of the event will be required, as well as an estimate of the financial effect (IAS 10, para 21).

FRS 102

If the financial statements of the O'Neill Group were prepared in accordance with FRS 102 *The Financial Reporting Standard applicable in the UK and Republic of Ireland*, the accounting treatment recommended in this case solution would apply, except in relation to the following issue.

Potential acquisition of Reid Enterprises Ltd (Issue 3 in this case solution)
It has been agreed in principle that the trade, assets and liabilities of Reid Enterprises will be purchased on 1 January 2x06. The accounting implications of this transaction have been outlined above in this case solution.

Additionally, FRS 102 states that goodwill shall be considered to have a finite life, and that it should be amortised on a systematic basis over its life. If an entity is unable to make a reliable estimate of the useful life of goodwill, the life shall not exceed five years (FRS 102, para 19.23).

Goodwill of €1,150,150 would arise as a result of the purchase of Reid Enterprises. On the assumption that goodwill is to be amortised over five years, annual amortisation of goodwill would be recorded as follows in the consolidated financial statements of the O'Neill Group.

	DR €000	CR €000
Amortisation of goodwill – P/L	230	
Goodwill		230

(Being annual amortisation of goodwill, i.e. €1,150,150 × 1/5)

SOLUTION TO
FITZWILLIAM GROUP

(a) **Fitzwilliam Construction Ltd**

Construction Contract under IFRS 15

Accounting treatment

The ultimate outcome of the contract should be estimated as follows:

	€000	€000
Contract price		1,700
Less:		
Costs to date	920	
Completion costs	850	
Provision for clean up	200	1,970
Estimated loss		270

This expected loss must be recognised in full.

Revenue for the period is computed as the value of work certified of €880,000. Allowing for the expected loss of €270,000, cost of sales will therefore be €1,150,000.

The contract account is shown below:

Contract Account

Bank	920,000	Cost of sales	1,150,000
Provision for clean up	200,000	Balance c/f	850,000
Revenue	880,000		
	2,000,000		2,000,000

Extract from Financial Statements

Statement of Comprehensive Income for the year ended 31/12/2x05

	€
Revenue	880,000
Cost of sales	(1,150,000)
Gross loss	270,000

Statement of Financial Position as at 31/12/2x05

	€
Current assets	
Amount recoverable on contract	850,000
Current liabilities	
Bank overdraft	920,000
Provision for clean up	200,000
Net liabilities	270,000
Equity	
Accumulated loss	270,000

Journal entries:

	DR €	CR €
Contract a/c	920,000	
Bank		920,000
(Being costs to date on contract)		
Cost of sales – P/L	1,150,000	
Contract a/c		1,150,000
(Being costs to date transferred to cost of sales)		
Contract a/c	880,000	
Revenue – P/L		880,000
(Being revenue recognised on contract)		

Provision

IAS 37 states that a provision should be recognised when (IAS 37, para 14):

- an entity has a present obligation (legal or constructive) as a result of a past event;
- *it is probable that an outflow of resources will be required to settle the obligation; and*
- a reliable estimate can be made of the amount of the obligation.

In the case of Fitzwilliam Construction, there is a constructive obligation (giving rise to a valid expectation on the part of those affected by it) that the entity will clear up contamination, together with the probable transfer of economic benefits; a provision of €200,000 is therefore required.

	DR €	CR €
Contract a/c	200,000	
Provision – SOFP		200,000

The following disclosures are required (IAS 37, para 84):

- Amount of the provision at the beginning and end of the period.
- Additional provisions made in the period.

- A brief description of the nature of the obligation and the expected timing of any resulting outflows of economic benefits.
- An indication of the uncertainties about the amount or timing of outflows.

Additional disclosures required

The disclosures required in respect of construction contracts are outlined in IAS 11, paras 39–45:

- Amount of contract revenue recognised as revenue in the period.
- Method for determining revenue.
- Method for determining stage of completion.
- Gross amount due from customers.
- Aggregate of costs incurred, recognised losses and retentions.
- Advances received.
- Amount of retentions.

(b) Fitzwilliam Rental Ltd

(i) Year ended 31 December 2x05

Docklands Property

The disused building was purchased at a cost of €1.5 million on 1 January 2x05. At that time the intention was to develop the property and subsequently to let it to professional firms. IAS 40 defines investment property as "… property … held to earn rentals or for capital appreciation or both" (IAS 40, para 5).

At the time of its purchase, the building purchased by Fitzwilliam Rental therefore qualifies as investment property under IAS 40. The acquisition cost of €1.5 million plus the renovation cost of €300,000 will be included as investment property in the statement of financial position.

On 31 December 2x05 the property will be carried at fair value of €2 million, in accordance with the accounting policy of Fitzwilliam Rental. The gain of €200,000 will be recognised in profit or loss for the year ended 31 December 2x05 (IAS 40, para 35).

	DR	CR
	€	€
Investment property	200,000	
Gain on revaluation of investment property – P/L		200,000

If it is considered material, the work carried out by Fitzwilliam Construction Ltd should be disclosed as a related party transaction under IAS 24 *Related Party Disclosures*. The following disclosures will be required by IAS 24, para 17:

- The nature of the related party relationship (parties subject to common control by Fitzwilliam Group Ltd).
- Information about the transaction (€200,000 work done by Fitzwilliam Construction Ltd).
- Details of outstanding balances.

(ii) Year ending 31 December 2x06

Docklands property

In February 2x06 the docklands property was valued at €2.1 million, and the Group decided to relocate its headquarters to this building. Owner-occupied property is excluded from being treated as investment property (IAS 40, para 9). Thus, the docklands property is reclassified at that date, and will then be dealt with under the rules of IAS 16.

At the time of commencement of owner-occupation, the fair value at the date of change of use is deemed to be the 'cost' of the property under its new classification (IAS 40, para 60). The increase in value of €100,000 (€2.1 million – €2 million) up to the date of transfer should be recorded in profit or loss.

	DR	CR
	€	€
Investment property	100,000	
Gain on revaluation of investment property – P/L		100,000
PPE	2,100,000	
Investment property		2,100,000

Disclosures

- The fact that Fitzwilliam Rental uses the revaluation model for investment property (IAS 40, para 75).
- Amounts recognised in profit or loss (IAS 40, para 75).

Old Group headquarters

In February 2x06 Fitzwilliam Rental managed to secure new tenants for this property. The old headquarters therefore become investment property at this date. This represents a transfer from owner-occupation to investment property, and the old headquarters will now be dealt with under IAS 40.

IAS 16 should be applied up to the date of reclassification. Any difference arising between the carrying amount under IAS 16 at that date, and the fair value, is accounted for as a revaluation under IAS 16 (IAS 40, para 61).

The book value of the property was €1.5 million, and the market value at the date of letting in February 2x06 was €1.8 million. Thus, the increase of €300,000 is recorded as a revaluation surplus prior to reclassification, and it is **not** included in profit or loss.

	DR	CR
	€	€
PPE	300,000	
Revaluation surplus – OCI		300,000
Investment property	1,800,000	
PPE		1,800,000

(iii) Air conditioning and heating system

IAS 16, para 13 states that parts of some property, plant and equipment may require replacement at regular intervals. Such parts will be included in property, plant and equipment when the cost is incurred, if the recognition criteria of the standard are met. The standard also requires that each significant part of an item of property, plant and equipment should be depreciated separately.

Thus, the building and air conditioning system are treated as separate assets and depreciated over their respective useful lives:

The depreciation of the building for the year ending 31 December 2x06 will be €1,900,000 × 10/12 × 1/50 = €31,667.

The depreciation of the heating system for the year ending 31 December 2x06 will be €200,000 × 10/12 × 1/10 = €16,667.

(c) Fitzwilliam Retail Ltd

In March 2x05, Fitzwilliam Retail sold one of its department stores to a third party and entered into a 10-year operating lease to lease back the store at a market rental.

IAS 17 *Leases* states that, if it is clear that the transaction is carried out at fair value, the profit or loss should be recognised immediately (IAS 17, para 61).

The following journal entry will be required:

	DR	CR
	€	€
Bank	2,500,000	
Property, plant and equipment		2,200,000
Profit on disposal – P/L		300,000
(Being disposal of property)		

(d) Fitzwilliam Group

(i) *Proposed dividend*

On 14 January 2x06 the Board of Fitzwilliam Group Ltd proposed a dividend of €750,000 in respect of the year ended 31 December 2x05. IAS 10 *Events After the Reporting Period,* states that dividends declared after the reporting period shall not be recognised as a liability at the end of the reporting period (IAS 10, para 12). Such dividends are disclosed in the notes in accordance with IAS 1 *Presentation of Financial Statements.*

(ii) *Share options*

The Board of Fitzwilliam Group Ltd agreed to grant 50 share options to each of its 100 employees with a commencement date of 1 January

2x06. This agreement is defined as an equity settled share-based payment under IFRS 2 *Share-based Payment.*

IFRS 2 requires that as the services received from the employees do not qualify as an asset they should be recognised as expenses (IFRS 2, para 8). It also requires that the charge should be measured at the fair value of the shares or share options at the date of grant of the options (IFRS 2, para 11). IFRS 2 further requires that the expense be recognised over the vesting period (IFRS 2, para 15).

The total of the fair value of share options granted equals:

$50 \times 100 \times 20 = €100,000.$

It is likely that 25% of employees will leave during the four-year vesting period, and will therefore forfeit their rights under the share option scheme.

The total cost of the scheme is therefore likely to be €75,000 (i.e. €100,000 × 0.75). This will be expensed over the four-year vesting period, giving rise to an annual charge in the statement of comprehensive income of €18,750.

The following journal entry will be required:

	DR	CR
	€	€
Share option expense – P/L	18,750	
Equity reserve – SOFP		18,750
(In each of years 1–4)		

Disclosure requirements

IFRS 2 requires that the following information be disclosed (IFRS 2, paras 44–50):

- Information that enables users of financial statements to understand the nature and extent of share-based payment arrangements.
- Information that enables users to understand how fair value was determined.
- Information that enables users to understand the effect of share-based transactions on the entity's profit or loss for the period and on its financial position.

FRS 102

If the financial statements of the Fitzwilliam Group were prepared in accordance with FRS 102 *The Financial Reporting Standard applicable in the UK and Republic of Ireland*, the accounting treatment recommended in this case solution would apply and no differences would arise as a result of the application of FRS 102.

SOLUTION TO
HARDING GROUP

Memorandum

From: **B. Inline**

To: **Group Financial Director, Harding plc**

Date: **1 March 2x07**

Further to our recent meeting, I have detailed below my views in respect of accounting issues arising in respect of the financial statements for the year ended 31 December 2x06.

(a) Disposal of Golf plc

(i) *Costs included in 'Other Operating Expenses'*

Operating costs incurred
The IASB's *Conceptual Framework* states that "...the definition of expenses encompasses losses as well as those expenses that arise in the course of the ordinary activities of the entity" (Paragraph 4.33).

Operating costs incurred of €92 million appear to comply with the above definition, and they are therefore correctly included as an expense in Golf's statement of comprehensive income for the year ended 31 December 2x06.

Provision for future operating losses

IAS 37 *Provisions, Contingent Liabilities and Contingent Assets* states that "provisions shall not be recognised for future operating losses" (IAS 37, para 63). The inclusion of a provision for future operating losses of €30 million in the statement of comprehensive income of Golf is therefore in breach of the rules of IAS 37. Such losses should instead be charged to expense as incurred.

Impairment of assets

IAS 36 *Impairment of Assets* requires that an entity shall assess, at each reporting date, whether there is any indication that an asset may be impaired. If any such indication exists, the entity shall estimate the recoverable amount of the asset (IAS 36, para 9).

IAS 36 requires that, if the recoverable amount of an asset is less than its carrying amount, the carrying amount of the asset shall be reduced to its recoverable amount (IAS 36, para 59). Should an impairment loss arise, it should be recognised immediately in profit or loss (IAS 36, para 60).

Thus, the inclusion by Golf of an impairment loss of €18 million in its statement of comprehensive income is in line with the requirements of IAS 36.

(ii) *Accounting treatment of Golf in the consolidated financial statements*
Golf plc has been a loss-making subsidiary for several years, and the Board of Harding plc agreed at a Board meeting in November 2x06 to sell Golf to a third party as a going concern. A price has been agreed and final negotiations are currently under way with an expected completion date of September 2x07. The Group Financial Director is keen to exclude Golf from the consolidated financial statements as it is no longer part of continuing group operations.

IFRS 10 *Consolidated Financial Statements*, however, requires that consolidation of an investee should cease only when an investor loses control of an investee (IFRS 10, para 20).

Thus, Golf should continue to be consolidated as part of the Harding Group in the 2x06 financial statements. However, IFRS 5 requires that an entity should classify a disposal group as held for sale if its carrying amount will be recovered principally through a sale, rather than through continuing use.

Therefore, Golf should be included in the 2x06 consolidated financial statements as a disposal group held for sale. The assets of Golf will be included in current assets as a single figure, classified as a disposal group held for sale. Golf's liabilities will also be presented separately from other liabilities in the consolidated statement of financial position.

The assets and liabilities of Golf should not be reclassified as held for sale in the consolidated SOFP of previous periods.

The question also arises as to whether Golf should be classified as a discontinued operation in the 2x06 consolidated financial statements. A discontinued operation is defined as a component of an entity that has either been disposed of or is classified as held for sale (IFRS 5, Appendix A). Golf should therefore be classified as a discontinued operation in the 2x06 consolidated financial statements. A single amount should be included in the statement of comprehensive income, comprising the total of:

(i)   Golf's post-tax loss (i.e. €80m to be adjusted for tax); and
(ii) the post-tax gain or loss recognised in the measurement to fair value less costs to sell of the disposal group.

The statement of comprehensive income of prior periods should be restated as if Golf had been a discontinued operation in those periods.

(b) Harding plc Properties

(i)   *Head office property*
      The treatment of Harding's head office property is determined by IAS 16 *Property, Plant and Equipment*.

      Harding has opted to apply the revaluation model as the company's accounting policy, as permitted by IAS 16 (IAS 16, para 29). If an asset's carrying amount is increased as a result of a revaluation, the increase shall be credited to other comprehensive income and accumulated in equity under the heading of revaluation surplus (IAS 16, para 39). Where an asset's carrying amount is decreased as a result of a revaluation, the decrease shall be recognised in other comprehensive income to the extent of any credit balance existing in the revaluation surplus in respect of that asset (IAS 16, para 40).

At 31 December 2x05, Harding revalued its head office property from €20 million to €31 million. The property has later fallen in value to €29 million at 31 December 2x06. As there is a revaluation surplus of €11 million at 31 December 2x05, the decrease in value a year later will be set against the revaluation surplus on the same property.

The following journal entry will be required:

	DR € million	CR € million
Revaluation surplus – OCI	2	
Property, plant and equipment		2
(Being decrease in value of head office property at 31 December 2x06)		

(ii) *Investment property*

IAS 40 permits an entity to choose as its accounting policy – either the fair value model or the cost model (IAS 40, para 30). Harding plc owns one investment property, purchased during 2x05, and included in the financial statements at 31 December 2x05 using the cost model.

The Board wishes to employ the fair value model in respect of investment property at 31 December 2x06. This represents a change in measurement basis – it is therefore a change in accounting policy as defined by IAS 8 *Accounting Policies, Changes in Accounting Estimates and Errors* (IAS 8, para 5).

IAS 8 states that an entity is permitted to change an accounting policy only if the change:

• is required by an IFRS; *or*

- results in the financial statements providing reliable and more relevant information about the effects of transactions, other events or conditions on the entity's financial position, financial performance or cash flows (IAS 8, para 14).

In respect of Harding plc's decision to adopt the fair value model for its investment property, this is *not* required by an IFRS. Thus, if the shift to the fair value model is to be permissible under IAS 8, it must result in the financial statements providing reliable and more relevant information. On the assumption that this is the case, Harding would be allowed to change its accounting policy and adopt the fair value model in respect of its investment property.

IAS 8 states that when an entity changes an accounting standard voluntarily it shall apply the change retrospectively (IAS 8, para 19(b)). Paragraph 23 of IAS 8 reiterates the need for retrospective application, except where it is impracticable to determine either the period-specific effects or the cumulative effect of the change.

In the case of Harding plc, therefore, the value of its investment property should be amended retrospectively at 31 December 2x05, if it is practicable to make this adjustment. If not, the increase in value should be effected entirely in the 2x06 financial statements.

On the assumption that retrospective adjustment is not practicable, the increase in value of €4 million should be recognised in profit or loss in the 2x06 financial statements (IAS 40, para 35). The following journal entry will be required:

	DR € million	CR € million
Investment property	4	
Revaluation gain – P/L		4
(Being gain on revaluation of investment property at 31 December 2x06)		

(c) Holly plc

(i)   *Final net asset valuation of Holly*

IFRS 3 *Business Combinations* recognises that it is not always possible to accurately determine the value of some assets at the date of acquisition. In these circumstances, IFRS 3 states that provisional values should be used in an entity's financial statements during the measurement period for the items for which the accounting is incomplete (IFRS 3, para 45). However, the measurement period shall not exceed one year from the acquisition date (IFRS 3, para 45).

In respect of the acquisition of Holly plc on 1 March 2x05, goodwill was provisionally computed based on a net asset value of €8 million. The final valuation, which became available in December 2x06, shows a net asset value of €7 million. As this information was not available within 12 months of the acquisition date, no adjustment to the provisional value is permitted under IFRS 3. An exception to this rule is only permissible in order to correct a material error, in accordance with IAS 8 *Accounting Policies, Changes in Accounting Estimates and Errors* (IFRS 3, para 50).

If the adjustment of €1 million relates to the correction of a material prior-period error, accounting for the business combination will be amended as follows;

	DR	CR
Goodwill	€1m	
Net assets		€1m

Otherwise, the €1million should be charged to profit or loss for the year ended 31 December 2x06:

	DR	CR
Impairment loss – P/L	€1m	
Net assets		€1m

(ii) *Development costs*

IAS 38 *Intangible Assets* distinguishes between the research phase and the development phase of work carried out by an entity (IAS 38, para 52).

Research phase

In the research phase of an internal project, an entity cannot demonstrate that an intangible asset exists that will generate probable future economic benefits (IAS 38, para 54). The standard states that no intangible asset arising from research shall be recognised (IAS 38, para 54). It goes on to require that expenditure on research should be recognised as an expense as it is incurred (IAS 38, para 54).

The research carried out by Holly plc in 2x05 was written off, as management was not sufficiently confident of the ultimate profitability of the project. This treatment was correct, as the project at that stage would have been regarded as being in a research phase.

IAS 38 states that expenditure on an intangible item that was initially recognised as an expense shall not be recognised as part of the cost of an intangible asset at a later date (IAS 38, para 71). Thus, the expenditure incurred by Holly in 2x05 cannot be capitalised in 2x06, even though the project may have entered a development phase by that time.

Development phase

IAS 38 sets out the criteria which must be satisfied if an intangible asset arising from the development phase of an internal project is to be recognised. An entity must be able to demonstrate all of the following (IAS 38, para 57):

- Technical feasibility.
- Intention to complete the intangible asset and use or sell it.
- Ability to use or sell the asset.
- How the intangible asset will generate probable future economic benefits.
- Availability of adequate technical, financial and other resources to complete the project.
- Ability to measure reliably the expenditure attributable to the intangible asset during its development.

Holly plc's research project to develop a new chemical appears to have entered the development phase in 2x06 – production is expected to commence in the next few months, trading profits from sales are estimated at €20 million and the Board has decided to complete the project.

Thus, the expenditure incurred during 2x06, amounting to €10 million, should be capitalised as an intangible asset at 31 December 2x06.

(d) Deferred Tax Issues Relating to Prospect plc

IAS 12 *Income Taxes* requires that a deferred tax liability be recognised for most taxable temporary differences (IAS 12, para 15).

The following issues arise in respect of the deferred tax position of Prospect plc, an acquisition target of the Harding Group.

(i) *Gains on readily marketable investments*
Prospect plc has made a gain of €5 million in respect of its investments, which has been recorded as income in its financial statements. This gain will be taxed only on disposal of the investments. Thus, there is a taxable temporary difference of €5 million as the carrying value of the asset in the financial statements (i.e. cost + €5m) exceeds its tax base (i.e. cost).

As the corporation tax rate is 30%, this will give rise to a deferred tax liability of €1.5 million. This should be charged to profit or loss.

(ii) *Accrual for pension contributions*
Prospect plc intends making an additional accrual for pension costs of €1 million, which will not be allowable for tax purposes until it is paid. This is a deductible temporary difference, as the amount of the liability in the financial statements (i.e. €1m) exceeds its tax base (i.e. €nil).

As the corporation tax rate is 30%, this will reduce Prospect's deferred tax liability by €300,000. This gain will also be included in profit or loss.

The net effect of these two temporary differences is an increase in the deferred tax liability of €1.2 million. Thus, a journal entry is required as follows:

	DR €000	CR €000
Deferred tax charge – P/L	1,200	
Deferred tax liability – SOFP		1,200

FRS 102

If the financial statements of the Harding Group were prepared in accordance with FRS 102 *The Financial Reporting Standard applicable in the UK and Republic of Ireland,* the accounting treatment recommended in this case solution would apply, except in relation to the following issues.

Investment property (Issue (b) (ii) in this case solution)
FRS 102 requires that investment property is carried at fair value, if its fair value can be measured reliably without undue cost or effort. As Harding plc has opted for the fair value model under IAS 40, the application of FRS 102 would not result in any change in accounting treatment.

Development costs (Issue (c) (ii) in this case solution)
The capitalisation of development expenditure that satisfies the qualifying criteria is optional under FRS 102 (FRS 102, para 18.8H).

Development costs of €10 million incurred during 2x06 have been capitalised in this case solution in accordance with IAS 38. This is a permissible treatment under FRS 102.

Alternatively, under FRS 102, Holly could opt to write off the €10 million development costs to profit or loss. In this event, the expenditure would be accounted for as follows.

	DR € million	CR € million
Research and development costs – P/L	10	
Bank/trade and other payables		10

SOLUTION TO DARCY GROUP

To: **Mr Fitzwilliam**

Subject: **Various Accounting Issues relating to the 2x07 Financial Statements of the Darcy Group of Companies**

Date: **September 2x08**

1.   Bingley plc

(a) *Transactions with Collins plc*

Under IAS 28 *Investments in Associates and Joint Ventures*, an associate is an entity over which the investor has significant influence and that is neither a subsidiary nor an interest in a joint venture. Significant influence is defined as the power to participate in the financial and operating policy decisions of the investee, but is neither control nor joint control over those policies.

As Collins plc has a majority shareholder, Bingley plc does not exercise control over it. However, such ownership by another investor does not preclude an investor from having significant influence (IAS 28, para 5).

An investor who holds less than 20%, as is the case with Bingley plc's holding in Collins plc, is presumed not to have significant influence unless such influence can be clearly demonstrated (IAS 28, para 5).

Bingley plc is, however, represented on the Board of Directors of Collins plc and thereby participates in all major operating and financial policy decisions of the company. Material transactions also regularly take place between the two companies. Accordingly, Bingley plc does exercise significant influence over Collins plc, and the latter company should be accounted for as an associate under IAS 28.

The investment in Collins plc should therefore be accounted for under the equity method in the consolidated financial statements of the Darcy plc group.

Under this method, the investment in an associate is initially recognised at cost in the financial statements of the group, and the carrying amount is increased or decreased to recognise the investor's share of the profit or loss of the associate after the date of acquisition. The investor's share of the profit or loss of the associate is recognised in the investor's consolidated statement of comprehensive income. Distributions received reduce the carrying amount of the investment. Adjustments to the carrying amount may also be necessary for changes in the investor's proportionate interest in the investee, arising from changes in the investee's other comprehensive income. Such changes include those arising from the revaluation of property, and from foreign exchange translation differences. The investor's share of those changes is recognised in other comprehensive income of the investor (IAS 28, para 11).

Profits and losses resulting from transactions between an investor and an associate are recognised in the investor's financial statements only to the extent of unrelated investors' interests in the associate (IAS 28, para 22).

Accordingly, in relation to the development land sold by Bingley plc to Collins plc, 18% of the €200,000 profit made on the sale, i.e. €36,000, should be eliminated in the consolidated financial statements of the group.

This is a consolidation adjustment, and the following journal entry is required:

	DR €	CR €
Cost of sales – P/L	36,000	
Investment in associate		36,000

It is also worthwhile to consider how the sale of the development site will have been recorded by Bingley (and therefore also in the accounts of the group). As Bingley is engaged in property developing, the sale of a land site will be included in revenue. It will also result in a reduction in inventory.

	DR €000	CR €000
Bank/receivables	2,000	
Revenue – P/L		2,000
Cost of sales	1,800	
Inventory		1,800

Disclosure of the transaction between Bingley plc and Collins plc is also required under IAS 24 *Related Party Transactions*, as follows:

- The nature of the relationship between the parties, i.e. investor and associate.
- The amount of the transaction, i.e. €2,000,000.
- Details in relation to outstanding balances at the year end.
- Any provisions for doubtful debts and bad debts written off.

(b)   Transactions with Phillips plc

The interest acquired by Bingley plc in Phillips plc during the period should be accounted for in accordance with IFRS 11 *Joint Arrangements*.

Under IFRS 11, a joint arrangement is defined as an arrangement in which two or more parties have joint control. This is clearly the case in relation to Phillips plc.

As Bingley and the other investor share joint control over the net assets of Phillips, the latter company is a joint venture.

As required by IFRS 11 *Joint Arrangements*, Bingley must account for its interest in Phillips using the equity method.

Under the **equity method**, the investment in Phillips plc would initially be recognised at cost, and the carrying amount increased or decreased to recognise the group's share of the post-acquisition change in the net assets of Phillips plc. The group statement of comprehensive income will recognise a share of the profit or loss of Phillips plc (IAS 28, para 10).

2.   Bennett plc

(a)   Acquisition of industrial saw

IAS 17 *Leases,* deals with the accounting treatment of operating and finance leases.

A finance lease is a lease that transfers substantially all of the risks and rewards, incidental to ownership, of an asset (IAS 17, para 4). The saw has an estimated life of four years and the lease period is initially for the same period, while Bennett has an option to extend the lease by a further two years. Therefore as the agreement transfers all of the risks and rewards of ownership of the saw to Bennett, this represents a finance lease.

Accounting treatment

At the *commencement of the lease term*, lessees shall recognise finance leases as assets and liabilities in their statement of financial position, at amounts equal to the fair value of the leased asset or, if lower, the present value of the minimum lease payments, each determined at the inception of the lease (IAS 17, para 20).

As the fair value of the industrial saw is not available, the present value of the minimum lease payments is used in this case.

IAS 17 requires that the minimum lease payments shall be apportioned between the finance charge and the reduction of the outstanding liability. The finance charge shall be allocated to each period so as to produce a constant periodic rate of interest on the remaining balance of the liability (IAS 17, para 25).

Workings

(i) *Present value of minimum lease payments*

Based on a discount rate of 12%:

			€
Year 0	5,000 × 1	=	5,000
Year 1	5,000 × 0.893	=	4,465
Year 2	5,000 × 0.797	=	3,985
Year 3	5,000 × 0.712	=	3,560
			17,010

(ii) *Initial record of the lease*

	DR €	CR €
PPE	17,010	
Lease obligation – SOFP		17,010

(iii) *Allocation of lease payments between capital and interest*

Year End	Opening Capital Balance	Lease Payment	Capital Repaid	Accrued Finance Charge @ 12%	Closing Capital Balance
	€	€	€	€	€
31.12.07	17,010	(5,000)	5,000	1,441 (a)	12,010
31.12.08	12,010	(5,000)	3,559 (b)	1,014 (c)	8,451
31.12.09	8,451	(5,000)	3,986 (d)	535 (e)	4,465
31.12.10	4,465	(5,000)	4,465 (f)	0	

(a) (€17,010 – €5,000) × 12%   = €1,441
(b) (€5,000 – €1,441)   = €3,559
(c) (€12,010 – €3,559) × 12%   = €1,014

(d) (€5,000 − €1,014   = €3,986

(e) (€8,451 − €3,986) × 12%   = €535

(f) (€5,000 − €535)   = €4,465

Extract from Statement of Comprehensive Income for the year ended 31 December 2x07

	€
Depreciation (17,010/4 Years)	4,253
Finance charge	1,441

Extract from Statement of Financial Position as at 31 December 2x07

	€
Non-current assets	
Cost	17,010
Accumulated depreciation	(4,253)
Net book value	12,757
Non-current liabilities	
Finance lease	8,451 (i.e. €5,000 + €5,000) − (€1,014 + €535)
Current liabilities	
Finance lease	3,559 (i.e. €5,000 − €1,441)
Accruals (finance charge)	1,441

(b) Shipment of timber products

In relation to the shipment to the new customer, the products have been delivered to the customer with a limited right of return. Although the customer has not contacted the company to confirm its acceptance of the goods, the time period for return has elapsed before the year-end of the company. Accordingly, it must be assumed that the customer has obtained control of the goods and there is, therefore, no further uncertainty about the possibility of return. Bennett has therefore satisfied its performance obligations in respect of its contract with the new customer, and revenue of €220,000 should be recognised in accordance with IFRS 15 *Revenue from Contracts with Customers*.

The following journal entry is required:

	DR €000	CR €000
Trade receivables	220	
Revenue – P/L		220
(Being sales of goods to customer)		

In determining the accounting treatment, one should also consider whether any further information (e.g. the late return of the goods) is available after 31 December 2x07.

(c) Inventories

(i) Change in basis of inventory valuation

Under IAS 2 *Inventories,* inventories shall be measured at the lower of cost and net realisable value (IAS 2, para 9).

The cost of inventories of items that are ordinarily interchangeable should be assigned using the first in first out (FIFO) or weighted average cost formula (IAS 2, para 25).

Bennett plc's large inventories of small 'Category C' products that cannot be separately identified, fall within this category. Therefore one of the above cost formulas should be used. The use of the last in first out (LIFO) formula is not permitted under IAS 2.

The inventories of the company at 31 December 2x07 should therefore be reduced by €110,000 to reflect the first-in, first-out basis of valuation. The following journal entry is required:

	DR €000	CR €000
Cost of sales – P/L	110	
Inventories – SOFP		110
(Being reduction in inventories to reflect the FIFO cost formula)		

A change from the LIFO basis of inventory valuation to the FIFO basis is the correction of an error, which must be treated in accordance with IAS 8 *Accounting Policies, Changes in Accounting Estimates and Errors.*

However, as the cost of these items did not move significantly in the past, it is likely that the FIFO and LIFO figures would not have been materially different. Therefore, it is not necessary to make a prior-period adjustment.

(ii) Reversal of NRV write-down

Where the cost of inventories may not be recoverable, it is appropriate to write the inventories down below cost to net realisable value (IAS 2, para 28).

Bennett plc undertook such a write-down in the year ended 31 December 2x06 in relation to Product X items included in its inventories. However, market conditions have now changed and the items could be sold for more than cost at 31 December 2x07.

In these circumstances it is appropriate to reverse the write-down so that the new carrying amount is the lower of cost and the revised net realisable value. The reversal is limited to the amount of the original write-down to ensure that the inventories are not valued at an amount that is higher than their cost (IAS 2, para 33).

Such a reversal should be treated as a reduction in the amount of inventories recognised as an expense in the period in which the reversal occurs (IAS 2, para 34).

In this case, the original cost of the inventory of €190,000 should be reinstated.

The following journal entry is required:

	DR €000	CR €000
Inventories – SOFP	60	
Cost of sales – P/L		60
(Being reversal of NRV write-down due to changed circumstances)		

(d) Grant Assistance

Under IAS 20 *Accounting for Government Grants and Disclosure of Government Assistance,* government grants should not be recognised until there is reasonable assurance that:

- the entity will comply with the conditions attaching to them; and
- the grants will be received (IAS 20, para 7).

Government grants related to assets may be presented in the statement of financial position either by setting up the grant as deferred income or by deducting the grant in arriving at the carrying amount of the asset. However, the latter method is prohibited by company law. The treatment of the grant as deferred income by Bennett plc is therefore appropriate (IAS 20, para 24).

Bennett plc has received a grant of €900,000 (€1,500,000 × 60%) during the year ended 31 December 2x07. The two conditions relevant to the grant are the hire of additional staff and the purchase of specified items of plant. While the former condition has been met, the latter has only been met in relation to €720,000 (€1,200,000 × 60%) of the grant. As the purchase of further plant is subject to cash flow considerations, Bennett plc's compliance with the conditions is not yet assured.

Accordingly, €720,000 of the grant should be accounted for as a separate category of deferred income in the year ended 31 December 2x07. The remaining €180,000 of the grant should be accounted for in the year to 31 December 2x08 when the directors incur the matching capital expenditure.

Under IAS 20, government grants should be recognised as income over the periods necessary, to match them with the related costs which they are intended to compensate, on a systematic basis (IAS 20, para 12).

Grants related to depreciable assets, as is the case here, are recognised as income over the periods and in the proportion in which the depreciation on those assets is charged (IAS 20, para 17).

As the plant is depreciated on a straight-line basis at 8% per annum, and a full year's depreciation has been deducted in the year to 31 December 2x07, a matching 8% of the grant of €720,000, i.e. €57,600, should be released from deferred income and recognised as income in the financial statements for the year.

The following journal entries are required to reflect the above treatment:

	DR €000	CR €000
Deferred income – SOFP	180	
Trade and other payables		180
(Being removal of government grant for which conditions may not be satisfied)		
Deferred income – SOFP	57.6	
Amortisation of government grants – P/L		57.6
(Being release of government grant to match with depreciation charge)		

The disclosures required are as follows:

- The accounting policy adopted for government grants, including the methods of presentation in the financial statements.
- The nature and extent of government grants recognised in the financial statements, and an indication of other forms of government assistance from which the entity has directly benefited.
- Unfulfilled conditions and other contingencies attaching to government assistance that has been recognised (IAS 20, para 39).

Drafting of disclosures

Accounting policy note:

Government grants relating to tangible non-current assets are recognised as deferred income, and are amortised to profit or loss over the estimated useful lives of the related assets in line with the depreciation policy of the company.

	€
Balance at beginning of year	X
Recognised during year	720,000
Amortised to profit or loss	(57,600)
Balance at end of year	X

The company received government grants of €900,000 during the year to aid the purchase of certain items of plant required in relation to the planned expansion of the manufacturing business. At the year-end, the conditions in relation to €720,000 of this grant had been fulfilled and accordingly this amount has been recognised in the financial statements. The remaining €180,000 will be recognised when further plant is purchased.

FRS 102

If the financial statements of the Darcy Group were prepared in accordance with FRS 102 *The Financial Reporting Standard applicable in the UK and Republic of Ireland*, the accounting treatment recommended in this case solution would apply, except in relation to the following issues.

Joint venture (Issue 1 (b) in this case solution)
FRS 102 identifies three types of investments in joint ventures. Bingley's investment in Phillips would be regarded as a jointly controlled entity (FRS 102, para 15.8). A venturer is required to account for a jointly controlled entity using the equity method. Therefore the method of accounting required under FRS 102 is the same as that required by IFRS 11 *Joint Arrangements*, which has been applied in this case solution.

Government grants (Issue 2 (d) in this case solution)

FRS 102 requires government grants to be recognised based on either the performance model or the accrual model (FRS 102, para 24.4). The use of the latter model is required by IAS 20.

The performance model requires an entity to recognise grants in income when performance-related conditions (if any) are satisfied, and when the grant proceeds are received or receivable.

In respect of grants of €900,000 received during 2x07, Bennett has the option of using the accrual model, which has been employed in this case solution.

Alternatively, Bennett could use the performance model. The performance model would result in the following journal entries in Bennett's financial statements for the year ended 31 December 2x07.

	DR €000	CR €000
Bank	720	
Grant income – P/L		720
(Being government grant received where the performance-related conditions have been satisfied)		
Bank	180	
Trade and other payables		180
(Being government grant received in respect of which the performance-related conditions have yet to be satisfied)		

SOLUTION TO
ROCKET GROUP

Memorandum

From: **A. Senior**

To: **Group Financial Director, Rocket plc**

Date: **1 March 2x08**

Further to our recent meeting, I have detailed below my views in respect of accounting issues arising in respect of the financial statements for the year ended 31 December 2x07.

(a) Launch plc

(i) Work in progress inventory

Work in progress inventory should be valued at the lower of cost and net realisable value (IAS 2.9). Cost is defined as the cost of purchase, costs of conversion and other costs incurred in bringing the inventories to their present location and condition (IAS 2.10). Costs of conversion include costs directly related to the units of production, such as direct labour. They also include a systematic allocation of fixed and variable production overheads (IAS 2.12).

The cost of the carpet inventory at 31 December 2x07 is therefore computed as follows:

	€'000
Materials (200 units @ €1,500 × 75%)	225
Labour (200 units @ €600 × 75%)	90
Fixed production overheads (Note 1)	47
Total cost	362

Note 1: The allocation of fixed production overheads to the costs of conversion is usually based on the normal capacity of the production facilities (IAS 2.13). However, in periods of abnormally high production, the amount of fixed overhead allocated to each unit of production is decreased so that inventories are not measured above cost (IAS 2.13).

During 2x07, Launch produced 12,000 finished carpets, compared to a normal output level of 10,000. On the basis that 12,000 represents an abnormally high production figure, fixed production overheads should be allocated to production in a way that avoids inventories being measured in excess of their cost. This can be achieved by allocating overheads based on the actual level of production achieved.

The fixed production overhead content of the carpets that were partially completed at 31 December 2x07 should be computed as follows:

Total fixed production overheads	€3.8 million
Production overhead per fully completed carpet, based on actual output of 12,000 carpets (€3.8 million/12,000)	€317

Therefore, the amount of fixed production overheads to be included in the cost of the 200 carpets, which are on average 75% complete, is computed as follows:
200 × .75 × €317 = €47,550

IAS 23 *Borrowing Costs* requires that costs that are directly attributable to the acquisition, construction or production of a qualifying asset shall be capitalised as part of the cost of that asset (IAS 23.8). A qualifying asset is an asset that necessarily takes a substantial period of time to get ready for its intended use or sale (IAS 23.5). As 10,000 carpets are produced annually by Launch, this category of asset does not represent a qualifying asset. Thus, the interest costs should be expensed as they are incurred.

Distribution costs, sales commissions and administration costs are not costs related to the production of the carpets, therefore they are not included in the valuation of inventory.

Carpet manufactured for the Regency Hotel

One of the carpets, which was 75% complete at the 31 December 2x07, was produced for the Regency Hotel, which closed in early January 2x08. The carpet can however be sold to another customer, giving rise to the following **net realisable value**:

	€
Selling price	3,000
Less:	
Completion costs (€362,000/200 × 1/3)	(603)
Selling and distribution costs	(800)
Net realisable value	1,597
Cost of carpet (€362,000/200)	1,810

Therefore, the Regency Hotel carpet should be valued at its net realisable value of €1,597.

Journal entries

	DR	CR
	€	€
Closing inventory – SOFP	362,000	
Cost of sales		362,000
(Being work in progress inventory at 31 December 2x07)		
Cost of sales	213	
Closing inventory – SOFP		213
(Being restatement of carpet to net realisable value i.e. €1,810 – €1,597)		

(ii) Carpet ends and floor mats

The carpet ends and floor mats represent a minor by-product, whose cost is not separable from the company's main product. In accordance with IAS 2, the inventories of such by-products, when immaterial, may be measured at net realisable value, and this value is deducted from the cost of the main product (IAS 2, para 14).

In the case of Launch plc, the following journal entries are required:

	DR €	CR €
Bank	130,000	
Revenue		130,000
(Being sales of carpet ends and floor mats during 2x08)		
Inventory of carpet ends and floor mats – SOFP	25,000	
Cost of sales		25,000
(Being NRV of by-product offset against the production costs of Launch plc's main product)		

(iii) Inventory of wool

The wool inventory held by Launch plc at 31 December 2x07 has a cost of €600,000, and a NRV of only €200,000. However, it is anticipated that this wool will be used for the production of carpets which are expected to be sold above cost.

Materials held for use in the production of inventories are **not** written down below cost if the finished products in which they will be incorporated are expected to be sold at or above cost (IAS 2, para 32). Consequently, the wool inventory of Launch plc should be included in the financial statements at cost on 31 December 2x07. As Launch plc has already reduced the inventory to €450,000, this write-down in value should be reversed as follows:

	DR €	CR €
Inventory of materials – SOFP	150,000	
Cost of sales		150,000
(Being reversal of write-down of wool inventory)		

(iv) *Sale and lease-back*

(I)   Factory lease

IAS 17 *Leases* defines a finance lease as a lease that transfers substantially all the risks and rewards, incidental to ownership, of an asset. In the case of the factory building it is clear that the lease agreement qualifies as a finance lease. This is so as the lease term of 50 years is in line with the asset's estimated useful life, and Launch plc has an option to extend the lease for a further 30 years by making a nominal annual payment.

Where a sale and lease-back transaction results in a finance lease, IAS 17 states that any excess of proceeds over the carrying amount of the asset is deferred and amortised over the lease term (IAS 17, para 59). Thus, the following journal entries will be required:

	DR €000	CR €000
Bank	12,000	
Buildings		10,000
Deferred income – SOFP		2,000
(Being sale of factory on 1 January 2x07)		
Revaluation surplus – SOFP	4,000	
Retained earnings – SOFP		4,000
(Being transfer of capital surplus on factory to realised reserves, following the sale of the asset)		
Buildings	12,000	
Lease obligation – SOFP		12,000
(Being finance lease signed on 1 January 2x07)		
Lease obligation	500	
Bank		500
(Being lease instalment paid on 1 January 2x07)		
Depreciation expense – P/L	240	
Accumulated depreciation		240
(Being depreciation of factory for 2x07)		
Lease interest – P/L	1,150	

Lease obligation – SOFP		1,150
(Being lease interest charge for 2x07		
at an implicit rate of interest of 10%;		
(€12m – €500,000) × 10%)		
Deferred income – SOFP	40	
Amortisation of deferred income – P/L		40
(Being amortisation of deferred income		
over lease term, i.e. €2m/50)		

(II)   Car park

The car park, which is the subject of the sale and lease-back agreement, is on a three-acre site. This car park is in the nature of land, consequently the asset has an indefinite life. It is appropriate therefore to treat the lease as an operating lease, which is defined by IAS 17 as a lease other than a finance lease (IAS 17, para 4).

Where a sale and lease-back transaction results in an operating lease and it is clear that the transaction is carried out at fair value, the profit or loss should be recognised immediately (IAS 17, para 61). Thus, the following journal entries will be required:

	DR €000	CR €000
Bank	9,000	
Land		7,000
Profit on disposal – P/L		2,000
(Being disposal of car park on 1 January 2x07)		
Revaluation surplus – SOFP	3,000	
Retained earnings – SOFP		3,000
(Being transfer of capital surplus on car park to		
realised reserves, following the sale of the asset)		
Lease charge – P/L	400	
Bank		400
(Being lease instalment paid by Launch plc on		
1 January 2x07)		

(b) Space plc

The following journal entries are required in respect of the purchase and disposal of the building by Space plc:

	DR €000	CR €000
Building	6,000	
Bank		6,000
(Being purchase of building on 1 January 2x03)		
Depreciation expense	120	
Accumulated depreciation		120
(Being depreciation of building for 2x03)		
Depreciation expense	120	
Accumulated depreciation		120
(Being depreciation of building for 2x04)		
Impairment write-down – P/L	1,760	
Building		1,760
(Being impairment write-down on 1 January 2x05)		
Depreciation expense	83	
Accumulated depreciation		83
(Being depreciation of building for 2x05, based on a net book value of €4 million/48 years)		
Depreciation expense	83	
Accumulated depreciation		83
(Being depreciation of building for 2x06, based on a net book value of €4 million/48 years)		
Accumulated depreciation	166	
Building		166
(Being elimination of accumulated depreciation prior to revaluation)		

Building	3,166	
Reversal of previous impairment – P/L		1,686*
Revaluation surplus – OCI		1,480

(Being revaluation of building to €7 million
on 1 Jan. 2x07)

* The write-back to the income statement is restricted to the original write-down, less the additional depreciation that would have been charged had the asset not become impaired in the first place (i.e. €1.76m less ((€120,000 – €83,000) × 2)).

The disposal of the building is an intragroup transaction, and will be cancelled in the consolidated financial statements.

Should the building be re-stated to fair value at 31 December 2x07, the following journal entry will be required in the consolidated financial statements:

	DR €000	CR €000
Building	1,000	
Accumulated depreciation	152*	
Revaluation surplus – OCI		1,152

* This is the reversal of depreciation charged in 2x07 (i.e. €7 million/46 years)

Space plc and Launch plc are members of the same group, thus they are related parties as defined by IAS 24 (IAS 24, para 9 (a) (i)). Therefore the sale of the building by Space to Launch constitutes a material-related party transaction, and disclosure should be made in the individual financial statements of both Space plc and Launch plc. No disclosure is required in the group financial statements, as the transaction will be cancelled on consolidation.

Disclosure of the following details is required (IAS 24, para 17):

- Description of the relationship between the related parties (fellow subsidiaries of Rocket plc).
- The amount of the transaction (sale of building for €8 million).

- Any other elements of the transaction necessary for an understanding of the financial statements.
- The amounts due or from the related parties at the reporting date.

FRS 102

If the financial statements of the Rocket group were prepared in accordance with FRS 102 *The Financial Reporting Standard applicable in the UK and Republic of Ireland*, the accounting treatment recommended in this case solution would apply, and no differences would arise in respect of the application of FRS 102.

SOLUTION TO TELFER GROUP

Memorandum

From: **A. Senior**

To: **Group Financial Director, Telfer Industrial Group**

Date: **1 July 2x09**

Further to our recent meeting, I have detailed below my views in respect of accounting issues arising in respect of the financial statements of the Telfer group of companies.

(1) Acquisition of Summit Limited

The acquisition of Summit Limited is achieved by what is termed a 'step acquisition' by IFRS 3 *Business Combinations*. This has the following implications in this case:

(i) Associate stage
Telfer Holdings Limited had significant influence over Summit Limited as and from its purchase of a 25% shareholding in that company on the 31 May 2x07. Summit Limited is defined as an associate of Telfer Holdings Limited at that date (IAS 28, para 3). Summit Limited is therefore accounted for under the equity method in the consolidated financial statements of the Telfer Group as and from that date (IAS 28, para 16).

The following journal entries are required in the financial statements of the Telfer Group:

	DR €000	CR €000
Investment in Summit Limited	2,500	
Bank		2,500
(Being purchase of 25% stake in Summit Limited)		
Investment in Summit Limited	250	
Retained earnings		250
(Being the Telfer Group share of the retained earnings of Summit for the year ended 31 May 2x08: ((€8m − €7m) × 25%))		

(ii) Subsidiary stage

On the 31 May 2x08, Telfer Holdings Limited acquired a further 65% of the shares in Summit Limited. IFRS 3 requires that, where a business combination is achieved in stages, the acquirer must remeasure its previously-held equity interest at acquisition-date fair value (IFRS 3, para 42). The resulting gain or loss, if any, should be recognised in profit or loss (IFRS 3, para 42).

Previously-held equity interest in Summit at acquisition-date fair value	€2.30m
Amount at which Summit was included in the financial statements of the Group (€2.5m + €0.25m)	€2.75m
Loss on remeasurement	€0.45m

Thus, a loss of €.45m will be recorded in the financial statements of the Telfer Group for the year ended 31 May 2x08.

Acquisition-related costs should be accounted for by the acquirer as an expense in the year ended 31 May 2x08 (IFRS 3, para 53).

The following journal entries are required in the financial statements of the Telfer Group:

	DR €000	CR €000
Loss on remeasurement – P/L	450	
Investment in Summit Limited		450
(Being remeasurement of previously held equity interest)		
Identifiable net assets	9,000	
Bank		7,800
Investment in Summit Limited		2,300
Non-controlling interest* (€9m × 10%)		900
Goodwill **	2,000	
Acquisition-related expenses – P/L of the Telfer Group for year ended 31 May 2x08	200	
Bank/trade and other payables		200
(Being acquisition costs incurred by Telfer Holdings Limited)		

* Non-controlling interest is computed above as a share of the fair value of the identifiable net assets of Summit Limited at acquisition date. IFRS 3 also permits non-controlling interest to be computed at its fair value (IFRS 3 Appendix B.44).

** IFRS 3 requires that goodwill is measured as the excess of (a) over (b) (IFRS 3.32) where:

(a) the aggregate of:

    (i) the consideration transferred (€7.8 million);

    (ii) the amount of any non-controlling interest in the acquiree (€.9 million); and

    (iii) in a business combination achieved in stages, the acquisition-date fair value of the acquirer's previously-held equity interest in the acquiree (€2.3 million);

(b) the net of the acquisition-date amounts of the identifiable assets acquired and the liabilities assumed (measured in accordance with IFRS 3) (€9 million).

Thus, goodwill = (€7.8m + €.9m + €2.3m) − €9m
= €2m

(iii) Disclosure

Appendix B of IFRS 3 requires that an acquirer shall disclose specific information for each business combination that occurs during the reporting period (IFRS 3, Appendix B, para 64).

The following disclosure note, relating to the acquisition of Summit Limited, is based on the illustrative examples in IFRS 3:

Para. ref.		€000
B64 (a-d)	On 31 May 2x07 Telfer Holdings acquired 25% of the outstanding ordinary shares of Summit Limited. On 31 May 2x08 Telfer Holdings acquired 65% of Summit Limited and obtained control of that company. As a result of the acquisition, the Telfer Group will have an increased presence in the high-margin industrial components market, an important and expanding market.	
B64 (e)	The goodwill of €2 million arising from the acquisition, consists largely of the increased market opportunities from combining the operations of Summit Limited and the Telfer Group.	

Para. ref.		€000
B64 (k)	The following table summarises the consideration paid for Summit Limited and the amounts of the assets acquired and liabilities assumed at the acquisition date, as well as the fair value at the acquisition date of the non-controlling interest in Summit Limited:	
	At 31 May 2x08	
	Consideration	
B64 (f)(i)	Cash	7,800
B64 p (i)	Fair value of Telfer's equity interest in Summit before the business combination	2,300
		10,100
B64 (m)	Acquisition-related costs (included in the Telfer Group's statement of comprehensive income for the year ended 31 May 2x08)	200
B64 (i)	Recognised amounts of identifiable assets acquired and liabilities assumed	9,000
B64 (o)	Non-controlling interest in Summit Limited	(900)
	Goodwill	2,000
		10,100

(iv) Disposal of shares

At the 31 May 2x08, Telfer Holdings Limited held 90% of the shares in Summit Limited. On the 28 February 2x09, a 20% stake in Summit Limited was sold, realising cash proceeds of €3 million.

IFRS 10 requires that when changes in a parent's ownership interest in a subsidiary do not result in a loss of control, that these changes are accounted for within shareholders' equity as transactions with owners acting in their capacity as owners (IFRS 10, para 23).

No gain or loss is recognised on such transactions, and goodwill is not re-measured. Any difference between the change in non-controlling interest and the fair value of consideration received is recognised directly in equity and attributed to the owners of the parent (IFRS 10, Appendix B, para. 96).

The following journal entries will be required in the financial statements of the Telfer Group:

	DR €000	CR €000
Bank	3,000	
Non-controlling interest*		2,015
Equity reserves – SOFP**		985

* (20% × fair value of net assets of Summit at 31 May 2x08) +
   (20% × profits of Summit for 9 months of the year ended 31 May 2x09)

$$= (20\% \times €9 \text{ million}) + (20\% \times €1,430,000 \times 9/12)$$

$$= €2,015,000$$

** The gain on disposal of €985,000 will be shown in the SOCIE for the year ended 31 May 2x09 as an amount attributable to owners of the parent.

(2) Property Asset

(i) Purchase of building

The building purchased by Rampton Limited for €2 million on the 1 June 2x06 would have been classified as a non-current asset at that time. On the 31 May 2x07, the property was restated at €2.5 million under the revaluation model of IAS 16.

The following journal entries would have been required in the financial statements of Rampton Limited in the year ended 31 May 2x07:

	DR €000	CR €000
Buildings	2,000	
Bank		2,000

(Being purchase of building on the 1 June 2x06)

Depreciation expense	40	
Accumulated depreciation		40
(Being depreciation of building for y/e 31 May 2x07)		
Accumulated depreciation	40	
Building		40
(Being elimination of accumulated depreciation at time of revaluation)		
Building	540	
Revaluation surplus – OCI		540
(Being revaluation of building at 31 May 2x07)		

(ii) Non-current asset held for sale

At the 31 May 2x08 it was decided to dispose of the building. IFRS 5 states that an entity shall classify a non-current asset as being held for sale if its carrying amount will be recovered principally through a sale transaction rather than through continuing use (IFRS 5, para 6). On the assumption that the building satisfies the further criteria of IFRS 5, paras 7 and 8, it should be reclassified as an asset held for sale at 31 May 2x08.

Prior to reclassification as held for sale, IFRS 5 requires that the building be accounted for in accordance with applicable IFRSs (IFRS 5, para 18). Thus, in accordance with IAS 16, depreciation should be fully up-to-date, and the building should be restated at its fair value of €3 million.

The following journal entries would have been required in the financial statements of Rampton Limited in the year ended 31 May 2x08:

	DR €000	CR €000
Depreciation expense	51	
Accumulated depreciation		51
(Being depreciation of building for y/e 31 May 2x08 i.e. €2.5 million/49)		
Accumulated depreciation	51	
Building		51
(Being elimination of accumulated depreciation at time of revaluation)		

Building	551	
Revaluation surplus – OCI		551

(Being revaluation of building at 31 May 2x08)

Asset held for sale	3,000	
Building – non-current asset		3,000

(Being classification of the building as an asset held for sale)

Impairment loss – P/L	100	
Asset held for sale		100

(Being set off of selling costs, after the asset is classified
as held for sale, so that the asset is valued at fair
value less costs to sell, in accordance with IFRS 5)

(iii) Change to a plan of sale

At 31 May 2x09 the property was withdrawn from sale.

IFRS 5 requires that if the criteria to be classified as held for sale are no longer met, an entity shall cease to classify an asset as held for sale (IFRS 5, para 26).

Such an asset (or disposal group) should be measured at the **lower of**:

(I)   its carrying amount before it was classified as held for sale, adjusted for any depreciation, amortisation or revaluations that would have been recognised had the asset (or disposal group) not been classified as held for sale; **or**

(II) its recoverable amount (i.e. higher of fair value less costs to sell, and value in use) at the date of the decision not to sell (IFRS 5, para 27).

The asset that is being held for sale by Rampton Limited should therefore be measured at the **lower of**:

(I)   €3 million less one year's depreciation (€3 million/48) = €2,937,500, and

(II) the asset's recoverable amount (i.e. the higher of its fair value less costs to sell of €1.8 million or its value in use of €1.5 million).

The asset should therefore be valued at its recoverable amount of €1.8 million.

Any required adjustment to the carrying value of a non-current asset that ceases to be classified as held for sale should be included in profit or loss for continuing operations (IFRS 5, para 28). However, the adjustment should be treated as a revaluation increase or decrease if the asset had been revalued in accordance with IAS 16 before its classification as held for sale (IFRS 5, para 28).

The following journal entry is therefore required in the financial statements of Rampton Limited for the year ended 31 May 2x09:

	DR €000	CR €000
Building	2,900	
Asset held for sale		2,900
(Being re-classification of building when it ceases to be held for sale)		
Revaluation surplus – OCI		
(€540,000 + €551,000 – €100,000)	991	
Impairment loss – P/L	109	
Building (€2.9m – €1.8m)		1,100
(Being adjustment on asset that ceases to be classified as held for sale)		

(3) Intragroup Sales

IFRS 10 requires that profits and losses resulting from intragroup transactions that are recognised in assets, such as inventory, should be eliminated in full (IFRS 10, Appendix B, para. 86).

Rampton Limited and Brink Limited are both subsidiaries of Telfer Holdings. Thus, to the extent that goods purchased from Brink Limited are held in inventory by Rampton at 31 May 2x09, any intragroup profit or loss must be eliminated.

It must be considered however that Brink Limited will have incurred a corporation tax charge on profits earned on goods sold to Rampton. Thus, from a group perspective, although the intragroup profit on goods held in inventory must be eliminated, the tax charge remains.

Therefore a group tax charge is being recorded in advance of the recognition of the related profit. This represents a deductible temporary difference, as defined by IAS 12 *Income Taxes*.

The following journal entries are required in the group financial statements at 31 May 2x09:

	DR €000	CR €000
Revenue	12,000	
Cost of sales		12,000
(Being elimination of intragroup sales)		
Cost of sales	800	
Inventory – SOFP		800
(Being elimination of unrealised intragroup profit on inventory: 12m x 1/3 x 20%)		
Deferred tax asset – SOFP	160	
Deferred tax credit – P/L		160
(Being deferred tax credit on unrealised intragroup profit on inventory i.e. 800k x 20%)		

Disclosure

As Rampton Limited and Brink Limited are members of the same group, they are defined as related parties by IAS 24 (IAS 24, para 9). Sales by Brink to Rampton are therefore related party transactions. Subject to the amounts involved being material, the following disclosure notes will be required.

Group financial statements

As intragroup sales are cancelled in the consolidated financial statements, no disclosure is required.

Financial statements of Rampton Limited

Brink Limited is a related party of Rampton Limited, by virtue of both parties being members of the Telfer Group. Sales by Brink to Rampton amounted to €12 million during the year ended 31 May 2x09. The amount outstanding at 31 May 2x09 in the statement of financial position of Rampton in respect of these transactions was €xxx.

(4) Sale of Goods

IFRS 15 states that, in determining the transaction price, an entity should adjust the promised amount of consideration for the effects of the time value of money. In this instance, an appropriate discount rate can be computed by identifying the rate that discounts the nominal amount of the promised consideration (i.e. €121,000) so that it equals the price that the customer would pay in cash for the goods (i.e. €100,000). The discount rate in this case is therefore 10% (i.e. $\frac{€121,000}{(1.1)^2} = €100,000$.

In the case of Rampton Limited, it is clear that nine units of product have been sold on normal credit terms of two months. Sales of these items should be recorded without adjustment to fair value.

In respect of the other item however, two years' credit has been allowed.

The following journal entries will be required in the financial statements of Rampton Limited during May 2x09:

	DR €000	CR €000
Trade receivables	900	
Revenue		900
(Being the sale of 9 integrated waste management systems)		
Trade receivables	100	
Revenue		100
(Being the sale of 1 system on extended credit: €121,000/(1.1)²		
Cost of sales	800	
Inventory – SOFP		800
(Being the cost of 10 waste management systems)		

The following journal entry will be required in the financial statements of Rampton Limited during the year ended 31 May 2x10:

	DR €000	CR €000
Trade receivables	10	
Interest revenue – P/L		10
(Being unwinding of discount on extended credit sale; €100,000 x 10%)		

IFRS 15 requires that interest revenue be presented separately from revenue from contracts in the SOCI (IFRS 15, para 65).

FRS 102

If the financial statements of the Telfer Industrial Group were prepared in accordance with FRS 102 *The Financial Reporting Standard applicable in the UK and Republic of Ireland*, the accounting treatment recommended in this case solution would apply, except in relation to the following issues.

Acquisition expenses (Issue (1) (ii) in this case solution)
FRS 102 states that the costs of a business combination will include any costs that are directly attributable to the business combination (FRS 102, para 19.11). Therefore the acquisition expenses of €200,000 would be included as part of the consideration paid by the Telfer Industrial Group and consequently:

- goodwill arising on the acquisition of Summit Limited would be increased by €200,000; and
- profit of the Telfer Industrial Group for the year ended 31 May 2x08 would be increased by €200,000.

Goodwill arising on the acquisition of Summit Limited (Issue (1) (ii) in this case solution)
FRS 102 states that goodwill shall be considered to have a finite life, and that it should be amortised on a systematic basis over its life. If an entity is unable to make a reliable estimate of the useful life of goodwill, the life shall not exceed five years (FRS 102, para 19.23).

Goodwill of €2.2 million (adjusted for acquisition expenses of €200,000) arose as a result of the acquisition of Summit Limited on 31 May 2x08. Assuming that goodwill is to be amortised over five years, the amortisation of goodwill will be recorded as follows in the consolidated financial statement of the Telfer Group for the year ended 31 May 2x09:

	DR €000	CR €000
Amortisation of goodwill – P/L	440	
Goodwill		440

(Being annual amortisation of goodwill; €2.2m × 1/5)

Non-current asset held for sale (Issue (2) (ii) in this case solution)
The concept of a non-current asset held for sale is not considered in FRS 102. Therefore, the re-classification of the property as an asset held for sale would not occur if Rampton Limited was preparing its financial statements in accordance with FRS 102.

SOLUTION TO CAMPBELL GROUP

Memorandum

From: **Sarah Mulhern**

To: **Martin Mangan, Chief Accountant**

Date: **1 February 2x11**

Further to our recent meeting, I have detailed below my views in respect of accounting issues arising in respect of the financial statements of the Campbell Group of companies.

The following issues are addressed:

(1) Computation of the basic and diluted EPS

(2) Employee benefits

(3) Additional disclosures for publicly listed companies

(4) Workings (Appendix 1)

(1) Computation of Basic and Diluted EPS

Basic earnings per share shall be calculated by dividing profit attributable to ordinary equity holders of the parent entity (the numerator) by the weighted average number of ordinary shares outstanding (the denominator) during the period (IAS 33, para 10).

Applying this requirement of IAS 33, the basic and diluted EPS are computed as follows:

(a) *Year ended 31 December 2x10*

	Earnings	No. of Shares	EPS	Incremental EPS
	€ *million*	*million*		
Basic EPS				
(W1) & (W2)	1,180	2,247	**52.51c** *basic EPS*	
Potential ordinary shares (W4):				
- Options	Nil	30		Nil *(dilutive)*
	1,180	2,277	51.82c	
- 8% conv. debentures	28	250		11.2c. *(dilutive)*
Diluted EPS	1,208	2,527.2	**47.8c** *diluted EPS*	

(b) *Year ended 31 December 2x09 – restated EPS*

Basic EPS for 2x09 as originally reported = €850m/800m shares (W1) = 106.25c

2009 EPS	×	Bonus Factor	×	Rights Multiplier (W3)	EPS Restated for 2009
106.25c	×	1/2	×	2.40/2.50	51.0c

Previously reported EPS for 2x09, restated for bonus issue and the bonus element of the rights issue that took place during 2x10.

(2) Employee Benefits

(a) Short-term employee benefits

IAS 19 defines short-term employee benefits as "... employee benefits (other than termination benefits) that are due to be settled within 12 months after the end of the period in which the employees render the related service" (IAS 19, para 7).

Short-term benefits should be recognised as:
- a liability, after deducting any amount already paid (IAS 19, para 10(a));
- an expense, unless another standard requires or permits the inclusion of the benefits in the cost of an asset (IAS 19, para 10(b)).

The Campbell Group has incurred a total of €16.5 million during December 2x10 in the provision of short-term employee benefits. In accordance with IAS 19, €15.3 million should be recorded in profit or loss and either credited to bank or accrued as a liability at 31 December 2x10.

IAS 16 *Property, Plant and Equipment* requires that directly attributable costs be included in the cost of an asset (IAS 16, para 16). IAS 16 specifies the costs of employee benefits arising from the construction of property as being an example of attributable costs for this purpose (IAS 16, para 17). Thus, the costs incurred by the Campbell Group in respect of the factory extension should be capitalised as part of the cost of land and buildings.

The following journal entry is required:

	€ million	€ million
Wages and salaries – P/L	15.3	
Land and buildings	1.2	
Bank		10.4
Trade and other payables (€3.6m + €1.1m + €0.6m + €0.8m)		6.1

IAS 19 also requires that an entity should recognise the cost of **bonus payments** when:
- the entity has a present legal or constructive obligation to make such payments as a result of past events; and
- a reliable estimate of the obligation can be made (IAS 19, para 19).

In respect of the commitments to staff in Auto Limited, bonus payments of €1.8 million should be recognised as follows:

	€ million	€ million
Wages and salaries – P/L	1.8	
Trade and other payables – SOFP		1.8

(b) Post-employment benefits

(i) Defined contribution plan

IAS 19 requires that when an employee has rendered service to an entity during a period, the entity should recognise the contribution payable to a defined contribution plan in exchange for that service (IAS 19, para 51):

- as a liability, after deducting any contribution already paid; and
- as an expense.

Thus, the following journal entry is required in respect of the defined contribution plan of the Campbell Group:

	€ million	€ million
Wages and salaries – P/L	120	
Bank		95
Trade and other payables – SOFP		25

Employee contributions will normally be a deduction from gross salary costs, and neither an expense nor a liability will arise from the perspective of the Campbell Group.

(ii) Defined benefit plan

Recognition of actuarial gains and losses in the period in which they occur

IAS 19 *Employee Benefits* requires that actuarial gains and losses are recognised in other comprehensive income in the period in which they occur. To prepare the financial statements of the Group for the year ended 31 December 2x10 it will be necessary to compute the following amounts in respect of the defined benefit pension plan:

- Charge to profit or loss for the year ended 31 December 2x10.
- Pension liability at 31 December 2x10.
- Actuarial gains/losses for the year ended 31 December 2x10.

- **Charge to profit or loss for the year ended 31 December 2x10**

  The defined benefit expense for the period can be computed as follows:

	€ million
Net interest cost	24
Current service cost for the year	390
Defined benefit expense for the period	414

- **Pension liability at 31 December 2x10**

Present value of defined benefit obligation at year end	2,300
Fair value of assets of plan at year end	1,650
Defined benefit liability at 31 December 2x10	650

  The defined benefit liability has increased by €50 million during the year (i.e. from €600m to €650m).

- **Remeasurement gains/losses for year ended 31 December 2x10**

  Remeasurement gain/loss on obligations of pension plan:

	€ million
Present value of defined benefit obligation at 1 January 2x10	1,680
Current service cost for the year	390
Interest cost	67
Benefits paid	(150)
	1,987
Remeasurement loss (balancing figure)	313
Present value of defined benefit obligation at end of year	2,300

  The above remeasurement loss of €313 million will be included in other comprehensive income for the year ended 31 December 2x10.

Remeasurement gain/loss on <u>assets</u> of pension plan:

	€ million
Fair value of assets of plan at 1 January 2x10	1,080
Employer contributions	400
Interest income on assets of plan	43
Benefits paid	(150)
	1,373
Remeasurement gain (balancing figure)	277
Fair value of assets of plan at end of year	1,650

The remeasurement gain of €277 million on the assets of the plan will be recognised as part of other comprehensive income for the year ended 31 December 2x10.

Consequently, there will be a net remeasurement loss of €36 million in other comprehensive income for the year ended 31 December 2x10 (i.e. remeasurement loss of €313m, less a remeasurement gain of €277m).

• **Journal entries**

The following journal entries will be required for the year ended 31 December 2x10:

	DR € million	CR € million
Defined benefit assets	400	
Bank		400
(Being employer contributions for the year)		
Defined benefit obligation — SOFP	150	
Defined benefit assets		150
(Being benefits paid for the year)		
Defined benefit assets	43	
Interest income – P/L		43
(Being return on assets: €1,080m × 4%)		
Interest cost – P/L	67	
Defined benefit obligation – SOFP		67

(Being interest cost for year: €1,680m × 4%)

Current service costs – P/L	390	
Defined benefit obligation – SOFP		390

(Being current service cost for year)

Remeasurement loss – OCI	313	
Defined benefit obligation		313

(Being remeasurement loss for year on defined
benefit pension obligation)

Defined benefit assets	277	
Remeasurement gain – OCI		277

(Being remeasurement gain on assets of plan)

The journal entries above will lead to a net increase of €50 million* in the defined benefit pension liability at 31 December 2x10. This will increase the pension liability in the statement of financial position from €600 million to €650 million.

* Increase in obligation (€390m – €150m + €67m + €313m) less increase in assets (€43m + €400m – €150m + €277m)

(3) Additional Disclosures Arising for a Listed Company

(a) Operating segments

IFRS 8 *Operating Segments* applies to entities whose equity instruments are traded on a stock exchange (IFRS 8, para 2). Thus, the Campbell Group, whose shares are listed on the Dublin and London exchanges, comes within the scope of the standard.

An operating segment is defined as a component of an entity:
*   that engages in business activities from which it may earn revenues and incur expenses;
*   whose operating results are regularly reviewed to make decisions; when allocating resources and assessing performance, and
*   for which discrete financial information is available (IFRS 8, para 5).

The strategy of the Campbell Group has been to form a separate company for each main area of operation, with separate subsidiaries being responsible for car sales, car hire, valeting and repairs, leasing and hire purchase, and sales of motor accessories. It seems reasonable to conclude that each of these subsidiaries represents an operating segment of the Campbell Group.

IFRS 8 requires an entity to report separately information about an operating segment that meets any of the following quantitative thresholds (IFRS 8, para 13):

(i)   Its reported revenue is 10% or more of the combined revenue of all operating segments.

(ii)   The amount of its reported profit or loss is 10% or more of the greater of (I) the combined profit of all operating segments that did not report a loss and (II) the combined reported loss of all operating segments that reported a loss.

(iii) Its assets are 10% or more of the combined assets of all operating segments.

Disclosure

The Campbell Group is required to disclose the factors used to identify its reportable segments and the types of products and services from which each reportable segment derives its revenue (IFRS 8, para 22). The Group will also be required to disclose the profit or loss and total assets for each of its reportable segments (IFRS 8, para 23).

The following additional disclosures are required for each reportable segment if the information is regularly reported to the chief operating decision maker (IFRS 8, para 23):

(i) segment liabilities

(ii) the following items of income and expense:

- revenues from external customers and from other operating segments of the Group;
- interest revenue and interest expense;
- depreciation, amortisation and other material non-cash items;
- items of income and expense that are sufficiently material to warrant separate disclosure;

- the Group's interest in the profit or loss of associates and joint ventures accounted for by the equity method;
- income tax expense or income.

IFRS 8 also requires entities to provide a number of reconciliations and to make certain entity-wide disclosures. The latter disclosures are not required if the information has already been provided as part of the information on reportable segments.

(b) Interim financial reporting

As the Campbell Group is listed on the Dublin and London stock markets, under Stock Exchange rules it is required to present interim financial statements. IAS 34 *Interim Financial Reporting* also encourages publicly traded entities to:

- provide interim financial reports at least as of the end of the first half of their financial year; and to
- make their interim financial reports available not later than 60 days after the end of the interim period (IAS 34, para 1).

The Campbell Group has the option of publishing a complete set of financial statements in its interim financial report (IAS 34, para 7). Alternatively, it may provide a condensed set of financial statements consisting, at a minimum, of the following components (IAS 34, para 8):

- a condensed statement of financial position;
- a condensed statement of comprehensive income;
- a condensed statement of changes in equity;
- a condensed statement of cash flows; and
- selected explanatory notes.

As the ordinary shares of the Campbell Group are quoted on the stock market, basic and diluted earnings per share for the interim period should be presented in the statement of comprehensive income, whether condensed or otherwise (IAS 34, para 11).

The principal selected explanatory notes that should be provided (if the information is material and not provided elsewhere in the report) are as follows (IAS 34, para 16A):

(i) A statement that the same accounting policies and methods of computation are used in the interim financial statements, as compared with the most recent annual financial statements, or a description of the nature and effect of any changes.

(ii) Explanatory comments about the seasonality or cyclicality of interim operations.

(iii) The nature and amount of changes to estimates reported in prior financial years.

(iv) Issues, repurchases and repayments of debt and equity.

(v) Dividends paid.

(vi) Certain segment information, if required by IFRS 8.

(vii) Material events subsequent to the end of the interim period that have not been reflected in the financial statements for the interim period.

(viii) The effect of changes in the composition of the Group during the interim period (e.g. business combinations).

(ix) Changes in contingent liabilities or contingent assets since the end of the last reporting period.

Appendix I – Workings

Basic EPS 2x10 and 2x09

(1) Earnings (the numerator)

Earnings for the purposes of computing EPS is defined as profit attributable to ordinary shareholders of the parent entity (IAS 33, para 10).

In the case of the Campbell Group, earnings will therefore be computed as follows:

	2x10 € million	2x09 € million
Profit for the year attributable to owners of the parent	1,200	870
Less: preference dividend – on 10% irredeemable pref. shares	(20)	(20)
Earnings	1,180	850

(2) Weighted Average Number of Shares for Basic EPS (the denominator)

Date	Particulars	Movement	Cum. Shares (M)	*No. x Time Prop. x Bonus Factor x Rights Multiplier*	Weighted Ave. No. (M)
01/01/10	B/fwd (W3)	-	800	[800m x 1/12 x 2/1 x €2.50/€2.40]	138.9
01/02/10	Rights issue	200	1,000	[1,000m x 2/12 x 2/1]	333.3
01/04/10	Issue at fair value	200	1,200	[1,200m x 3/12 x 2/1]	600
01/07/10	Bonus issue	1,200	2,400	[2,400m x 3/12]	600
01/01/10	Treasury purchase	(100)	2,300	[2,300m x 3/12]	575
	Weighted average number of shares for basic EPS				2,247.2

(3) Theoretical Ex-rights Price (TERP)

				€
Cum. rights	4	@ €2.50		10.00
Rights	1	@ €2.00		2.00
Ex-rights	5			12.00

Theoretical ex-rights price = €12.00/5 = €2.40 per share.

Therefore, the rights multiplier is €2.50/€2.40.

(4) Diluted Earnings per Share for 2x10

Entities are required to calculate diluted earnings per share attributable to ordinary equity shareholders of the parent company (IAS 33, para 30).

For the purpose of calculating diluted EPS, an entity shall adjust profit or loss, and the weighted average number of shares outstanding for the effects of all dilutive potential ordinary shares (IAS 33, para 31).

For the Campbell Group, there are two sources of dilutive potential ordinary shares:

- Share options issued on the 1 April 2x10
- €500 million of 8% convertible debentures.

The computation of diluted EPS may require adjustments to be made to both earnings and the number of shares:

Earnings

In the case of the 8% **convertible debentures**, the profit attributable to ordinary equity holders of the parent entity should be adjusted by the after-tax effect of interest recognised in the period (IAS 33, para 33). For the Campbell Group, profit will be increased by €28 million (i.e. €500m × 8% × 0.7).

In respect of the **share options**, there is no effect on earnings.

Shares

For the purpose of calculating diluted EPS, the number of ordinary shares is the weighted average number of issued ordinary shares, plus the weighted average number of ordinary shares that *would* be issued on the conversion of all the dilutive potential ordinary shares into ordinary shares (IAS 33, para 36). Dilutive potential ordinary shares should be deemed to have been converted into ordinary shares at the beginning of the period, or the date of issue if later (IAS 33, para 36).

For the **8% convertible debentures**, the additional number of ordinary shares is 250m (i.e. €500m/100 x 50).

For **share options**, potential ordinary shares are treated as consisting of both of the following (IAS 33, para 46):

(i) **A contract to issue ordinary shares at their average market price during the period.** Such ordinary shares are assumed to be fairly priced and to be neither dilutive nor anti-dilutive. For the Campbell Group this will be computed as follows:

- Average market price of one ordinary share during 2x10 = €2.50
- Weighted average number of shares under option during 2x10 = 150m (i.e.10 x 20m x 9/12)

- Exercise price for shares under option during 2x10 = €2
- Weighted average number of shares that would have been issued at average market price = 120m (i.e. 150m x €2/€2.5)

(ii) **A contract to issue the remaining ordinary shares for no considera-tion.** Such ordinary shares generate no proceeds and have no effect on profit or loss attributable to ordinary shares outstanding. Therefore such shares are dilutive and are added to the number of ordinary shares outstanding in the calculation of diluted EPS.

For the Campbell Group, the number of shares deemed to be issued for no consideration will be 30m (i.e. 150m – 120m).

Calculation of Diluted EPS

In considering whether potential ordinary shares are dilutive or anti-dilutive, each issue is considered separately, in sequence, from the most dilutive to the least dilutive. Thus, dilutive potential ordinary shares with the lowest 'earnings per incremental share' are included in the diluted EPS calculation before those that have a higher earnings per incremental share (IAS 33, para 44). This is to avoid an anti-dilutive issue being allowed to impact on the diluted EPS figure.

This requirement of IAS 33 is applied as follows:

	Increase in earnings	Increase in number of ordinary shares	Earnings per incremental share
Share options	Nil	Shares for no consideration = 30m	Nil
8% convertible debentures	€28m	250m	11.2 cent

Potential ordinary shares should be treated as dilutive only when their conversion to ordinary shares would decrease EPS from continuing operations (IAS 33, para 41). Potential ordinary shares are only included in the computation of diluted EPS when their effect on EPS is dilutive (IAS 33, para 43).

FRS 102

If the financial statements of the Campbell Group were prepared in accordance with FRS 102 *The Financial Reporting Standard applicable in the UK and Republic of Ireland*, the accounting treatment recommended in this case solution would apply, and no differences would arise in respect of the application of FRS 102.

INDEX